UNCIVIL MIRTH

Uncivil Mirth

RIDICULE IN ENLIGHTENMENT BRITAIN

Ross Carroll

PRINCETON UNIVERSITY PRESS

PRINCETON & OXFORD

Published by Princeton University Press
41 William Street, Princeton, New Jersey 08540
6 Oxford Street, Woodstock, Oxfordshire OX20 1TR

press.princeton.edu

Library of Congress Cataloging-in-Publication Data

Names: Carroll, Ross, 1981– author.
Title: Uncivil mirth : ridicule in enlightenment Britain / Ross Carroll.
Description: Princeton : Princeton University Press, [2021] | Includes bibliographical references and index.
Identifiers: LCCN 2020040571 (print) | LCCN 2020040572 (ebook) | ISBN 9780691182551 (acid-free paper) | ISBN 9780691220536 (ebook)
Subjects: LCSH: Ridicule. | Great Britain—History. | Enlightenment—Great Britain. | Shaftesbury, Anthony Ashley Cooper, Earl of, 1801–1885.
Classification: LCC BJ1535.R5 C37 2021 (print) | LCC BJ1535.R5 (ebook) | DDC 179/.8–dc23
LC record available at https://lccn.loc.gov/2020040571
LC ebook record available at https://lccn.loc.gov/2020040572

British Library Cataloging-in-Publication Data is available

Editorial: Ben Tate and Josh Drake
Production Editorial: Kathleen Cioffi
Jacket Design: Chris Ferrante
Production: Danielle Amatucci
Publicity: Alyssa Sanford and Amy Stewart
Copyeditor: Tash Siddiqui

Jacket art: Composite of (1) William Hogarth, *The Laughing Audience*, 1733. Metropolitan Museum of Art, Harris Brisbane Dick Fund, 1932, and (2) Thomas Rowlandson, *Comedy Spectators, Tragedy Spectators*, 1789. Metropolitan Museum of Art, The Elisha Whittelsey Fund, 1959

This book has been composed in Miller

Printed on acid-free paper. ∞

Printed in the United Kingdom

10 9 8 7 6 5 4 3 2 1

For my parents, Sheila and Geoff

Out burst the frannion into open laugh:
She blush'd, and frown'd at his uncivil mirth.
Then, soften'd to a smile, as hiding half
What moste offend if boldly utter'd forth,
He seem'd t'essay to give his answer birth:
But stopp'd, and chang'd his smiles to looks of ruth.
'Is this,' quoth he, 'fit guerdon for thy worth?
'Does Cupid thus impose upon thy youth?
'Dwells, then, in heav'n, such envy, void of love and truth?

—ANONYMOUS, *PSYCHE: OR THE
GREAT METAMORPHOSIS*

CONTENTS

ACKNOWLEDGEMENTS

THIS BOOK HAS BEEN a long time in the making (arguably too long) and I have accumulated many debts along the way. The idea for the project took shape towards the end of my doctoral studies at Northwestern University where I had the pleasure of learning from some terrific teachers. My adviser, Mary Dietz, gave me freedom when I needed it, reined me in when she had to, and read my work with the same keen eye which I had seen her cast over hundreds of manuscript submissions for *Political Theory*. Working under her guidance at that journal for three years provided me with an invaluable professional apprenticeship that will stand to me always. More generally, Mary's indefatigable good humour and phenomenal work ethic, of which I remain in awe, colours all that I do professionally, even if I can scarce hope to match either. Jim Farr taught me that genuine curiosity about the past could have a home in a political science department and enabled me to turn a deaf ear to those who insinuated that any project that did not directly address contemporary questions was unworthy of pursuit. Sara Monoson's refreshingly frank questioning still resonates whenever I find myself making fanciful claims about historical texts (which is often).

Numerous friends and colleagues have either given feedback on material related to this project or provided much needed encouragement at crucial moments. Tim Stuart-Buttle provided copious commentary on the penultimate draft and I am certain that the final book was much improved by his efforts. Paul Sagar prompted me to think more carefully about sociability than I might have otherwise. I had the pleasure of having Chris Brooke and Teresa Bejan discuss the manuscript at the Association for Political Theory, Britain and Ireland conference in Oxford in January 2020. I enjoyed every minute of that event, which is just as well as in-person conferences were soon to become a rarity. Christine Jackson-Holzberg knows more about Shaftesbury than anyone I know and generously shared information and insight with me over the course of a long and fruitful correspondence (I hope we actually meet someday!). Daniel Kapust deserves special mention, not only for commenting on my work, but also for digging out refences for me from his home in Wisconsin when I had no way of accessing my office or a library during the coronavirus lockdown. I have also benefitted immensely from the encouragement and feedback of Jonathan Barry, Eileen Hunt-Botting, Richard Bourke, Theo Christov, Josh Cherniss, Greg Conti, Aurelian Craiutu, Robin Douglass, Mark Goldie, David Marshall, Andy Sabl, Joanna Vecchiarelli Scott, Quentin Skinner and David Williams. Many of the arguments contained in this book had their first outings before audiences at Cambridge, Oxford, Exeter, Harvard, Madison, Georgetown, Washington, Chicago, Evanston, Dublin, Shaftesbury (in Dorset) and Lausanne.

The graciousness, support, and good cheer of my editor, Ben Tate, made my experience with Princeton University Press a thoroughly enjoyable one from beginning to end. Three anonymous reviewers for Princeton provided detailed and helpful scrutiny of the manuscript. Kathleen Cioffi steered the book through production with a steady hand. Tash Siddiqui was an excellent copy-editor and I hope I didn't test her patience too much. Material from chapter 2 appeared as 'Ridicule, Censorship, and the Regulation of Public Speech: The Case of Shaftesbury' in *Modern Intellectual History* (vol. 15, no. 2, 2018). Some of chapter 6 appeared originally as 'Wollstonecraft and the Political Value of Contempt' in *European Journal of Political Theory* (vol. 18, no. 1, 2019).

I am fortunate to have been part of several vibrant and sustaining intellectual communities over the past few years. At Northwestern University my fellow political theorists Crina Archer, Lexi Neame, Menaka Philips, Anna Terwiel, Jennifer Forestal, Gent Carrabregu, Desiree Weber, Chris Sardo, Ilya Winham and many others helped to make the slog of doctoral study far more enjoyable than it otherwise might have been. Special mention here must go to Doug Thompson. Doug started working on Montaigne around the same time that I discovered Shaftesbury and our conversations have always proved the best of intellectual tonics for me. It is more than likely that the idea of writing a book on ridicule entered my subconscious during an afternoon laughing with Doug about something or other (possibly even the philosophy of the great de Selby) in the *Political Theory* editorial office in Evanston. After we had both left Northwestern and I needed reassurance that ridicule could be a serious topic of intellectual history, Doug provided it in spades. At the College of William & Mary, John Lombardini, Adam Potkay, Rebekah Sterling, and Simon Stow were always forthcoming with advice, insight and encouragement. The staff at the Newberry Library in Chicago, the National Archives at Kew and the British Library were excellent as always. Finally, the heartiest of thanks must go to my colleagues at the Centre for Political Thought here at Exeter, especially Sarah Drews Lucas, Dario Castiglione, Robin Durie, Robert Lamb, Iain Hampsher-Monk, Catriona McKinnon, James

Muldoon and Andy Schaap. They have made the University of Exeter a wonderful place to do political theory and have been incredibly generous with their counsel, support and friendship.

It is rightly said that books are made by lives rather than minds. Terah Walkup was a huge and precious part of my life during the early years of this project. There are several friends in Ireland, America and the UK that I have leaned on too (you know who you are). However, I have depended upon no one so much as Celeste McNamara. Celeste offered endless reserves of support of every conceivable kind—intellectual, moral, and practical—at every juncture. To her I owe an incalculable debt. My parents, Geoff and Sheila (to whom I dedicate this book), sister Sarah, and brother-in-law Glenn have not allowed their mystification at what exactly I have been doing to diminish their support for me one bit. I owe them more than they can know.

UNCIVIL MIRTH

Introduction

WHEN JOHN LOCKE DIED in 1704 his friends mourned the loss of a philosopher who combined seriousness of thought with a special talent for raillery. Locke, they recalled, often relied on this skill to pierce through affectation and conceitedness, making it an important part of his philosophical practice. Because he considered 'gravity' a sign of imposture, one friend noted, Locke would mimic anyone adopting an overly serious demeanour to make them an object of 'ridicule'.[1] Another reported that Locke practised raillery 'better than anyone' and even managed to blend 'mirth with instruction'.[2] For Locke, ridicule was no mere pleasant diversion; it was an instrument of enlightenment and an aid to inquiry.

Although he found ridicule useful, Locke was also keenly aware of its risks. He often 'spoke against raillery' to his friends and judged it of 'dangerous consequence if not well manag'd'.[3] In his writings on education Locke proved even more reticent, warning that youth should 'carefully abstain from *raillery*' if they wished to 'secure themselves from provoking others'.[4] Those who jest may not even be aware that they have created an enemy, he cautioned, because the object of the joke may laugh along just to save face. The 'right management of so nice and ticklish a business' was

---

1. Pierre Coste, 'The Life and Character of Mr. Locke in a Letter to the Author of the Nouvelles de La Republique Des Lettres by Mr. P. Coste', in *A Collection of Several Pieces of Mr. John Locke. Publish'd by Mr. Desmaizeaux, under the Direction of Anthony Collins, Esq.* (London: R. Francklin, 1739), iv–v.

2. Masham to Le Clerc, 12 January 1704, in Roger Woolhouse, 'Lady Masham's Account of Locke', *Locke Studies* 3 (2003), 189.

3. Ibid., 190.

4. John Locke, *Some Thoughts Concerning Education*, ed. Nathan Tarcov (Indianapolis, IN: Hackett, 1996), 108. Emphasis in original.

'not everyone's talent', Locke insisted, as even 'a little slip may spoil all', causing needless injury and offence.[5] If mirth could correct and enlighten, it could also wound and diminish, hurting the pride of those on the receiving end and endangering civility.

As this book demonstrates, Locke was far from alone among Enlightenment philosophers in viewing laughing, raillery, and jesting as ambiguous and fraught. The questions of why humans laugh and when it was appropriate for them to do so had been continuous preoccupations of philosophers at least since Aristotle. The century after Locke's death, however, saw philosophical scrutiny of the subject rise to a pitch and intensity rarely seen before or since. It is at this time, moreover, that philosophers in Britain placed the *politics* of ridicule at the foreground of their investigations. That is, they concerned themselves less with the physical or mental origins of laughing than with how jesting and raillery could disrupt or sustain social life. They were in equal measure fascinated and perturbed by the power of ridicule to embarrass or provoke its targets, and expended great energy probing the limits of its propriety. There was more at stake here than fixing standards of decorum; rather the aversion to being laughed at reflected an all too human need for recognition and esteem, a need that had to be balanced against the undeniable utility of ridicule as a corrective to pride and pretension.

The debate began in earnest with one of Locke's own pupils, Anthony Ashley Cooper, the third Earl of Shaftesbury and grandson of one of the architects of England's Glorious Revolution.[6] In the treatises that made up his *Characteristics of Men, Manners, Opinions, Times* (1711), Shaftesbury tried to rescue ridicule from the charge of incivility and demonstrate its usefulness against the bigoted, fanatical and proud. Few others expressed such confidence that the abusiveness of ridicule would decline with time, as citizens grew accustomed to mocking and being mocked in turn. The social value of ridicule was so great, Shaftesbury alleged, that preserving its free use in debate was among the most critical tasks that philosophy could perform. And although he inherited Locke's fears about the offensiveness of this behaviour, he did not shy away from deploying what he defended, particularly against religious enthusiasts, clerics and philosophical rivals. For Shaftesbury, ridicule was not a trifling conversational technique; it was a force for enlightenment and a necessary antidote

5. Ibid., 108.
6. For the sake of consistency I will always refer to Anthony Ashley Cooper as 'Shaftesbury' even though for some of the period I cover he had not yet assumed the title of Earl.

to the pedantic scholasticism that had dominated European intellectual life for too long.

In the chapters that follow we will encounter a wide range of philosophers who drew on Shaftesbury's example by avowing the power of ridicule to unsettle prejudice, demarcate the boundaries of sociable behaviour, and attack entrenched systems of thought and power. Far from constituting a school, they varied hugely in their intellectual affinities and philosophical temperaments. They ranged from the philosophical sceptic David Hume to his Aberdonian critics Thomas Reid and James Beattie, to enthusiastic defenders of the rights of man such as Mary Wollstonecraft and Alexander Geddes. And while they shared a fascination with the promise of ridicule as a mode of criticism, few celebrated or indulged in it without misgivings. All engaged in intense handwringing over the damage that even well-intentioned ridicule could cause to civility and social peace.

What lay behind this surge of philosophical interest in ridicule? Part of the explanation lies in what Jürgen Habermas long ago identified as the transformation of the public sphere. The relaxing of censorship and deregulation of the printing trade in the 1690s led to an explosion of political and religious parodies, burlesques, satires, squibs and scoffs. In such an atmosphere, the model of polite conversation popularized by coffee-house magazines like the *Spectator* was little more than a faint aspiration, as Whig and Tory partisans went out of their way to belittle, demean and pour scorn on their rivals.[7] Many satirists aggressively sought to mobilize public opinion around the issues of toleration, the still-contested revolution settlement of 1688, and seemingly endless wars with France. Whigs and Tories alike expressed unease about the new discursive climate and it was not long before ridicule ceased to be merely a feature of public debate but an *object* of it as well. Beginning with Shaftesbury, philosophers made it their business to determine whether ridicule was an unfortunate

7. There is now a substantial literature on the gulf separating eighteenth-century ideals of politeness from the reality of actual public speech. See especially Kate Davison, 'Occasional Politeness and Gentlemen's Laughter in 18th Century England', *The Historical Journal* 57, 4 (2014), 921–45. Also Simon Dickie, *Cruelty and Laughter: Forgotten Comic Literature and the Unsentimental Eighteenth Century* (Chicago: University of Chicago Press, 2011) and Vic Gatrell, *City of Laughter: Sex and Satire in Eighteenth-Century London* (London: Atlantic Books, 2006). The culture of politeness, Helen Berry writes, cultivated an 'underbelly of impolite resistance'. Helen Berry, 'Rethinking Politeness in Eighteenth-Century England: Moll King's Coffee House and the Significance of "Flash Talk": The Alexander Prize Lecture', *Transactions of the Royal Historical Society* 1 (2001), 68. For Michael Brown the Enlightenment, especially in Britain and Ireland, was 'intrinsically impolite'. Michael Brown, 'The Biter Bitten: Ireland and the Rude Enlightenment', *Eighteenth-Century Studies* 45, 3 (2012), 394.

by-product of this new freedom of debate or, on the contrary, one of the most valuable features of it.

The troubling role that ridicule played in reflecting and solidifying social hierarchies also prompted reflection on the limits of its propriety. As Simon Dickie has shown, the British upper and merchant classes had a voracious appetite for jokes targeted at the poor, labourers, servants, the Welsh, Black people, and women.[8] Jest-books full of the sort of stereotyped characters that would make many modern readers wince were wildly popular. This prompted concern less about the potential harm to those who served as the butt of the jokes than for the corrupting effects on those encouraged to laugh along. Locke himself worried that gentlemen overly accustomed to mocking their social inferiors would develop a haughtiness that they would struggle to shake when dealing with members of their own class.[9] The habit of laughing down could too easily develop into the habit of laughing at one's peers.

A final explanation relates to a philosophical topic that was keenly debated at the turn of the eighteenth century. As intellectual historians and political theorists have long emphasized, a key question in eighteenth-century philosophy was that of sociability or the extent to which humans were (or could be made) fit for political society.[10] The place afforded to laughter and ridicule within that debate, however, has so far been neglected. It is no coincidence that philosophers who pondered how to theorize, promote and manage peaceable co-existence also took an interest in ridicule. For theorists of natural sociability indebted to the Stoic tradition, such as Shaftesbury and Francis Hutcheson, humans have a natural inclination to associate with one another. To them, the practice of laughing and joking was, fundamentally, a benevolent expression of that natural desire for community. This contrasts with a rival Epicurean and Augustinian tradition—featuring the likes of Thomas Hobbes and Bernard Mandeville—that emphasized how the ungovernable pride of post-lapsarian humans locked them into a perpetual struggle for positional superiority. Looked at from the perspective of this tradition, ridicule starts to look more ominous. While it might have some utility as a method for

---

8. Dickie, *Cruelty and Laughter*, chapter 5.

9. Locke, *Some Thoughts Concerning Education*, 92.

10. For the sociability debate, the focus of chapter 2, see Paul Sagar, *The Opinion of Mankind: Sociability and the Theory of the State from Hobbes to Smith* (Princeton, NJ: Princeton University Press, 2018); Istvan Hont, *Politics in Commercial Society* (Cambridge, MA: Harvard University Press, 2015); Christopher Brooke, *Philosophic Pride: Stoicism and Political Thought from Lipsius to Rousseau* (Princeton, NJ: Princeton University Press, 2012).

shaming the unsociable into reforming their behaviour, it was also a troubling expression of contempt that could bruise fragile egos and frustrate
the project of corralling prideful humans into a tolerable co-existence.
Although the sociability debate did not map precisely onto the controversy over ridicule (where a thinker stands on one issue is never a precise
predictor of how they view the other), it nevertheless provides a useful lens
through which the stakes of the ridicule debate become clearer.

I argue that the ridicule debate in Enlightenment Britain should be
taken seriously not only by historians, but also by political theorists confronting the problem of how to harness the critical power of ridicule without wielding it as a weapon of gratuitous humiliation or abuse. By excavat-
ing the debate that Shaftesbury started, we can glimpse earlier attempts to
guard against ridicule's dangers without forsaking the contemptuousness
and bite from which it draws power. Ridicule, I will conclude, is a political force to be regarded warily but never disavowed. For now, however, we
need to look more closely at the two broad ways of thinking about ridicule
that structured that eighteenth-century debate.

Hobbesian Laughter and the Danger of Contempt

According to the tradition of thought that Shaftesbury challenged, ridicule was inextricably bound up with contempt, the passion we experience
when we behold something lowly, beneath consideration, or even worth-
less. It was a tradition faithful to the etymology of the term itself. 'Ridicule' derives from the Latin *ridere* (to laugh) but, as its cognate 'deride'
(from *deridere*) suggests, the laughter of ridicule communicated contempt rather than mere joy. According to Laurent Joubert's influential
Traité du ris (1579), we laugh when beholding something 'ugly, deformed,
improper, indecent, unfitting, and indecorous'.[11] To laugh at something
was always to elevate oneself above it. As a social practice, therefore, ridicule was heavily associated with the vice of pride. To ridicule someone
was to laugh disdainfully at their expense and encourage others to do the
same.[12]

11. Laurent Joubert, *Treatise on Laughter*, trans. Gregory David de Rocher (Tuscaloosa:
University of Alabama Press, 1980), 20.

12. In 'all the situations' that produce laughter, René Descartes put it, 'there is always
some element of hatred'. René Descartes, *The Passions of the Soul* (Oxford: Oxford
University Press, 2015), 245. Unlike Hobbes, however, Descartes reserved a role for a 'moderate ridicule' that could 'helpfully rebuke the vices by making them appear ridiculous'.
Ibid., 268.

It was precisely the troubling disdainfulness of laughter that inspired one of the most infamous statements on the topic in the early modern period: that of Thomas Hobbes. In the chapters that follow I frequently use the adjective 'Hobbesian' as shorthand for an understanding of laughter as an expression of prideful superiority. To take a Hobbesian approach to the politics of ridicule, I will show, was to emphasize how laughter injured the self-worth of those on the receiving end and robbed them of their social standing. To look at ridicule through a Hobbesian lens was to call into doubt the very possibility of a safe or inoffensive jest. And while few (if any) of the thinkers examined here bought into this account entirely, it nonetheless offers a useful heuristic for understanding why and how so many philosophers saw ridicule as a problem for politics.

It is worth noting at the outset, however, that what Hobbes himself actually wrote about laughter was a good deal more complicated. Over the course of three works, Hobbes scrutinized the origins of laughter both to situate it within his taxonomy of the passions and to better understand its destructive power. The first and most important ingredient in laughter that Hobbes identified, and that most neglected by his later critics, was surprise. Whatever makes us laugh, he asserted in *Elements of Law* (1640), must be 'new and unexpected'.[13] If something that made us laugh in the past has grown 'stale or usual' then it will lose the capacity to amuse us again. He repeated the point in *Leviathan* (1651), insisting there that habituation or custom reduces our propensity to both laugh and weep because 'no man laughs at old jests' or 'weeps for an old calamity'.[14]

What sorts of surprises did Hobbes have in mind? In *Elements of Law*, Hobbes allowed that a gathering of people may laugh together when surprised by some general absurdity that is 'abstracted from persons'.[15] For the most part, however, we laugh when made suddenly aware of some ability in *ourselves*. If we have underestimated our ability to carry out a task, but then manage to pull it off against our expectations, we may emit a laugh in surprise. The mysterious passion that is the source of laughter is, then, a 'sudden conception of ability in himself that laugheth'.[16]

13. Thomas Hobbes, *The Elements of Law: Human Nature and De Corpore Politico*, ed. J.C.A Gaskin (Oxford: Oxford University Press, 1994), 54. On the centrality of suddenness to Hobbes's account of laughter see David Heyd, 'The Place of Laughter in Hobbes's Theory of Emotions', *Journal of the History of Ideas* 43, 2 (1982), 287.

14. Thomas Hobbes, *Leviathan*, ed. Richard Tuck (Cambridge: Cambridge University Press, 1991), 43.

15. Hobbes, *The Elements of Law*, 55.

16. Ibid., 54.

There are two things to note about this definition. First, despite what Hobbes's critics claimed, there is nothing in it that suggests that laughter must arise from a triumph over someone else. Surprise at having surpassed our expectations of our own ability is quite enough. A hiker who laughs at the summit of a mountain having convinced herself she would never make it is as much a Hobbesian laugher as someone who laughs in scorn at a beaten opponent. So too is the person who laughs at general human folly, which can prompt a laugh that offends no one.[17] Second, there is nothing in Hobbes's theory that implies that the superior will necessarily laugh at those weaker than themselves. In *Leviathan*, laughter emerges from what Hobbes calls 'a sudden glory arising from a sudden conception of some eminency in ourselves, by comparison with the infirmities of others, or with our own formerly'.[18] The term *conception* here is key. The 'eminency' in question often exists solely in the laugher's own imagination, a point Hobbes stresses repeatedly. The proud who are 'greedy of applause from everything they do well', he says, are particularly disposed to laugh because they are actually insecure about their self-worth and giddily surprised by any act they happen to perform well.[19] Even in cases where their sense of superiority is justified, these laughers are mistaken in their belief that the 'infirmities' of others constitute 'sufficient matter' for triumph.[20]

The definitions of laughter contained in *Elements of Law* and *Leviathan* were not Hobbes's final word on the subject, however. In *De Homine* (1658) Hobbes revised his position slightly by rephrasing one of the conditions of laughter and adding another. Rather than writing of inferiority, Hobbes now employed the language of 'unseemliness' to describe what it is in an object that prompts us to laugh, implying a more general inappropriateness rather than weakness.[21] More significantly, Hobbes now added 'strangeness' as a necessary condition for laughter, suggesting that we never laugh at 'friends and kindred' even if they act in an unseemly manner.[22] There are then, Hobbes concluded, '*three* things conjoined that move one to laughter: unseemliness, strangers [*sic*], and suddenness'.[23] By stipulating that these three elements must be 'conjoined', Hobbes made

---

17. As Ewin notes, 'inoffensive laughter' is entirely possible in Hobbes's schema. R. E. Ewin, 'Hobbes on Laughter', *The Philosophical Quarterly* 51, 202 (2001), 31.

18. Hobbes, *Leviathan*, 54–55.

19. Ibid., 54.

20. Ibid., 55.

21. Thomas Hobbes, *Man and Citizen (De Homine and De Cive)*, ed. Bernard Gert (Indianapolis, IN: Hackett, 1991), 59.

22. Ibid.

23. Ibid.

clear that one element on its own was insufficient and that laughter could not arise solely from egoistical interpersonal comparison. Bonds of friendship were sufficient to stifle laughter on his theory, just as familiarity was.

For Hobbes, then, the problem was not that the strong would constantly laugh at the weak but that vainglorious mockers would provoke angry retaliation from those whose dignity they managed to offend. If, as Hobbes maintained, social life was an arena for contests over honour, then to be ridiculed in this way was no laughing matter. Because 'men take it heinously to be laughed at or derided', he warned, they will risk life and limb to settle the score, with dire consequences for social peace.[24] Hobbes had witnessed enough duels to realize how quickly a jest could lead to violence and unsurprisingly included derision among the provocations to 'quarrel and battle' prohibited under his laws of nature.[25]

Hobbes was forced to admit, however, that this particular law of nature was 'very little practiced', as the psychic satisfactions to be had from expressing contempt towards others were simply too great.[26] Since, as he argued in *De Cive* (1642), 'all the pleasure and jollity of the mind' consisted in besting others, it is 'impossible but men must declare themselves some mutual scorn and contempt, either by laughter, or by words, or by gesture'.[27] This did not stop him trying to impress upon his aristocratic tutee, William Cavendish, the importance of attempting restraint when the occasion to mock someone presented itself. Adopting the 'Satyricall way of nipping' that haughty aristocrats were fond of, Hobbes cautioned Cavendish, was a sure way to lose friends and become embroiled in duels.[28] A gentleman should instead

24. Hobbes, *The Elements of Law*, 92.

25. Ibid.

26. Ibid. As Kinch Hoekstra observes, this is why Hobbes urges us to *acknowledge* each other as equals for the sake of peace, even when our pride prompts us to announce our superiority to others instead. Kinch Hoekstra, 'Hobbesian Equality', in *Hobbes Today: Insights for the 21st Century*, ed. S. A. Lloyd (Cambridge: Cambridge University Press, 2013), 77.

27. Hobbes, *Man and Citizen (De Homine and De Cive)*, 115. As Quentin Skinner has shown, Hobbes's wariness towards ridicule (notwithstanding his frequent use of it himself against scholastics and clerics of all stripes) stemmed from the inclusion of ridicule among the most prized weapons in the tradition of classic and Renaissance rhetoric. See Quentin Skinner, 'Hobbes and the Classical Theory of Laughter', in *Visions of Politics*, vol. 3, *Hobbes and Civil Science* (Cambridge: Cambridge University Press, 2001). For an account of Hobbes's wit that situates it within the Lucianic tradition of *serio ludere* see Conal Condren, *Hobbes, the Scriblerians and the History of Philosophy* (London: Pickering and Chatto, 2012).

28. Hobbes to Charles Cavendish, 1 September 1638, in *Electronic Enlightenment Scholarly Edition of Correspondence*, ed. Robert McNamee et al., University of Oxford, https://www.e-enlightenment.com. For Hobbes's criticism of duelling culture see Markku Peltonen, *The Duel in Early Modern England: Civility, Politeness and Honour* (Cambridge: Cambridge University Press, 2003), 170–71.

display his nobility by assisting those in 'danger of being laughed at' and so guard them from humiliation.[29]

Hobbes's critics, several of whom we will meet later on, lambasted him for his views on laughter and the philosophy of human nature they reflected. But although the specifics of Hobbes's argument were unique to him, his general worry that vainglorious men laughing at each other could produce discord was commonplace, especially among writers working in a more religious idiom. The Quaker Robert Barclay denied that 'jesting' could qualify as 'harmless mirth' largely on this basis.[30] Others interpreted St Paul's admonishment to indulge in neither 'foolish talking, nor jesting' in his Epistle to the Ephesians as having far-reaching consequences for how Christians should and should not laugh at one another.[31] The theologian Isaac Barrow insisted that Paul's words forbade any 'injurious, abusive' or 'scurrilous' jests that tended towards the 'disgrace, damage, vexation, or prejudice' of a neighbour or that raised 'animosities, dissensions, and feuds'.[32] The Presbyterian Daniel Burgess, in his 1694 *Foolish Talking and Jesting Described and Condemned*, similarly declared that those who threaten 'God and Men's peace' for the 'tickle of their fancies in prejudicial and disgraceful jibes' were making an 'unwise bargain'.[33] Jean Baptiste Bellegarde cautioned readers in his *Reflexions upon Ridicule* to 'keep that jest within your teeth that is ready to burst' for although it might raise a momentary laugh, it would also 'make an eternal wound in the heart' of the person targeted and 'he will never pardon you'.[34] For 'they who seem to take it patiently, have a secret rage within'.[35]

At the beginning of the eighteenth century, worries about the fractiousness of ridicule continued to mount, even as the worst of the violence and turmoil that so alarmed Hobbes seemed to have abated. For Quentin Skinner, from this moment on there was a sustained effort to 'outlaw' laughter as displaying an uncivil lack of self-restraint, one that

---

29. Hobbes to Cavendish, *Electronic Enlightenment*.

30. Robert Barclay, *An Apology for the True Christian Divinity: Being an Explanation and Vindication of the Principles and Doctrines of the People Called Quakers* (London, 1678), 352.

31. King James Bible, Ephesians 5:4.

32. Isaac Barrow, *The Theological Works of Isaac Barrow*, vol. 1 (Oxford: Clarendon, 1818), 320.

33. Daniel Burgess, *Foolish Talking and Jesting Described and Condemned* (London: Andrew Bell and Jonas Lumley, 1694), 59.

34. Jean Bellegarde, *Reflexions Upon Ridicule and the Means to Avoid It* (London: Tho. Newborough, D. Midwinter, and Benj. Tooke, 1706), 56.

35. Ibid., 31.

needed to be 'governed' by manners or 'preferably eliminated' altogether from polite society.[36] Lord Chesterfield's admonishments to his to son to avoid laughing aloud in company became emblematic of the restraints that society placed on mirth.[37] As Norbert Elias put it, the civilizing process demanded that laughter be 'pruned' and jesting curtailed.[38] The possibility that ridicule could serve any valuable social function seemed to have receded.

The Shaftesburian Alternative

Although the tradition of regarding laughter as an uncivil expression of contempt was dominant in early modern Britain, it co-existed with a separate tradition of *civil* mirth that Shaftesbury could later tap into. In many cases, these competing traditions could be found in the same author.[39] Indeed, the majority of the philosophers we will encounter in this book believed that both traditions contained a grain of truth, even as they leaned more towards one than the other. Those who raised doubts about the contemptuousness of laughter often acknowledged a legitimate role for it as an innocent diversion or a corrective to error and vice. In his *Government and Improvement of Mirth According to the Laws of Christianity* (1707), Benjamin Colman regretted that most jesting was little more than the 'froth and noxious blast of a corrupt heart' but praised the 'loveliness' of a 'civil mirth'.[40] Similarly Barrow, in his interpretation of Paul's instruction in Ephesians, noticed that the term used to signify jesting, *eutrapelia*,

36. Skinner, 'Hobbes and the Classical Theory of Laughter', 172.

37. Philip Dormer Stanhope, *Letters written by the late Right Honourable Philip Dormer Stanhope, Earl of Chesterfield, to his son Philip Stanhope*, vol. 1 (Dublin: John Chambers, 1776), 376.

38. Norbert Elias, 'Essay on Laughter', ed. Anca Parvulescu, *Critical Inquiry* 43 (Winter 2017), 284.

39. As Morton notes, although criticisms of laughter were ubiquitous, categorical prohibitions were rare. Adam Morton, 'Laughter as a Polemical Act in Late Seventeenth-Century England', in *The Power of Laughter and Satire in Early Modern Britain*, ed. Mark Knights and Adam Morton (Woodbridge: The Boydell Press, 2018), 108. As Curtis notes, some sixteenth-century philosophers such as Erasmus and Thomas More 'gave licence to the use of laughter as a means of making necessary and health-giving criticism'. Catherine Curtis, 'From Sir Thomas More to Robert Burton: The Laughing Philosopher in the Early Modern Period', in *The Philosopher in Early Modern Europe: The Nature of a Contested Identity*, ed. Conal Condren, Stephen Gaukroger and Ian Hunter (Cambridge: Cambridge University Press, 2006), 112.

40. Benjamin Colman, *The Government and Improvement of Mirth According to the Laws of Christianity* (Boston: B Green, 1707), 20 and 18. Colman echoed Locke in arguing that 'Youth is more especially the Age of Levity and Laughter, and needs Correction'. Ibid., 3.

was used by Aristotle in the *Nicomachean Ethics* to mark a key social virtue, and declared it unlikely that Paul would have ruled out what Aristotle approved.[41] On Barrow's account, Paul was summoning the Ephesians not to forgo jesting altogether, but to seek out a mean between buffoonery and moroseness. For it was, he maintained, ill advised to be 'always dumpish' or 'seriously pensive' in the company of others.[42] Burgess, in his own gloss on Ephesians, agreed. What he termed 'lawful jesting' was occasionally needed to 'raise drooping spirits and sharpen blunted minds'.[43]

For those seeking concrete exemplars of civil mirth, scripture was again at hand. A defence of good humour was readily available in Christ's miracle at the wedding at Cana, an intervention that, in Colman's words, authorized 'regular mirth'.[44] But the Bible also contained at least one example of a godly person laughing *at* others. In the book of Kings, the prophet Elijah tests the worshippers of Baal by challenging them to have their deity ignite a pyre. When it becomes clear that their efforts have failed, Elijah taunts them by sarcastically suggesting that Baal might be on a journey, or even asleep, and that perhaps a louder prayer might rouse him. For many early modern critics, no further proof was needed to sanctify the use of ridicule to counter idolatry and presumption. John Edwards, in his *Theologica Reformata* (1713), held that all 'jeering is forbidden excepting the jeering of idols' and leaned for his argument upon the fact that 'Elijah, in a deriding manner, bids the Priests of Baal cry aloud'.[45] The dissenter Isaac Watts found that there were 'Seasons wherein a wise Man or Christian may treat some criminal or silly Characters with *Ridicule* and *Mockery*' for 'Elijah condescended thus to correct the *Priests* and *Worshippers* of Baal'.[46] Barrow also drew on the example of Elijah to demonstrate how facetiousness

41. For Aristotle the *eutrapelos* occupies an intermediate position between the buffoon (*bōmolochoi*) who seeks to raise a laugh at all times regardless of the consequences, and the boor (*agroikoi*) who disapproves of all laughter whether appropriate or not and so fails to recognize the importance of playful conversation to a flourishing life. Aristotle, *Nicomachean Ethics*, 1128a3–10. In the *Rhetoric* Aristotle describes *eutrapelia* as a kind of 'cultured insolence', implying that there was a way of laughing at others and being laughed at in turn that was commensurate with civility. Aristotle, *Art of Rhetoric*, 1389b12. For an insightful analysis of Aristotle's *eutrapelia* as a political virtue see John Lombardini, *The Politics of Socratic Humor* (Oakland, CA: University of California Press, 2018), chapter 4.

42. Barrow, *The Theological Works of Isaac Barrow*, vol. 1, 308.

43. Burgess, *Foolish Talking and Jesting Described and Condemned*, 53.

44. Colman, *Government and Improvement of Mirth*, 91.

45. John Edwards, *Theologica Reformata, or the Body and Substance of the Christian Religion* (London: John Lawrence, at the Angel in the Poultry, 1713), 344.

46. Isaac Watts, *Sermons on Various Subjects* (London: John and Barham Clark, Eman. Mathews, and Richard Ford, 1723), 241–42.

could expose 'things apparently base and vile to due contempt'.[47] For when 'plain declarations will not enlighten people, to discern the truth and weight of things, and blunt arguments will not penetrate', he argued, 'then doth reason resign freely its place to wit, allowing it to undertake its work of instruction and reproof'.[48]

Shaftesbury also sought to rehabilitate mirth but did so in a more secular idiom. His ambition was to drain from English culture a gloomy Calvinist mindset that reduced social life to a contest for recognition between proud individuals and emphasize instead the human capacity for sympathetic connection and reasonable disagreement. For the Earl and his followers, achieving this required discrediting the Hobbesian account of why we laugh. Over the course of the eighteenth century they turned Hobbes into a straw man and his theory into a caricature. But as Jon Parkin has shown, straw men have their uses and have played an underappreciated role in the generation of new philosophical ideas.[49] The slaying of a straw man Hobbes, I will show, paved the way for an alternative paradigm, one that made laughter once again a thoroughly social (and sociable) practice.

What was special about this alternative way of thinking about laughter? I analyse Shaftesbury's writings in the first two chapters and show how, as in the case of Hobbes, what he said was crudely misinterpreted by followers and critics alike. But for now I will outline four particularly salient features of the new mode of thinking that he inaugurated. First, unlike the Hobbesian variety, Shaftesburian laughter could be more easily *shared* in company without anyone present feeling slighted or diminished. And while Hobbesian laughter placed a strain on community by giving vent to an unsociable feeling of contempt, Shaftesburian laughter was agreeably contagious. For Shaftesburians, no philosophy that grounded laughter in individual self-glory could account for how shared laughter

47. Barrow, *The Theological Works of Isaac Barrow*, vol. 1, 308.
48. Ibid., 309. Those who cited Elijah's actions as a precedent, however, were forced to downplay the violence that his ridicule portended. No one who consulted the entirety of this episode from the book of Kings could conclude that Elijah mocked the worshipers of Baal in a spirit of correction. On the contrary, Elijah, having already tricked these false prophets into exposing their misplaced faith in Baal, used ridicule to compound their humiliation. Nor did he present the prophets with a chance to recognize their error and reform. Instead, flush with victory, Elijah ordered their massacre. This was not ridicule with an eye to education; it was a verbal chastisement that foreshadowed a far worse punishment to come.
49. Jon Parkin, 'Straw Men and Political Philosophy: The Case of Hobbes', *Political Studies* 59, 3 (2011).

forged friendship and conviviality. Instead, they insisted, laughter generally resulted from surprising incongruities in persons, objects, or situations that could be appreciated collectively at the expense of no one's honour or dignity.[50]

Second, Shaftesburians were more sanguine about ridicule as a mode
of moral criticism because they clung to a teleological world view that
posited a strict demarcation between what was natural or virtuous, on
the one hand, and what was unnatural or vicious, on the other. Ridicule,
on this view, was effective against vice because, once exposed, vice *naturally* inspires contempt in anyone with an uncorrupted moral sense. For
Shaftesburians, certain behaviours and traits were intrinsically ridiculous,
meaning that any properly constituted mind should dismiss them with
laughter once exposed. On the Hobbesian account, whether something is
found to be ridiculous or not is a relative and contingent matter, depending more on the skill of the ridiculer than on any qualities inherent in
the object itself. Conversely, for Shaftesburians, directing ridicule against
whatever was natural or virtuous was impossible and would only result
in the ridiculer themselves becoming an object of derision. And while the
Shaftesburian notion that ridicule was a 'test of truth' became a well-worn
trope that critics occasionally interpreted too literally (see chapter 2) many
of Shaftesbury's readers adopted a version of it and held that ridicule could
indeed be used to test for verity and worth.

Third, Shaftesburians were, by and large, interested in tapping ridicule's potential as an *everyday* social practice and critical method. Certainly, they recognized that great wits such as Swift, Dryden and Pope
were particularly gifted in the arts of mimicry, irony, sarcasm, or mock
praise. But they also recognized that these writers hardly monopolized
such practices. Shaftesbury took pains to criticize the writing style of
authors and refine conversational practice in the drawing rooms of the
gentry. But he was also interested in the puppet shows mocking Protestant enthusiasts performed in London's markets and in the power of
such performances to shape public perception of religious dissent. Mary
Wollstonecraft was more concerned by the everyday use of ridicule by
men to demean women, even as she recognized that the likes of Swift led
the way. Scottish abolitionists like Alexander Geddes were hardly master

---

50. Matthew Bevis, *Comedy: A Very Short Introduction* (Oxford: Oxford University Press, 2012), 80. For many students of laughter today the incongruity theory is still
largely unsurpassed and remains, in Terry Eagleton's words, the 'most plausible account
of why we laugh'. Terry Eagleton, *On Humour* (New Haven, CT: Yale University Press,
2019), 67.

satirists, but they nevertheless saw value in using satire to educate public opinion on the evils of the African slave trade.

Finally, on the Shaftesburian view, the element of contempt that had been so central to the Hobbesian view could never be disavowed completely. On the contrary, it was from contempt that ridicule derived both its danger *and* its practical efficacy as an instrument of enlightenment. Even those philosophers most solicitous of civility saw the need to communicate their own contempt and excite contempt in others. In some cases, they judged that a true civility demanded contempt. For Hutcheson, the potential for ridicule to serve as an instrument of sociability often depended on its power to deflate its object. For the Aberdonian philosopher James Beattie, scoffing contemptuously at sceptics like David Hume was not only permissible but required if civil society was to hold together. For Shaftesburians, if a ridiculous doctrine, person, or institution has taken on an air of authority, then a gentle jibe might not be sufficient to expose it. In those circumstances, a more withering ridicule was the order of the day.

Ridicule and Political Theory

Recovering the ridicule debate in Enlightenment Britain is of more than historical interest. Teresa Bejan has made the case for returning to the seventeenth century to enrich our understanding of the current divide between those calling for greater civility in public life and those who see in such calls a thinly veiled attempt to suppress marginalized voices.[51] My similar wager is that returning to the eighteenth-century debate on ridicule will speak to the disagreement between those who see forms of speech such as sarcasm, satire and mockery as essential to a healthy politics and those who fear them irrational, trivializing or abusive. The principal problem with this dispute, I want to show now, is that its participants are too indebted to either the Hobbesian or Shaftesburian manner of approaching the issue and so neglect the insights of the other.

To begin with, there are strong Hobbesian overtones in the argument made by some political theorists that contemptuous speech brutalizes politics by converting disputants into belligerents and discussion into the silence of mutual disdain.[52] For some liberals, the concern goes deeper

51. Teresa M. Bejan, *Mere Civility: Disagreement and the Limits of Toleration* (Cambridge, MA: Harvard University Press, 2017).

52. Karen Stohr, 'Our New Age of Contempt', *New York Times*, 23 January 2017. On the 'civilitarian' critique of insulting public speech see Bejan, *Mere Civility*. For Bejan and

still. Jeremy Waldron has argued that contemptuous speech can remove from those subjected to it the reassurance that they enjoy equal standing within the polity, making it a potent weapon of civic exclusion.[53] This applies also to racist or misogynistic jokes; such jokes are never just humour but also implicit attempts at humiliation that endanger the minimal sense of self-worth necessary for membership in a political community.[54] Looked at through a Hobbesian lens, those who object to such jokes are not humourless killjoys, but are voicing a legitimate worry about a real injury deserving of redress.

Traces of the Hobbesian understanding of laughter can also be glimpsed in the realist critique of attempts to substitute moralistic condemnation for political contestation.[55] Speakers who frequently have recourse to ridicule inject precisely the kind of simplistic moralism into political contests that realists abhor. After all, those who publicly mock others often presume that once their opponents have been exposed as ridiculous then the contest will be settled in their favour, obviating the need for further contestation and exchange. The Hobbesian objection is that these ridiculers mistakenly believe that their mockery constitutes a real triumph for virtue and truth, as opposed to an illusory, contingent, or easily reversible victory. From a realist point of view, the destructiveness of this presumption extends beyond any harm done to its immediate target. For it also inflicts (or attempts to inflict) shame on those who hesitate before piling on or who dare acknowledge that what is ridiculous to some may not be so to others.

There are Shaftesburian elements too lurking in our contemporary politics, particularly among those who see ridicule as a *guarantor* of civility rather than a threat to it. If, as Henri Bergson claimed, it is the arrogant, vain, or otherwise 'unsociable' that are most horrified at being laughed at,

Garsten, 'mutual contempt can corrode the affective bonds of democratic citizenship'. Teresa Bejan and Bryan Garsten, 'The Difficult Work of Liberal Civility', in *Civility, Legality and Justice in America*, ed. Austin Sarat (Cambridge: Cambridge University Press, 2014), 18.

53. The power of contemptuous utterances as a force for civic exclusion is discussed at length in Jeremy Waldron, *The Harm in Hate Speech* (Cambridge, MA: Harvard University Press, 2012).

54. On the dangers of humiliation, conceived of as behaviour that 'constitutes a sound reason for a person to consider his or her self-respect injured' see Avishai Margalit, *The Decent Society* (Cambridge, MA: Harvard University Press, 1996), 9.

55. The literature on realism in political theory is large and growing. For some of the best recent work in this tradition see the essays collected in Matt Sleat, ed., *Politics Recovered: Realist Thought in Theory and Practice* (New York: Columbia University Press, 2018).

then ridicule may prove an effective means of protecting politics from just those sorts of characters.[56] More recently, several political theorists and historians have championed ridicule as a weapon against authoritarian personalities.[57] According to another version of this argument, ridicule is valuable less for what it accomplishes than for what it replaces. When we ridicule someone, we are pointedly *not* treating them seriously, or with the deference they demand. Ridicule can thus function as a way of refusing terms of engagement perceived to be unjust or otherwise skewed against the speaker. Even the relatively powerless, after all, can laugh in defiance at the folly and vice of the powerful. And while ridicule can do little to substantially alter asymmetries of power, it can nevertheless bolster the laugher's determination to resist the interpretation of the social world that the powerful may wish to foist upon them. As Miranda Fricker has written, declaring 'something potentially authoritative to be absurd gives one critical courage' as 'one hermeneutical rebellion inspires another'.[58]

Finally, echoes of Shaftesbury can be heard in the argument made by some political theorists that ridicule *enables* exchange because it is a form of criticism that, while severe, nevertheless invites reply. On this view even contemptuous jests are better for politics than silently regarding someone with disdain. For some, the demise of mutual mockery between individuals and groups is actually an ominous sign that an altogether nastier form of exchange is about to commence. The adage that when the jokes stop the shooting might be about to start expresses a real worry that laughing at each other might be the last thing propping up civility in conditions of heightened social and political tension. If, as Iris Marion Young argued, humour merits inclusion among 'the forms of speech that often lubricate

56. Henri Bergson, 'Laughter', in *Comedy*, ed. Wylie Sypher (Garden City, NY: Doubleday Anchor Books, 1956), 154.

57. Ronald Dworkin, 'The Right to Ridicule', *New York Review of Books*, 23 March 2006. Robert Darnton, 'To Deal with Trump, Look to Voltaire', *New York Times*, 27 December 2018. For Elizabeth Markovits the 'idea that irony's victims are always unfairly ridiculed is spurious; some characters call for deflation, and irony is a less aggressive . . . way than frank speech to deflate another's arrogance'. Elizabeth Markovits, *The Politics of Sincerity* (University Park: Pennsylvania State University Press, 2008), 102. The liberal philosopher Kwame Anthony Appiah has made the ambitious claim that 'carefully calibrated ridicule' could be a more powerful resource against injustice than appeals to moral argument. Kwame Anthony Appiah, *The Honor Code: How Moral Revolutions Happen* (London: Norton, 2010), 172.

58. Miranda Fricker, *Epistemic Injustice: Power and the Ethics of Knowing* (Oxford: Oxford University Press, 2007), 167.

ongoing discussion' then an excessive earnestness may spell more trouble for civility than ridicule itself.[59]

I contend that the tension between these perspectives is where the most fruitful thinking about the politics of ridicule is to be found. To declare ridicule uncivil is to deny its sociable and emancipatory potential. On the other hand, it is no less problematic to overlook ridicule's capacity to humiliate the already vulnerable or to embrace a teleological view that presents it as the friend of virtue and the scourge of vice. The best British Enlightenment thinking on the topic recognized that neither aspect of ridicule—the oppressive nor the emancipatory—could be discarded without cost. Political theorists who want to take ridicule seriously must do the same.

Overview of the Book

Shaftesbury first earned notoriety for defending ridicule in his *Letter Concerning Enthusiasm* of 1708. Commentators have generally interpreted Shaftesbury's *Letter* as targeting religious fanatics, High Church clerics, and other deviants from the Whig common sense of his day. In the first chapter I upend this view by revealing how Shaftesbury's project was far more ambitious in scope. The Earl, I argue, did not limit his ridicule to enthusiasts or priests but instead, drawing on the ancient Stoics and Cynics, sought to shock his readers into revising their beliefs and adopting a sociable religious disposition more conducive to toleration. It was the first indication that Shaftesbury was elevating ridicule from a conversational art to a vehicle for enlightenment.

Shaftesbury died in Naples in 1713, having fled both the English cold (he was a chronic asthmatic) and the political disappointment of a Tory electoral triumph. But by then he had already published what would become the urtext of the ridicule debate for the remainder of the century, *Sensus Communis: an Essay on the Freedom of Wit and Humour* (1709). Chapter 2 situates *Sensus Communis* in its political context and shows how Shaftesbury's commitment to ridicule received an early test when the High Churchman Henry Sacheverell used a sermon at St Paul's Cathedral to mock Whig pieties concerning toleration. By agreeing with Whig efforts

---

59. Iris Marion Young, 'Communication and the Other: Beyond Deliberative Democracy', in *Democracy and Difference: Contesting the Boundaries of the Political*, ed. Seyla Benhabib (Princeton, NJ: Princeton University Press, 1996), 129.

to suppress Sacheverell's sermonizing through Parliamentary impeachment, Shaftesbury conceded that the coercive power of the state was sometimes needed to create space for the more sociable exchanges he preferred. The chapter concludes in the 1720s with two of Shaftesbury's most influential early readers: Bernard Mandeville and Francis Hutcheson. I show that it was in the disagreement between these two philosophers (one a champion of Shaftesbury, the other his most trenchant critic), that the significance of ridicule to the debate on sociability comes truly into focus.

In the third chapter we turn to David Hume and to reactions to Shaftesbury's experiment in Scotland. To many of his early critics, it appeared that Hume had followed Shaftesbury in making ridicule central to his philosophical practice, particularly when it came to religion. Even today several commentators agree that Hume either deliberately sought to provoke laughter in his readers or simply lacked the self-control necessary to keep his own derision hidden. I complicate this picture by revealing Hume's ambivalence towards the Shaftesburian programme. If good humour was a virtue for Hume, it was one that could conceal worse vices. And while he indulged his taste for ridicule frequently, he also harboured Hobbesian doubts about its capacity to distort debate and sow discord.

Hume's Aberdonian adversaries, Thomas Reid and James Beattie, are the focus of chapter 4. These Common Sense philosophers took a keen interest in the psychology of laughter and were anxious to undermine Hobbes's argument that laughter was ultimately an expression of contempt. But they never disavowed ridicule in philosophical argumentation and public debate. On the contrary, Beattie in particular championed it as an antidote to scepticism, a philosophy he deemed both absurd (and hence immune to rational refutation) and dangerously persuasive. Far from being a frivolous or uncivil mode of speech, therefore, Reid and Beattie made ridicule into a shield for the common sense understandings that held society together.

The final chapters of the book turn to two more radical incarnations of Shaftesbury's experiment to be found in the revolutionary atmosphere of the 1790s. In the fifth chapter we turn to a group of critics on the fringes of the Scottish Enlightenment who deployed ridicule for a very different political cause: the campaign against the Atlantic slave trade. William Dickson, Alexander Geddes and James Tytler all set out to expose defenders of African slavery as not merely mistaken but contemptible, and their arguments as an absurd affront to humanity. Taking their cue from Montesquieu's *Spirit of the Laws*, the form of ridicule they often adopted was a mock endorsement of the very pro-slavery arguments they sought to discredit. In adopting this rhetorical strategy, I argue, these abolitionists found that some prejudiced or self-interested claims on behalf of slavery could not be countered by argument alone and that presenting them as beneath refutation was essential to defeating them.

Chapter 6 brings us to the role of ridicule in the work of one of the century's foremost critics of men and women's subordination. In her *Vindication of the Rights of Men*, Mary Wollstonecraft, referencing Shaftesbury, accused Edmund Burke of using ridicule to humiliate his political opponents, including her own mentor, Richard Price. Yet she herself showed few qualms about returning like with like. Rather than demonstrating inconsistency, I argue, Wollstonecraft's rhetorical strategy reveals her appreciation for the power of ridicule to expose prejudice and undercut illegitimate claims to authority. Particularly in her two *Vindications*, Wollstonecraft deployed ridicule as a weapon against haughty elites and made a case for teaching young women to laugh contemptuously at the cultural products (mainly sentimental novels) that contributed to their subordination.

In recovering these experiments with ridicule my aim is not to exhaust the full range of reactions to Shaftesbury's project or trace every intervention into the debate he inspired. Shaftesbury's *Characteristics of Men, Manners, Opinions, Times* went through eleven editions during the eighteenth century (so far as philosophical texts go only Locke's *Essay Concerning Human Understanding* went through more) and tracking every response to its claims about ridicule would be tedious and not especially instructive. Nor have I scoured these texts for models ripe for contemporary imitation. Ridicule is nothing if not contextual and the same applies to arguments about how it might be used. What I have offered, however, is an exercise in historical recovery that can help us recognize what might be transpiring when a critic, comedian, politician or journalist reaches for ridicule, and what effects this can have on our social and political life. Ridicule does not currently lack for champions. Nor have we a shortage of critics lamenting its tendency to trivialize, distract and wound. Less common are historically informed analyses of what ridicule can and cannot do, drawn from an era in which the promise and pitfalls of ridicule were subjected to greater scrutiny than any other. This book, I hope, will begin to fill that gap.

CHAPTER ONE

A Polite Diogenes?

RIDICULE IN SHAFTESBURY'S
POLITICS OF TOLERATION

IN THE SUMMER of 1706 three Huguenot refugees—Elie Marion, Durand Fage, and Jean Cavalier—arrived in London from the Cévennes region of southern France, fleeing war and religious persecution. A large number of their co-religionists had already settled in the city, but the new arrivals quickly found themselves shunned by the more established Huguenot community. The divisive issue was their reputation for ecstatic acts of devotion, false miracles, and (particularly from Marion) millenarian prophesies, one of which foretold the destruction of London itself. More alarming still was that members of the gentry soon began imitating the French Prophets (as they came to be known) sparking fears of a general contagion. Sir John Lacy and Sir Richard Bulkley allowed the prophets to use their homes as meeting houses, helped publicize their activities, and even began speaking in tongues and uttering their own prophecies. By 1708 the ranks of the French Prophets had swelled considerably and although the group had no explicit political agenda, they caused enough of a stir to strain the government's commitment to religious toleration.

Shaftesbury was among those who personally bore witness to the prophesizing of these new converts and was present for one of Lacy's spiritual agitations.[1] Reflecting on what he had seen, the Earl composed

---

1. Shaftesbury wrote of Lacy: 'I saw him lately under an agitation (as they call it), uttering prophecy in a pompous Latin style, of which, out of his ecstasy, it seems he is wholly incapable.' Shaftesbury, 'A Letter Concerning Enthusiasm', in *Characteristics of Men, Manners, Opinions, Times*, ed. Lawrence E. Klein (Cambridge: Cambridge University Press, 1999), 24. On Shaftesbury's presence at Lacy's house see Shaftesbury, *Standard Edition:*

a letter to former Lord Chancellor John Baron Somers that, when published anonymously in 1708 as the *Letter Concerning Enthusiasm*, quickly
became one of the most controversial religious tracts of the early eighteenth century. Its darkly humorous tone led some early readers to suspect Jonathan Swift the author, a misattribution that amused Swift far
more than it did Shaftesbury.[2] However, Shaftesbury's *Letter* was not only
humorously written; it also championed ridicule as an antidote to the religious enthusiasms the French Prophets had generated. The effectiveness
of this antidote could, he further alleged, already be seen. As Shaftesbury
saw matters, the puppet shows that parodied Marion and his colleagues
in Smithfield's Bartholomew Fair had already diminished their standing
in the eyes of the public, obviating the need for more repressive measures
inconsistent with toleration.

Had he stopped there, Shaftesbury's *Letter* might have served as an
unremarkable addition to the enormous outpouring of pamphlets occa-
sioned by the French Prophet controversy.[3] After all, the Earl had not even
been the first to recommend ridicule as an appropriate response to the crisis. Richard Kingston in his *Enthusiastick Impostors No Inspired Prophets*
(1707) reckoned that no one should 'forebare ridiculing and exposing a
Buffoon' who was 'usurping the Office and Name of a Prophet'.[4] What set
Shaftesbury's *Letter* apart, however, was that it seemed to elevate ridicule

---

Complete Works, Correspondence and Posthumous Writings, vol. 3,1, *Correspondence. Letters 1–100 (December 1683–February 1700*, ed. Christine Jackson-Holzberg, Patrick Müller
and Friedrich A. Uehlein (Stuttgart/Bad Cannstatt: Frommann-Holzboog, 2017), 168. Also
Hillel Schwartz, *The French Prophets: The History of a Millenarian Group in Eighteenth-
Century England* (Berkeley: University of California Press, 1980), 93n.

2. On 14 September 1708 Swift wrote to his friend Philip Ambrose: 'Here has been an
Essay of Enthusiasm lately publisht that has run mightily, and is very well writt. All my
friends will have me to be the Author . . . By the free Whiggish thinking I should rather take
it to be yours: But mine it is not.' Swift cited in Ronald Paulson, *Don Quixote in England:
The Aesthetics of Laughter* (Baltimore, MD: Johns Hopkins University Press, 1998), 121.
Shaftesbury wrote again to Somers (the dedicatee of Swift's *Tale of the Tub*) around the same
time expressing his worry that the *Letter* would be published as the work of Swift. Ibid., 122.

3. More than eighty tracts appeared attacking the prophets between 1707 and 1708.
Georgia Cosmos, *Huguenot Prophecy and Clandestine Worship in the Eighteenth Century:
'The Sacred Theatre of the Cévennes'* (Burlington, VT: Ashgate, 2005), 156.

4. Richard Kingston, *Enthusiastick Impostors No Inspired Prophets* (London: J. Morphew, 1707), 20. The notion that good humour or 'mirth' could counteract enthusiasm
was at least as old as Burton's 1621 *Anatomy of Melancholy*. Ofspring Blackall similarly
demanded that the French Prophets be subjected to a trial but advised more sober methods
of distinguishing true prophets from false. Ofspring Blackall, *The Way of Trying Prophets*
(London: W. Rogers, 1707).

from a light-hearted response to enthusiasm into a general test of religious imposture. The 'test of ridicule', he suggested, could and should be applied to all religious doctrines to verify if they were genuinely worthy of respect or only spuriously so.[5]

Unsurprisingly, this ambitious proposal met with stiff resistance. Some readers suspected that the *Letter*'s author had used the affair of the French Prophets as a smokescreen for a disparagement of Christianity itself. The Tory pamphleteer Mary Astell accused Shaftesbury of inviting readers to treat religion 'with less respect and reverence' and predicted that ridicule, once given free reign, would quickly become 'boundless', with the innocent and sincerely pious suffering humiliation alongside false prophets and enthusiasts.[6] Edward Fowler, the Bishop of Gloucester, was similarly in no doubt that the *Letter* aimed at 'Rejecting entirely the Church of God' and balked at the notion that ridicule could serve any useful purpose in religious life.[7]

Much of the difficulty surrounding Shaftesbury's proposal stemmed from his use of the term 'ridicule' ahead of less ominous alternatives. Whereas humour could be good-natured, amiable, and self-deprecating, ridicule was flinty and contemptuous, closer to a scoff or sneer than a laugh. Writing later in the century the poet and polemicist John Brown accused Shaftesbury of conflating 'good humour' (which he found unobjectionable)

5. Shaftesbury, 'Letter Concerning Enthusiasm', 8.

6. Mary Astell, *Bart'lemy Fair, or An Inquiry After Wit; in Which Due Respect Is Had to a Letter Concerning Enthusiasm, to My Lord: Answer a Fool According to His Folly, Lest He Be Wise in His Own Conceits* (London: R. Wilkin, 1709), 71.

7. Edward Fowler, *Reflections upon a Letter Concerning Enthusiasm* (London: H. Clemens, 1709), 17. Shaftesbury's own son, the fourth Earl, later pleaded that his father only sought a more tolerant response to the French Prophets and selected ridicule merely to 'suppress' their 'vain and idle delusions' rather than undermine religion as such. The Fourth Earl of Shaftesbury, 'A Sketch of the Life of the Third Earl of Shaftesbury by His Son, the Fourth Earl', in *The Life, Unpublished Letters, and Philosophical Regimen of Anthony, Earl of Shaftesbury*, ed. Benjamin Rand (New York: Macmillan, 1900), xxvi. Even those who sympathized with Shaftesbury's desire for a less solemn environment for religious debate nevertheless worried that using ridicule to correct religious extravagance might endanger religious peace and, by extension, toleration itself. Shaftesbury's own tutor John Locke had no shortage of disdain for religious enthusiasts led astray by their overheated imaginations. But he never went so far as to advocate mocking them and stressed the need for religious disputants to comport themselves with civility regardless of how strongly they felt the other side to be mistaken. Bejan, *Mere Civility*, 131–35. Shaftesbury himself recommended 'Mr Lock's *Essay of Human Understanding*' as a resource in the 'fight against the enthusiasts' in a letter to a young protégé, but he took to that fight weapons that Locke himself never approved of using. Shaftesbury, 'The Ainsworth Correspondence', in *Standard Edition: Complete Works, Correspondence and Posthumous Writings, Moral and Political Philosophy*, vol. 2,4, *Select Sermons of Dr. Whichcote u.a.*, ed. Wolfram Benda, Christine Jackson-Holzberg, Friedrich A. Uehlein and Erwin Wolff (Stuttgart/Bad Cannstatt: Frommann-Holzboog, 2004), 346 and 348.

with 'ridicule', a form of speech whose sole purpose was to 'excite contempt' in an audience.[8] And while good humour, Brown asserted, was a
boon to religion, ridicule was a 'broiler and incendiary' that could discredit
religious truths, expose the innocent to harm, and 'destroy mutual charity between Christians'.[9] John Leland, in an influential overview of Deist
writers, was similarly convinced that Shaftesbury was 'making merry with
his reader' by equating 'raillery and ridicule' with 'good-humour'.[10] Even
Shaftesbury's most ardent sympathizers recognized the troubling ambigu-
ity surrounding the Earl's choice of terms, explaining it away by supposing
that 'his Lordship uses the word ridicule as synonimous [*sic*] with freedom, familiarity, good humour and the like'.[11] More recent scholars have
echoed this interpretation, arguing that Shaftesbury's loose terminology
reflected his style as a writer and that his aim was merely to inject levity
into a religious culture plagued by an oppressive solemnity.[12]

In this chapter I argue that neither his critics nor his defenders appreciated the complexity of Shaftesbury's test of ridicule and its role in his
religious politics. Shaftesbury defended ridicule in full awareness of its
troubling association with contempt. In spite of this, and of his own misgivings about the practice, he refused to draw the sting out of ridicule by
equating it with affability or good-natured raillery.[13] Instead, Shaftesbury

8. John Brown, *Essays on the Characteristics* (London: C. Davis, 1751), 42.

9. Ibid., 70 and 100.

10. John Leland, *A View of the Principal Deistical Writers That Have Appeared in
England in the Last and Present Century*, vol. 1 (London: W. Richardson and S. Clark, for
R. and J. Dodsley, and T. Longman, 1766), 62.

11. Charles Bulkley, *A Vindication of My Lord Shaftesbury, on the Subject of Ridicule.
Being Remarks upon a Book, Intitled, Essays on the Characteristics* (London: John Noon,
1751), 19–20. Cf Paulson, *Don Quixote in England*, 119. Bulkley's interpretation was her-
meneutically over-generous. Shaftesbury conceded that he was sometimes loose in his use
of terms but the example he chose of a term lacking a 'precise definition' was 'enthusiasm' itself, whose meaning Shaftesbury had deliberately pluralized in a bid to distinguish
a 'noble' variety of enthusiasm from fanaticism. To plead that 'ridicule' had been only a
stand-in for good humour was an option available to Shaftesbury; it is not, however, one he
chose to pursue. Shaftesbury, 'Miscellaneous Reflections', in *Characteristics of Men, Manners, Opinions, Times*, 351. The Irish freethinker John Toland similarly argued that the *Letter* reflected nothing more than its author's 'innate disposition' to 'Innocent Raillery'. John
Toland, 'Introduction', in *Letters from the Right Honourable the Late Earl of Shaftesbury,
to Robert Molesworth* (London: W. Wilkins, 1721), viii.

12. Stuart Tave holds that Shaftesbury had no interest in developing a 'satirical method'
but only sought a 'sober kind of cheerfulness'. Stuart Tave, *The Amiable Humourist: A
Study in the Comic Theory and Criticism of the Eighteenth and Early Nineteenth Centuries*
(Chicago: University of Chicago Press, 1960), 37.

13. John Redwood was similarly sceptical of the notion that Shaftesbury was just being
slippery with his terminology. 'Shaftesbury', he wrote, 'was not unaware of what he was

in the *Letter* offered a multi-layered defence of ridicule, one that made full and unapologetic use of its corrosive potential. Superficially, the Earl celebrated ridicule as an alternative to persecution for those concerned about the spread of enthusiasm. More fundamentally, he identified a particular kind of ridicule that could therapeutically treat the passions that gave rise to persecution in the first place. Drawing on Stoic interpretations of the ancient Cynics, I argue Shaftesbury saw the test of ridicule as a way of shocking his readers into re-evaluating their religious beliefs and becoming better humoured in their disposition towards God, the universe, and ultimately each other.[14] The good humour he sought to instil by this shock therapy was not an insipid cheerfulness or polite amiability but rather a radical transformation of character indispensable for a tolerant society. Appreciating this, I maintain, can help explain why a philosopher sensitive to the dangers of ridicule would rely on it so often in his own religious criticism.

Early Misgivings about Ridicule in Shaftesbury's Manuscripts

Shaftesbury began assessing the dangers associated with ridicule long before he sat down to write the *Letter*. We can say this with some confidence thanks to the survival of two unpublished *Askêmata* or 'exercise' journals that the Earl kept during two periods of self-imposed political exile in Rotterdam, the first of which he began in 1698 after a demanding stint in the House of Commons (he would not ascend to the title of Earl until the following year). Temporarily freed from the demands of public life, Shaftesbury embarked during these retreats on what he called, in a letter to his mentor John Locke, 'a hearty application to the ancients', a course of study heavily emphasizing the Stoic philosophers Epictetus and Marcus Aurelius.[15] The *Askêmata* provide a partial record of these intel-

---

saying and its implications.' John Redwood, *Reason, Ridicule and Religion: The Age of Enlightenment in England 1660–1750* (London: Thames and Hudson, 1976), 183. The classic statement of Shaftesburian politeness as Whig ideology remains Lawrence E. Klein, *Shaftesbury and the Culture of Politeness: Moral Discourse and Cultural Politics in Early Eighteenth-Century England* (Cambridge: Cambridge University Press, 1994).

14. On the importance of Cynic 'shock therapy' to the Enlightenment see Michael Sonenscher, *Sans-Culottes: An Eighteenth-Century Emblem in the French Revolution* (Princeton, NJ: Princeton University Press, 2008), 141.

15. Shaftesbury to Locke, 9 April 1698, in *The Life, Unpublished Letters, and Philosophical Regimen of Anthony, Earl of Shaftesbury*, 306. The Roman Stoics evidently dominated this programme of study, with the notebooks consisting mostly of translations of, and

lectual pursuits. More than that, however, they contain the collected remnants of intense, even violent, exercises in Stoic self-examination.

Several of these exercises directly concerned Shaftesbury's laughing habits and how he might amend them. In one particularly jarring entry he severely admonished himself for his witty behaviour and tried to purge his desire to excite laughter in others. Even 'tho' Laughter be a Passion which may be employed . . . against the Pomp and rediculouse solemnity of human affaires', he wrote, 'yet there is nothing more unsafe, or more difficult of management.'[16] If others considered him to have crossed the fine line between polite restraint and downright moroseness, to have 'grown dull' and lost 'whatever he had either of Witt or humour' then so much the better. On such occasions, he told himself, 'all is well and thou must rejoice'.[17]

What made laughter so risky for the aspirant to Stoic virtue? From Shaftesbury's scattered warnings to himself in the *Askêmata* we can identify a number of key dangers. The first concerns Shaftesbury's preoccupation with cultivating self-mastery. For Shaftesbury, the desire to laugh along with companions or generate new laughter in their company was a subset of a more general yearning for the 'pleasure in pleasing', a pleasure which compromised his independence by making his happiness contingent upon the response of the company around him.[18] If he was to laugh at all then it must be within the tightly controlled environment of his own

commentaries on, excerpts from Epictetus's *Encheiridion*, Arrian's *Discourses of Epictetus* and Marcus Aurelius's *Meditations*. Shaftesbury's friends in Rotterdam took notice of this curious immersion in Stoic philosophy. A remark in the *General Dictionary* (an English adaptation of Pierre Bayle's *Dictionnaire historique et critique*) reveals that Shaftesbury 'carried always with him' the works of Xenophon, Horace, Epictetus and Marcus Aurelius. Pierre Bayle, 'Shaftesbury', in *A General Dictionary, Historical and Critical: In Which a New and Accurate Translation of That of the Celebrated Mr. Bayle . . . Is Included*, ed. and trans. John Peter Bernard, Thomas Birch and John Lockman, vol. 9 (London: James Bettenham, 1739), 186. Klein likewise acknowledges Shaftesbury's debt to Stoicism but nevertheless concludes that the centrality of sociability to Shaftesbury's political philosophy led him to 'ultimately reject . . . the austerer claims of stoic sagacity'. Klein, *Shaftesbury and the Culture of Politeness*, 79. Christopher Brooke has suggested that the text is less a collation of Stoic doctrines than a variety of 'spiritual exercises' designed to effect some desired change in their user. Brooke, *Philosophic Pride*, 123.

16. Shaftesbury, 'Askêmata', in *Standard Edition: Complete Works, Correspondence and Posthumous Writings*, vol. 2,6, *Moral and Political Philosophy. Askemata I (Englisch)*, ed. Wolfram Benda, Christine Jackson-Holzberg, Patrick Müller and Friedrich A. Uehlein (Stuttgart/Bad Cannstatt: Frommann-Holzboog, 2011), 245.

17. Ibid., 247.

18. Ibid., 65.

private exercises. 'Laugh alone', Shaftesbury implored himself, 'at Seriouse times' and so 'excite to it rather than be carried to it by Temper'.[19] The logic was that by therapeutically administering small doses of laughter to himself Shaftesbury could thereby 'Chuse it' rather than having 'it' choose him.[20]

Shaftesbury also shared Hobbes's concern about the unsociability of laughter and worried that it ultimately arose from a feeling of contempt or scorn. Seeking the essence of laughter ('in itself' or at 'Bottom') he arrived at the alarming conclusion that behind every laugh lurks one of the passions the student of Stoicism must learn to extirpate from the self: 'That, Anger; this, Contempt. That, Reproof: this, Reproach.'[21] He refined this view in a Latin manuscript entitled *Pathologia* that Shaftesbury composed as a personal study of Stoic doctrine in 1706 but never intended for publication. The *Pathologia* contains a revealing passage that Shaftesbury transcribed directly into the *Askêmata* to round off his entry on laughter in January 1707, nine months before writing the *Letter*. According to Stoic doctrine the passions (*pathē*) derive from false evaluations of what is good or placing value in externals that should be considered indifferent. Extending this theory to laughter, Shaftesbury found that the pleasure we take in ridicule (*jocositas*) derives from falsely treating 'some ugliness in external things and other people' as 'if it were a good for us', a failing that made this form of laughter a 'species of malice or malignity'.[22] And while Shaftesbury allowed that not all laughter was necessarily grounded in mockery of others, he nevertheless implied that even the remaining, milder form of laughter (*hilaritas*) also ultimately originated in admiration for something 'fancied beautiful' and so fell foul of his Stoic strictures.[23]

For Shaftesbury's contemporaries the worry that laughter sprung from contempt usually resulted in stern cautions against jesting when in company, on the basis that one could never be sure how others would react. The *Askêmata* reveal that Shaftesbury shared this fear and he advised himself there to avoid 'Railleries Ironyes or Mockeryes'.[24] The Earl even urged himself to recollect the 'sad Example & Experience' of his own previous experiments with humour, a probable allusion to an earlier satire of

19. Ibid., 451.
20. Ibid., 451.
21. Ibid., 445.
22. I rely here on the translation of the *Pathologia* contained in Laurent Jaffro, Christian Maurer and Alain Petit, 'Pathologia, A Theory of the Passions', *History of European Ideas* 39, 2 (2013), 240.
23. Ibid.
24. Shaftesbury, '*Askêmata*', 64.

enthusiasm, *The Adept Ladies or the Angelick Sect*, which he composed around 1701 but never published. This text, inspired in part by Shaftesbury's earlier contact with Huguenot enthusiasts, has always been something of a stumbling block for those who wish to present the Earl as a consistent champion of polite wit.[25] His son, the fourth Earl, described it as a 'little treatise' on enthusiasm, a kind of precursor to the *Letter*, but there is little in it by way of argument.[26] Instead, Shaftesbury outdid Swift for scatological portraits of the religiously deluded, including one of a woman who believed she could eat human waste and miraculously excrete it as gold.[27]

If his own past shame were not enough, there was always the memory of Shaftesbury's grandfather, the first Earl, to contend with. The first Earl had an enormous influence on Shaftesbury's upbringing and was largely responsible for setting him on the path to classical learning by ensuring that he acquired fluency in Latin and Greek from a young age.[28] Grateful though Shaftesbury may have been for this early boost to his classical education, however, he was far less sure that the first Earl's legendary wit was worthy of imitation: 'And Remember the treacherouse Pleasure: *reviving chearing entertaining moving, affecting, imprinting:* Imitation of Gd Fr [Grandfather]—Perniciouse! Ruinouse!'[29] John Dryden's caricature of the first Earl in *Absalom and Achitophel* as a rogue whose fervent and ungoverned wit led him to insanity ('Great Witts are sure to Madness near ally'd') stuck deep in the public's imagination, and evidently also in Shaftesbury's.[30]

25. *The Adept Ladies* may have been inspired by an earlier encounter of Shaftesbury's with Nicolas Fatio de Duillier, later associated with the French Prophets and subjected to public humiliation on the scaffold. See *Correspondence. Letters 1–100 (December 1683–February 1700)*, 375 and 168.

26. Shaftesbury, 'A Sketch of the Life of the Third Earl of Shaftesbury by His Son, the Fourth Earl', xxvi.

27. Alfred Owen Aldridge, 'Shaftesbury's Rosicrucian Ladies', *Anglia*, no. 103 (1985), 297.

28. Shaftesbury, 'A Sketch of the Life of the Third Earl of Shaftesbury by His Son, the Fourth Earl', xix.

29. Shaftesbury, 'Askêmata', 65. In a letter to Jean Le Clerc, Shaftesbury complained of his grandfather's 'over fondness of wit' which made him act 'very unnaturally'. Shaftesbury to Jean le Clerc, 8 February 1705. *The Life, Unpublished Letters, and Philosophical Regimen of Anthony, Earl of Shaftesbury*, 334.

30. Dryden cited in K.H.D. Haley, *The First Earl of Shaftesbury* (Oxford: Clarendon University Press, 1968), 2. Shaftesbury would avenge himself on Dryden in the *Characteristics*, accusing him of exemplifying the 'pedantic manner', 'vanity', and 'defiance of criticism' prevalent among the authors of his day. Shaftesbury, 'Miscellaneous Reflections', 455.

Laughter at physical disability or mental impairment, a phenomenon he encountered with depressing frequency in London, struck Shaftesbury as particularly abhorrent. Too many Londoners for Shaftesbury's taste took pleasure in mocking the mentally impaired and would pay admission at Bedlam asylum in order to laugh at the inmates there.[31] The *Askêmata* reveal just how deeply Shaftesbury deplored this 'Divertion of Seeing Bedlam'.[32] Similarly odious to him was the Court practice of laughing at 'Dwarf Man-Monkey' jesters.[33] It is possible that memory of his grandfather loomed large again here. Shaftesbury would have been keenly aware that the first Earl's enemies persistently mocked him for his physical appearance (a copper tube Locke devised to transfer fluid from the Earl's hydatid cyst earned him the nickname 'Count Tapski').[34]

Ridicule was dangerous not only because of its capacity to *express* contempt, however. Shaftesbury also worried that it could *excite* contempt in those made to laugh, corrupting their sentiments and, in the worst cases, even encouraging them to violence. We can find evidence for this in yet another of Shaftesbury's unpublished manuscripts. Around the time of his first retreat in Rotterdam, Shaftesbury began making detailed notes to himself for a book he was planning to write on the life of Socrates. Deliberating on how he should present the events that led to Socrates's trial and execution, Shaftesbury followed Plato and Xenophon in singling out Aristophanes's parody of the philosopher in *The Clouds* as particularly influential in priming the Athenians to convict: 'Remember at the ending of this part of the discourse relating to Aristophanes', he reminded himself, to stress the 'hard fate' suffered by Socrates for having been 'laughed at as an Enthousiast' (the fate that would later befall the French Prophets). Whatever his later views on the merits of mocking those accused of enthusiasm, Shaftesbury at this stage was clear that such behaviour was reckless and had encouraged those who laughed at Socrates to take further measures to silence him. Notwithstanding the two decades that elapsed between the performance of Aristophanes's play and the trial itself, Shaftesbury bluntly condemned Aristophanes as Socrates's 'Murderer', so powerful was his ridicule in stoking Athenian animosity towards the philosopher.[35] For the young lord, then, ridicule was iniquitous both as an injury in itself and

31. Gatrell, *City of Laughter*, 62.

32. Shaftesbury, 'Askêmata', 447.

33. Ibid.

34. Dickie, *Cruelty and Laughter*, 76.

35. Shaftesbury, 'Chartae Socraticae,' in *Standard Edition: Complete Works, Correspondence and Posthumous Writings*, vol. 2,5, *Chartae Socraticae: Design of a Socratick*

because it could expose its object to severer forms of treatment further down the line.

To these ethical worries Shaftesbury added a further reservation about the damage ridicule could do in the context of religious debate. Again, the example of Locke may have been important here. In his *Vindication of the Reasonableness of Christianity* (1695), Locke condemned 'frothy Discourses concerning the Serious Matters of Religion' and warned that 'misbecoming *Wit*' was 'not of the least causes of Atheism'.[36] Shaftesbury shared his concern. Indeed, for a thinker soon to publicly defend the use of ridicule in religious matters, Shaftesbury in the *Askêmata* comes across as remarkably reluctant to deploy it in any religious controversy at all. Not only did he disavow '*free talking* about matters of Religion and the Established Rites of Worship', he also eschewed any criticism of the devout communicated 'rediculingly [*sic*] and with Contempt'.[37] Some commentators have gone so far as to say that in these personal studies Shaftesbury effectively ruled out 'the possibility of a rational use of *jocositas* to ridicule fanatics and zealots', the precise role he would reserve for it in the *Letter*.[38]

Considered against the backdrop of this extensive set of doubts, Shaftesbury's embrace of ridicule in the *Letter* begs some troubling questions. If the Earl previously flinched at the idea of laughter grounded in contempt, why did he now approve of exposing the French Prophets to mockery? And given the role he attributed to ridicule in bringing about the demise of Socrates, why did he now appear so sanguine about its effects? Laurent Jaffro, puzzled at how an author wracked by doubts about laughter could later endorse ridicule, speculates that Shaftesbury simply 'changed his

---

History, ed. Wolfram Benda, Christine Jackson-Holzberg, Friedrich A. Uehlein and Erwin Wolff (Stuttgart/Bad Cannstatt: Frommann-Holzboog, 2008), 181–83.

36. John Locke, *Writings on Religion*, ed. Victor Nuovo (Oxford: Clarendon Press, 2004), 220.

37. Shaftesbury, 'Askêmata', 108. Klein notes that it is unclear who exactly Shaftesbury had in mind here but suspects that these lines show Shaftesbury's reticence at being associated with freethinkers like Toland and Collins. Klein, *Shaftesbury and the Culture of Politeness*, 157.

38. Christian Maurer and Laurent Jaffro, 'Reading Shaftesbury's *Pathologia*: An Illustration and Defense of the Stoic Account of the Emotions', *History of European Ideas* 39, 2 (2013), 218. Although in a more recent essay Jaffro wavers on this reading of the *Pathologia*, stating now that 'Shaftesbury rejects the use of ridicule, or rather explains that the Stoics reject it'. Laurent Jaffro, 'The Passions and Actions of Laughter in Shaftesbury and Hutcheson', in *Thinking about the Emotions: A Philosophical History*, ed. Alix Cohen and Robert Stern (Oxford: Oxford University Press, 2017), 137.

mind' about this particular passion in the months between his final entry on laughter in the *Askêmata* and composing the *Letter* in 1707 (it was not published until the following year).[39] There are, however, two less ad hoc explanations for the Earl's move available. The first requires a closer look at the substance of Shaftesbury's argument for ridicule in the opening sections of the *Letter*, and in particular his explanation for why ridiculing the Prophets was preferable to any other form of response. The second calls for us to look again at Shaftesbury's engagement with ancient Stoic philosophy, and particularly his appreciation for the humour of the ancient Cynics.

Ridicule as a Tolerant Alternative to Persecution

The opening of Shaftesbury's *Letter* looks like proof that the Earl's efforts to therapeutically wean himself off a taste for ridicule were a failure. However, agonizing over the appropriateness of ridicule within a Stoic programme of self-improvement was a task distinct from evaluating its role within an increasingly turbulent public sphere. 'Never was there in our nation a time known, when folly and extravagance of every kind were more sharply inspected, or more wittily ridiculed', Shaftesbury now gushed.[40] Relaxed too was his worry that religion was too sombre a subject for levity: 'I have often wondered to see men of sense so mightily alarmed at the approach of anything like ridicule on certain subjects; as if they mistrusted their own judgment.'[41] The Earl now saw no reason why anyone should be 'afraid to stand the *test* of ridicule', so safe was this method of criticism. Welcoming ridicule as a corollary to intellectual freedom, the *Letter* depicted the public's appetite for mirth not as a symptom of declining civility but as a sign that it was flexing its critical muscle. If 'gravity is of the very essence of imposture', Shaftesbury now claimed, then ridicule was an indispensable protection against baseless claims to authority.[42] What this in turn implied was that the growth of ridicule in speech and print was not the temporary effusion of a giddy public getting used to its new freedom. Nor was it a crude behaviour that would gradually subside with 'refinement in manners, good breeding, and politeness'.[43] Rather rid-

---

39. Maurer and Jaffro, 'Reading Shaftesbury's *Pathologia*', 217. Another commentator finds that Shaftesbury 'seems to forget about the destructive ends to which humour . . . may be put'. Stanley Green, *Shaftesbury's Philosophy of Religion and Ethics* (Athens: Ohio University Press, 1967), 126.

40. Shaftesbury, 'Letter Concerning Enthusiasm', 7.

41. Ibid., 8.

42. Ibid.

43. Ibid., 7.

icule was required as a *permanent* check against those who project an air of seriousness in order to procure unwarranted protection from scrutiny.

It was precisely the seriousness surrounding the French Prophet controversy that Shaftesbury sought to dispel. Instead of presenting them as serious claimants to divine inspiration the Earl sought to spoil the awe that the Prophets strove to cultivate, ultimately rendering them so harmless that persecuting them would be pointless. In Section III of the *Letter*, Shaftesbury portrayed Marion and his associates as mentally fragile obsessives who foolishly prioritized martyrdom over physical safety. As such, persecuting them would not only be excessive, but would also spare the Prophets their most dreaded punishment of all: toleration itself. Because, Shaftesbury jested, some 'heathenishly cruel' and 'tolerating Englishmen' had subjected them to ridicule instead of being 'so obliging as to break their bones for them' the suffering of the French Prophets had already been excruciating.[44] For millenarian enthusiasts pining for a dose of persecution to indulge their 'spirit of martyrdom' a tolerant ridicule was itself as the utmost form of torture.[45]

But how tolerant was this ridicule really and to what extent did it serve as an alternative to more severe forms of correction? What Shaftesbury overlooked was the difficulty of neatly separating ridicule from the violence he imagined it could replace. Commenting on this portion of the *Letter*, the German philosopher Leibniz agreed that religious enthusiasts were likely to 'take raillery to be a form of martyrdom' because ridicule could harm just as easily as more physical forms of abuse.[46] Unlike Shaftesbury, however, Leibniz considered this a reason to *refrain* from such tactics. To Leibniz's horror, Shaftesbury's mockery of the French Prophets tacitly acknowledged that, in their case, ridicule and physical abuse had gone hand in hand. Appealing to English pride, Shaftesbury jokingly insisted that his compatriots would never 'stone' the Prophets in the 'open street' as their 'own mob' had already done, a reference to the rough treatment the Prophets had received from fellow Huguenots.[47]

44. Ibid., 15.

45. Ibid.

46. Gottfried Wilhelm Freiherr von Leibniz, 'Remarques Sur Le Livre Anglois Intitulé, Lettre Sur l'Enthousiasme', in *Recueil de Diverses Pieces, Sur La Philosophie, La Religion Naturelle, l'histoire, Les Matematiques, Etc. Par Mrs. Leibniz, Clarke, Newton, et Autres Auteurs Célèbres*, vol. 2 (Amsterdam: François Changuion, 1740), 320. My translation.

47. Shaftesbury, 'Letter Concerning Enthusiasm', 15. On how French Huguenots, anxious to demonstrate loyalty to their English hosts, led the opposition to the prophets see Lionel Laborie, *Enlightening Enthusiasm: Prophecy and Religious Experience in Early Eighteenth Century England* (Manchester: Manchester University Press, 2015), 172–75.

What Shaftesbury declined to mention was that attempts to violently suppress the Prophet's activities extended far beyond the Huguenot community. In April 1707 rioters attacked Lacy's house and the homes of other English members of the French Prophets' circle, smashing their windows. Fage and Cavalier were obliged to seek safety at the home of a judge after a similar assault on a supporter's house (stones and even dead animals were thrown at them as they fled). Later Marion and two of his scribes, Jean Daudé and Nicolas Fatio de Duillier, were brought into court charged with blasphemy, sedition and the spreading of terror among the people of London.[48] Upon being found guilty they were spared the pillory but were instead made to face hostile crowds on the scaffold on two consecutive days, during which they suffered severe injuries (Marion to the face, Fatio to the eye) from hurled stones.[49] Further trouble followed in May 1708 (just prior to the publication of Shaftesbury's *Letter*) when a large crowd gathered at Bunhill Fields to witness the resurrection of Dr Thomas Emes, a follower of the group who had died during a particularly violent agitation the previous December but whom the Prophets predicted would be resurrected. Anti-Prophet pamphlets became more menacing as the day of reckoning approached. One enjoined the 'Fools' who came to see Emes 'rise in May' to instead 'Piss on his Presumptive Clay'.[50]

Shaftesbury not only played down this violence, but the tone of the *Letter* also chimed with the satires that had helped stoke it. Most troublingly, Shaftesbury followed other anti-prophet publications in blurring the distinction between the wider London Huguenot community and the new arrivals from France (one such pamphlet compared the London

See also Lionel Laborie, 'The Huguenot Offensive against the Camisard Prophets in the English Refuge', in *The Huguenots: France, Exile and Diaspora*, ed. Jane McKee and Randolph Vigne (Brighton: Sussex Academic Press, 2013), 125–33.

48. Schwartz, *The French Prophets*, 111. Witnesses in support of the prophets had their testimony dismissed as 'almost ridiculous' by the Court. Anon., *An Account of the Tryal, Examination and Conviction of the Pretended French Prophets* (London: J.B, 1707), 1.

49. Laborie, 'The Huguenot Offensive against the Camisard Prophets', 129.

50. Anon., *An Epitaph on the French Prophet* (London, 1707), 1. There was later a suggestion that the government may have intervened to spur on the humiliation of the Prophets. Commenting on the affair in 1766, Lord Chesterfield insinuated that although Queen Anne's government 'loved a little persecution well enough', they instead 'ordered' Martin Powell, the Irish marionette artist who is credited with the earliest version of Punch and Judy, to 'make Punch turn Prophet' and thereby put an end to the 'prophets and their prophecies'. Philip Stanhope to Solomon Dayrolles, London, 26 January 1766. Philip Dormer Stanhope, *Miscellaneous Works of the Late Philip Dormer Stanhope, Earl of Chesterfield*, vol. 4 (London: Edward and Charles Dilly, 1779), 310.

Huguenots to ingrates who had abused the 'merciful protection of this Realm' by allowing religious fanatics to emerge from their community).[51] By sarcastically suggesting that the French Prophets only had something to fear from their 'own' people, Shaftesbury presented the French Prophet disturbance as an entirely Huguenot émigré affair, hardly a welcome gesture towards a vulnerable group still struggling with assimilation. Moreover, by intimating that the Prophets were thin-skinned enough to experience ridicule as the 'cruelest contempt in the world', the Earl echoed popular satires that had already presented the three men on the scaffold as cowards begging to be released from name-calling and jeering.[52] The anonymous author of *Pillory Disappointed, or the False Prophets Advancement* (sung to the tune of *Rotten Eggs, Turnop Tops, Pieces of Dirt, & Brick-Batts*) invented a scaffold speech for Marion in which he implored the crowds to 'spare' their eggs as otherwise he would soil his britches in response (the pamphlet also made reference to how the 'once glittering windows' at the Prophets' Barbican meeting place were now 'shattered in pieces').[53] There is no indication that Marion or his companions made any scaffold speeches during their two-day ordeal. Nor is it at all clear that the Prophets crumpled under ridicule in the manner that Shaftesbury and these other satirists suggested. As Georgia Cosmos has noted, the Prophets did not actually shy away from the sentence of public humiliation passed down to them. If they had 'acknowledged their error in printing and publishing false prophecies' they would have been spared the entire episode.[54] Instead they endured it and resumed their activities undeterred afterwards.

That Shaftesbury participated at all in this clamour against the French Prophets (even if to urge that they be tolerated and their behaviour deemed harmless) is, on one level, surprising. As his mentor Locke had done, the Earl developed extensive personal ties to the Huguenot *refuge* in Rotterdam during his stay in that city and advocated for the Huguenot cause in his dealings with figures close to the English government.[55] Locke had recommended Fatio, one of those injured on the scaffold, as a tutor

---

51. Anon., *A Full and True Account of the Apprehending and Taking Six French Prophets* (London, 1707), 1.

52. Shaftesbury, 'Letter Concerning Enthusiasm', 15.

53. Anon., *Pillory Disappointed, or the False Prophets Advancement* (London: Robert du Chemin, 1707), 1.

54. Cosmos, *Huguenot Prophecy and Clandestine Worship in the Eighteenth Century*, 135.

55. Gerald Cerny, *Theology, Politics, and Letters at the Crossroads of European Civilization: Jacques Basnage and the Baylean Hugenot Refugees in the Dutch Republic* (Dordrecht: Martinus Nijhoof, 1987), 129.

to the heir of the Duke of Bedford (Shaftesbury would also have been familiar with Fatio's scientific work as a Fellow of the Royal Society and his close association with Isaac Newton).[56] The Earl had even lamented in a letter from January 1707 how 'naturall Inhospitallity and Aversion to Strangers' among the English had hindered the 'Naturalization' of the 'Poor French Protestants'.[57] And while many of Shaftesbury's Huguenot connections might have been tempted to distance themselves from the French Prophets, some of his closest acquaintances in that circle did the opposite. The prominent Quaker, Benjamin Furly, at whose house Shaftesbury and Locke had stayed during their respective stays in Rotterdam, had supported the French Prophets in 1708.[58] Similarly, Leibniz was indignant on their behalf, mainly out of respect for Fatio. The 'affair of the French Prophets has had a bad ending', he wrote to an English friend, and 'that angers me'.[59] Shaftesbury, by contrast, seems to have been undisturbed by events. Nor did he express remorse over how he had portrayed them.

It would seem difficult therefore to describe Shaftesbury's ridicule as bearing the stamp of toleration. But this is only the case if we think of toleration as requiring a warm or respectful disposition towards the object tolerated. As critics of toleration (and some of its defenders) have long argued, toleration is perfectly compatible with intense negative judgments and feelings of dislike, contempt and dismissal.[60] That Shaftesbury considered the Prophets contemptible is clear. Equally clear, however, is that he considered ridicule to be a far more palatable outlet for such a judgment than the alternative options those in authority were then considering. The decision of the French Prophets to continue proselytizing after their trial eventually stretched the government's patience to breaking

56. On Locke's recommendation of Fatio see Scott Mandelbrote, 'The Heterodox Career of Nicolas Fatio de Duillier', in *Heterodoxy in Early Modern Science and Religion*, ed. John Hedley Brooke and Ian Maclean (Oxford: Oxford University Press, 2005), 282. In a letter to Locke Shaftesbury referred to Fatio as an 'extraordinary person'. Shaftesbury to Locke, 25 February 1692. *Correspondence. Letters 1–100 (December 1683–February 1700*, 168.

57. Shaftesbury to Jacques Basnage, 21 January 1707. National Archives, Kew, PRO 30/24/22/4.

58. Laborie, *Enlightening Enthusiasm*, 87.

59. Leibniz to Thomas Burnet, 16 March 1708. Cited in Mandelbrote, 'The Heterodox Career of Nicolas Fatio de Duillier', 268 n.18. Leibniz's anger was mainly stoked by his affection for Fatio, whose contributions to mathematics he admired.

60. For critiques of toleration's complicity with injustice and violence see Herbert Marcuse, 'Repressive Tolerance', in *A Critique of Pure Tolerance*, ed. Robert Paul Wolff, Barrington Moore and Herbert Marcuse (Boston: Beacon Press, 1969) 95–137. Also Wendy Brown, *Regulating Aversion: Tolerance in the Age of Identity and Empire* (Princeton, NJ: Princeton University Press, 2008).

point, notwithstanding the fact that, as Trinitarian Protestants, they could claim protection under the Toleration Act. In December 1707 Queen Anne signalled her intention to prosecute the Prophets and their English sup- porters, a fate avoided only because her government decided that allow- ing the Prophets to make failed predictions would prove more effective in suppressing their influence than legal intervention.[61] By advocating (and enacting) ridicule at the Prophets' expense and advertising its effective- ness as an antidote to religious enthusiasm more generally, Shaftesbury was prompting magistrates to stay the course whenever their commitment to toleration became strained. His method of dealing with the Prophets reflected not so much a dropping of the Earl's earlier qualms about ridi- cule, but a grudging recognition that if outbreaks of religious fanaticism were to be contained in a manner supportive of toleration then ridicule might yet be the best method available, its dangers notwithstanding.

Finally, it would be a mistake to think of Shaftesbury's ridicule in the *Letter* as directed solely against the Prophets. For in the very act of diminishing them Shaftesbury also cut down to size those who had been so alarmed by their activities. Throughout the *Letter* Shaftesbury went to great lengths to show that the enthusiasm seizing the Prophets was a natural effervescent that was entirely 'innocent' in its effects and should therefore be left to harmlessly run its course.[62] The more he naturalized enthusiasm in this way, the more Shaftesbury made a mockery of those who either sought to criminalize it or who demanded violent measures to contain it. Those who take fright at something ridiculous, Shaftesbury insinuated, become a little bit ridiculous themselves.

The 'Divine Facetiousness' of Diogenes

By celebrating ridicule as 'test' that could be tried out on all manner of religious opinions, Shaftesbury seemed to delight in its anarchic quality. But he also made clear in the *Letter* that not all jests were equal. Nor did they all serve the same purpose. Puppeteers in the booths at Smithfield might usefully deny would-be Prophets the gravity from which they drew their power, but Shaftesbury also alluded to more refined forms of ridicule that could advance more positive ends, including educating people into 'piety and true religion'.[63]

61. Laborie, *Enlightening Enthusiasm*, 186–87.
62. Shaftesbury, 'Letter Concerning Enthusiasm', 9.
63. Ibid., 13.

What kind of ridicule could perform this ambitious task? A crucial clue can be found in the same *Askêmata* notebooks that contain the Earl's most wrenching doubts about laughter. After expressing horror at the laughers in Bedlam, Shaftesbury tentatively raised the possibility that a 'civil polite humane' laughter may be found that the Stoic might affirm. So foreign was this laugh from all others, he maintained, it 'hardly' qualified as laughter at all, containing nothing of the convulsions, guffaws, or shakes usually associated with laughter. This 'serene', 'peaceful' and 'mild' laughter, he concluded, was the laugh of Socrates and 'those that followed the Socratic way', a laugh distinct from the abusiveness of Aristophanes and the modern wits who followed his example.[64]

It is immediately tempting to infer that this humane laughter must be some variant of Socratic irony, a form of humour Shaftesbury would explicitly defend in later writings.[65] This is the conclusion drawn by Jaffro who finds here that humane laughter is being 'eulogized as akin to Socratic irony'.[66] However, the exemplars of this laughter that Shaftesbury cites are very much at odds with that conclusion. The first such exemplar is 'Socrates's laugh with Appolodorus in the Prison'.[67] In the prison scene from Xenophon's *Apology*, Socrates teasingly responds to Appolodorus's lament that his good friend is to die 'unjustly' by asking whether he

64. Shaftesbury, 'Askêmata', 447. By raising the possibility of a 'civil polite humane' laughter, Shaftesbury may have gone beyond the Stoics to draw on a Renaissance tradition associated variously with Hippocrates and Democritus that presented laughter as a kind of safety valve, allowing us to vent humours that could otherwise manifest themselves more malignantly. Ronald Paulson, drawing exclusively on Shaftesbury's published writings, has with good reason situated the third Earl in this 'cathartic' tradition of laughter. Paulson, *Don Quixote in England*, 117. I am reluctant to embrace that conclusion. In the passage just cited Shaftesbury is not yet describing his preferred form of laughter in these terms and he in any case considered Democritus an anticipator of the very Epicurean philosophy he opposed. In his much-cited 1706 letter to Pierre Coste, Shaftesbury follows Horace in reducing the entire history of philosophy to a struggle between only two 'real distinct philosophies'. The first is a 'civil, social' philosophy that he traces from Socrates through to Stoicism and which emphasizes 'concernment in civil affairs'. The second is an unsociable philosophy originating with Democritus and ending up as Epicureanism. Shaftesbury makes clear in the letter that his allegiance lies with the first camp. Shaftesbury to Pierre Coste, 1 October 1706, in *The Life, Unpublished Letters, and Philosophical Regimen of Anthony, Earl of Shaftesbury*, 359.

65. In the *Soliloquy, or Advice to an Author* he describes Socratic irony as an 'exquisite and refined raillery which belonged in his manner and by virtue of which he could treat the highest subjects and those of the commonest capacity both together and render them explanatory to each other'. Shaftesbury, 'Soliloquy, or Advice to an Author', in *Characteristics of Men, Manners, Opinions, Times*, 87.

66. Maurer and Jaffro, 'Reading Shaftesbury's *Pathologia*', 218.

67. Shaftesbury, 'Askêmata', 448.

would 'rather see me put to death justly'.[68] This is an instance of Socratic humour, to be sure, but it bears few traces of irony. It is better described as an illustration of Socrates's tenderness towards a friend whose sorrow he temporarily relieves through the gentlest of jibes. (Socrates affectionately strokes Appolodorus's head as he delivers the tease, removing even the slightest suggestion of mocking intent.)[69]

By contrast, the two other exemplars Shaftesbury presents, the Cynic 'geniuses' Diogenes and Demonax, were considered neither practitioners of irony nor reputed to be particularly mild in their manner. Diogenes and his fellow Cynics were widely associated in the eighteenth century with indecency and the compulsive mockery of others, qualities seemingly anti-thetical to polite or humane laughter, and to Socratic irony as well. Not only were the Cynics considered impolite, they were accused of selecting the very kind of social conventions conveyed by the term 'politeness' as the primary target of their ridicule. Anecdotes concerning Diogenes's public masturbation, his spitting of phlegm in the face of his rich host (with the excuse that he could find no more suitable surface to spoil), and his gen-eral determination to flout of all standards of decency, abounded.[70]

Even Shaftesbury's fellow travellers in the republic of letters looked upon the Cynics with suspicion. His friend in Rotterdam, Pierre Bayle, found that Diogenes's laughter originated in a raw disdain for those around him and he compared the Cynic to Bion the Borysthenite, an impious philosopher whose 'impudence in turning religion into ridicule ought to be repressed' (*réprimé*).[71] Shaftesbury's selection of Demonax as another exemplary laugher was no less curious. As Shaftesbury would have read in his copy of Lucian (his only source on Demonax), this Cynic explicitly disavowed Socratic irony in favour of a more chastising, pointed

---

68. Xenophon, *Conversations of Socrates*, ed. Hugh Tredennick and Robin Waterfield (London: Penguin, 1990), 48.

69. Ibid.

70. Samuel Johnson, in a *Dictionary* entry of 1755, defined the 'Cynick' as a 'philoso-pher of the snarling or currish sort; a follower of Diogenes; a rude man; a snarler; a misan-thrope'. Cited in David Mazella, *The Making of Modern Cynicism* (Charlottesville: Univer-sity of Virginia Press, 2007), 15. For an account of the *philosophes'* attempt to domesticate Diogenes and appropriate his frankness of speech for criticism see Louisa Shea, *The Cynic Enlightenment: Diogenes in the Salon* (Baltimore, MD: Johns Hopkins University Press, 2010), chapter 3. For a brilliant account that presents Diogenes's unashamed behaviour as a form of democratic criticism see Jill Locke, *Democracy and the Death of Shame: Political Equality and Social Disturbance* (Cambridge: Cambridge University Press, 2016), chapter 2.

71. Bayle, 'Bion', *A General Dictionary, Historical and Critical: In Which a New and Accu-rate Translation of That of the Celebrated Mr. Bayle . . . Is Included*, ed. and trans. John Peter Bernard, Thomas Birch and John Lockman, vol. 3 (London: James Bettenham, 1735), 355.

form of mockery.[72] In an example of the very kind of mockery of physical deformity Shaftesbury had seemed to disdain, Demonax even jeered the lame Peripatetic philosopher Cyprian Rufinus for having the gumption to call himself a 'Walking Philosopher' (a rough translation of 'peripatetic').[73]

What are we to make of this celebration of some of the rougher characters in the Socratic tradition from the pen of a thinker famed as a theorist of politeness? Certainly Shaftesbury's choice of the Cynics as his exemplary laughers casts doubt on Michael Gill's claim that Shaftesbury would have 'scorned any attempt, Cynic or otherwise, to justify rudeness'.[74] There is less need for puzzlement, however, when we consider that Shaftesbury was drawing on earlier attempts in the Stoic tradition to rehabilitate Cynic ridicule. As Stephen Halliwell has shown, there is 'no intrinsic Stoic aversion to laughter' and several ancient Stoics combined sensitivity to the dangers of laughter with the use of ridicule to cajole students (and themselves) along the path to virtue.[75] They particularly admired the hectoring style of Diogenes to the point where Epictetus incorporated the Cynic into the Stoic canon.[76]

Let me illustrate this point with an example with which Shaftesbury was familiar. In a chapter of Arrian's *Discourses* entitled 'On the Cynic Calling' Epictetus chides imitators of the Cynic who think that carrying a staff, wearing a tattered cloak, and mocking passers-by for their pretentions would suffice to live up to as Diogenes's example. For Epictetus,

72. Lucian says of Demonax that 'there was no Socratic irony about him'. See his 'Demonax the Philosopher' in Lucian, *Chattering Courtesans and Other Sardonic Sketches*, trans. Keith Sidwell (London: Penguin, 2004), 36. For an alternative reading of Demonax, one that contrasts the conviviality, spontaneity and self-reflexiveness of his humour with the aggression of Diogenes's ridicule see Inger N.I. Kuin, 'Diogenes vs. Demonax: Laughter as Philosophy in Lucian', in *Laughter, Humor, and Comedy in Ancient Philosophy*, ed. Pierre Destrée and Franco V. Trivigno (Oxford: Oxford University Press, 2019).

73. Shaftesbury's fascination with Demonax ran deep. In his manuscript on Hieronymus Wolf's translation of Epictetus he speculated that Epictetus's addressee in 3.22 ('On the Cynic Calling') might have been 'the very Demonax' whom Lucian had 'Cynicized'. Shaftesbury Papers, National Archives at Kew, PRO 30/24/27/16.

74. Michael Gill, 'Shaftesbury on Politeness, Honesty, and Virtue', in *New Ages, New Opinions: Shaftesbury in His World and Today*, ed. Patrick Müeller (Frankfurt am Main: Peter Lang, 2014), 168.

75. Stephen Halliwell, *Greek Laughter: A Study of Cultural Psychology from Homer to Early Christianity* (Cambridge: Cambridge University Press, 2008), 304.

76. Similarly, Martha Nussbaum describes 'Stoic laughter' as an educative comic form that turns on the 'discrepancy between pretension and real worth' or 'the picture fools have of worldly goods and the reality of the worthlessness of those goods'. Martha Nussbaum, 'Stoic Laughter: A Reading of Seneca's Apocolocyntosis', in *Seneca and the Self*, ed. Shadi Bartsch and David Wray (Cambridge: Cambridge University Press, 2009), 87.

Diogenes alone could ridicule his contemporaries because he had puri-
fied his character through rigorous self-discipline.[77] Moreover, Epictetus affirmed, Diogenes's antics were unique in that they enjoyed divine
sanction. Unlike his charlatan imitators, Diogenes was a kind of divine
messenger (*angelos*) tasked with disabusing his fellow humans of their
false beliefs. Far from wantonly abusing his fellow Greeks, then, Diogenes
only ever ridiculed them 'as a father, a brother' and as a 'servant' of Zeus.
If he never offered a positive moral doctrine of his own it was because
Diogenes's role was to prepare his fellow human beings to receive the
positive teachings of Zeno, the first philosopher to present Stoic doctrine
systematically.[78]

Shaftesbury followed this Stoic tradition closely in the *Askêmata*, presenting Diogenes not as the ribald misanthrope his contemporaries took
him for but as one of the 'Great Ones', charged with preparing the ground
for later Stoic teachers by admonishing his fellows to live in accordance
with nature.[79] Further evidence from the *Askêmata* reveals just how seriously Shaftesbury took Epictetus's interpretation of Diogenes's career. In
accordance with the Hieronymous Wolf translation of Epictetus he anno-
tated, the Earl referred to Diogenes as 'the *Explorator*', a divine messenger
tasked with warning his fellow humans of their waywardness and pointing
towards a new path by his example.[80]

77. Shaftesbury's insistence on Diogenes's purity is also evident from an exchange of
letters he had with Pierre Coste in September 1709, the Shaftesbury half of which is missing. Coste, who was translating Shaftesbury's *Sensus Communis* into French at the time,
objected to the Earl's insistence in that text on the moral importance of personal cleanliness, and cited Diogenes as an example of one who was physically dirty but morally pure.
From Coste's letter of 26 September Shaftesbury's response seems to have been that Diogenes was an exception in that his dirty behaviour was part of his divine mission. The rest
of us remain duty bound to pursue cleanliness and robust physical health. Pierre Coste to
Shaftesbury, 26 September 1709. Hampshire Record Office. Malmesbury Papers 9M73/
G255/29.

78. Epictetus, *Discourses, Fragments, Handbook*, trans. Robin Hard (Oxford: Oxford
University Press, 2014), 181.

79. Shaftesbury, 'Askêmata', 424. By assimilating Diogenes to the Stoics in this manner,
Shaftesbury parted ways with other Cynic sympathizers who preferred to contrast Diogenes's good humour to Stoic surliness. The anonymous author of a 1711 periodical *The
Grouler: or Diogenes Robb'd of his Tub* saw little common ground between the hapless,
'sniveling Stoick' and Diogenes, whose task was to 'rally men into reason and cudgel em'
into good manners'. For Shaftesbury, it was precisely Diogenes' proto-Stoic commitment
to living in accordance with nature that licensed him to 'cudgel' people at all. Anon., *The
Grouler, or Diogenes Robbed of His Tub* (London: S. Popping, 1711), 1.

80. Shaftesbury, 'Askêmata', 104. Shaftesbury continued to make Diogenes's ridicule
an exception to his Stoic doubts about ridicule in his *Soliloquy, or Advice to an Author* of
1710, the only of his published works to directly reference the Cynic. Again, Shaftesbury

Shaftesbury not only championed Diogenes in the abstract; he also took a particular interest in his mockery of his fellow Greeks' efforts to win over the gods to their side. The Cynic tradition abounds with anecdotes of Diogenes scoffing at religious rituals and those superstitious enough to assign them importance. Bayle had been doubtful whether these jests revealed much of anything about Diogenes's own religious affiliations.[81] Shaftesbury, by contrast, found in them reliable indications of Diogenes's theism. One anecdote that Shaftesbury seized upon finds Diogenes responding to an accuser who asked if he were the same Diogenes who did not believe in any gods. 'How can I not believe in the Gods', Diogenes retorts 'when I find you wretched to them?' In the gloss on these lines from his manuscript notes on Epictetus, Shaftesbury contended that whilst Diogenes had 'called this Reproacher a *Wretch*' his true meaning was that 'all were Wretches and far distant from the Deity or anything Divine who lived as [the Reproacher] did', that is, 'vitiously and corruptly'.[82] For Shaftesbury, then, Diogenes did not merely deflect the accusation of atheism with a witty rebuff, but rather turned the accusation back on his 'Reproacher' and all who acted like him. *He*, Diogenes, was the true theist; his accuser was the one guilty of impiety.

For all his admiration for Cynic ridicule, Shaftesbury was acutely aware that its example was nearly impossible to safely imitate. In the first place, the sort of elite audience that Shaftesbury's writings aimed at was entirely

---

situated Diogenes in a philosophical lineage stretching back to Socrates, only this time he divided up Socrates's legacy into a '*sublime* part' (taken up by Plato) and a 'reproving part' that Antisthenes converted into satire before 'his better humoured and more agreeable successor [Diogenes] turned [it] into the *comic*, and went upon the model of that ancient comedy that was then prevalent'. Shaftesbury, 'Soliloquy, or Advice to an Author', 114. In a recent interpretation of these lines, David Mazella has remarked on the 'oddity' of Shaftesbury's presentation of Diogenes as an agreeable comic character. If we bear in mind Shaftesbury's celebration of Diogenes in the *Askêmata*, however, then there is less need for puzzlement. As Shaftesbury read him, Diogenes refined the 'reproving' role of Antisthenes (whose friendship with Socrates provided the vital link in the Stoic succession story) by drawing on the comic resources of Aristophanes and the Old Comedians to ridicule the illusions and misplaced values of his society. For while Aristophanes pandered to his audience and selected his targets with a steady eye to their approval, Diogenes, for all his seeming lack of restraint, was far more discriminating, using ridicule only to teach the importance of living in accordance of nature. Bayle's worry that Diogenes was a panderer after laughs like modern wits was, on Shaftesbury's own interpretation of Diogenes's career, totally unfounded. Mazella, *The Making of Modern Cynicism*, 92.

81. Pierre Bayle, 'Diogenes', in *A General Dictionary, Historical and Critical*, vol. 4 (London: James Bettenham, 1736), 606.

82. Shaftesbury Papers, PRO 30/24/27/16.

too thin-skinned to tolerate such treatment. Even Epictetus, Shaftesbury noted, only drew on the 'roughness of Diogenes' when admonishing students of the 'lower sort' who could endure such treatment more easily (he chose a less harsh approach when addressing those of 'better rank').[83] And even if Shaftesbury's readers could overcome the indignation of being spoken to in the manner of a Cynic, they were unlikely to experience this as anything other than a verbal assault. In the *Askêmata* Shaftesbury registered regret at the failure of his contemporaries to adequately comprehend the ethical significance of Diogenes's project. For whereas Aristophanes bore sufficient resemblance to 'modern Witts' to be well received, he complained, the 'Divine Facetiousness' of Diogenes had been so obscured that 'no one now sees or understands' it.[84] In spite of these obstacles, I argue next, Shaftesbury attempted to play the part of Diogenes in his own religious critique, a critique that went far beyond a discrediting of the French Prophets to touch on the essentials of Christianity itself.

Playing the Cynic

Shaftesbury's Cynic tactics are most in evidence in Section III of the *Letter*. In choosing to ridicule the French Prophets, Shaftesbury seemed to comfort his readers that only fanatics talking in tongues need fear such treatment. But if his readers laughed at this point then they may have done so nervously. Shaftesbury's examples from sacred history heavily suggested that the category of those with something to fear from ridicule extended far beyond the religiously extravagant or melancholic. The English Reformation may have faltered, he hinted, if the clerics at the time had countered it in a 'merrier' way.[85] Worst of all from the perspective of later critics, Jesus himself might have been vulnerable to the effects of ridicule (even prior to his humiliation with the crown of thorns): had the Jews 'taken the fancy to act . . . puppet-shows in his contempt' then they may have 'done our religion more harm than by all their other ways of severity'.[86]

If these examples were intended to convince the Earl's readers to embrace ridicule as a method of criticism, then they were peculiar choices. For, as several early critics recognized, they pointed to only one of two

---

83. Ibid.
84. Shaftesbury, 'Askêmata', 448. Shaftesbury listed among his fears the possibility that 'Socrates & Diogenes be forgot, or most ridiculously represented' before despondently admitting to himself that any efforts at 'reviving' their example would fail. Ibid, 152.
85. Shaftesbury, 'Letter Concerning Enthusiasm', 16.
86. Ibid.

conclusions: either ridicule really *did* have the power to harm even worthy characters and doctrines (and thus was not nearly so safe as Shaftesbury claimed) or Jesus and Christianity did not qualify as such.[87] Shaftesbury's insinuation was that Jesus and the French Prophets shared an uncomfortably large amount in common in that each depended upon martyrdom (or the threat of it) for their reputation as God-sent to take hold.

That Shaftesbury was belittling Christ here was made still clearer by his choice of an example of someone who *had* been genuinely invulnerable to ridicule: Socrates. Reversing course entirely from his *Design of a Socratick History*, Shaftesbury now insisted in the *Letter* that Socrates's endurance of Aristophanes's parody of him in *The Clouds*, far from endangering the philosopher, actually enhanced his reputation in Athens. Drawing on a popular anecdote from Aelianus's *Varia Historia*, Shaftesbury used Socrates's case to illustrate how to avoid the humiliation and reputational damage those publicly ridiculed normally suffer:

> The divinest man who had ever appeared in the heathen world was in the height of witty times and by the wittiest of all poets abominably ridiculed in a whole comedy, written and acted on purpose. But so far was this from sinking his reputation or suppressing his philosophy that they each increased the more for it, and he apparently grew to be more the envy of other teachers. He was not only contented to be ridiculed, but, that he might help the poet as much as possible, he presented himself openly in the theatre, that his real figure (which was no advantageous one) might be compared with that which the witty poet had brought as his representative on stage. Such was his good humour![88]

As Aelianus describes the incident in the theatre, some non-Athenians present in the audience during the performance of *The Clouds* asked aloud about the identity of the philosopher being parodied on stage. Overhearing them, Socrates stood up to announce his presence and 'remained standing in full view throughout the play as the actors performed it'.[89] For the most recent editors of Shaftesbury's corpus, the Earl's retelling of this story meant to imply that 'resentment of Socrates was fuelled by

87. For Tim Stuart-Buttle, Shaftesbury's Stoicism made him so wary of Jesus's teachings regarding sin, repentance and salvation that he effectively denied that Christ could be a moral exemplar. Tim Stuart-Buttle, *From Moral Theology to Moral Philosophy: Cicero and Visions of Humanity from Locke to Hume* (Oxford: Oxford University Press, 2019), 93.

88. Shaftesbury, 'Letter Concerning Enthusiasm', 17.

89. Claudius Aelianus, *Historical Miscellany*, ed. N. G. Wilson (Cambridge, MA: Harvard University Press, 1997), 85.

the victory of good humour' in the theatre and 'ultimately led to his trial and death'.[90] But there is reason to doubt this. Although the passage does imply that Socrates's good humour inoculated him against the pain of ridicule, Shaftesbury makes no suggestion that the Athenians resented him for that. Mention of Socrates's eventual trial and death at the hands of the Athenians was now, in fact, conspicuously absent from the Earl's version of the story. Instead, Shaftesbury left his readers with the impression that Aristophanes had done nothing worse than provide Socrates with an opportunity to demonstrate his good nature.[91] This is despite the fact that his principal source for the anecdote, Aelianus, had presented Aristophanes as a successful character assassin hired by Socrates's enemies to begin the work that they would eventually finish with their indictment.

Still more remarkable about Shaftesbury's version of this story was the degree to which Socrates was willing to undergo this ordeal. François Charpentier, whose *Vie de Socrate* (1650) features prominently among the sources Shaftesbury consulted for his unfinished *Socratick History*, claimed that Socrates had been attracted by the 'opportunity to draw offence on himself' (*l'ocassion de s'offenser*) before enacting revenge on Aristophanes by being the 'first to laugh' at his play.[92] Shaftesbury stopped short of claiming that Socrates laughed aloud, but his version of the story nevertheless hinted that Socrates did not just bear up under an unwanted ridicule but rather deliberately sought it out. In this respect, Socrates (a favourite of Epictetus as well as Shaftesbury) exemplified the Stoic practice of willingly placing oneself in testing circumstances and flourishing nonetheless. [93]

90. Shaftesbury, 'Chartae Socraticae', 29.

91. 'Socrates', Peter Gay wrote, 'was a symbol for the Enlightenment more through his death than through his ideas.' Peter Gay, *The Enlightenment: The Rise of Modern Paganism* (New York: Norton, 1966), 82. To some extent this was as true for Shaftesbury as for anyone else. In an *Askêmata* entry from 1703–4 Shaftesbury calls Socrates's demise a 'Death so much lamented: for which Providence has been so oft questioned: for which thou thyself so often hast been disturbed'. If Socrates's death troubled the Earl deeply, he managed to conceal his disturbance carefully in the *Letter*.

92. François Charpentier, *Vie de Socrate* (Amsterdam: Chez F. L'Honore, 1650), 272 and 276.

93. The controversy over this passage from the *Letter* would continue for four decades. The bishop of Norwich, John Leng, himself a translator of *The Clouds*, conceded that Socrates's reputation was enhanced after the Athenians 'came to themselves'. But for Leng this was beside the point. Ridicule could still corrupt the minds of its audience and was 'no more commendable, because truth and sincerity' were 'able to stand the shock of it'. John Leng, *Natural Obligations to Believe the Principles of Religion, and Divine Revelation: In XVI Sermons, Preached in the Church of St. Mary Le Bow* (London: W.B. for Robert Knaplock, 1719), 52 and 54. Similarly, for George Berkeley, Aristophanes's comedy

Where Socrates succeeded, Christ would have failed. By declaring that Christianity could have been smothered at its origins by a Roman parody of Christ, Shaftesbury implied that Jesus lacked something that Socrates possessed. Not surprisingly, Shaftesbury's early critics were not amused at this mixture of a defence of ridicule with ridicule itself. 'How hideous it sounds from one who calls himself a Christian', Samuel Parker replied in the August 1708 edition of his *Censura Temporum*, 'that he could have shewn the Jews and Romans a better way of suppressing Christianity than they had the wit to think of themselves; when in the very suggestion too he puts his own method in practice.'[94] Parker found the contrasting treatments of Socrates and Christ to be particularly offensive. For while Shaftesbury had given the former the 'Athenian theater' as a stage, Jesus and the Apostles were to 'take their trial in a *Smithfield Booth*'.[95] Little wonder that Parker could not read this 'flagrant Buffoonry [*sic*] Raillery and Ridicule upon all Religion' without 'trembling'.[96]

The more attentive among Shaftesbury's readers may have discovered an early clue to the surprise awaiting them in the Earl's choice of epigraph, Horace *Satires* 1.1.24–5: *'What prevents the man of mirth from telling the*

---

illustrated how 'men in a laughing fit' may 'applaud a ridicule' and be driven to actions they later regret. George Berkeley, *Alciphron: Or, the Minute Philosopher* (Dublin: William Williamson, 1757), 130. William Warburton used the example of Socrates to show that it was naïve to think that the virtuous will not suffer if they are dressed in a 'fool's coat'. William Warburton, *The Divine Legation of Moses Demonstrated* (London: Fletcher Gyles, 1742), xix. Mark Akenside, replying to Warburton, held that even though Aristophanes had misrepresented him, Socrates could not be prevented from 'detecting and disclaiming' the parody. Mark Akenside, *The Pleasures of Imagination* (London: R. Dodsley, 1744), 83. Warburton was unimpressed. What a 'mighty consolation', he retorted, that Socrates had 'disclaimed the fool's coat they had put on him' even though it 'at last brought him to his execution'. William Warburton, *Remarks on Several Occasional Reflections* (London: John and Paul Knapton, 1744), xiii. Warburton's protégé, John Brown, was similarly in no doubt that Aristophanes had 'whetted the rage of a misled multitude' against Socrates. Brown, *Essays on the Characteristics*, 58. Finally, James White, in his 1759 translation of *The Clouds*, took Shaftesbury's side against Brown: 'Aristophanes, with all his Wit, could not injure the Cause of Virtue and Truth, or render the character of Socrates ridiculous, or his conduct odious.' James White, *The Clouds: A Comedy. Written by Aristophanes, the Wittiest Man of His Age, against Socrates* (London: T. Payne, 1759), vi–vii. As Raymond Anselment put it: 'Shaftesbury could not disregard the growing belief that Aristophanes' ridicule ultimately destroyed Socrates.' Raymond A. Anselment, 'Socrates and *The Clouds*: Shaftesbury and a Socratic Tradition', *Journal of the History of Ideas* 39, 2 (1978), 175.

94. Samuel Parker, *Censura Temporum* (London: John Morphew, 1708), 245.

95. Ibid., 246.

96. Ibid., 244.

truth?[97] Though the line may have appeared innocuous at first, the satire from which it was drawn similarly ridicules exaggeratedly foolish characters before suddenly directing the joke back upon the unsuspecting reader. Having poked fun at a miser who applauds himself silently while gazing upon the wealth he has amassed, Horace cuts short the reader's joy: 'why do you laugh? The name has been changed but you're the one the story is about.'[98] At a stroke, Horace removes the reader's window onto the miser's foolish extravagance and replaces it with a mirror, prompting his readers to reflect instead on their own folly. In the same way, Shaftesbury spoiled his own reader's laughter at the French Prophets by diminishing the distance separating them. It was not only enthusiastic sectarians that suffered from an overly inflamed imagination. All religion, he now implied, gave rise to melancholic 'panics' when the 'spirits of men are low'.[99] Christians gripped by such panics try to placate God by endlessly debating the liturgical forms that will win his approval, debates Shaftesbury compares to beggars disagreeing on how to address the occupants of a coach ('your Lordship' or 'your Honour'?) in order to encourage them to part with their money.[100] French Prophets might embarrass themselves with false predictions, but English Christians were also capable of making a spectacle of themselves in their efforts to 'beg right' from God.[101] Diogenes's mockery of Greek religion finds here its modern equivalent.

It might be supposed that Cynic tactics like these were entirely too crass to persuade Shaftesbury's readers of anything (as we have seen Shaftesbury himself was doubtful whether Diogenes's example could ever be revived). Certainly, if the Earl sought to convince his readers to adopt an alternative way of thinking about religion then it is unlikely that portraying those invested in liturgical disputes as deluded sycophants was going to succeed. Worse again, this sort of bantering was grist to the mill of High Church critics who had long warned that the more open print environment ushered in by the lapsing of pre-publication censorship in 1695 had emboldened the profaners of revealed religion. Unsurprisingly, then, a host of commentators have concluded that Shaftesbury in the *Letter* overstepped the mark and essentially disregarded his own

97. Shaftesbury, 'Letter Concerning Enthusiasm', 4.
98. Horace, *Satires and Epistles*, trans. John David (Oxford: Oxford University Press, 2011), 4.
99. Shaftesbury, 'Letter Concerning Enthusiasm', 10.
100. Ibid., 19.
101. Ibid.

warnings. For Richard Wolf 'the irreverence of Shaftesbury's wit' had overshadowed 'the range of satiric refinements embodied in his performance'.[102] Jaffro is more unequivocally negative in his judgment, concluding that Shaftesbury simply 'failed' to 'elaborate a polite criticism of Christianity'.[103]

To interpret the *Letter* as a betrayal or failure, however, is misleading. For a start, such a reading overlooks the extensive pedagogical use that Shaftesbury and his preferred Stoics made of ridicule as a mode of criticism, *even* as they voiced suspicions of laughter. But it should also be kept in mind that Shaftesbury only failed to be polite in the same way Diogenes so failed. The priority for both was to challenge existing systems of belief. In doing so they knew they would cause widespread upset and so draw accusations of impoliteness. At the same time, however, they tended not to engage in petty humiliation or points-scoring that made ridicule frequently so uncivil. That embarrassment for individuals was never Shaftesbury's primary objective is borne out by the fact that he (unlike Swift) scrupulously avoided implicating any individuals in his mockery (even the 'French Protestants' were left anonymous, though few would have missed the reference).[104] The closest he came to doing so was a tease he directed at a 'truly Christian prelate' who could provide a 'full account of his belief in fairies'.[105] Pierre Coste's 1709 French translation of the *Letter* identified Edward Fowler as the prelate in question, but Shaftesbury was careful not to expose Fowler in any edition that he personally supervised into print.[106] He even expressed worry to his friends that the allusion to Fowler might have been too easily discoverable and made amendments to take some

102. Richard B. Wolf, 'Shaftesbury's Just Measure of Irony', *Studies in English Literature, 1500–1900* 33, 3 (1993), 581.

103. Laurent Jaffro, 'Shaftesbury on the Natural Secretion and the Philosophical Personae', *Intellectual History Review* 18, 3 (2008), 358. On Shaftesbury's abandonment of Socratic irony see Laurent Jaffro, 'Le Socrate de Shaftesbury: Comment raconter aux modernes l'histoire de Socrate', in *Socrate in Occidente* (Florence: Le Monnier Università, 2004), 90. Shaftesbury's biographer Robert Voitle was similarly perplexed by Shaftesbury's tactics in the *Letter*. Why, he asked, did the Earl 'expose his ideas on Christ and the Church in a public controversy when he could have implied these things elsewhere, politely, with a fraction of the risk to his reputation for piety?' Robert Voitle, *The Third Earl of Shaftesbury 1671–1713* (Baton Rouge: Louisiana State University Press, 1984), 328.

104. Shaftesbury, 'A Letter Concerning Enthusiasm', 15.

105. Ibid., 6.

106. According to Hillel Schwartz, Fowler was also 'passionately interested in ghost stories'. Shaftesbury may have selected him as his object of fun because the French Prophets themselves counted him among their followers. See Hillel Schwartz, *Knaves, Fools, Madmen, and That Subtle Effluvium: A Study of the Opposition to the French Prophets in England, 1706–1710* (Gainesville: University of Florida Press, 1978), 42.

of the sting out of it.[107] For Shaftesbury, Fowler's belief in fairies was the product of a risible delusion, to be sure, but his aim was to highlight the folly of a particular category of belief, not asperse an innocuous individual.

Transitioning to a Good-Humoured Religion

To achieve its aim Cynic ridicule as imagined in the Stoic tradition must not only surprise or disturb but also render its target receptive to a new way of thinking. Just as Epictetus saw Diogenes's rebukes as preparing his fellow Greeks to receive the positive doctrines of Zeno, so Shaftesbury used the *Letter* to shock his readers out of one manner of evaluating the world and prepare them to be lured towards another. When he incorporated the *Letter* into the *Characteristics* Shaftesbury placed it first so that, as he later explained, its 'unraveling humour' could prepare the reader for the formal presentation of his philosophy in the *Inquiry Concerning Virtue or Merit* (originally published in 1699 but included in the *Characteristics* as the fourth treatise in 1711).[108] Having played the Cynic in the *Letter* the Earl now showed that he could take on the role of Zeno.

If Shaftesbury used ridicule as a Cynic shock tactic then what alternative way of thinking about religion was he trying to edge his readers towards? At the beginning of the *Inquiry*, Shaftesbury acknowledged that 'men of wit and raillery' enjoyed exposing the 'weak sides of religion' but could never seriously discuss how to improve it.[109] The *Inquiry* set out to do just that by making the case for a good-humoured religion built on a Latitudinarian understanding of God as thoroughly benevolent. Christians had only been melancholic, Shaftesbury affirmed, because they were gripped by the 'thought of living in a distracted universe' ruled by a capricious God who manufactured obedience through 'rewards and punishments'.[110] Such a view of the divine was not only mistaken, Shaftesbury argued, but carried with it horrific social consequences. Christians convinced that eviscerating heresy or ensuring religious uniformity would earn them high celestial rewards were, he argued, incentivized to commit all manner of atrocities. More troubling still, projecting the qualities of 'malignity, arbitrariness, partiality or

107. Richard B. Wolf, 'The Publication of Shaftesbury's "Letter Concerning Enthusiasm"', *Studies in Bibliography: Papers of the Bibliographical Society of the University of Virginia* 32 (1979), 238.

108. Shaftesbury, 'Miscellaneous Reflections', 396. John Toland published an unauthorized edition of the *Inquiry* in 1699, much to Shaftesbury's annoyance.

109. Shaftesbury, 'An Inquiry Concerning Virtue or Merit', in *Characteristics of Men, Manners, Opinions, Times*, 164.

110. Ibid., 189 and 183.

revengefulness' onto God himself could, Shaftesbury warned, gradually cause Christians to become 'reconciled' to those same qualities and consider the 'most cruel, unjust and barbarous acts . . . not only as just and lawful but as divine and worthy of imitation'.[111]

A good-humoured religion, by contrast, required working oneself into the belief that everything was 'governed, ordered, or regulated for the best by a designing principle or mind'.[112] There is nothing in the *Inquiry* that directly indicates the Stoic pedigree of this doctrine, and other Latitudinarians such as Benjamin Whichote (an edition of whose sermons Shaftesbury published) had long argued for a religious attitude emphasizing the benevolence of God. Again, it is the *Askêmata* that reveals the Stoic origin of Shaftesbury's argument. The *Askêmata* laid bare Shaftesbury's personal quest to achieve good humour, a quest that relied again on Stoic self-examination and the application of what Stephen Darwall calls 'self-analytical reality therapy'.[113] In Shaftesbury's Stoic view, those who succeed in becoming good-humoured would never 'feel any of those Gripes and Knawings of Discontent and bitter Sadness' but instead 'preserve a steady countenance' and meet their 'Fate not only undauntedly but cheerfully'.[114]

The boast from the Stoics that they alone could meet their fate 'undauntedly' frequently attracted the derision of critics who considered it a sign of a humourless stubbornness. Henry More had argued as much in *Enthusiasmus Triumphatus*, comparing the capability of enthusiasts to endure misfortune to a 'sullen and insolent Stoicism'.[115] For Shaftesbury, however, a sullen endurance was a radically insufficient posture towards the universe because it still implied that whatever had to be endured was hostile or an evil of some sort. Shaftesbury's good humour required, instead, a revaluation of what had been considered evil as a sign of a benevolent and harmonious cosmos at work. It could even help to imagine a series of awful counterfactuals and affirm them using a technique known as the *praemeditatio malorum* or the pre-meditation of misfortunes: 'Whenever any Melancholly

111. Ibid., 181. For an account of Shaftesbury's philosophy as a repudiation of revealed Christianity (including its more Latitudinarian variants) see Tim Stuart-Buttle, 'Shaftesbury Reconsidered: Stoic Ethics and the Unreasonableness of Christianity', *Locke Studies* 15 (2015), 163–213.

112. Shaftesbury, 'Inquiry Concerning Virtue or Merit', 165.

113. Stephen Darwall, *The British Moralists and the Internal 'Ought': 1640–1740* (Cambridge: Cambridge University Press, 1995), 199.

114. Shaftesbury, 'Askêmata', 244–45.

115. Henry More, *Enthusiasmus Triumphatus; or, A Brief Discourse of The Nature, Causes, Kinds, and Cure of Enthusiasm* (Los Angeles: William Andrews Clark Memorial Library, University of California, 1966, repr. of 2nd edn., 1662), 41.

Fancy occurs', the Earl implored himself, do not 'compound' it but 'run straight to whatever is furthest, and suppose the worst: suppose all to have allready happen'd that can happen'.[116]

This was an extremely ambitious project in revaluation. But the pay-off could be considerable for the individual and society alike. The good-humoured, as Shaftesbury describes them, were tolerant less out of political prudence than out of a desire to imitate God at his benevolent best. What is more, unwavering good humour in one's view of the cosmos allowed for flexibility in other areas, including in the particularities of religious doctrine. In his *Miscellaneous Reflections* (a set of commentaries on his earlier writings published in 1710 that eventually formed the third volume of the *Characteristics*) Shaftesbury went so far as to claim that good humour was, for this reason, the best means of healing religious division. If persecution had in the past frequently 'forced people to divide [from the established Church] who at first had never any such intention' then good humour had the capacity to 'reconcile persons to a belief in which they were never bred, or to which they had conceived a former prejudice'.[117] If ridicule misused could occasionally threaten religious peace, good humour, as Shaftesbury presented it, could only ever work in its favour.

Cultivating good humour was thus a deadly serious business; nothing less than the preservation of religious concord hinged upon it. But as a doctrine it was next to impossible to promulgate widely. Even if Shaftesbury's readers had been surprised by his ridicule into critically examining their own beliefs, it was demanding a lot for them to rid themselves of cosmic resentment entirely. In his *Askêmata* he contemplated the futility of convincing most people

> that to be affronted, to be despised, to be poor, to smart, is not to *suffer*: that Banishment and Death are not Ill; that Plagues, Earth-quakes, the Sack or Ruine of cityes and Destruction of Mankind are not in themselves Ill; and that with respect to the Whole these things are orderly, good and beautiful. Inculcate this. Make them understand it. But if this be rediculouse to think of; how much more rediculouse is it to endeavour to chang [*sic*] their other Opinions, or if they seem convincd of any thing, to think this should stand a moment, thus propt, without that other Foundation?[118]

116. Shaftesbury, 'Askêmata', 292–93. On the significance of *praemeditatio malorum* for Stoic self-therapy see Pierre Hadot, *Philosophy as a Way of Life: Spiritual Exercises from Socrates to Foucault* (Oxford: Blackwell, 1995), 85.

117. Shaftesbury, 'Miscellaneous Reflections', 383.

118. Shaftesbury, 'Askêmata', 111.

Even alerting others to Stoic texts so that they might attempt this philosophical training themselves on their own terms seemed to have been ruled out: 'what is it to Thee, whose business is only to improve by these [rules] not publish them, profess or teach them'.[119] The clergy, however, were a slightly different matter and if they could be encouraged to preach good humour along Shaftesbury's preferred lines then, he believed, the chances of ridding society of melancholic religion could be improved. Even if convincing the people at large to affirm Providence unreservedly was unfeasible, it was still possible to convince members of the clergy to represent the workings of the divine in a more benign light. Over the course of his correspondence with Michael Ainsworth, a young protégé who was preparing to embark on a career in the clergy, we catch sight of Shaftesbury doing just that: 'never do we more need a just Chearfulness, *good Humour*, or Alacrity of Mind' he advises the cleric-in-training, 'than when we are contemplating God', otherwise people will 'make the Idea of God so much after their own bitter Spirit'.[120] If the wholesale revaluation of the universe by the public at large was several bridges too far then a watered-down, Christianized Stoicism transmitted from the pulpit by a new generation of clerics might still reduce the melancholy that fuelled both the religious enthusiasms of the French Prophet sort and the persecution that frequently accompanied them.

Conclusion

Shaftesbury, I have argued, was a philosopher both plagued with doubts about ridicule and yet strangely optimistic about its potential to both replace persecution as a response to religious enthusiasm, and edge Christianity itself in a more tolerant direction. How successful was he? In his *Lectures on Rhetoric and Belles Lettres*, Adam Smith would later claim that in attempting to 'overthrow the present fabric of theology', Shaftesbury 'judged rightly, that the destruction would be easier accomplished,

---

119. Ibid., 318.

120. 'Letter V', Shaftesbury to Ainsworth, 28 January 1709. Shaftesbury, 'The Ainsworth Correspondence', 378. Emphasis in original. Shaftesbury placed great hope in the possibility that a new breed of cleric could have a moderating impact on English religion. As Ashley Walsh points out, Shaftesbury, for all his anticlericalism, envisaged a 'positive role' for a Protestant national Church staffed by clerics committed to toleration and moderation. Ashley Walsh, *Civil Religion and the Enlightenment in England, 1707–1800* (Woodbridge: The Boydell Press, 2020), 40.

and more to the taste of the times, by ridicule than by confutation'.[121] There were two assumptions buried in this assessment, each of which is doubtful. First, Smith assumed that Shaftesbury had indeed forsaken argument (or 'confutation') altogether, overlooking how Shaftesbury's humour served as preparation for the systematic presentation of his philosophy in the *Inquiry*. Shaftesbury's decision to switch to a more formal style itself conveyed recognition on his part that ridicule alone could only achieve so much. For the Stoic, it is never sufficient to embarrass the *idotai* into reforming themselves; they also needed to understand the rational basis for doing so. In the *Inquiry*, Shaftesbury set out to provide exactly that by explaining why any Christian theology that presented God as a whimsical tyrant must be flawed. Without an argument to follow the ridicule of the *Letter*, Shaftesbury's readers would have been justified in rating Shaftesbury as precisely the kind of profane mocker of religion they took Diogenes to be.

Furthermore, Smith assumed that in choosing ridicule as his mode of attack against the dominant theology of his day Shaftesbury had taken the path of least resistance. The Earl 'judged rightly' because the time was apparently ripe for this form of criticism to succeed. Shaftesbury's critique, Smith seemed to imply, was not as untimely as the Earl himself seemed to fear, but instead chimed well enough with the mood in England to achieve his purpose. In the next chapter, I explore why Smith's assessment here was again awry by situating Shaftesbury's defence of ridicule against the backdrop of another public controversy relating to toleration, one that gained momentum right as the affair of the French Prophets petered out. What Smith failed to understand in retrospect, and the Earl could not see at the time, was that the freedom to ridicule did not grant any particular advantage to the cause of toleration in the way Shaftesbury hoped. Even if the posthumous success of the *Characteristics* gave later readers like Smith the impression that Shaftesbury had won the culture war, by the Earl's death in 1713 he had been given every reason to believe the opposite.

121. Adam Smith, 'Lectures on Rhetoric and Belles Lettres', in *The Glasgow Edition of the Works and Correspondence of Adam Smith*, vol. 4, ed. J. C. Bryce (Oxford: Oxford University Press, 1983), 60.

CHAPTER TWO

Sociability, Censorship and the Limits of Ridicule from Shaftesbury to Hutcheson

Whether a character is good or bad is of little moment; granted he is unsociable, he is capable of being comic.

—HENRI BERGSON, 'LAUGHTER'

APART FROM HIS RELIGIOUS CRITICISM and moral philosophy, Shaftesbury is best known today for his efforts to civilize the manners and public speech of his compatriots. That they needed civilizing was only too evident to the Earl and many of his contemporaries. Queen Anne's England was marked by intense domestic factionalism fuelled by disagreement over the legacy of the 1688 revolution, religious toleration, and continuous war against France. The Triennial Act of 1694 (mandating elections every three years) and the relaxation of pre-publication censorship in 1695 allowed this factionalism to be played out in aggressive spats between Whigs anxious that the 1688 settlement could yet be overturned and Tories fearful that toleration of dissent had imperilled the Church. Publications poured forth on how the press should be restrained, printing regulated, and abusive speech curtailed.[1]

At the heart of the debate on how to reform this raucous public sphere lay the question of whether or not humans were naturally sociable. If, as Hobbes

---

1. See for instance John How, *Some Thoughts on the Present State of Printing and Bookselling* (London: How, 1709). On the fierce debate about censorship and press regulation characteristic of this period see Kevin Sharpe, *Rebranding Rule: The Restoration and Revolution Monarchy, 1660–1714* (New Haven, CT: Yale University Press, 2013), 649–51.

had argued, humans entered social life mainly to extort recognition of their imagined superiority, then magistrates were required to keep a watchful eye on abusive speech, particularly as wounded egos could turn to violence to restore their or their party's lost honour. By contrast, if humans were, at bottom, naturally sociable, then they could be relied upon to preserve peaceful relations among themselves without heavy interference from the state.

A year after his *Letter Concerning Enthusiasm*, Shaftesbury published a treatise that placed him unequivocally on one side of this debate. In *Sensus Communis: An Essay on the Freedom of Wit and Humour* (1709) Shaftesbury declared that sociability was as natural to mankind as 'eating and drinking', and that the desire for community could successfully compete with pride as a motivator of human conduct.[2] However hard 'narrow-minded philosophers' such as Hobbes might try, they could only reduce social behaviour to selfishness by abusing language and ignoring the 'force of nature'.[3] Even the factionalism afflicting England, Shaftesbury wryly suggested, was only a misdirected form of the 'social love' that drove humans to associate with each other.[4] Nothing could better express and preserve that natural sociability, he further claimed, than the free use of humour in the public sphere. Citizens left free to banter and laugh would in time learn to 'polish one another', curbing unsociable behaviour in the process.[5] Far from threatening civility in the public sphere, therefore, ridicule in Shaftesbury's view could humble the uncivil and serve as a 'lenitive remedy against vice'.[6]

An important corollary of Shaftesbury's argument was that humour itself required little by way of regulation, least of all by the state. Unfavourably comparing the stewardship of humour to the stifling of commerce through trade restrictions, he insisted that it would 'refine itself', if care was taken 'not to tamper with it'.[7] The 'only danger', he added, was in 'laying an embargo' and denying it a 'free port'.[8] If anyone tried to abuse this freedom by mocking what was natural or good then the laughter would rebound on them. Switching metaphors to hydraulics, Shaftesbury insisted that attempts to impose sobriety or earnestness by fiat would only

2. Shaftesbury, 'Sensus Communis, An Essay on the Freedom of Wit and Humour', in *Characteristics of Men, Manners, Opinions, Times*, ed. Lawrence E. Klein (Cambridge: Cambridge University Press, 1999), 51.

3. Ibid., 54–55.

4. Ibid., 53.

5. Ibid., 31.

6. Ibid., 59.

7. Ibid., 31.

8. Ibid.

backfire as the 'greater the weight' pressing down on the human spirit 'the bitterer will be the satire' (for it was the 'persecuting spirit' that 'raised the bantering one').[9] According to one recent interpreter, Shaftesbury was now defending free humour 'unconditionally' and trusted entirely in its 'auto-regulation'.[10] To another, Shaftesbury was proposing that ridicule could even 'replace censorship' altogether as a guarantor of sociability.[11]

In this chapter I argue that Shaftesbury's position on the freedom of humour in *Sensus Communis* was less straightforwardly optimistic than these passages suggest and that commentators have supposed. I begin by showing that although Shaftesbury insisted that wit and humour could be sociable, he was forthcoming about their limits and never presented them as an alternative to censorship. Next I situate Shaftesbury within a controversy over the appropriateness of using ridicule to discredit High Churchmen whose slandering of the Whigs threatened liberty and toleration. During the commotion surrounding the 1710 impeachment trial of the High Church-man Henry Sacheverell, I show, Shaftesbury considered ridicule insufficient to tame the High Church party's intransigence and approved of using the law to quell their unsociable behaviour. In this respect he distanced him-self from other Whig sympathizers, such as Daniel Defoe, who were more optimistic that Sacheverell and his supporters could be laughed away into irrelevance.

The last sections of the chapter examine two particularly influential responses to Shaftesbury's *Sensus Communis* written during the 1720s, each of which offered a novel take on the relationship between ridicule and sociability. Bernard Mandeville (1670–1733) defended a Whig politics

---

9. Ibid., 34–35. Terry Eagleton sees in these lines the origin of the so-called 'relief' theory of laughter (latest associated with Freud) according to which laughter is a kind of relief of psychic tension. Eagleton, *On Humour*, 10. John Morreall finds instead an 'overlap' between the relief theory and Hobbesian theory in that to laugh 'in breaking free of constraint can also be to laugh in scorn at those who have been constraining one'. John Morreall, *Taking Laughter Seriously* (Albany: State University of New York Press, 1983), 20.

10. Lydia B. Amir, *Humour and the Good Life in Modern Philosophy: Shaftesbury, Hamann, Kierkegaard* (Albany: State University of New York Press, 2015), 40 and 43. Jaf-fro similarly argues that the 'self-regulation' of ridicule is 'taken for granted by Shaftesbury'. Jaffro, 'The Passions and Actions of Laughter in Shaftesbury and Hutcheson', 144. Georges Minois also defends the thesis that Shaftesburian ridicule will auto-regulate. Georges Minois, *Histoire du Rire et de la Dérision* (Paris: Librairie Arthème Fayard, 2000), 410.

11. Mogens Laerke, 'G.W. Leibniz: Moderation and Censorship', in *The Use of Censor-ship in the Enlightenment*, ed. Mogens Laerke (Leiden: Koninklijke Brill NV, 2009), 171. According to Thomas Keymer, Shaftesbury considered censorship 'beneath the dignity of a civilized modern government' and a 'clumsy, counterproductive means of addressing dissent'. Thomas Keymer, *Poetics of the Pillory: English Literature and Seditious Libel, 1660–1820* (Oxford: Oxford University Press, 2019), 90.

of toleration using Shaftesburian arguments but dismantled the Earl's case for natural sociability in the second volume of the *Fable of the Bees*. In the process he also called into question Shaftesbury's views on what ridicule was good for. Mandeville, I show, adopted a modified Hobbesianism in relation to ridicule, considering it a product of pride that could be turned against the proud (Mandeville's own preferred use for it was to expose the conceitedness of moralists such as Shaftesbury himself). Departing slightly from Hobbes, Mandeville also presented laughter as a form of psychic release, or a temporary escape from the demands that performing civility places on the mind and body.

Mandeville's attack encouraged other Whigs to fly to Shaftesbury's defence by reinstating ridicule as a guarantor of natural sociability. The Irish Presbyterian Francis Hutcheson (1694–1746), the subject of the chapter's final section, led the way in a set of contributions to the *Dublin Weekly Journal*. Hutcheson endeavoured to prove that the practice of laughing with and at others revealed our inclination to sociability more than our pride. Nevertheless, even Hutcheson was forced to admit that ridicule was too dangerous to be left to refine itself, particularly in an Ireland where the battles between Sacheverellite High Churchmen and Whigs continued unabated well into the 1720s. Rules were needed to govern its use and Hutcheson took it upon himself to stipulate what they should be. This placed him at odds with Shaftesbury, who was generally more content to allow citizens search out the limits of ridicule on their own, albeit with the magistrate stepping in when needed.

Sensus Communis *and the Case against Hobbes*

Often treated as an extension of the *Letter Concerning Enthusiasm*, Shaftesbury's *Sensus Communis* differs from the latter in subject matter, style and argument. Although the Earl struck out at critics like Astell and Fowler for overstating the dangers of ridicule to religion, he now avoided any obviously irreligious innuendo (making a probable reference to the reception of the *Letter*, he declared it reprehensible for writers to 'offend the public ear' or cause 'scandal or disturbance').[12] Instead, his new task was to illustrate the place of wit and humour in sustaining civil society

---

12. Shaftesbury, 'Sensus Communis', 36. The aim, he stressed, was never to accost or 'press rudely' with no 'regard to time or place' but instead for gentlemen who 'know each other perfectly well' to speak with frankness among themselves. Ibid., 49 and 36. For Gadamer, what Shaftesbury had in mind was a 'virtue of social intercourse' and for that reason limited truly free humour to conversation among friends. Hans-Georg Gadamer, *Truth and Method* (London: Continuum, 2004), 22.

and polite conversation. Shaftesbury's wager was that permitting gentlemen to laugh freely could not only encourage them to curb bad behaviour in each other, but also heighten awareness of their own nature as sociable creatures.

Shaftesbury's first step was to refute the Hobbesian view that introducing ridicule into conversation would prick the pride of those on the receiving end and lead to rancour. Laughing, Shaftesbury suggested, was the 'very life' of conversation, particularly among trusted familiars in a salon, drawing room, or coffee house. By lubricating discussion it had the power to convert even a moment of intense disagreement over a matter of politics, religion, or morality into an enjoyable event.[13] By learning to laugh at each other and be 'laughed at' in turn, he held, participants in conversation could be drawn into an edifying and sociable exchange even as their positions on the question at hand sharply diverged.[14]

By insisting on the reciprocal nature of these exchanges, Shaftesbury parted ways from some of his favourite ancient philosophers, particularly the Cynics and Stoics. As we saw in the previous chapter, Cynic ridicule does not invite reply or encourage a convivial, back-and-forth exchange of views (Diogenes's retorts invariably *end* conversations by putting the arrogant, the vain, and the vice-ridden firmly in their place).[15] Similarly, as Martha Nussbaum notes, Stoic ridicule was so harsh precisely because it was directed at the 'fool' who does not yet share the Stoic view of the world.[16] The possibility that the 'fool' might have something valid to say in response, and so keep the conversation going for a while longer, is never considered. By contrast, the kind of exchanges Shaftesbury now sought to encourage in *Sensus Communis* were designed to end inconclusively in a 'pleasant confusion' with the participants feeling 'agreeable' enough not to be 'discouraged from resuming the debate' in the future.[17]

13. Shaftesbury, 'Sensus Communis', 37.

14. Shaftesbury, 'Sensus Communis', 68. As Sophia Rosenfeld notes, Shaftesbury's *Sensus Communis* was part of an attempt to reform the tastes of gentlemen while at the same time laying the foundation of an ever-expanding 'participatory, moral and political order'. Making conversation enjoyable was key to that project. Sophia Rosenfeld, *Common Sense: A Political History* (Cambridge, MA: Harvard University Press, 2011), 32 and 23.

15. Kuin argues similarly that Cynic laughter is 'exclusive, premeditated, and self-immune'. Kuin, 'Diogenes vs. Demonax', 266.

16. Nussbaum, 'Stoic Laughter', 90.

17. Shaftesbury, 'Sensus Communis', 37. For Daniel Carey, Shaftesbury's understanding of humour was ultimately normative. The 'exercise of raillery recalled adversaries to a more reasonable view' of the matter at hand. Daniel Carey, *Locke, Shaftesbury and Hutcheson: Contesting Diversity in the Enlightenment and Beyond* (Cambridge: Cambridge University Press, 2006), 148.

At stake here was not just social concord, but the ability to reason collectively about matters of importance. For 'without wit and
humour', Shaftesbury now alleged, 'reason can hardly have its proof or be
distinguished'.[18] Note that wit and humour here are not *substitutes* for
reason.[19] Rather, their value lies in creating the kind of atmosphere in
which the promptings of reason, particularly about human nature, can
be heard.[20] This point can be easily lost sight of because of Shaftesbury's
occasional references in *Sensus Communis* to ridicule as a mechanism for
discovering truth:

> Truth, it is supposed, may bear all lights, and one of those principal
> lights, or natural mediums, by which things are to be viewed, in order
> to a thorough recognition, is ridicule itself, or that manner of proof by
> which we discern whatever is liable to just raillery in any subject.[21]

Commentators on this passage then and since have seized on the phrase
'manner of proof' as evidence that Shaftesbury sought to convert ridicule
into a crude measure of truth-value, as if the tendency of a proposition
to provoke laughter was sufficient proof that it was false.[22] Shaftesbury
himself gave this impression by inserting the phrase 'Ridicule a Light,

18. Shaftesbury, 'Sensus Communis', 35.
19. Critics had frequently accused Shaftesbury of trying to replace reason with ridicule.
See, for instance, William Shorey, *Reason, and Not Raillery, the Proper Test of Religion*
(London: W. and J. Innys, 1720), 9.
20. In this respect I disagree with Jure Gantar who sums up Shaftesbury's position as
follows: 'ridicule as a vehicle is parallel to reason and helps us reach similar objectives to
the ones achieved by rational introspection.' Jure Gantar, *Pleasure of Fools: Essays in the
Ethics of Laughter* (Montreal: McGill-Queen's University Press, 2005), 74.
21. Shaftesbury, 'Sensus Communis', 30.
22. Peter Berger, following a long interpretive tradition, suggests that Shaftesbury here
presented ridicule as a straightforward 'means of distinguishing between truth and falsehood'. Peter L. Berger, *Redeeming Laughter: The Comic Dimension of Human Experience*
(Berlin: Walter de Gruyter, 1997), 22. Roger Lund makes a similar claim, but suspects that
the kind of ridicule Shaftesbury recommends is 'entirely too negligible to reveal the truth of
anything'. Roger D. Lund, *Ridicule, Religion and the Politics of Wit in Augustan England*
(Burlington, VT: Ashgate, 2012), 147. Isabel Rivers finds that Shaftesbury simply leaves
'undefined precisely the nature of the truth that will bear ridicule'. Isabel Rivers, *Reason,
Grace and Sentiment: A Study of the Language of Religion and Ethics in England, 1660–
1780*, vol. 2, *Shaftesbury to Hume* (Cambridge: Cambridge University Press, 2000), 40.
Stanley Grean relates how Shaftesbury's doctrine was 'compressed into the words "ridicule
the test of truth"' by those same interpreters. Grean, *Shaftesbury's Philosophy of Religion
and Ethics*, 123. For Lawrence Klein, Shaftesbury's test was mainly a 'method for leeching a
passion [enthusiasm], not contesting a proposition'. Lawrence E. Klein, 'Ridicule as a Tool
for Discovering Truth', in *The Oxford Handbook of Eighteenth-Century Satire*, ed. Paddy
Bullard (Oxford: Oxford University Press, 2019), 580.

Criterion to Truth' in the Index to the *Characteristics*.[23] Even so, ridicule in the above passage is only *a* medium for viewing a given object and not necessarily the decisive one. Shaftesbury's real worry was that if ridicule were pre-emptively disqualified from conversation out of fear of causing offence, then certain truths about human nature would remain buried. His claim, less epistemological than psychological, was that while fear disables our reason, gaiety activates it:

> I can very well suppose that men may be frightened out of their wits; but I have no apprehension they should be laugh'd out of 'em. I can hardly imagine that in a pleasant way they shou'd ever be talk'd out of their love for society, or reason'd out of humanity and common sense.[24]

An important assumption Shaftesbury makes here is that those still in possession of their 'wits' will have a 'love for society' by default. In other words, one of the key truths that ridicule should help us recognize is that sociability is our natural state. Only the terror of coercion or censorship could dislodge that natural feeling and distract us from that truth.

It was a point that Shaftesbury saw fit to illustrate with a criticism of a philosopher who spent his life consumed by fear: Thomas Hobbes. So terrified of popular government was Hobbes, Shaftesbury implied, that he could not even tolerate Englishmen reading about it in a 'Roman or Greek historian' and so recommended the 'extirpation of ancient literature in favour of his Leviathan hypothesis'.[25] In religion, too, Hobbes's horror of sectarians and enthusiasts drove him to spend his life frantically warning whoever would listen that preachers were out to deceive them. Had he been less fearful, Shaftesbury implied, Hobbes might have spotted the contradiction between his selfless efforts to educate his readers and his philosophical denial of natural human sociability. For how could it be, Shaftesbury asked in mock disbelief, that such an 'able and witty philosopher' convinced that 'by nature we are all wolves' could work so tirelessly to disabuse people of their illusions: 'But pray, whence this Zeal in our behalf? What are *We* to *You* . . . why this Concern for Us? . . . why all this danger on our account?'[26] Revealing himself to be the 'good sociable man' his philosophy denied, Hobbes was even willing to run 'the risk of being

23. 'Shaftesbury's Index', in *Characteristics of Men, Manners, Opinions, Times*, ed. Douglas J. Den Uyl, vol. 3 (Indianapolis, IN: Liberty Fund, 2001), 289.
  24. Shaftesbury, 'Sensus Communis', 45.
  25. Ibid., 42.
  26. Ibid., 43.

a martyr for our deliverance' (a reference to the accusations of heresy that dogged Hobbes in his later life).[27]

Writing in the early 1750s the Baptist minister Charles Bulkley found that this list of questions perfectly exemplified how ridicule was integral to Shaftesburyian reasoning about human nature. If the Earl's sarcasm was undeniably a mockery of Hobbes, he asked rhetorically, was it 'not reasoning too?'[28] Had Shaftesbury disavowed ridicule on the grounds that it was unphilosophical or uncivil, Bulkley held, he would have needlessly denied himself a valuable argumentative resource. Using sarcasm to expose the lack of congruity between a philosopher's words and his actions was not a cheap *ad hominem* attack but a way of placing deniers of natural sociability onto the back foot and nudging them into the kind of self-reflection that cast their philosophy into doubt.

Adam Smith was far less impressed than Bulkley with Shaftesbury's choice of tactics in rebutting Hobbes's account of human nature. 'In his treatise, where he ridicules Mr Hobbes', he complained of *Sensus Communis*, 'there is not one passage which would make us laugh.'[29] Twisting the knife still further, Smith even implied that Hobbes would emerge the winner in any battle of wits: 'Mr Hobbes' book would make us laugh, but [Shaftesbury's] ridicule of it would never affect us.'[30] That Smith vaunted Hobbes over Shaftesbury here is noteworthy, not least given Smith's hostility to what he elsewhere called Hobbes's 'odious' moral doctrines.[31] But there is also a sense in which Smith may have missed Shaftesbury's point. The kind of humour that aids reflection on our sociable nature does not necessarily generate laughter. In this case, Shaftesbury could just as well

27. Shaftesbury, 42–43. There was nothing remotely original about this joke. In the *Discourses* Epictetus sarcastically alluded to Epicurus's strenuous efforts to educate humanity as proof that his denial of human sociability was impossible to sustain in practice. Subjecting Epicurus to a mock interrogation, he implied that a *true* denier of sociability would never have taken such trouble to help his fellow human beings: 'Why is it that you care then? Let us be deceived . . . Why do you worry about us, man; why write such lengthy books?' Epictetus's answer was that Epicurus was impelled by nature to write for the benefit of others and in doing so denounce his own doctrine. Epictetus, *Discourses, Fragments, Handbook*, 121.

28. Bulkley, *A Vindication of My Lord Shaftesbury, on the Subject of Ridicule*, 26.

29. Smith, 'Lectures on Rhetoric and Belles Lettres', 60.

30. Ibid. Smith's fellow Belles Lettrist Hugh Blair seconded Smith's judgment of Shaftesbury's 'raillery': 'He attempts it often, but always awkwardly; he is stiff even in his pleasantry and laughs in form like an author, not like a man.' Hugh Blair, *Lectures on Rhetoric and Belles Lettres*, vol. 3 (Basel: J. J. Tourneisen, 1788), 40.

31. Adam Smith, *The Theory of Moral Sentiments*, ed. Knud Haakonssen (Cambridge: Cambridge University Press, 2002), 376.

have been prompting readers to scrutinize Hobbes's position more closely than take delight in the joke at his expense.

Not all jests smoothened conversation or aided the process of collective reasoning, however. For Shaftesbury, keeping the conversation going required that the use of humour itself be closely monitored by the participants. As he explained in an unorthodox gloss on a passage from Aristotle's *Rhetoric*, abuses of humour should be corrected just as swiftly as excessive earnestness:

> It was the saying of an ancient sage [Gorgias] that 'humour was the only test of gravity, and gravity, of humour. For a subject which would not bear raillery was suspicious, and a jest which would not bear a serious examination was certainly false wit.'[32]

In the original text (*Rhetoric* 3.18) Aristotle has Gorgias advise orators to respond to their opponent's earnestness with jesting and their jesting with earnestness. Shaftesbury's critics indignantly pounced on the Earl's alternative rendering of the passage. John Brown, Shaftesbury's most influential critic in the 1750s, accused him of providing a 'maimed translation' of Aristotle's words, perverting their meaning by presenting a specific piece of advice intended for orators under the 'fantastical appearance' of a philosophical 'maxim'.[33] The elevation of humour into the 'only test' of gravity was, Brown insisted, Shaftesbury's own unwarranted insertion, a move of which Aristotle was 'entirely innocent'.[34] The German philosopher Moses Mendelssohn similarly complained that while Aristotle's Gorgias had 'merely wanted to teach a rhetorical technique which could be useful in public disputation', Shaftesbury had once again converted 'the laughable into a criterion of truth'.[35]

But it is far from evident that Shaftesbury wished to remove humour from the context of persuasion and collective deliberation.[36] What he exposed was that speakers insisting on seriousness were themselves engaged

32. As Karen Collis notes, Shaftesbury quotes a Latin 'Translator' in a footnote, but the text he reproduces there 'was not an accurate reproduction of any Latin text then printed'. Karen Collis, 'Shaftesbury and Literary Criticism: Philosophers and Critics in Early Eighteenth-Century England', *The Review of English Studies* 67, 279 (2015), 307.

33. Brown, *Essays on the Characteristics*, 84.

34. Ibid.

35. Moses Mendelssohn, *Philosophical Writings*, ed. Daniel Dahlstrom (Cambridge: Cambridge University Press, 1997), 112–13.

36. Particularly as, for Shaftesbury, the 'persuasive arts' were the life-blood of a free community governed by 'consent and voluntary association'. Shaftesbury, 'Soliloquy, or Advice to an Author', 107.

in a rhetorical ploy that should be challenged and that humour was often the best way to do so. As Lawrence Klein has observed of Shaftesbury, when the 'serious person insisted on acting out seriousness, this was its own form of pandering to an audience'.[37] Importantly, these critics also ignored Shaftesbury's call for the 'serious examination' of jests. Speakers who used humour were no more entitled to have their views go unchallenged than those adopting a more serious demeanour. By the end of *Sensus Communis* Shaftesbury was at pains to show that those who mock compulsively or indiscriminately could expect no sympathy from him. There was, after all, a big difference between 'seeking how to raise a laugh from everything and seeking in everything what justly may be laughed at'.[38]

Of course, what may be justly laughed at may not be *worth* laughing at or *advisable* to laugh at. Outside the context of a polite exchange between peers, deploying humour in public debate carried considerable risks. This was to become particularly evident to Shaftesbury and his Whig colleagues in the immediate aftermath of the publication of *Sensus Communis* in 1709. For it was then that Shaftesbury and his Whig colleagues were confronted by an opponent, Henry Sacheverell, whose attacks on the Whig junto provided plenty of fodder to satirists but whose success in shaping public opinion exposed the limits of engaging in a major political contest armed, in Roger Lund's words, 'with weapons designed for the drawing room'.[39] Not all forms of unsociability could be gently remedied with humour. Censuring would occasionally have to give way to censorship.

Silencing the Unsociable Dr Sacheverell

On 5 November 1709 Henry Sacheverell delivered a sermon at St Paul's Cathedral entitled *The Perils of False Brethren Both in Church and State*.[40] Sacheverell's avowed purpose in the sermon was to weed out the equivalent 'False Brethren' of his own time by exposing a conspiracy that had been

37. Klein, *Shaftesbury and the Culture of Politeness*, 95.

38. Shaftesbury, 'Sensus Communis', 59. As Roger Crisp notes, Shaftesbury's 'virtuous person will be grave about what is truly serious'. Roger Crisp, *Sacrifice Regained: Morality and Self-Interest in British Moral Philosophy from Hobbes to Bentham* (Oxford: Oxford University Press, 2019), 83.

39. Lund, *Ridicule, Religion and the Politics of Wit in Augustan England*, 147.

40. Henry Sacheverell, *The Perils of False Brethren Both in Church and State: Set Forth in a Sermon Preach'd before The Right Honourable, The Lord Mayor, Alderman, and Citizens of London, at the Cathedral Church of St Paul, on the 5th of November, 1709* (London: Henry Clements, 1709), 6.

'hatch'd in the cabinet-council of hell'.[41] Implicated in this plot were not only religious dissenters or 'self-conceited Enthusiast[s]' but also anyone who declared even the mildest sympathy for the 'principles of forty one', a reference to the doctrines justifying the Parliamentary revolt against Charles I.[42] The majority of Sacheverell's sermon consisted of him pouring scorn on these principles, and those who abided by them, one by one: the doctrine of *'Resistance'* was not only 'illegal' but had been already 'redicul'd out of countenance';[43] 'toleration' served no other purpose than to indulge 'monsters' and 'vipers' in the 'bosom' of the Church.[44] Most insidious of all, however, were those 'occasional conformists', the false brethren of the sermon's title, who feigned conformity to the established religion and loyalty to the state, but who will 'betray either whenever it is within their power'.[45]

For all its bluster and seeming lack of self-restraint, Sacheverell's sermon was carefully calibrated to inflict maximum discomfort on Shaftesbury's Whig colleagues, who had consistently opposed High Church attempts to ban occasional conformists from holding political office. But his timing was still more impeccably chosen. 5 November was a date doubly significant to Whig political mythology, coincidentally marking both the foiling of Guy Fawkes's Gunpowder Plot in 1605, and the landing of William of Orange's army at the culmination of the 1688 revolution. Even Sacheverell's language and turns of phrase, dismissed by one contemporary observer as resulting in an 'incoherent jumble', were precisely chosen so as to be maximally goading without being defamatory.[46] Apart from a single oblique reference to the recently fallen High Lord Treasurer Sidney Godolphin ('Wiley Volpones') the sermon avoided directly accusing any individual of conspiring against the state, and Sacheverell cleared it for traces of libel with three different lawyers in advance of going to print.[47]

41. Ibid., 2.
42. Ibid., 2 and 21.
43. Ibid., 19.
44. Ibid., 25.
45. Ibid., 33. An occasional conformist was anyone who received communion in the established Anglican Church in order to gain eligibility for office but who nevertheless continued to worship as a dissenter. Mark Knights, *The Devil in Disguise: Deception, Delusion and Fanaticism in the Early English Enlightenment* (Oxford: Oxford University Press, 2011), 144.
46. Alexander Cunningham, *The History of Great Britain: From the Revolution in 1688, to the Accession of George the First*, vol. 2 (London: Thomas Hollingbery, 1787), 276. Cunningham was a contemporary observer whose Latin history of the period was translated and published in 1787.
47. Sacheverell, *Perils of False Brethren*, 40; Geoffrey Holmes, *The Trial of Doctor Sacheverell* (London: Eyre Methuen, 1973), 73.

Once published the sermon became a sensation, prompting an urgent debate among the Whigs on how best to respond. Troublesome for the Whigs was not so much the content of Sacheverell's accusation (which advanced little beyond what earlier defenders of the High Church had offered) but rather his extraordinary rhetorical success in delivering it. Consistently among the reactions to his sermon we find a reluctant concession that what Sacheverell lacked in argumentative finesse, he more than made up for with his 'Talent' at 'railing'.[48] Even though Sacheverell had been mindful to avoid libelling any individuals, he had, in the eyes of the Whigs, brazenly ridiculed the Constitution itself and gotten away with it: 'will not the world think that we do not value as we ought our happy constitution', the Irish freethinker John Toland asked indignantly, 'if they see its greatest enemies permitted twice a week to banter, ridicule, libel and insult it?'[49] Up for urgent deliberation was whether defenders of toleration and liberty of conscience should respond in turn with ridicules of their own, or seek to silence Sacheverell using another instrument at their disposal, namely law. I will touch upon each of these proposed strategies in turn, before turning to Shaftesbury's own complex relationship to the Sacheverell controversy.

Daniel Defoe, writing in his *Review of the State of the English Nation* in December 1709, was among the first to propose ridicule as the best means of containing Sacheverell's influence: if the Whigs would just 'laugh at him', he predicted, the 'beast' would soon 'vent his gall' and be 'quiet'.[50] Defoe's proposal was enthusiastically taken up by a wide variety of aspiring satirists eager to present Sacheverell as unworthy of more earnest attention. Some opted for unsophisticated forms of character assassination, bluntly accusing Sacheverell of 'drunkenness', 'lewdness', 'gaming', 'unfaithfulness', 'foul dealing' and 'forgery'.[51] Others concocted comic personas, dubbing

48. John Dunton, *The Bull-Baiting: Or, Sacheverell Dress'd up in Fire-Works* (London: John Morphew, 1709), 43.

49. John Toland, *The Jacobitism, Perjury, and Popery of High Church Priests* (London: J. Baker, 1710), 14. Justin Champion, *Republican Learning: John Toland and the Crisis of Christian Culture, 1696–1722* (Manchester: Manchester University Press, 2003), 142.

50. Defoe cited in William Lee, *Daniel Defoe: His Life and Recently Discovered Writings: Extending from 1716 to 1729*, vol. 1 (London: John Camden Hotten, Piccadilly, 1869), 159. Defoe's own parody *The Shortest-Way with Dissenters* was directed at an earlier sermon of Sacheverell's. W. A. Speck, 'The Current State of Sacheverell Scholarship', in *Faction Displayed: Reconsidering the Impeachment of Dr Henry Sacheverell*, ed. Mark Knights (Singapore: Wiley-Blackwell, 2012), 19.

51. William Bisset, *The Modern Fanatick. With a Large and True Account of the Life, Actions, Endowments, Etc of the Famous Dr. Sacheverell* (London: A. Baldwin: and T. Harrison, 1710), 27–31.

him, in one instance, 'Don Henrico Furioso de Sacheverellio', a descendent of the hapless Don Quixote.[52] Still others adopted a more indirect approach by presenting Sacheverell's text as *already* approximating self-parody and so advertising its own ridiculousness.[53] The best example of this was the anonymously authored poem *The Priest Turn'd Poet or, The Best Way of Answering Dr. Sacheverell's Sermon . . . Being His Discourse paraphras'd in Burlesque Rhime.* This satire announced its strategy with a biblical citation that Astell had used against Shaftesbury: '*Answer a Fool according to his folly, lest he be wise to his own conceits.*'[54] For its author, to treat Sacheverell seriously would be futile, or possibly even dangerous. Even to call his speech a sermon would grant him undeserved dignity:

> Had I thought Dr. Sacheverell's Performance to have deserv'd the name of a sermon, I should have been far from treating it in this manner; but since, in my Opinion, he has burlesqu'd the Text, and all that Men of Sense account sacred and valuable, I conceive myself to have transgrest no Rule of Decency or Good Manners, by exposing his Ridiculous Prose in Bantering Verse. I only do that which he ought to have done himself, viz. to make it Rhime.[55]

The poem itself highlights both the promise and limitation of ridicule as a response to Sacheverell. On the one hand, the reproduction of Sacheverell's sermon line-by-line in rhyming couplets hinted at how little tampering was required to convert a serious sermon into 'Ridiculous Prose and Bantering Verse'. The problem, however, was that it only appeared ridiculous to those 'Men of Sense' the author appealed to in the above Preface. Of course, appealing to 'Men of Sense' was itself a rhetorical ploy; if readers were undecided as to whether or not to laugh, the prospect of inclusion among the sensible might remove their inhibition. The flip side of such an appeal, however, was that if 'Men of Sense' denoted those who already detested Sacheverell, then treating them to a laugh at the preacher's expense would achieve little. If parody could only reinforce

52. John Distaff, *A Character of Don Sacheverellio, Knight of the Firebrand; in a Letter to Isaac Bickerstaff, Esq; Censor of Great Britain* (Dublin: Francis Higgins, 1710).

53. John Dunton, likewise, asserted that there was 'no way in the World to be serious' with Sacheverell, and that any attempt to 'Gravely answer' his sermon would make the author 'almost as ridiculous as he'. Dunton, *The Bull-Baiting: Or, Sacheverell Dress'd up in Fire-Works*, 43.

54. Anon., *The Priest Turn'd Poet or, The Best Way of Answering Dr. Sacheverell's Sermon . . . Being His Discourse Paraphras'd in Burlesque Rhime* (London: the booksellers of London and Westminster, 1709), 1.

55. Ibid.

morale among Sacheverell's determined opponents, rather than persuade those on the fence to join their ranks, then it was a severely limited form of persuasion.

There was an even more substantial risk attached to parodying Sacheverell, however. A successful parody required that the author's intentions be veiled enough to achieve the effect of irony, but apparent enough to make clear who was being subjected to ridicule and why. Defoe himself had learned this the hard way when he parodied an earlier sermon of Sacheverell's in his 1702 *The Shortest-Way with the Dissenters*, a text that appeared to recommend the extermination of dissenters as the most efficient way of restoring religious uniformity.[56] The difficulty here, by contrast with *The Priest-Turn'd Poet*, is that it was never sufficiently clear who was supposed to laugh, or even whether the pamphlet was a satire at all or rather a counterfeit, warning readers about the extreme measures Sacheverell's ilk were capable of.[57] (Some Tory readers initially greeted it with approval, and only became outraged when they learned the identity of its author.[58]) What is more, even readers sensitive to the possible ironies at work in the text felt compelled to condemn it anyway on the grounds that less discerning readers would be corrupted by its literal message. The following angry reaction to Defoe's pamphlet is as a case in point:

> there are various Conjectures as to the Author and his Party: Some think him a Papist, some a non-Jurant parson, and others think him a Dissenter. I don't much concern myself which of the three he belongs to, or what his design may be, or if he act in disguise; for be that how it will, he is certainly one of the worst of Men. But since he speaks the language of the two former, I attack him as such.[59]

56. Daniel Defoe, *The Shortest-Way with the Dissenters* (London, 1702).

57. Roger Lund is confident that Defoe's text was intended as a satire. Lund, *Ridicule, Religion and the Politics of Wit in Augustan England*, 166. Ashley Marshall, by contrast, is adamant that Defoe intended the piece to be taken literally and thereby serve as a warning to Defoe's like-minded readers of the extreme measures that High Churchmen were willing to contemplate against dissenters. Ashley Marshall, 'The Generic Context of Defoe's *The Shortest-Way with the Dissenters* and the Problem of Irony', *The Review of English Studies* 61, 249 (2009), 243. Keymer blends both interpretation and declares Defoe's text to be 'both irony and hoax at once, or each in turn'. Keymer, *Poetics of the Pillory*, 130.

58. As Marshall puts it: 'Some High-Churchmen clearly recognized the similarities between Defoe's pamphlet and their own political idiom.' Marshall, 'The Generic Context of Defoe's *The Shortest-Way with the Dissenters*', 240.

59. Charles Leslie, *Reflections upon a Late Scandalous and Malicious Pamphlet Entitul'd, The Shortest Way with the Dissenters; or Proposals for the Establishment of the Church. To Which the Said Pamphlet Is Prefix'd Entire by It Self* (London, 1703), iii. In a brilliant recent analysis, Michael Prince suggests that Leslie was as much (if not more) the

The author, the High Churchman Charles Leslie, recognizes that Defoe may have written ironically but is indifferent to that possibility. Seditious words, regardless of authorial intention, were liable to have seditious effects and so must be suppressed. The state censors, once they discovered Defoe's authorship, were of a similar mind and sentenced him to the pillory.

Defoe's suggestion that laughing at Sacheverell would suffice failed, however, to carry the day with the Whigs. Somers, to whom Shaftesbury had dedicated his *Letter Concerning Enthusiasm*, recommended that Godolphin initiate legal action, but cautioned that if Sacheverell were to be tried it would be preferable to do so with minimum fuss behind the closed doors of a courtroom. It was a warning that would go unheeded: the Whig members of Parliament had by this point, in Holmes's words, been 'goaded beyond endurance' and decided to publicly impeach Sacheverell before the House of Lords.[60] Wishing to make an example, the Whigs subjected him to what in essence was a show-trial, designed to signal to the public that the state would brook no slander from critics of toleration. Ridicule alone was deemed insufficient; the objective was now, in the words of one Whig Lord, to 'quash' Sacheverell and 'damn him'.[61]

How did Shaftesbury position himself in the debate on how best to respond to Sacheverell? Shaftesbury's defence of ridicule as an instrument of sociability in *Sensus Communis* might lead us to expect him to have inclined towards Defoe's proposal of answering Sacheverell with counter-ridicules in print rather than turning to the law. Nevertheless, there is evidence that Shaftesbury was sympathetic to the Whig decision to use the law to hit back at anti-toleration opposition, even if his own relationship with the Whig leadership was tense at best.[62]

Shaftesbury's personal involvement in the impeachment was peripheral, his chronic ill-health precluding him from attending the House of

---

target of Defoe's pamphlet as Sacheverell. Leslie, Prince notes, was 'a far more important *thinker* than Sacheverell' in the High Church cause and 'just as scurrilous'. Defoe loathed him. Michael B. Prince, *The Shortest Way with Defoe: Robinson Crusoe, Deism, and the Novel* (Charlottesville: University of Virginia Press, 2020), 7.

60. Holmes, *The Trial of Doctor Sacheverell*, 85.

61. Lord Wharton, cited ibid., 97.

62. On Shaftesbury's ambivalence towards the 'Whig politicos' see Voitle, *The Third Earl of Shaftesbury 1671–1713*, 307. We also know that Shaftesbury kept a copy of *The Tryal of Dr. Henry Sacheverell*, the official account of the impeachment proceedings, at the property in Reigate where he prepared *Soliloquy*. This copy featured among four books that the Earl gifted to the local Cranston library in December 1711. https://www.angam.phil.fau.de/fields/enst/lit/shaftesbury/reading-room/cranston/.

Lords during the proceedings.[63] It is certain he kept a close eye on events, however, because there is a hand-written account of the debate on the first article of impeachment among the Shaftesbury papers that was prepared for the Earl's own private reading.[64] Friends and allies also kept him informed of events and of the urgent need to shape public perception of the proceedings against Sacheverell. In late December 1709 Toland sent him his *Lettre d'un Anglois à un Hollandois, au sujet du Docteur Sacheverell* explaining that he intended by it to remedy any misinterpretation of Sacheverell's 'infamous libel' that 'foreners' reading translations of his sermon might be prone to.[65] More importantly, we also can surmise from his correspondence what way Shaftesbury was leaning on the issue of how best to counter Sacheverell's influence. Writing to his protégé Michael Ainsworth, the Earl expressed satisfaction that the Parliament 'at this instant' was proceeding 'against Sacheveril'.[66] The letter is dated 30 December 1709, a little over two weeks after Parliament voted to initiate impeachment proceedings (the trial itself would not begin until late February 1710). Thus, although we cannot know whether Shaftesbury was fully apprised as to the set of options available to the Whig Parliamentarians, he seems to have been comfortable with their ultimate recourse to the unorthodox method of Parliamentary impeachment.

Shaftesbury's appetite for high-profile punishments that would allow Whig statesmen a platform to demonstrate their commitment to the public good was already clear from *Sensus Communis* itself. Thinking, no doubt, of Cicero's exposure of the Catiline conspiracy, he declared that there was 'nothing greater or nobler than the undertaking or management of some important Accusation; by which some High Criminal of State,

63. Although he could not attend, Shaftesbury did play an indirect role in the trial itself. In order to demonstrate that Sacheverell's warnings of a conspiracy against the Church had a basis in fact, lawyers for his defence read aloud from a number of putatively blasphemous works, including six passages from Shaftesbury's *Letter Concerning Enthusiasm*. *Collections of Passages Referr'd to by Dr. Henry Sacheverell in His Answer to the Articles of His Impeachment* (London, 1710). The passages from Shaftesbury's *Letter* are cited on pages 23–24 and 28. When Parliament ordered Sacheverell's sermons to be publicly burned as part of his sentence, it ordered the volume containing the Shaftesbury excerpts to be burned alongside them. Philip Connell, *Secular Chains: Poetry and the Politics of Religion from Milton to Pope* (Oxford: Oxford University Press, 2016), 169.

64. Clyve Jones, 'Debates in the House of Lords on "The Church in Danger", 1705 and on Dr Sacheverell's Impeachment, 1710', *The Historical Journal* 19, 3 (1976), 764. Jones reproduced the full text in this article.

65. John Toland to Shaftesbury, December 1709. Hampshire Record Office, Malmesbury Papers 9M73/G258/7.

66. Shaftesbury, 'The Ainsworth Correspondence', 411.

some form'd Body of Conspirators against the Publick, may be arraigned and brought to punishment, through the honest zeal and publick affection of a Private Man'.[67] It is unlikely that Shaftesbury had Sacheverell particularly in mind here (he published *Sensus Communis* before Sacheverell had caused a stir). Nevertheless, it is clear that by the summer of 1710 Shaftesbury believed Sacheverell's actions to be deserving of a dramatic punishment of some sort. When explaining to the Huguenot scholar Jean Le Clerc why he had to flee 'instantly' to his country estate at Wimborne St Giles in July of 1710, he blamed the 'ferment which the seditious High Churchman (Sacheverell) has raised'.[68] There is nothing in this letter to suggest that the tumultuous fallout from the trial had anything to do with Whig overreach. Instead, Sacheverell's 'seditious' (implying illegal) behaviour was entirely to blame.

Shaftesbury's approval of the Whig decision to impeach Sacheverell shows that, to his mind, there were limits to what ridicule could achieve in public debate. Laughing at Sacheverell had only gotten the Whigs so far, and the impeachment itself backfired. (By the end of the year Sacheverell had processed in triumph throughout the country, having only received a mild sentence, and the Tories trounced the Whigs in a general election.) More than that, by this time Shaftesbury had reneged on his earlier insistence that humour be free of regulation by the state. In his *Soliloquy* (written during the height of the Sacheverell affair) he endorsed the use of law by ancient Athens and Rome to regulate offensive humour. Earlier commentators on ancient attitudes towards censorship, such as Hobbes, had insisted that ancient societies were notable for their *lack* of any censorship laws.[69] Shaftesbury, by contrast, not only claimed that the ancients *did* enact such laws but also commented approvingly on their efficacy.[70] He warned against the 'great Error' of supposing that 'restraining' the more

67. Shaftesbury, 'Sensus Communis', 59.

68. Shaftesbury to Benjamin Furly, 19 July 1710, in *The Life, Unpublished Letters, and Philosophical Regimen of Anthony, Earl of Shaftesbury*, 424.

69. On Hobbes's interpretation, if the harm caused by what he termed 'contumely' did not extend beyond personal offence of the victim then ancient societies had little interest in criminalizing it. Hobbes, *Leviathan*, 213.

70. The existence of such laws in Athens has long been the subject of controversy. Stephen Halliwell maintains that, far from being tightly regulated by law, comedy enjoyed an exceptional degree of freedom in Athens. Stephen Halliwell, 'Comic Satire and Freedom of Speech in Classical Athens', *The Journal of Hellenic Studies* 111 (1991), 48–70. Robert Wallace suggests that the Athenians may have introduced legal restrictions on ridicule in 440 BCE in response to the war with Sparta but that they likely lifted them three years later. Robert Wallace, 'Law, Attic Comedy, and the Regulation of Comic Speech', in *Cambridge Companion to Ancient Greek Law*, ed. Michael Gagarin and David Cohen (Cambridge,

'licentious manner of Wit, *by Law*' was a 'violation of the liberty of the Athenian state'.[71] Augustus's Rome too had prohibited the Fescennine verses and the *fabulae Atellanae* 'for the public's sake' having found them 'contrary to the just liberty of the people'.[72] In both of these examples Shaftesbury presented the law as a legitimate instrument that states had used to curb humour that threatened the public good.[73]

Shaftesbury's position on censorship is thus quite a bit more complicated than usually presented. Certainly, the space in which citizens could use humour to express their natural sociability was more tightly circumscribed than often supposed. In his *Miscellaneous Reflections* Shaftesbury narrowed it still further, all but declaring ridicule the exclusive preserve of Whig gentlemen. By adopting an 'air of breeding and Gentility' Shaftesbury suggests, Sacheverell's party had hoped to 'laugh Gentlemen into their Religion, who had unfortunately been laugh'd out of it'.[74] For there was no reason to believe that 'Orthodoxy shou'd not be able to laugh as agreeably' as 'Heresy or Infidelity'.[75] As ever with Shaftesbury, however, this concession carried a sting in the tail. The Earl's assurance that ridicule was equally available to all sides was an empty one. When confronted by parodies of themselves or their arguments, 'real Gentlemen' will not recognize themselves and so 'will hardly be apt to think they are

---

2005), 364. Shaftesbury's own sources for the law are Horace's epistle on *The Art of Poetry* and Marcus Aurelius's *Meditations* 11.6.

71. Shaftesbury, 'Soliloquy, or Advice to an Author', 111. Shaftesbury's followers felt obliged to gloss over this aspect of the *Soliloquy* because it seemed so plainly at odds with his earlier championing of the freedom to ridicule in *Sensus Communis*. For example, Anthony Collins in his *Discourse Concerning Ridicule and Irony in Writing* copiously cited Shaftesbury, but was obliged to depart from the Earl's line of argument when it came to the topic of ancient censorship. The central pillar of Collins's argument was the historical claim that 'all polite Governments' had refrained from legally regulating ridicule, permitting it instead as a means of employing 'innocently and usefully the vacant hours of many, who know not how to employ their Time, or would employ it amiss by entering into factions and Cabals to disturb the state'. The lesson to be drawn was that any 'attempt to make a *Law* to restrain such speech in a modern society would 'prove abortive' and be 'deem'd the Effect of . . . present Anger at a poor Jest'. This was a cogent historical argument against censorship, but it was not Shaftesbury's. Anthony Collins, *A Discourse Concerning Ridicule and Irony in Writing, in a Letter to the Reverend Dr. Nathaniel Marshall* (London: J. Brotherton, 1729), 18 and 74.

72. Shaftesbury, 'Soliloquy, or Advice to an Author', 113.

73. As Lawrence Klein reads it, on Shaftesbury's interpretation these legal curtailments 'expressed not the limiting of freedom' but rather a 'new and more sophisticated grasp of it'. Klein, *Shaftesbury and the Culture of Politeness*, 206.

74. Shaftesbury, 'Miscellaneous Reflections', 461.

75. Ibid.

refuted'.[76] These gentlemen might laugh along but, Shaftesbury warned the Sacheverellites, the 'laugh may perhaps be different from what you intend'.[77] Rather than laughing along in agreement they instead would instead 'inwardly smile' at any attempt to fight against Whig gentlemen using 'their own arms'.[78] While ridicule might in theory be available to everyone, Shaftesbury implied, Whig gentlemen were both more practised in its use and, because they had no need to shelter behind solemnity, impervious to whatever ridicules the Sacheverellites might throw at them.

Mandeville and Shaftesbury's Hypocrisy

By insinuating that ridicule was the special weapon of Whig gentleman, Shaftesbury once again left himself open to the charge that his project was little more than cover for a conspiracy against Tories and the High Church. It is unsurprising, therefore, that in the decades following his death in 1713 his writings endured a mixed fate. And while much of the controversy revolved around his heterodox religious beliefs, the claim in *Sensus Communis* that ridicule was safe because largely self-regulating also drew considerable fire. Clerics such as John Tottie, preaching at Oxford, baulked at the suggestion that ridicule could be its 'own Corrector' and warned that permitting it too freely would cause many 'friendly contest[s] for the truth' to descend into 'spiteful trial[s] of wit'.[79]

Even readers who largely shared Shaftesbury's Whig politics expressed unease. One such critic was the Dutch medic, philosopher and satirist Bernard Mandeville. In his *Free Thoughts on Religion, the Church, and National Happiness* (1720), Mandeville stood unequivocally with Shaftesbury and the Whigs on the issue of toleration, citing with approval 'one of the most polite authors of the age' on the futility of using persecution to eradicate dissent.[80] On the question of how best to deal with intolerant speech, however, Mandeville hedged his bets. Securing public peace, he maintained, required that magistrates keep a handle on the speech of all parties, penalizing equally 'fiery pulpiteers' like Sacheverell along with the

76. Ibid., 463.
77. Ibid.
78. Ibid.
79. John Tottie, *Ridicule, so Far as It Affects Religion, Consider'd and Censur'd* (Oxford, 1735), 11 and 14.
80. Bernard Mandeville, *Free Thoughts on Religion, the Church, and National Happiness* (London: T. Jauncy, 1720), 239.

'scurrilous jests' of dissenters.[81] Distancing himself from the freethinkers, Mandeville concluded that religion and the sacred could never be the 'proper objects of ridicule', not least because to 'scoff at religion' was 'affronting to God'.[82]

It might seem unlikely that Mandeville, of all writers, could be squeamish about using ridicule, least of all when discussing religion. After all, among his first works was a satirical poem, *The Grumbling Hive: or Knaves Turn'd Honest*, that celebrated the contribution of vice to a flourishing commercial society. In case the irreligious implications of the poem were not evident enough, Mandeville published the *Fable of the Bees: or, Private Vices Publick Benefits*, an extensive commentary on the *Grumbling Hive* that explicitly denied that religion was the source of virtue. The Middlesex Grand Jury denounced the extended 1723 edition of the *Fable* as impious, placing it in the same category as the irreligious satires that Mandeville had condemned in *Free Thoughts*. But although his critics lumped him together with freethinkers railing at superstition and clericalism, Mandeville was far more concerned with exposing the hypocrisy of moralists, which explains why he presented Shaftesbury in a dramatically different light in 'A Search into the Nature of Society', an essay added to the 1723 edition of the *Fable*. A close examination of that essay makes clear that, for Mandeville, the 'proper object of ridicule' was not (or not only) religious delusion, but the hypocrisy engendered by moralistic preening about vice.[83]

Commentators on 'A Search into the Nature of Society' have focused, with good reason, on its philosophical rejection of Shaftesbury's views on

81. Ibid., 361. Runciman considers *Free Thoughts* a partisan defence of the Whigs. David Runciman, *Political Hypocrisy: The Mask of Power from Hobbes to Orwell and Beyond* (Princeton, NJ: Princeton University Press, 2018), 69. Hundert describes the early career Mandeville as a 'Whig propagandist' and calls *Free Thoughts* a 'party political tract'. E. J. Hundert, *The Enlightenment's Fable: Bernard Mandeville and the Discovery of Society* (Cambridge: Cambridge University Press, 1994), 6. Turner is less sure, and doubts that Mandeville had any 'party fervor' at all. Brandon P. Turner, 'Mandeville against Luxury', *Political Theory* 44, 1 (2016), 35.

82. Hundert, *Enlightenment's Fable*, 122.

83. Istvan Hont rightly pointed out that Mandeville's first volume of the *Fable*, taken as a whole, had more to do with attacking Fénelon's austere political economy than satirizing moralistic hypocrisy. The engagement with Shaftesbury in 'A Search into the Nature of Society', however, unquestionably has the latter as its focus. Istvan Hont, 'The Early Enlightenment Debate on Commerce and Luxury', in *The Cambridge History of Eighteenth-Century Political Thought*, ed. Mark Goldie and Robert Wokler (Cambridge: Cambridge University Press, 2008), 387–95.

natural sociability.[84] Just as important, however, was the manner in which Mandeville carried out this refutation. Mandeville did not limit himself to arguing with Shaftesbury; he also made an example of the Earl's character to display to his readers how self-deluded moralists can be. Alluding to the Earl's insistence that war was the only way to check French hegemonic ambitions, Mandeville asked how it could be that a man enfeebled by asthma could be so bellicose in his politics. A philosopher claiming to be unafraid of death, he sneered, should surely have never passed up the chance to 'follow Arms when his Country was involved in War', knowing full well that Shaftesbury never intended to go near a battlefield.[85] (Part of the blame here, Mandeville continued, lay with Locke, a 'great Philosopher' who had coddled the young lord into overestimating his own virtue.[86]) The fact that Shaftesbury had only ever encountered imaginary deaths from the safety of his 'closet', Mandeville further implied, leeched credibility from whatever he might say about disciplining the passions, and threatened to nurture similar self-delusions in others.[87]

Note that Mandeville here repeats the move that Shaftesbury had performed against Hobbes in *Sensus Communis*. Just as Shaftesbury used Hobbes's own sociable behaviour to cast doubt on the plausibility of Hobbes's account of human nature, so Mandeville warned his readers not to heed philosophers who implore their readers to perform virtuous feats that they themselves could only contemplate. In his entry for Shaftesbury in the index for the first volume of the *Fable*, Mandeville made this strategy explicit, pointing to this portion of the text as the place where Shaftesbury is 'Refuted by his own Character'.[88]

84. Sagar, *The Opinion of Mankind*, 42–46. Tim Stuart-Buttle notes that Mandeville has been 'dismissed' by historians of philosophy as 'primarily a satirist' mainly owing to neglect of his writings from the later 1720s onwards, writings that 'betray a greater seriousness of purpose'. While this is largely correct, it suggests that Mandeville is unserious when satirizing. Mandeville's attack on Shaftesbury demonstrates how his satirical method was integral to achieving his philosophical aims. Stuart-Buttle, *From Moral Theology to Moral Philosophy*, 120.

85. Bernard Mandeville, *The Fable of the Bees: or, Private Vices, Publick Benefits*, vol. 1, ed. F. B. Kaye (Oxford: Clarendon Press, 1924), 332.

86. Ibid.

87. Ibid.

88. Mandeville, 378. Because Shaftesbury's *Askêmata* journals were not available to him, Mandeville could not have known just how correct he was about the Earl's efforts to cure his fear of death through imaginary encounters with it in his 'closet'. Equally, however, if he had known something of Shaftesbury's tortuous attempts to achieve virtue, he might not have attacked the Earl so virulently for presenting virtue as easy to achieve. In a recent analysis, Tim Stuart-Buttle has suggested that Mandeville was not mistaken about Shaftesbury's position in that he knew full well that Shaftesbury thought virtue 'profoundly demanding'. Stuart-Buttle, *From Moral Theology to Moral Philosophy*, 122. Though as

Mandeville's precise motivation for skewering Shaftesbury in this way is difficult to discern. It is possible that he thought he could gain notoriety from exposing one of the most celebrated moralists of the age as a hypocrite. More likely, however, is that Mandeville was making a point about what the sociability Shaftesbury called for actually entailed. As Mandeville saw it, Shaftesbury had committed two errors. The first was to assume that we seek out the company of others from a natural desire for sociability. In fact, Mandeville countered, everyone enters conversation to satisfy their own interests. This applies most obviously to the vainglorious boor seeking to score points or show off. But it applies also to Shaftesbury's 'Good-humour'd' gentleman who is difficult to offend, non-confrontational, and seems to enjoy conversation for its own sake.[89] While the latter might be better company than the former, Mandeville explains, both act from self-interest. It just so happens that the good-humoured man's pride is satisfied by becoming the 'Darling of the Company', whereas the boor craves the esteem that comes from beating an opponent in argument.[90]

The second failing of Shaftesbury's that Mandeville tried to expose was the foolishness of thinking that natural sociability (if there were such a thing) would be advantageous to society. The suppression of our unsociable passions was not just implausible, Mandeville argued, but would also spell disaster if attempted on a large scale, draining commercial society of the avidity that kept it going. Genuine Shaftesburian sociability, Mandeville insisted, would be 'good for nothing but to breed drones' and 'qualify a man for the stupid enjoyments of a monastic life'.[91] Better to recognize that most citizens of a commercial society only act sociably out of shame, concealing (but not obliterating) the pride that drives them to work, compete and produce.[92] For Mandeville, Shaftesbury's insistence

---

Robin Douglass points out, Mandeville's accusation that Shaftesbury made virtue easy was not entirely without basis. Shaftesbury does allow that those who are free of 'ill-passions' may be 'cheaply virtuous' by following their natural temperament. Shaftesbury, 'Inquiry Concerning Virtue or Merit', 176. Robin Douglass, 'Mandeville on the Origins of Virtue', *British Journal for the History of Philosophy* 28, 2 (2020), 282.

89. Mandeville, *Fable of the Bees*, 342.

90. Ibid.

91. Ibid., 333.

92. Ibid., 72. Robin Douglass points out that Mandeville vacillated on the issue on whether polite behaviour motivated by shame was truly virtuous or not. In the 1714 edition of the *Fable* he seemed to suggest that virtue arose from shame. By the 1723 *Fable*, by contrast, polite behaviour is a counterfeit virtue that we achieve by concealing our true passions and appetites. Some of this difference can be accounted for by Mandeville's determination to 'accentuate the differences between his own position' and Shaftesbury's. Because Shaftesbury held that virtue came to us naturally, Mandeville doubled down on his argument that true virtue required the actual conquest of our passions rather than

that sociability was natural had devalued the artifices that made society such an impressive accomplishment in the first place.[93]

Mandeville's mockery of Shaftesbury did not end there. In the second volume of the *Fable*, published in 1728, he swapped *ad hominem* sarcasm for parody to attack what he saw as the elitism of the natural sociability doctrine. This second *Fable* is structured as a dialogue between Cleomenes (generally the spokesman for Mandeville) and Horatio (a stand-in for Shaftesbury). The 'First Dialogue' opens with Cleomones successfully feigning conversion to Shaftesbury's philosophy in order to entice a reluctant Horatio to debate with him. Having owned up to this ruse, Cleomenes then rounds on the Earl for promulgating a hopelessly demanding notion of social virtue while making a 'Jest of all reveal'd Religion'.[94] If he had succeeded, Cleomenes complains, the labouring poor that made up the majority of society would have found themselves both excluded from virtue and bereft of any alternative moral guide. Horatio, disgruntled at having been duped, retorts that parodying Shaftesbury proves nothing against his philosophy, for 'the best Things, you know, may be ridicul'd'.[95] Cleomenes objects that Shaftesbury himself had said quite the opposite:

> Lord *Shaftsbury* [*sic*] has flatly denied [that the best things can be ridiculed] and takes Jokes and Banter to be the best and surest Touchstone to prove the Worth of Things; his Lordship made use of that Test to try the Scriptures and the Christian Religion by, and expos'd them because it seems they could not stand it.[96]

Although hardly charitable, Mandeville's interpretation here of Shaftesbury's argument in *Sensus Communis* is more accurate than the more common accusation that the Earl had made ridicule a test of truth. Shaftesbury certainly did imply that testing a French Prophet or a Socrates with ridicule could tell us something about their respective 'Worth'. What Mandeville sought to expose was the Earl's excessive confidence that aristocratic gentlemen had sufficient virtue to stand the test, while ordinary people would not.

---

their concealment behind a veneer of politeness. Douglass, 'Mandeville on the Origins of Virtue', 286.

93. As Stuart-Buttle notes, 'society', for Mandeville, should be celebrated as 'mankind's greatest achievement', one that Shaftesbury's thesis that we are naturally sociable seemed to deny. Stuart-Buttle, *From Moral Theology to Moral Philosophy*, 124.

94. Bernard Mandeville, *The Fable of the Bees: Or, Private Vices, Publick Benefits*, vol. 2, ed. F. B. Kaye (Oxford: Clarendon Press, 1924), 47.

95. Ibid., 52.

96. Ibid., 53.

When Cleomenes and Horatio return to the same subject in their 'Third Dialogue' Mandeville made clear that his own thoughts on ridicule were far closer to Hobbes's. Explaining the difference between our instinct for self-preservation (self-love) and the hankering for recognition of our superiority over others (self-liking), Cleomenes describes a man driven by the latter: 'Whenever he met with any visible Marks in others of Inferiority to himself, he would laugh, and do the same with their misfortunes, as far as his own Pity would give him Leave.'[97] As F. B. Kaye notes, this is clearly an 'adaptation of Hobbes's theory of laughter'.[98] For the moment, the only qualification that Mandeville makes is that in his version perceiving defects in others gives rise to two competing emotions, meaning that laughter will only ensue if self-liking succeeds in overpowering pity, something that cannot be taken for granted. Even this was to confirm rather than deny Mandeville's general Hobbesianism, however, not least because Mandeville reduced pity itself to yet another expression of our prideful natures. For when we pity others, we only experience unease because we imagine a similar discomfort occurring to us.[99] If laughing at another's misfortune is more obviously unsociable, the more respectable emotion of pity is no less self-centred.

Later, in 'The Fourth Dialogue', Mandeville delivered a more exacting critique of Hobbes's thinking on laughter, while pouring further scorn on Shaftesbury's. Resuming their discussion, Horatio challenges Cleomenes to clarify whether he truly thinks that laughter can be reduced to pride. Although '*Hobbes* is of that Opinion', Cleomenes replies, pride cannot account for *every* laugh.[100] To improve on Hobbes's account, Cleomenes defines laughter more broadly as a 'Mechanical Motion, which we are

---

97. Ibid., 134.

98. Ibid., F. B. Kaye, editor's footnote, 134. Daniel Kapust similarly finds that Mandeville 'shares the Hobbesian understanding of laughter as fundamentally derisive'. Daniel J. Kapust, *Flattery and the History of Political Thought: That Glib and Oily Art* (Cambridge: Cambridge University Press, 2018), 146 n.38.

99. When we pity others, Mandeville argued, we are really only imagining a similar discomfort for ourselves. See Mandeville, *Fable of the Bees*, vol. 1, 66. As Adam Smith observed in a famous letter to the editors of the *Edinburgh Review*, this was a bone of contention between Mandeville and Rousseau. On Smith's gloss, Mandeville considered pity the 'only amiable principle' natural to man but denied that it could be a foundation for virtue. Rousseau disagreed. Adam Smith, 'A Letter to the Authors of the Edinburgh Review', in *The Glasgow Edition of the Works and Correspondence of Adam Smith*, vol. 3, *Essays on Philosophical Subjects*, ed. W.P.D. Wightman, J. C. Bryce, and I. S. Ross (Oxford: Oxford University Press, 1980), 251. See also Istvan Hont, *Politics in Commercial Society*, 20.

100. Mandeville, *Fable of the Bees*, vol. 2, 156.

naturally thrown into, when we are unaccountably pleased'.[101] But the range of things that might unexpectedly please us in this way, Cleomenes continues, often have little do with our pride. We laugh when we behold an object or behaviour that is 'odd and out of the way' and delights us for reasons we cannot explain.[102] What Cleomenes ultimately arrives at, then, is an argument that grounds laughter in the perception of pleasing absurdities rather than superiority or self-liking.

Concluding the discussion, Mandeville muddies the waters further by having Horatio (usually the stand-in for Shaftesbury) renew the case for Hobbes. What we usually laugh at, Horatio objects, are things that are 'mortifying, unbecoming, or prejudicial to others'.[103] Cleomenes, however, is not convinced, and accuses Horatio of overlooking too many causes of laughter, not least physical touch or tickling. He then launches into a more detailed account of the physiology of laughter (Mandeville's experience as a physician is fully in evidence here) and makes the case that laughter, much like weeping, offers periodic relief from the physical strain that comes from bottling up emotion. Society's expectation that we hold ourselves together to avoid making a scene or displaying unseemliness, Mandeville here implies, places severe burdens on the body. Laughter provides a much needed 'Relaxation to all the Muscles' and cathartic release, a use that Hobbes never envisaged.[104]

We can see now why Mandeville's criticism of the Hobbesian argument should not be confused for an endorsement of the Shaftesburian alternative. By having Horatio endorse Hobbes, Mandeville tried to show that Shaftesbury had clung too closely to a Stoic understanding of ridicule as a controlled rhetorical act that conveys judgment and embarrasses the foolish or vice-ridden. Missing in this picture, for Mandeville, is the valuable role that laugher can play as a *relinquishment* of control. In other words, by associating laughter with a pleasantly irrational relaxation of our self-composure, Mandeville had taken yet another jab at Shaftesbury's Stoic austerity.

A final notable implication of Mandeville's quasi-Hobbesian analysis is that ridicule cannot be left to refine itself as Shaftesbury had suggested in *Sensus Communis*. We have to refine it ourselves; and that entails being judicious about how we use it. It is not enough, on Mandeville's account, to mock freely, confident that worthy people and things will be immune.

101. Ibid., 157.
102. Ibid.
103. Ibid.
104. Ibid., 158.

Mandeville's point is that refining ridicule to a point where it can usefully shame unsociable behaviour but not degenerate into abuse, can never be that easy. Nature provides no shield to deflect undeserved mockery. Much better, on Mandeville's view, to appreciate ridicule as another arbitrary tool of social discipline that plays on our craving for esteem and what he calls the 'fear of shame'.[105]

Hutcheson and the Sociability of Laughter

Mandeville's critique of Shaftesbury in the first volume of the *Fable* drew a sharp reply from one of the most influential theorists of sociability of the eighteenth century, Francis Hutcheson. Today Hutcheson is best known for his impact on Scottish moral philosophy, particularly from 1729 onwards when he took up the Chair of Moral Philosophy at his *alma mater*, the University of Glasgow. The core elements of Hutcheson's anti-Mandevillian philosophy, however, had already formed during years spent in Dublin teaching at a Presbyterian academy.[106] In his *Inquiry into the Original of our Ideas of Beauty and Virtue* (1725) Hutcheson held that Mandeville's reduction of sociability to a kind of hypocrisy that we selfishly deploy to earn praise and avoid shame ignored how a 'disinterested affection' for others actuates much of our social behaviour.[107] Hutcheson had no problem acknowledging that people often act selfishly, but he believed that Mandeville's denial that people ever act from benevolence was poor observational psychology masquerading as realism. A philosopher who is prepared to claim that familial affection or patriotism were just different varieties of selfishness has not, Hutcheson implied, met many parents or patriots.

To reject Mandeville on this point was to embrace Shaftesbury, and Hutcheson went out of his way during his Dublin career to associate

---

105. Ibid., 95.

106. As James Moore noted, Hutcheson's years in Dublin saw him develop a 'coherent public philosophy' that formed part of a campaign to reform higher education in Ireland and Scotland along Shaftesburian lines. James Moore, 'The Two Systems of Francis Hutcheson: On the Origins of the Scottish Enlightenment', in *Studies in the Philosophy of the Scottish Enlightenment*, ed. M. A. Stewart (Oxford: Oxford University Press, 1990), 41. That philosophy constituted, in Paul Sagar's words, a 'sustained rejection' of the Hobbesian and Mandevillian view that 'positional competition for recognition characterised humans' central psychological processes'. Sagar, *The Opinion of Mankind*, 92.

107. Francis Hutcheson, *An Inquiry into the Original of Our Ideas of Beauty and Virtue* (London: John Darby, 1725), 143. This is the second imprint of the first edition.

himself with the Earl's legacy. This had as much to do with his social connections as it did philosophical affinity. Hutcheson was a member of the
Molesworth circle, a loose association of Whig reformers determined to
improve the manners and morals of the Irish by implementing a Shaftesburian programme of religious toleration and cultural renewal.[108] So
strong was his allegiance to this agenda that Hutcheson occasionally presented himself as an explicator and defender of Shaftesbury's doctrines
rather than an original philosopher in his own right (the subtitle to the
Inquiry described the book's aim as explaining and justifying the '*principles of the late Earl of Shaftesbury*' against '*the author of the Fable of the
Bees*').[109] Broad adherence to Shaftesbury's principles, however, did not
imply uncritical agreement with everything the Earl had written, particularly when it came to the relationship between ridicule and sociability.[110]
Indeed, if we are too hasty in reading Hutcheson's contribution to the ridicule debate as a mere endorsement of Shaftesbury then we will miss much
of what made Hutcheson's position distinctive.

Hutcheson presented his thoughts on laughter in June 1725 in three
'letters to Hibernicus' that appeared in the *Dublin Weekly Journal*, a
publication edited by his friend James Arbuckle, another member of
Molesworth's circle. Arbuckle had been appalled at how Irish clerics, chief
among them Jonathan Swift, had made themselves instruments of the
Sacheverellite High Church, and believed their slurs against dissenters
would exacerbate Irish religious factionalism.[111] In response, he made it

108. On Molesworth as a 'propagandist for Shaftesbury's thought' in 1720s Dublin see
Rivers, *Reason, Grace and Sentiment*, vol. 2, *Shaftesbury to Hume*, 155.

109. In subsequent editions Hutcheson removed this subtitle but included a paragraph
in the preface recommending Shaftesbury's writing and expressing regret for how they had
been misused. Ibid., 159–60. Daniel Carey speculates that Hutcheson may have removed
the references to Shaftesbury in the title to the *Inquiry* because the death of Molesworth
in May 1725 'freed him from the need to advertise himself so prominently as Shaftesbury's
defender'. Carey, *Locke, Shaftesbury, and Hutcheson*, 153 n.4.

110. Hutcheson's biographer William Robert Scott argued that 'instead of following
Shaftesbury's analysis of ridicule' Hutcheson become 'more independent, assigning an
ethical rather than intellectual "use" for its exercise'. This is a mischaracterisation of Shaftesbury's ridicule which, as we have seen, certainly had an ethical content. But Scott was
correct to place distance between Hutcheson and the Earl. William Robert Scott, *Francis
Hutcheson: His Life, Teaching and Position in the History of Philosophy* (Cambridge: Cambridge University Press, 1900), 32.

111. On Swift's attack on freethinking see Jeffrey R. Wigelsworth, *Deism in Enlightenment England* (Manchester: Manchester University Press, 2009), 123. As Brown points
out, Swift was 'no arch-Tory'. During the upheavals following the Sacheverell trial it was
still possible to defend the established Church from within the 'constellation of the Whig
party'. Michael Brown, 'Swift, Satire, and the Problem of Whig Regeneration', *Restoration:*

his mission to do for the Irish what Joseph Addison and Richard Steele's *Spectator* had attempted for the English; polish their manners by publishing short, edifying essays that could serve as starting points for polite conversation.

Defining the appropriate place for laughter in such conversations was key to this enterprise. Arbuckle himself took the first steps, devoting one of his own Hibernicus letters to lamenting how wit in Ireland was no longer 'subservient to Virtue and good Manners'.[112] There was again a partisan edge to this complaint. The deterioration of Irish wit, Arbuckle held, was exclusively the fault of Swift and his friends in Trinity College, whose taste for scatological abuse had been illustrated by the *Wonderful Wonder of Wonders*, a satire 'on human posteriors' that Arbuckle condemned despite imitating its style (copies of the piece should, he recommended, be 'applied to the use of the Party offended').[113] Arbuckle concluded by assuring readers that his condemnation of Swift and his acolytes did not apply to humour as such. Invoking Shaftesbury's *Sensus Communis*, Arbuckle proclaimed that 'nothing in Nature is ridiculous' and that consequently there was 'no harm in Mirth, provided it be managed so as not to be shocking to Decency and Good Manners'.[114]

Hutcheson's first Hibernicus letter took up where Arbuckle had left off. Rather than attack Tory satire, Hutcheson set out to articulate a more positive vision of laughter as a social practice that could draw people together rather than set them at odds.[115] Making good on that vision first required

---

Studies in English Literary Culture, 1660–1700 39, 1–2 (2015), 89. On Arbuckle's clash with Swift and his circle see Richard Holmes, 'James Arbuckle and Dean Swift: Cultural Politics in the Irish Confessional State', *Irish Studies Review* 16, 4 (2008), 431–44. For an alternative account that emphasizes Arbuckle's personal loathing of Swift and his willingness to reply to Swift's rudeness in kind see Brown, 'The Biter Bitten: Ireland and the Rude Enlightenment'.

112. James Arbuckle, 'No. 9' in *Hibernicus's Letters: Or, a Philosophical Miscellany*, vol. 1 (London: J. Clark, T. Hatchet, E. Symon; J. Gray; C. Rivington; and 6 others, 1734), 70.

113. Arbuckle, 'No. 9', 72–73. *The Wonderful Wonder of Wonders* was published anonymously but is attributed to Swift. It appears to have been a satire on finance and on the push to establish a Bank of Ireland to issue paper currency in particular. For this context see Sean Moore, 'Swift's Financial Satires and the Bank of Ireland Controversy of 1720–1', *Eighteenth-Century Ireland / Iris an Dá Chultúr* 17 (2002), 39–40. Arbuckle was ostensibly more offended by the satire's reference to bodily functions than its specific polemical content.

114. Arbuckle, 'No. 9', 76.

115. As Michael Brown aptly puts it, Hutcheson set out to show that laughter was a 'social pleasure' that played an important part in the 'creation and sustaining of a moral community'. Michael Brown, *Francis Hutcheson in Dublin, 1719–1730* (Dublin: Four Courts Press, 2002), 117.

negating the Hobbesian argument that laughter was grounded in a contest for positional superiority. Hobbes's basic error, Hutcheson maintained, had been to take Aristotle's discussion of the ridiculous and generalize it to laughter as such. The result was that laughter at 'some Mistake, or some Turpitude' in another was the only form captured by Hobbes's theory.[116] Hutcheson attributed this implausible narrowing of the scope of laughter to Hobbes's denial of natural sociability and his consequent determination to 'deduce all human Actions from Self-Love'.[117] 'All', Hutcheson wrote in paraphrase of Hobbes, 'must be interest, and some selfish view' and so 'laughter itself must be a joy from the same spring'.[118]

If Hobbes's general theory of laughter was reductive, Hutcheson reasoned next, his understanding of the passion that triggers it was preposterous. More specifically, Hobbes's characterization of that passion as sudden glory forced him to embrace two absurd conclusions. The first was that a feeling of superiority was a necessary condition for laughter. This, for Hutcheson, excluded the countless instances where we laugh at incongruities or oddities without feeling in any way superior to the object of our laughter (an argument that anticipated Mandeville's own critique of the Hobbesian theory in volume 2 of the Fable). The second absurdity was that feeling superior to another was sufficient to make us laugh. If, Hutcheson alleged, Hobbes was correct that 'Laughter arose from our imagined Superiority' then 'the more that any object appear'd inferior to us, the greater would be the Jest'.[119] What Hobbes had supposedly failed to see was that the feeling of superiority was just as likely to result in a feeling of 'sedate Joy' as a peal of laughter.[120] This was all to imply, however, that the feeling of superiority was the sole driver of laughter, a position Hobbes never affirmed.[121]

Having undermined Hobbes's account of laughter, Hutcheson ventured in his second letter to replace it with an account that retained Hobbes's

116. Francis Hutcheson, 'No. 10' in Hibernicus's Letters, vol. 1, 77. On Hutcheson's criticism of Hobbes's 'failure to distinguish humor and ridicule' see Gordon Graham, 'Francis Hutcheson and Adam Ferguson on Sociability', History of Philosophy Quarterly 31, 4 (2014), 321.

117. Hutcheson, 'No. 10', 78.

118. Ibid., 79.

119. Ibid., 82.

120. Ibid., 86.

121. Had Hutcheson restricted his analysis to Leviathan then such an accusation against Hobbes might have been justified. But Hutcheson instead targeted the discussion of laughter in the Elements of Law, a text in which, as we have seen, Hobbes allows for laughter at incongruities or absurdities. See Introduction above.

emphasis on suddenness and surprise, but which decentred prideful comparison between self and object. The definition he arrived at placed some distance between himself and Shaftesbury. Rather than point to unnaturalness as the essence of the ridiculous, Hutcheson emphasized the contrast of dignity and meanness. In most cases, Hutcheson alleged, we laugh when struck by images that present a contrast between 'ideas of *Grandeur*' on the one hand, and of '*Meanness*' on the other.[122] Because the notions of dignity informing these contrasts were culturally variable, however, what is laughable in one country will not be so in another, a relativistic conclusion anathema to Shaftesbury.

Hutcheson's third and final letter on laughter made his divergence from Shaftesbury even starker. Given that our ability to laugh had been 'implanted' by nature, Hutcheson now asserted, it must have a use.[123] Setting aside psychological speculation in favour of practical ethics, Hutcheson identified two different uses for laughter, before assigning two further tasks to ridicule specifically. The first use he ascribed to laughter (and the most conventional) was to raise spirits oppressed by anxiety or sorrow. The second related more directly to the issue of sociability. The sheer contagiousness of laughter, Hutcheson noted, meant that it came into its own in social contexts, solidifying community and forming one of the most crucial 'bonds of human friendship'.[124]

As for ridicule, it too could serve the ends of sociability, despite the discomfort it can cause, by gently correcting 'smaller *Faults*' in our behaviour.[125] Echoing Shaftesbury's *Letter Concerning Enthusiasm*, Hutcheson further recommended ridicule as a way to restore perspective to inflamed imaginations and emphasized its usefulness against the 'wild *Enthusiastick Apprehensions*' of false prophets.[126] Rather than choose a contemporary example of false prophets to illustrate the point, like Shaftesbury

122. Hutcheson, 'No. 11' in *Hibernicus's Letters*, vol. 1, 90.

123. Hutcheson, 'No. 12' in *Hibernicus's Letters*, vol. 1, 96. Hutcheson repeated the argument that our sense of the ridiculous is innate in his 1744 *Synopsis metaphysicae, ontologiam et pneumatologiam complectens*. What he now called the *sensus ridiculi* was, he there argued, a 'reflexive sense' that was awakened when a 'thing arouses contrary sensations at one and the same time'. With Hobbes clearly in his sights, Hutcheson insisted that the *sensus ridiculi* could be spurred by entirely innocuous combinations of the low with the high (a child dressed in adult's clothing), combinations that had nothing to do with feelings of superiority. Francis Hutcheson, *Logic, Metaphysics, and the Natural Sociability of Mankind*, ed. James Moore and Michael Silverthorne, trans. Michael Silverthorne (Indianapolis, IN: Liberty Fund, 2006), 120.

124. Hutcheson, 'No. 12', 97.

125. Ibid., 101.

126. Ibid., 102.

had done, Hutcheson turned to scripture, invoking Elijah's mockery of the prophets of Baal to show how ridicule could temper '*false Grandeur*' and 'rectify' religious error.[127]

This choice of precedent, although in keeping with earlier Christian justifications for ridicule, was a bit naïve. After all, Elijah did not so much steer the prophets of Baal towards truth as jeer them in preparation for massacring them. In attempting to demonstrate the utility of ridicule as a corrective, Hutcheson hinted at the violence it portends. Towards the end of the third letter, he had to concede that ridicule was a risky instrument that 'fools' could either 'cut their fingers with' or injure an 'unwary By-stander'.[128] This was in all likelihood another sideswipe at Swift. Hutcheson will have been aware that Swift and his allies considered nothing off-limits in their abuse of Arbuckle, nicknaming him 'Witt-upon-crutches' on account of his lameness, and later advising (in a manner consistent with the theme of *The Wonderful Wonder of Wonders*) that his *Dublin Weekly Journal* was good for nothing but 'bum fodder'.[129]

How, then, could abuses of this sort be prevented? Where Shaftesbury trusted in a combination of mutual polishing and (for the worst abuses of the Sacheverellites) intervention by the magistrate, Hutcheson proposed a different safeguard entirely, namely a set of rules for the safe use of ridicule.[130] Attending to the specific nature of the object or person we intend to mock was paramount. If we are tempted mock something '*every way great*' (the likely reference is to religion), Hutcheson proposed as his first rule, then we should at least ensure that impressionable people are not around to hear.[131] For objects of a '*mixed nature*', ridicule of the 'mean' part must be followed by a gesture of respect towards the 'great' part.[132] The final 'necessary Rule' Hutcheson insists on is that when using mockery to correct unsociable behaviour, we should add some respectful phrases to make sure that the ridiculed are aware that we acted from benevolence and that humiliation was not our intent.[133] Taken together, then, Hutcheson's strategy to contain abuses of ridicule was one of

127. Ibid., 103.

128. Ibid., 104.

129. Scott, *Francis Hutcheson*, 33. For the mockery of Arbuckle's journal see Anon., *The Printers Petition to the Poetical Senate Assembled in Grub-Street* (Dublin, 1726), 1.

130. Laurent Jaffro similarly identifies Hutcheson's decision to specify rules for the use of ridicule as a significant departure from Shaftesbury. Jaffro, 'The Passions and Actions of Laughter in Shaftesbury and Hutcheson', 144.

131. Hutcheson, 'No. 12', 104.

132. Ibid., 105.

133. Ibid.

compensation or counterbalance. Ridicule will be safe provided we target it at undignified objects and actions, and then compensate by making clear our respect for whatever dignified bit remains.

This is a curious set of recommendations. By following up mockery with praise, Hutcheson's idea was to correct foolish behaviour while sparing the ridiculed from humiliation. What he never considers is that the ridiculed could easily reject the follow-up gesture of respect as insincere or inadequate. Hutcheson requires that the ridiculed keep separate their personal dignity from their foolish behaviour, so that they may retain the former when the latter is mocked. On the Hobbesian argument this is all but impossible as any signs of goodwill or benevolence will arrive too late to be meaningful. For once we have been laughed at, the Hobbesian would retort, it is too late to reverse the damage; our status in the eyes of others has already been compromised.

Arbuckle rounded off the series on laughter in *The Dublin Weekly Journal* by expressing pessimism about whether Hutcheson's rules would be heeded. The growing cynicism in Irish society, Arbuckle lamented, would make it fertile ground for Mandeville's 'jocular philosophy', resulting in a public 'perpetually *sneering*' at anything that resembled social virtue.[134] More pessimistically still, Arbuckle doubted whether any scheme for regulating abuses of ridicule could succeed, given the anarchic quality of laughter itself. 'Let it once open upon the Vanity of Some Great Men', he archly concluded, 'and it will be ready the next time to fall upon the Love of True Glory in Others.'[135] Neither Shaftesbury's polishing nor Hutcheson's counterbalancing, Arbuckle despaired, could do much to prevent this.

Conclusion

In the last chapter we saw Shaftesbury overcome his early hesitations about ridicule to fashion it into a potent weapon of religious criticism, one that he hoped would diminish or even dissolve the most intolerant aspects of English Christianity. In this chapter our focus switched from the corrosive power of humour to its sociable potential. For Shaftesbury and Hutcheson, if ridicule could bite it could also mollify, facilitating convivial disagreement on questions of moral and political importance. Indeed, the core message of *Sensus Communis* was that people permitted to discuss

134. Arbuckle, 'No. 57' in *Hibernicus's Letters: Or, a Philosophical Miscellany*, vol. 2 (London: J. Clark, T. Hatchet, E. Symon; J. Gray; C. Rivington; and 6 others, 1734), 20–21.
135. Ibid., 23.

matters freely among themselves will naturally have recourse to banter, fun-making, and laughter, and the conversation will be the better for it. Any political, social, or religious authority that tried to make conversers behave otherwise was threatening 'civility, good breeding, and even charity itself, under pretense of maintaining it'. But Shaftesbury was not naïve about the coercive forces that needed to be marshalled in order to provide a public space in which 'amicable collision' between citizens could occur.[136] In 1710 such a space was, in his eyes, not yet fully secure, and he was willing to condone some aggressive curtailment of clerical speech to ensure that it would be.

If Shaftesbury was not naïve about censorship, however, he was complacent in another respect. Like many who champion the use of humour in debate, Shaftesbury was overconfident that the laughter would ultimately fall on his side. As a kind of Stoic, he was convinced that nature could not be mocked, and that virtue would fare better than vice under the test of ridicule. And although Shaftesbury recognized that the weapon of ridicule could be wielded by anyone, he clung to the notion that certain behaviours and traits were intrinsically ridiculous, and that these happened to be found among his opponents. Given time, he reckoned, the bigots and the pedants, the deniers of natural sociability, the proud and the socially stiff, would all be exposed as ridiculous, and society would be the better for it. Hutcheson, too, was similarly assured that ridicule, correctly managed, would cut the unsociable (particularly High Churchmen) down to size, even when they had the likes of Swift as their spokesmen. The abusive mockers would be discredited, and sociability would win out in the end.

Mandeville offered no such assurances. Although he was attuned to the power of ridicule as a form of corrective (not least against moralists like Shaftesbury), Mandeville also appreciated its arbitrariness. For Hobbesians like him, if a person or idea happened to be ridiculed, this was a contingent fact that revealed nothing about their intrinsic naturalness or worth. Those who are mocked today will mock others tomorrow, and contempt need not always stick. In the next chapter, we encounter a philosopher, David Hume, who steered a path between these two positions, rejecting the teleology underpinning Shaftesburian ridicule while refusing the Hobbesian line that to laugh was to arbitrarily contempt.

136. Shaftesbury, 'Sensus Communis', 31.

CHAPTER THREE

Against 'Dissolute Mirth'

HUME'S SCEPTICISM ABOUT RIDICULE

'TELL YOUR SISTER MISS BETTY', David Hume wrote to his friend William Mure in 1743, 'that I am as grave as she imagines a philosopher should be: Laugh only once a fortnight: Sigh tenderly once a week: But look sullen every moment.'[1] Hume here poked fun at the pretentious austerity of philosophers who, even if they permitted themselves the occasional laugh in private, always strove to maintain a serious demeanour in front of others. As Mure would have instantly detected, however, Hume's inclusion of himself among these grave philosophers was ironic. Hume's jocularity was the stuff of legend and it continues to inform our image of the jovial *bon David* who delighted companions in conversation from the Edinburgh Select Society to the salons of Paris.[2]

Good humour was so significant an aspect of Hume's character that Adam Smith devoted a substantial portion of a famous obituary letter to describing how Hume laughed, who he laughed at, and how others responded to his humour. Smith acknowledged that 'what is called wit in other men' was often the product of 'malignity'.[3] Hume's wit, by contrast, was always so good-natured that even those on the receiving end

1. David Hume to William Mure, 10 September 1743. David Hume, *The Letters of David Hume*, ed. J.Y.T Greig, 2 vols (Oxford: Clarendon Press, 1932), vol. 1, 53.

2. On Hume's reputation for 'jovial hedonism' see Thomas W. Merrill, *Hume and the Politics of Enlightenment* (Cambridge: Cambridge University Press, 2015), 21. Hume himself makes reference to his reputation for good humour in his brief autobiography. David Hume, 'My Own Life', in *Essays Moral, Political and Literary*, ed. Eugene F. Miller (Indianapolis, IN: Liberty Fund, 1987), xl.

3. Adam Smith to William Strahan, 9 November 1776, in *The Letters of David Hume*, vol. 2, 452.

experienced it as benign. It 'never was the meaning of his raillery to mortify', Smith explained, and 'far from offending, it seldom failed to please and delight, even those who were the objects of it'.[4] This was no minor compliment. For the many writers on polite conversation who followed Shaftesbury, making the target of a joke laugh along was a special feat that only those who combined amiability with wit could pull off. In his 'Essay on Conversation' (published in the same year as Hume's letter to Mure), Henry Fielding proclaimed that the ideal jest should be so 'delicate that the object of it should be capable of joining in the mirth it occasions'.[5] But Fielding was clear that few could hope to accomplish this because almost all ridicule was offensive. By far the safest option, Fielding concluded, was 'totally abstaining' from raillery altogether.[6] Against the backdrop of strictures like these, Smith's description of Hume's wit constituted high praise indeed.[7] By diverting many and humiliating no one, Hume supposedly refuted the Hobbesian reduction of laughter to an offensive expression of contempt.

Not only did Hume enjoy a reputation for wit and good humour, he also celebrated their effects on society. Like Shaftesbury and Hutcheson, he maintained that a society starved of good humour was ripe for dogmatism, bigotry and persecution. Hume blamed the gloomy enthusiasts among the English dissenters for many of the worst deformations of English social life, even as he credited the arrival of English liberty to their antinomian excesses.[8] Moreover, he irritated critics by categorizing wit and good humour as genuine virtues rather than frivolous attributes. What Hume called the 'art of society and conversation' was integral to a flourishing civilization, and wit and humour were, to his mind, indispensable

4. Smith to Strahan. Ibid. Hume also prided himself on his ability to take a joke even (or especially) when his physical heft was the target and confided to one correspondent that it was the fate of 'we fat people' to constantly shrug off 'jests' with patience. Ever the philosopher, Hume in that same letter launched a mock inquiry into the question of 'why fat people shou'd be so much the object of mirth, rather than the lean'. The answer, he speculated, was that jesters either assume the fat are unwitty (and so will prove an 'easy conquest') or that they are so good natured that there is 'no risque [*sic*] of offending us'. Hume to Charles Erskine, 13 February 1748, ibid., vol. 1, 111.

5. Henry Fielding, 'An Essay on Conversation', in *Miscellanies*, vol. 1 (London: A. Millar, 1743), 174.

6. Ibid., 176.

7. Smith's verdict was far from universal among Hume's acquaintances. Hume's fellow historian Williams Robertson thought his humour a bit 'infantine' (*sic*). Dugald Stewart, *Biographical Memoirs of Smith, Robertson, and Reid* (Edinburgh: George Ramsay and Company, 1811), 211.

8. David Hume, 'Of Superstition and Enthusiasm', in *Essays Moral, Political, and Literary*, 73–79.

components of that art. Sociability, wit and good humour ran together for Hume, and a society lacking any of them would fast degenerate into barbarism.[9]

Various forms of humour were also central to Hume's writing style, even though he often failed to carry over into print the ability to avoid offence that had so impressed Smith. This was especially evident whenever Hume touched on the subject of religion. Irreligious jokes were one of his specialities, and commentators have cited some of the more pungent examples as evidence that Hume was closer to the radical Enlightenment of the Parisian salons than has usually been assumed (it is doubtful that a philosopher who wanted all churches converted into 'Riding Schools, Manufactories, Tennis Courts or Playhouses' belongs unequivocally in the moderate Enlightenment).[10] And while Hume placed great stock in a polite writing style, numerous scholars have interpreted the derisive tone of his writing on religion as deliberately shocking.[11] On this interpretation

9. Hume placed 'mutual deference or civility' among the most pleasing of the 'arts of conversation'. David Hume, 'Of the Rise and Progress of the Arts and Sciences', in *Essays Moral, Political and Literary*, 126. On Hume's ambivalent relationship to polite sociability see Nicholas Phillipson, 'Hume as a Moralist: A Social Historian's Perspective', *Royal Institute of Philosophy Supplements* 12 (1978).

10. Hume to Andrew Stuart, 1 August 1775. The letter is included as an appendix to Moritz Baumstark, 'The End of Empire and the Death of Religion: A Reconsideration of Hume's Later Political Thought', in *Philosophy and Religion in Enlightenment Britain: New Case Studies*, ed. Ruth Savage (Oxford: Oxford University Press, 2012). Baumstark interprets this remark as evidence that Hume was close to the *philosophes* in his attitude to religion. On Hume as a member of the moderate Enlightenment see Jonathan Israel, *A Revolution of the Mind: Radical Enlightenment and the Intellectual Origins of Modern Democracy* (Princeton, NJ: Princeton University Press, 2011), 15.

11. Recent commentators have agreed that Hume laced his writings with sarcasm, irony and wit, and that he sought to exploit the rhetorical power of ridicule to good effect. Marc Hanvelt has remarked on the 'rhetorical force' that Hume ascribes to ridicule and notes that, for him, a 'joke often packs a bigger punch than could any rational argument'. Marc Hanvelt, *The Politics of Eloquence: David Hume's Polite Rhetoric* (Toronto: University of Toronto Press, 2012), 48. The most extensive study of Hume's humour remains John Vladimir Price, *The Ironic Hume* (Austin: University of Texas Press, 1965). M. A. Box notices a 'marked reversal of tone when Hume touches on religion'. M. A. Box, *The Suasive Art of David Hume* (Princeton, NJ: Princeton University Press, 2014), 180. For Bernard Williams, Hume 'couldn't resist expressing himself in a manner designed to upset his conventional readers'. Bernard Williams, 'Hume on Religion', in *The Sense of the Past: Essays in the History of Philosophy*, ed. Myles Burnyeat (Cambridge: Cambridge University Press, 2007), 268. Greg Conti claims Hume 'cannot suppress his contempt' for religious enthusiasts. Greg Conti, 'Hume's Low Road to Toleration', *History of Political Thought* 36, 1 (2015), 176. For Isabel Rivers, Hume was inconsistent in his attitude to ridicule, in that he both disavowed and practised it. Rivers, *Reason, Grace and Sentiment*, vol. 2, *Shaftesbury to Hume*, 278.

Hume exploited the power of ridicule to undermine folly and superstition, but did so by finessed irony rather than outright scoffing.

In this chapter I argue that although Hume valued wit and humour as essential to sociability, he was far less sanguine about ridicule than Shaftesbury had been. Hume was too much of a sceptic to credit the notion that ridicule could dissolve the unnatural or conceited while sparing the true or worthy. For him, ridicule could deceive as easily as it could enlighten and could humiliate its target more egregiously than other forms of criticism. Hume also sympathized with the Hobbesian view that those who indulged frequently in ridicule displayed excessive confidence in their own views rather than a truly sceptical or critical spirit. He was even wary of its use in controversies over religion and had little faith that it could definitively settle anything. In this regard Hume was a rarity among eighteenth-century men of letters in that he was a skilled ridiculer who deflated the pretentions of ridicule itself.

The chapter begins by examining the place of wit, humour and ridicule in Hume's early philosophy. Although Hume took the unorthodox step of elevating wit and humour to the status of moral virtues, he was suspicious of writers who substituted wit for argument and deplored philosophers who used ridicule to wean their readers away from the customs essential to civilized society. Next, I situate Hume within the controversy over Shaftesbury's defence of ridicule, a controversy revived by John Brown's hugely influential 1751 *Essays on the Characteristics*. Although Hume never participated in this debate directly, he took a dim view of the Shaftesburian argument that ridicule could be deployed in public debate without much danger. The fourth section turns to Hume's views on the relationship between ridicule and hypocrisy. Hume, like Shaftesbury, saw great potential in using ridicule to expose gaps between professed principles and actual deeds, particularly when it came to clerics. Unlike Shaftesbury, however, he was far more attuned to how good humour itself could function as a screen for hypocrites. Finally, I show that while Hume saw a danger in treating religion too earnestly, he was deeply sceptical of ridicule as a method of religious criticism.

Hume against Philosophical Scoffers

Hume had no theory of laughter in the vein of a Hobbes or a Hutcheson, or at least the task of reconstructing one from his scattered remarks on mirth and amusement would not amount to much. He was, however, well versed in the text at the centre of the controversy over ridicule, having acquired a copy of the third (1726) edition of Shaftesbury's *Characteristics of Men, Manners, Opinions, Times* when he was just fifteen.[12] Shaftesbury's ethical naturalism and exhortations to virtue struck a chord with Hume and edged him towards the kind of intense introspection that the Earl had urged would-be authors to pursue. By 1729, however, Hume's confidence in Shaftesbury's philosophy had begun to falter, mainly as a result of an intellectual crisis that bears some resemblance to what the Earl himself went through. If Shaftesbury's writing was supposed to nourish a good-humoured disposition towards a benign deity and receptivity to Stoic wisdom, in Hume they fostered melancholic introversion and a suspicion of ancient moralists and their modern defenders.[13] As we shall see, Hume's ambivalence towards Shaftesbury's legacy only grew over time.

Hume's treatment of wit and humour in his first book, *A Treatise of Human Nature*, reflected Shaftesbury's influence. In Part III of that work, he followed the Earl in emphasizing the importance of wit and humour to sociability, even going so far as to list them as *virtues* (as opposed to merely desirable qualities). This was not a trivial move. Conversationalists endowed with wit and humour, Hume was saying, were not only pleasant or likable, but could make legitimate claims to esteem. Wit and humour both command respect, Hume maintained, though for slightly different reasons. Wit, he writes, is *'immediately agreeable'*, making the conversation of the witty 'very satisfactory' to those fortunate enough to hear it.[14]

12. James Harris suggests that Hume's discovery of Shaftesbury was among the most significant things that happened to him during his post-college years and that reading the *Characteristics* gave him a 'sense of direction and purpose'. James A. Harris, *Hume: An Intellectual Biography* (Cambridge: Cambridge University Press, 2015), 44. M. A. Stewart similarly finds that the impact of Shaftesbury on Hume was 'fairly clear' and continued through Hume's career as an essayist. M. A. Stewart, 'Hume's Intellectual Development, 1711–1752', in *Impressions of Hume*, ed. Marina Frasca-Spada and P.J.E. Kail (Oxford: Oxford University Press, 2005), 38.

13. Although Hume listed the Earl among the philosophers in England who had placed the science of man on a 'new footing' in the introduction to the *Treatise of Human Nature* (1739), by that stage Shaftesbury mainly served as a foil against which his own arguments could be developed. David Hume, *A Treatise of Human Nature*, ed. David Fate Norton and Mary J. Norton (Oxford: Clarendon Press, 2011), 5.

14. Hume, *Treatise of Human Nature*, 389. The 'very essence' of wit, Hume argues, is the 'power of bestowing' pleasure. Ibid., 194. As Jacqueline Taylor notes, knowing that we have this power of producing pleasure in others is what makes possessing wit a source of pride in Hume's philosophy. Jacqueline Taylor, *Reflecting Subjects: Passion, Sympathy, and Society in Hume's Philosophy* (Oxford: Oxford University Press, 2015), 18.

The satisfaction produced by the good-humoured is more indirect but no less potent. For while good humour is at first only agreeable to the person experiencing it, the operation of sympathy means that it soon 'diffuses a joy over the whole company'.[15] The good-humoured may not be as sharp as the witty, in other words, but they were pleasantly contagious, and so equally valuable as company. For these reasons, Hume held, ordinary people correctly praise both wit and humour as virtues.

Others were not so convinced. Several critics condemned Hume for stretching the concept of a virtue to breaking point and granting too much nobility to qualities that few moral agents could consciously develop in themselves. An anonymous critic complained that Hume had extended 'the moral sentiment or approbation to qualities of an inferior nature' such as 'chearfulness [sic] of temper'.[16] The philosopher James Balfour went further still, objecting that such traits were 'not moral qualities' at all because they 'may be misapplied to the worst of purposes'.[17] But Hume anticipated these objections and countered that the distinction between natural abilities and virtues was overdrawn. While it is true that we do not choose to have abilities like wit, Hume argued, other more readily acknowledged virtues such bravery and magnanimity are 'equally involuntary'.[18] That wit and good humour are rare qualities possessed only by a few is not enough, on Hume's account, to disqualify them as virtues.

Not *all* wit was virtuous, however. The kind of wit Hume praised was agreeable because it could divert and edify without unduly unsettling anyone. By contrast, elsewhere in the *Treatise* Hume showed nothing but

15. Hume, *Treatise of Human Nature*, 389. He repeated the point in the *Enquiry Concerning the Principles of Morals* (1751). There, Hume echoed Hutcheson's remarks on the sociable contagiousness of good humour, dismissing Horace's claim that the 'melancholy hate the merry' on the grounds that where the 'jollity is moderate and decent' even the glum will be delighted by it. David Hume, *Enquiries Concerning Human Understanding and Concerning the Principles of Morals*, ed. L. A. Selby-Bigge (Oxford: Clarendon Press, 1975), 250.

16. Anon., *Some Late Opinions Concerning the Foundation of Morality, Examined.* (London: R. Dodsley; and M. Cooper, 1753), 27. For a comprehensive overview of this controversy see James Fieser, 'Hume's Wide View of the Virtues: An Analysis of His Early Critics', *Hume Studies* 24, no. 2 (1998), 295–311. As Colin Heydt makes clear, however, Hume courted controversy not only by *adding* traits like wit to his list of virtues, but also by *excluding* religious virtues such as piety. Colin Heydt, 'Hume's Innovative Taxonomy of the Virtues', in *Reading Hume on the Principles of Morals*, ed. Jacqueline Taylor (Oxford: Oxford University Press, 2020), 118–36.

17. James Balfour, *A Delineation of the Nature and Obligation of Morality* (Edinburgh: Hamilton, Balfour, and Neill, 1753), 132.

18. Hume, *Treatise of Human Nature*, 388.

disdain for those who used their wit to undermine confidence in social customs, habits and institutions. Shaftesbury's favourites, the Cynics, were a case in point. By jeering passers-by and drawing ridicule on themselves by their outlandish behaviour, the Cynics hoped to force their audience to reflect on whether the conventions they flouted truly reflected nature and reason. But in the end, Hume reckoned, all they achieved was to make themselves look bizarre and cultish:

> The CYNICS are an extraordinary instance of philosophers, who, from reasonings purely philosophical, ran into as great extravagances of conduct as any *Monk* or *Dervise* that ever was in the world. Generally speaking, the errors in religion are dangerous; those in philosophy only ridiculous.[19]

It is tempting to interpret these lines as Hume providing strategic cover for his own philosophical activities; if philosophers who stray from the truth are merely ridiculous, then sceptics like Hume could be safely left to their own devices rather than harassed as menaces to society. That interpretation is bolstered by Hume's later characterization of scepticism as a harmless 'philosophical amusement' that by 'destroying *every Thing*, really affects *nothing*'.[20] But the Cynics in this passage are not stand-ins for sceptics. Hume downplays the danger posed by philosophy generally while also highlighting the delusiveness of the Cynic belief that mocking the artificial clears the way for appreciation of the natural. For Hume, philosophers like the Cynics who make a show of themselves in the name of such a project will *only* ever be ridiculous, their antics provoking bemusement rather than encouraging reform.[21]

At other moments, Hume presented philosophical wits as not just deluded or irritating but socially pathological. In an early essay 'Of Moral Prejudices' he condemned the 'insipid raillery' of those who satirized every respectable custom from marriage to friendship.[22] To illustrate his point, Hume tells the story of Diogenes's request that his corpse be thrown into a

---

19. Ibid., 176.

20. David Hume, 'A Letter from a Gentleman to His Friend in Edinburgh', ibid., 426.

21. Hence Hume's desire, in Thomas Merrill's evocative phrase, to bring philosophy 'back down to earth'. His hero in this task is the sober citizen of commercial society who will regard philosophical extremists as 'bizarre and rather pathetic beings'. Merrill, *Hume and the Politics of Enlightenment*, 23–24. Similarly, as Donald Livingston has pointed out, Hume considered philosophical sects like the Cynics 'fertile breeding grounds for hypocrisy'. Donald W. Livingston, *Philosophical Melancholy and Delirium: Hume's Pathology of Philosophy* (Chicago: University of Chicago Press, 1998), 96.

22. David Hume, 'Of Moral Prejudices', in *Essays Moral, Political, and Literary*, 538.

field to be eaten by birds and animals instead of buried. Sensing his friends'
alarm, Diogenes jokes that they should '*Place a Cudgel*' at his side to fend
off scavengers. 'I know none of the sayings of that philosopher', Hume
writes, 'which shows more evidently both the liveliness and ferocity of his
temper.'[23] For Hume, Diogenes had not only rejected a funeral for himself
but also branded anyone who might want one a fool and reduced the desire
to mourn to a gullible superstition. And while Hume implied that the bad
effects of such ferocious Cynicism would be mostly limited to 'those who
indulge it' he nevertheless feared that the 'virtuous and tender sentiments'
vital to civilized life had 'suffered mightily' as a result of its influence.[24]

Hume withdrew 'Of Moral Prejudice' from subsequent editions of his
Essays, a possible sign that he considered its argument too alarmist or
trivial to be worth the attention of future readers. In other essays, however,
Hume extended the criticism of Diogenes's scoffing to Shaftesbury's other
preferred ancients. With the possible exceptions of Lucian and Xenophon,
Hume declared in 'Of the Rise and Progress of the Arts and Sciences', the
ancients had produced 'not one piece of pleasantry that is excellent'.[25]
Even Horace, Shaftesbury's favourite humourist by some distance, lacked
a refined 'talent for ridicule', an uncompromising verdict that had much to

23. Ibid., 540.
24. Ibid., 539. Hume in the early 1740s was not alone in considering Cynicism a breeding ground for conceitedness and misanthropy. Henry Fielding's reconstruction of a conversation between a sunbathing Diogenes and Alexander the Great, published in his 1743
Miscellanies, made a similar point. According to most versions of the story, Alexander is
so impressed with Diogenes's fierce austerity that he offers to do anything he can for the
philosopher. Diogenes responds by asking the great conqueror to stop blocking his sun.
The anecdote had classically served as an illustration of the Cynic's disdain for worldly
goods and honours, but Fielding added a crucial twist. Early in Fielding's dialogue, Diogenes justifies his mockery of the Athenians on the same grounds Shaftesbury had cited;
namely that his 'snarling' aimed only to 'frighten' the Athenians away from vice. Alexander
is unconvinced and, as if to prove that Diogenes's ruling passion was resentment rather
than benevolence, tables a fresh offer. Instead of the Cynic relying only on 'raillery and
curses' to educate the vice-ridden Athenians, Alexander proposes instead to invade the city
and massacre the inhabitants on Diogenes's behalf (along with the populations of equally
corrupt Corinth and Sparta for good measure). Diogenes, who up to that point had dismissed Alexander's appetite for conquest as vainglorious, agrees on the basis that such an
act would make a 'good example' to the vice-ridden everywhere. However, when Alexander
suggests that the property of the massacred be set aside for his soldiers, Diogenes demurs.
Eventually the Cynic demands half of the plunder for himself because it would give him
an opportunity to 'show the world that I despise riches when I possess them, as much as
I did before in my poverty'. Alexander, convinced now that Diogenes's disdain for power
and wealth is a sham, rescinds the offer and departs, appalled that Diogenes was willing to
destroy three cities to satisfy his 'wrath and revenge'. Henry Fielding, 'A Dialogue Between
Alexander the Great and Diogenes the Cynic', in *Miscellanies*, vol. 1, 322–39.
25. Hume, 'Of the Rise and Progress of the Arts and Sciences', 134.

do with Hume's quest to vindicate modern refinements from Shaftesbury's Stoic criticism.[26] Elsewhere, Hume acknowledged that adopting a posture of amused detachment towards society could mollify the more unsociable passions, but wryly countered that it would also 'counterwork the artifice of nature, who has happily deceived us in an opinion, that human life is of some importance'.[27] When enough people are divested of their belief in the value of human endeavours, Hume warned, then the result will be a widespread 'dissolute mirth', a nihilistic gaiety that was disastrous for society.[28]

Hume also had little time for Shaftesbury's claim that while artifice withers under ridicule, nature is invincible to it and 'will not be mocked'.[29] Philosophers who ridicule artifice in the name of nature were themselves the most artificial characters of all, a point Hume made with particular force in the dialogue that concludes the *Enquiry Concerning the Principles of Morals* (1751). There, Hume allowed that Diogenes the Cynic had sociable intentions and that he considered himself duty-bound to 'love his friends, and to rail at them, and reprove them, and scold them' into living more in accordance with nature.[30] But again Hume flatly denied that Diogenes was any more natural in his behaviour than those he hectored. On the contrary, Hume invoked the Cynic only to demonstrate how 'philosophical enthusiasm' can lead to a life that is thoroughly 'artificial'.[31]

Hume in the *Enquiry* also questioned other teleological assumptions that underlay Shaftesbury's project. He regarded as perverse the Shaftesburian assumption that the cosmos is providentially organized for the best and that therefore we should remain good-humoured in spite of our sufferings. Writing of the Stoics, he rejected the thesis that the universe was 'ordered with perfect benevolence' and disparaged those who 'taught their pupils that those ills under which they laboured were, in reality, goods to the universe' and every event the 'object of joy'.[32] For Hume, preaching good humour to those in distress, or teasingly suggesting that their pains

26. Ibid. In *The Moralists*, Shaftesbury had attacked the 'courtly humour' of his day as 'foppish', particularly in the unnatural exchanges it demanded between men and women. Hume retorted that gallantry was not only natural, but that it was responsible for the superiority of modern humour. In a modern monarchy with an extensive class of leisured men striving for court preferment and female attention, 'wit' and 'civility' carried a premium. Shaftesbury, 'The Moralists', in *Characteristics of Men, Manners, Opinions, Times*, 237. Hume, 'Of the Rise and Progress of the Arts and Sciences', 126.

27. David Hume, 'The Sceptic', in *Essays Moral, Political, and Literary*, 176.

28. Ibid.

29. Shaftesbury, 'Soliloquy, or Advice to an Author', 158.

30. Hume, *Enquiries Concerning Human Understanding and Concerning the Principles of Morals*, 342.

31. Ibid., 343.

32. Ibid., 101.

are only illusory, will only annoy them: 'You would surely more irritate than appease a man lying under the racking pains of gout', he pointed out, if you were to lecture him on the 'rectitude of those general laws which produced the malignant humours in his body'.[33]

Beyond criticizing ancient philosophical wits and their modern imitators, the early Hume also used his own wit to counteract their influence and encourage appreciation for the refinements of modern society. The best example of Hume's anti-Stoic wit in action is *A True Account of the Behaviour and Conduct of Archibald Stewart Esq*, his only published satire. In 1747 Hume was prompted to write this pamphlet out of sympathy for his friend Archibald Stewart, who had been Provost of Edinburgh at the time of Prince Charles Stuart's occupation of the city at the climax of the 1745 Jacobite uprising. Stewart quickly realized that marching out to meet the invaders was unwise and that the prudent course of action was to await English reinforcements from the south (he waited in vain and the Highlanders eventually forced their way in). The ordeal was harrowing for Stewart and he was later accused, *inter alia*, of surrendering the city without resistance. Although he was eventually acquitted, Hume was disgusted that those accusations had been levelled against him in the first place and took issue with the people of Edinburgh for behaving like a gullible mob searching for scapegoats to hide their own failings.

In his biography of Hume, Ernest Mossner called the *Account of Stewart* a 'pious act of friendship' written in an 'urbane' and 'witty' style.[34] But the tone of the pamphlet is also by turns biting, sardonic and scatological. Hume's strategy for vindicating Stewart was to mock the people of Edinburgh for thinking that a militia composed of commerce-obsessed urbanites would be able to hold out against Jacobite Highlanders who lacked discipline but who had superior martial valour. In previous centuries the lowland Scots had been as warlike as anyone. But 'when men have fallen into a more civilized life, and have allowed to addict themselves entirely to the cultivation of arts and manufactures, the habit of mind, still more of their body, soon renders them entirely unfit for the use of arms'.[35] Even the city's feeble fortifications had been given over to commercial development and were now 'overlooked by houses' that were 'impossible to destroy because of their number and value'.[36] When such a city is faced with an event as violent

---

33. Ibid.

34. Ernest Mossner, *The Life of David Hume* (Oxford: Oxford University Press, 2001), 183.

35. David Hume, 'A True Account of the Behaviour and Conduct of Archibald Stewart Esq; Late Lord Provost of Edinburgh', in *The Ironic Hume*, 156.

36. Ibid., 161.

and atavistic as a siege, capitulation was a foregone conclusion. To pretend otherwise was, in Hume's mind, grossly disingenuous.

Had he written this satire in a Cynic or Stoic vein, Hume might have condemned the residents of Edinburgh for allowing their fondness for commerce to sap their martial prowess. But nothing could be further from Hume's point. As Andrew Sabl observes, Hume had contempt for the martial habits of pre-commercial societies and thought it mad that the outcome of a battle could hinge on luck or valour.[37] Modern warfare may prove destructive, but at least it was easier for the weaker side to gauge the likelihood of defeat and refuse a futile battle, sparing lives and property. Stewart had correctly made such a calculation, and so should have been lauded instead of pilloried. Hume's aim, then, was not to chastise the people of Edinburgh for failing to prioritize military virtue, but rather to mock their inability to recognize that the decision to privilege commerce over military defences (a sensible trade-off in his view) inevitably comes at a cost. Calling on Stewart to repel Highland invaders with an army of men with 'little inclination' to fight was an impossible ask, not least because the content of their chamber pots (a 'very formidable machine in Edinburgh') was about the most potent weapon they possessed.[38] Lacking self-awareness, the crowd blamed Stewart for failings that were entirely their own.

Stewart was unanimously acquitted before Hume managed to get his pamphlet into print. But Hume had made his point and it is unlikely he hoped that his *Account of Stewart* would move public opinion decisively. Hume had too chastened a view of what ridicule was capable of to think otherwise. Four years later, the controversy over what exactly ridicule *could* accomplish received new impetus as the Shaftesburians and their critics faced off again. This time it was an ally of William Warburton, bishop of Gloucester and one of Hume's most determined critics, who breathed new life into that debate by publishing the most forensic criticism yet of Shaftesbury's defence of ridicule. It is to this intervention, and Hume's indirect response to it, that we now turn.

Brown and the Revival of the Ridicule Debate

No one was more influential in reviving the controversy over ridicule in Hume's day than John 'Estimate' Brown, a member of what Hume dismissively referred to as the 'Warburtonian school', a group of critics with

37. Andrew Sabl, *Hume's Politics: Coordination and Crisis in the History of England* (Princeton, NJ: Princeton University Press, 2012), 62.

38. Hume, 'Account of Stewart', 161 and 160.

whom Hume refused to engage on account of their 'illiberal petulance, arrogance, and scurrility'.[39] Brown rose to fame as the author of the *Estimate of the Manners and Principles of the Times* (1757), a satire on English moral decay written in the wake of early defeats to France in the Seven Years' War. But he cut his teeth as a critic of Shaftesbury and his *Essays on the Characteristics* (1751) provided new 'heavy artillery' to critics of the Earl.[40]

In his opening essay, 'On Ridicule Considered as a Test of Truth', Brown accused Shaftesbury of failing to understand that ridicule was a form of rhetoric and as such was divorced from matters of truth altogether. To support his case Brown turned to Hume's own writings on rhetoric and style. In 'Of Eloquence' Hume had contrasted a pathetic form of eloquence aimed at moving the passions to a more modern variety designed to convince the audience through appeals to reason. As a form of eloquence whose sole purpose was to excite 'contempt with laughter', Brown argued, ridicule fell unequivocally on the pathetic side of Hume's dichotomy and therefore could 'befriend either truth or falsehood'.[41] To pretend otherwise, Brown scoffed, was to be as simple as the 'honest Irishman' who shone his candle on a sundial during the night to tell the time.[42]

Brown not only challenged Shaftesbury's association of ridicule with reasoning; he also attacked followers of the Earl, such as the freethinker Anthony Collins, who placed great faith in ridicule as an instrument of moral and religious reform. In his *Discourse Concerning Ridicule and Irony in Writing* (1729) Collins had argued that although all parties to religious disputes had profited from ridiculing their adversaries at one time or another, the Church of England had made especially good use of this method against libertines, atheists and dissenters. Hobbes may have been a 'philosophic drole', Collins urged, but he had soon been matched by Bramhall and by Eachard whose *Dialogues* were 'recommended to the Youth' to 'make them laugh' at Hobbes in turn.[43] Even partisans of the

---

39. Hume, 'My Own Life', xxxvii.

40. Thomas B. Gilmore, Jr., 'The Eighteenth Century Controversy over Ridicule: A Reconsideration', *Georgia State University School of Arts and Sciences Research Papers*, no. 25 (1970), 4. As Lawrence Klein has recently noted, Brown wrote at a 'moment of transition in discussions of ridicule' as the fierce religious combat characteristic of Queen Anne's reign gave way to more 'enlightened' study of the place of ridicule in the refinement of taste. As this chapter shows, however, the older form of the controversy could still flare up, particularly in Hume's Scotland. Klein, 'Ridicule as a Tool for Discovering Truth', 575.

41. Brown, *Essays on the Characteristics*, 42 and 46.

42. Ibid., 107.

43. Collins, *Discourse Concerning Ridicule*, 43 and 13. In Cato's Letters, Thomas

Glorious Revolution, Collins alleged, owed more of their success to mockery than to argument. It was more likely, he wrote, that 'King James II and Popery' were 'laughed' out of the country than that they were 'argued' out of it.[44] 'Popery', Collins insisted, 'must make men laugh' and it was easier to keep a straight face when reading a 'Stage-Comedy or Farce' than when contemplating the 'Comedy and Farce of Popery'.[45]

By showcasing how ridicule had been used by all sides in religious dispute, Collins had done little to dispel the worry that this was a weapon that could discredit the true as easily as it could unmask the false. This did not escape the notice of Brown, who seized upon Collins's lengthy list of religious mockers from history to show how ridicule was especially ill-suited to settling theological disputes. That ridicule had been 'successfully applied by every sect of Religionists and Infidels to the Destruction of each other's Tenets' was, Brown affirmed, no argument in its favour and served only to show just how easily ridicule could be used to defend error.[46]

Brown reserved the brunt of his attack, however, for Shaftesbury's intimation in the *Letter Concerning Enthusiasm* that Queen Mary had chosen poorly by preferring persecution to ridicule in her effort to strangle the English Reformation at birth. Baffled that the Earl could so quickly 'forget . . . his part' as a 'believer and a protestant' Brown held that Shaftesbury would have done better to depart from hypotheticals and look instead to a real historical episode more supportive of his claims, namely the spate of anti-clerical comedies performed in English Churches during the early 1540s.[47] For Brown, the unease these comedies prompted among early English reformers revealed their preference for a more sober campaign against the clergy. Quoting extensively from Burnet's *History*

Gordon recalled how the 'sarcasms' of the primitive Fathers 'against the heathenish worship' gave them a crucial early advantage in their struggle to establish Christianity on a more popular basis. Thomas Gordon, *Cato's Letters*, no. 53 (London, 1721).

44. Collins, *Discourse Concerning Ridicule*, 35.

45. Ibid., 31. It had, after all, been taken for granted among English reformers that belief in Catholic doctrine was unsustainable because the mind would eventually revolt into laughter at its absurdity. The Puritan controversialist Humphrey Lynde insisted that it could never be uncivil to mock Catholic doctrine because laughter was the only possible response to it. Catholics *themselves* were, for Lynde, compelled to laugh inwardly at their own beliefs and 'smile' knowingly when they met each other to quietly signal awareness of the ludicrousness of their own beliefs. Humphrey Lynde, *The Ancient Doctrine of the Church of England Maintained in Its Primitive Purity* (London: Austin Rice, 1660), 144.

46. Brown, *Essays on the Characteristics*, 73.

47. Ibid., 75.

of the Reformation (a key source for Hume's later discussion of the same incident) Brown noted that more serious-minded reformers opposed these 'Mock-Representations' even as they bore witness to their effectiveness in furthering the reform agenda.[48] These 'graver sort of reformers', Brown held, were determined to convince the public to embrace reform through argument and reason rather than play on their passions and so rightly disavowed ridicule completely.[49]

Shaftesbury's followers responded to Brown by questioning the strict opposition between reason and rhetoric that Brown supposedly found support for in Hume's essay. In his *Vindication of My Lord Shaftesbury on the Subject of Ridicule* Charles Bulkley insisted that the kind of ridicule Shaftesbury defended should itself be categorized as a 'method of reasoning', one appropriate to deliberation on all topics, including religion.[50] Not long after, Hume's friend and fellow founding member of the Edinburgh Select Society, Allan Ramsay, similarly defended ridicule's rational credentials in his *Essay on Ridicule* (1753). Taking issue with Brown's assumption that ridicule could only ever feature among the 'pathetic kinds of eloquence', Ramsay identified a form of 'argumentative ridicule' that should rank among the 'most forcible and expeditious of all the methods of reasoning'.[51] This form of ridicule, he argued, was most fruitfully used against statements that were not only false but that also made some claim to significance. An error in arithmetic was false but not vulnerable to ridicule because its claim to importance was negligible. Conversely, Diogenes may have won the laughter of an audience by displaying a plucked chicken to mock Plato's definition of man as a featherless biped but this in itself did not prove Plato wrong. False religion, however, comfortably satisfied both of Ramsay's criteria, explaining why 'of all the different absurdities, which have disgraced the human species' none 'has been the cause' of more 'wit and ridicule'.[52]

48. Ibid., 76.

49. Ibid., 77.

50. Bulkley, *A Vindication of My Lord Shaftesbury, on the Subject of Ridicule. Being Remarks upon a Book, Intitled, Essays on the Characteristics*, 17.

51. Allan Ramsay, *Essay on Ridicule* (London, 1753), 15, 17 and 22.

52. Ibid., 40. Ramsay may well have been drawing on a popular earlier attempt to specify precisely the kind of help that ridicule could provide to reason. In *The Pleasures of the Imagination* an exasperated Mark Akenside complained that Shaftesbury never intended to help discover 'speculative truths' through ridicule. Instead, judgments of praise or blame constituted its special domain. The 'faculty of ridicule', he explained, 'urges the mind to reject with laughter and contempt' whatever falsely lays claim to praise and thus helps to 'convince the world how ridiculous the claim is'. Ridicule did not only move the passions arbitrarily in one direction or another; it could also help people arrive at correct judgments 'sooner than in the way of speculative inquiry'. Akenside, *The Pleasures of Imagination*, 72.

Even if Brown was correct that ridicule had proven dangerous in the past, Ramsay further argued, the basis of religious debate had now changed in ways that rendered it safer. The most significant of these changes, Ramsay held, was that details of liturgy and ceremony had declined in importance to the extent that mocking a rival sect's practices no longer carried the force it once did. Whereas previously members of rival denominations were prepared to go to war over 'trifling distinctions', those distinctions were no longer significant at a time when religion had finally become a 'private concern'.[53]

The problem of the appropriateness of ridicule in religious debate also arose in the context of a dispute that, for Hume at least, struck close to home. The year of Ramsay's essay, 1753, also saw the orthodox Presbyterian clergyman John Witherspoon wade into a fracas over patronage in the Scottish Kirk by launching a satirical attack on the so-called moderate party, several members of which would go on to defend Hume against excommunication.[54] The title, *The Ecclesiastical Characteristics*, announced that this was a parody of the Shaftesburian approach to religion that Witherspoon feared was gaining too much ground in Scotland. Witherspoon's text comprises a list of maxims for how a moderate churchman should live (look for authority to 'heathen writers' rather than scripture, be 'polite' and 'imitate a fine gentleman', despise 'the common people', 'have charity for atheists and deists' but none for the religious),[55] a list of recommended reading ('Leibniz's *Theodicie* and his *Letters*, Shaftesbury's *Characteristics*', and 'Collins' *Enquiry into Human Liberty*'), and even a re-written version of the Lord's Prayer that gave thanks for sceptical philosophy ('O Lord we thank thee for M. Bayle's Dictionary. Amen.').[56]

Witherspoon's decision to use Shaftesbury's own preferred weapon of ridicule to attack the moderates, however, required some justification. In *A Serious Apology for the Ecclesiastical Characteristics* he defended the 'lawfulness' of using ridicule as a weapon against the heterodox and accused Shaftesbury of having merely misused it.[57] Those living 'under the

---

53. Ramsay, *Essay on Ridicule*, 54–55.

54. The term 'moderate party' was originally devised by Witherspoon but was later appropriated by those he meant to target by it. Thomas Ahnert, *The Moral Culture of the Scottish Enlightenment: 1690–1805* (New Haven, CT: Yale University Press, 2014), 67.

55. John Witherspoon, *The Ecclesiastical Characteristics, or the Arcana of Church Policy, Being an Humble Attempt to Open Up the Mystery of Moderation* (Glasgow, n.p., 1753), 15–47.

56. Ibid., 27 and 30.

57. John Witherspoon, *A Serious Apology for the Ecclesiastical Characteristics* (Edinburgh: William Gray, 1763), 15.

dominion of error', Witherspoon pleaded, suffer from a pride that makes them 'deaf to advice, and impregnable to grave and serious reasoning'. Such cases, he continued, required that we 'inlist [*sic*] ridicule in the service of reason'.[58] For Witherspoon, then, Shaftesbury had not been wrong to stress the compatibility of ridicule with reason. His mistake, rather, lay in assuming that his own version of polite religion would emerge from such a method of scrutiny unscathed.

Hume's Doubts about Ridicule in Writing, Conversation and Philosophy

On the surface we might have expected Hume to have some sympathy for the Shaftesburians in this dispute. As late as the 1741 *Essays*, Hume still referred to Shaftesbury's treatment of the sociable passions as containing the 'greatest force of argument and eloquence', notwithstanding the fact that Hume had long since rejected Shaftesbury's moral teleology.[59] The Select Society in Edinburgh, of which Hume was a founding member, embodied the Shaftesburian ethos of polite sociability.[60] Hume's own critics freely associated him with Shaftesbury, in one case presenting him as having extended the Earl's critique of Christianity to all religion, both revealed and natural.[61] As for Brown, Hume dismissed him as a 'flatterer' of Warburton and was incensed when the latter got hold of a personal letter from Hume to his publisher Andrew Millar and then used it to

58. Ibid., 18.

59. Hume, *Essays Moral, Political and Literary*, 620. This quote praising Shaftesbury originally appeared in the essay 'Of the Dignity or Meanness of Human Nature' but was removed from later editions of the *Essays*.

60. Carlyle described the Select Society using Shaftesburian language: 'It was those meetings in particular that rubbed off all corners, as we call it, by collision, and made the literati of Edinburgh less captious and pedantic than they were elsewhere.' The 'as we call it' is significant. It suggests that Shaftesbury's phrase was part of the society's creed. Alexander Carlyle, *Autobiography of the Rev. Dr. Alexander Carlyle, Minister of Inveresk: Containing Memorials of the Men and Events of His Time* (Edinburgh: W. Blackwood and sons, 1860), 298. See also Dennis C. Rasmussen, *The Infidel and the Professor: David Hume, Adam Smith, and the Friendship That Shaped Modern Thought* (Princeton, NJ: Princeton University Press, 2017), 70.

61. 'His lordship of Shaftesbury blames Christianity for disqualifying a man for the duties of the present life: but the Esquire [Hume] blames natural religion: for if that religion teaches anything of greater influence than atheism, it teaches that a future life is more to be regarded than the present. And if he cannot imagine a natural religion, but such as necessarily disables him for the practice of any one thing virtuous or reasonable; he can have no religion at all.' George Anderson, *An Estimate of the Profit and Loss of Religion, Personally and Publicly Stated* (Edinburgh, 1753), 249.

attack him.[62] It is also difficult to imagine Hume having much sympathy for Witherspoon, who branded him a 'wicked skeptic sage' in yet another satirical attack on the moderates and their allies.[63]

Yet there are several indications that Hume remained wary of the Shaftesburian defence of ridicule. In the first place he shared Brown's suspicion that ridicule could just as easily be distorting as truth-revealing. Hume acknowledged that playing loose with the truth for comic effect was sometimes justified (in his second *Enquiry* he allowed that telling a humorous story often entailed a kind of 'harmless' lying).[64] But while moralists occasionally could sacrifice accuracy for polemical effect, they usually pushed these distortions too far. In such cases, Hume found, the truth conveyed was rendered as doubtful as the exaggerations used to convey it. This made relying on satirists for insight dangerous *even* when their audiences were wise to their tricks. In 'Of the Populousness of Ancient Nations', published in his *Political Discourses* of 1752, Hume warned against depending on 'writers who deal in ridicule and satyr' as sources for precisely this reason.[65] Far better, he recommended, to look to 'historians, orators, and philosophers' whose 'testimony is unquestioned' (a remarkable sentence for a sceptic to write).[66]

To illustrate his point, Hume invoked the example of Swift. Citing a lengthy passage from *Gulliver's Travels* about the corrupt inhabitants of

62. Hume to Andrew Millar. 20 May 1757. Hume, *The Letters of David Hume*, 1932, vol. 1, 249. According to Mossner, Hume regarded Brown as 'beneath contempt'. Mossner, *The Life of David Hume*, 308. Brown accused Hume of taking a mercenary attitude towards religion and suggested that he had only removed the irreligious humour when sales of the first editions of his history had proven weak among the 'serious part of mankind'. John Brown, *An Estimate of the Manners and Principles of the Times* (London: L. Davis, and C. Reymers, 1757), 58.

63. John Witherspoon, *The Moderator*, no. 2 (1757), 12. *The Moderator* was published anonymously but Mossner identifies Witherspoon as the author of this particular issue. Mossner, *The Life of David Hume*, 356.

64. Hume, *Enquiries Concerning Human Understanding and Concerning the Principles of Morals*, 263. In his *Essays*, Hume found that witty authors, far from communicating truths, were usually compensating for their lack of insight. The 'strong flashes of wit' that they indulged in, he complained, could only ever deliver short-lived delight to the reader rather than long-term edification. For these reasons, Hume advised, authors concerned with striking a balance between wit and simplicity in their prose should err on the side of the latter. David Hume, 'Of Simplicity and Refinement in Writing', in *Essays Moral, Political, and Literary*, 193. Hume even criticized Montesquieu's *Spirit of the Laws*, a work greatly admired by his contemporaries, as compromised by the excessive 'glare' of its author's wit. Hume to Hugh Blair, 1 April 1767. *The Letters of David Hume*, vol. 2, 133.

65. David Hume, 'Of the Populousness of Ancient Nations', in *Essays Moral, Political, and Literary*, 414.

66. Ibid.

Lanngdon (London), Hume doubted whether Swift's description could apply to England, a country governed with 'humanity, justice, and liberty'.[67] In his gloss on these lines, John Vladimir Price deems it 'plain enough' that Hume himself is being ironic here, given the misgivings he would express about English society elsewhere. Be that as it may, Hume's warning about over-reliance on satirists is, I think, sincere. His worry was not that future historians would somehow fail to identify *Gulliver's Travels* as a satire. His far subtler point was that writers who gravitate towards ridicule should always be suspected of exaggerating beyond what is necessary for the joke to work.[68]

Truth was not the only casualty where ridicule was concerned. Sociability could also suffer. Hume was far more reticent than the Shaftesburians concerning the extent to which ridicule could be safely incorporated into polite conversation. Hume's experience as secretary of the Philosophical Society of Edinburgh taught him that even among gentlemen ostensibly committed to politeness the use of ridicule (no matter how well meaning) was best avoided. One incident in particular drove that lesson home. When the Professor of Natural Philosophy at Edinburgh, John Stewart, scorned Henry Home in a reply to the latter's essay 'Of the Laws of Motion', Hume was placed in the awkward position of having to smooth relations between them. As secretary of the society Hume was charged with editing (jointly) its *Essays and Observations* for that year, which included Home's essay, and there was some expectation that he might address the controversy in his Preface. Writing to Stewart, Hume reassured him he would make no mention of it but took the opportunity to lecture the professor on the ethics of dispute. His first point was to refute the Shaftesburian case for ridicule, imploring Stewart to disavow all 'raillery', of whatever kind, in debate.[69] Not only were such tactics 'unphilosophical', he complained, but no matter how 'gentle' the jibe might be it 'cannot but be offensive'.[70] Hume even warned Stewart to stay away from the next meeting of the society and to send friends to speak on his behalf instead.[71]

67. Ibid.

68. Hume's comments on Swift in his later correspondence make the point clearer still. Although Hume considered Swift an author he could often 'laugh with', he told the historian William Robertson, he lamented his lack of 'correctness'. Swift was an author with 'more humour than knowledge' whose 'spleen' and 'prejudice' outweighed any of his better qualities. Hume gave no indication that Whig satirists had fared any better. Hume to William Robertson. November or December 1768. Hume, *The Letters of David Hume*, vol. 2, 194.

69. Hume to John Stewart, February 1754. Ibid., vol. 1, 186.

70. Ibid.

71. Ibid.

That Hume advised Stewart not to attend the next meeting in person is significant. As Mossner reports, the original paper that Stewart presented to the society contained no sarcasms.[72] These were only added in the published version, suggesting that Stewart was prepared to alter his tone only when not face-to-face with his opponent. Hume's letter reveals just how stung Hume was by this, not least perhaps because Hume himself was mocked in the same essay (Stewart imputes views on causality to Hume that he never held and scoffs that Hume's theory of personal identity meant that he thought himself 'nothing but a bundle' of his own perceptions).[73] When confronted by attacks from a critic like Warburton, Hume tells Stewart, he can 'laugh at him'.[74] Even when critics used sarcasm to misrepresent his views and portray him as an incurable sceptic or atheist Hume refused to be baited.[75] Stewart, by contrast, was a respected acquaintance and so abuse from him, Hume explained, was far more wounding (it is not insignificant that this is the same letter in which Hume disavows his *Treatise of Human Nature* as a juvenile work; if even the likes of Stewart could so badly misconstrue its meaning then it must, Hume thought, be flawed). In any case, the incident served as a reminder to Hume that the search for a polite ridicule that lubricates conversations without causing aggravation was difficult and easily sabotaged. The safer course was to steer clear of ridicule altogether.

Later, Hume was party to another dispute among philosophers that similarly laid bare the power of ridicule to wound and humiliate. The incident began with an act of generosity on Hume's part that he would later have cause to regret. Having seen that the Genevan philosopher Jean-Jacques Rousseau was hounded wherever he went on the continent, Hume welcomed him to England, arranged accommodation for him in rural Staffordshire, and even secured a royal pension so that Rousseau could live comfortably at a safe distance from his harassers. This kindness soon blew up in Hume's face, however, when Rousseau publicly attacked him, going so far as to insinuate that his Scottish benefactor was conspiring

72. Mossner, *The Life of David Hume*, 259

73. *Essays and Observations, Physical and Literary. Read before a Society in Edinburgh, and Published by Them* (Edinburgh: G. Hamilton and J. Balfour, 1754), 117.

74. Hume to John Stewart, February 1754. *The Letters of David Hume*, vol. 1, 186.

75. Hume was subjected to all manner of abuse in the 1750s from Warburton, who would go so far as to threaten legal action if Hume's *Four Dissertations*, which included Hume's 'Natural History of Religion' were published (it eventually was in 1757).

with his enemies and intercepting his mail.[76] Hume was incensed and felt that he could not allow the accusation to go unanswered. Writing from Paris, Smith urged Hume not to escalate the spat: 'Stand this ridicule', and 'if you can, laugh at yourself'.[77]

That Smith encouraged Hume to temper his pride with self-laughter suggests an awareness on his part that Hume's good humour could be worn down if tested. He was right to be worried. After much deliberation, Hume sent his own side of the story to d'Alembert, hoping that its publication would not only vindicate his own character but discredit Rousseau. He hoped, he confided to Smith, to 'blast' Rousseau and his writings (writings, Hume tetchily added, that were overrated anyway).[78] When a number of satires on the affair appeared, Hume took pleasure in the fact that he came off better than Rousseau and that all of the 'raillery' in the English press was directed 'against that unhappy man' rather than against him.[79] One satire, *The Savage Man*, depicting Hume as a kindly farmer feeding an ungrateful and savage Rousseau, so delighted Hume that he sent a detailed description of it to Madame de Boufflers, his closest Parisian friend and the person who had urged Hume to help Rousseau in the first place. As he described to Boufflers: 'I am represented as a farmer who caresses him and offers him some oats to eat', but which Rousseau 'refuses in a rage'.[80]

Similarly, Hume praised William Strahan for publishing a mock indictment of his mistreatment of Rousseau (*The Heads of an Indictment Laid by J.J. Rousseau, Philosopher, Against D. Hume, ESQ.*) and was pleased to find that it contained 'some good humoured raillery against him and Voltaire and me'.[81] In reality, Hume knew that the mockery was directed almost solely at Rousseau and that the spoof vindicated him by sarcastically presenting all of the favours that Hume performed for Rousseau as crimes (among the outrages Hume is alleged to have committed were 'settling [Rousseau] to his heart's content').[82] As Hume knew, anyone even

76. For a thorough account of the dispute between Hume and Rousseau see Robert Zaretsky and John T. Scott, *The Philosopher's Quarrel* (New Haven, CT: Yale University Press, 2009).

77. Smith to Hume, 6 July 1776. Adam Smith, *The Glasgow Edition of the Works and Correspondence of Adam Smith*, vol. 6, *Correspondence (Second Edition)*, ed. Ernest Mossner and Ian Simpson Ross (Oxford: Oxford University Press, 1987), 113.

78. Hume to Adam Smith, 9 September 1766, in *The Letters of David Hume*, vol. 2, 82–83.

79. Hume to the Comtesse de Boufflers. 2 February 1767, ibid., vol. 2, 119.

80. Ibid.

81. Hume to William Strahan. 10 March 1767, ibid., vol. 2, 125.

82. The text of the indictment is reproduced in full in *Reviews of Literature and Spirit of Foreign Magazines*, vol. 8 (Philadelphia: John P. Watson, 1812), 79–81.

dimly aware of the dispute would recognize this as a ridicule of Rousseau's paranoia, and a vindication of everything Hume had done.

In a recent account of this affair, Dennis Rasmussen argues that the fallout from his split with Rousseau 'did not show Hume at his best' and that it sits uneasily with 'our usual image of *le bon David*.[83] But it reveals as much about Hume's appreciation for the malevolent power of ridicule as it does about his character. Hume was aware that the satires directed against Rousseau, however 'good humoured' the intention, were humiliating and was glad not to be the target himself. It was another indication that, for Hume, public mockery was often grounded in hostility and could too easily generate resentment in its object.

Good Humour and Hypocrisy

If Hume had misgivings about the use of ridicule in public clashes between philosophers, he was more comfortable with deploying it for another purpose that Shaftesbury had recommended; exposing hypocrisy. As we saw above, Hume abhorred cynical philosophers who mocked polite society as a hypocritical sham. But he saw great value in using it against more mundane hypocrisies, or to call out those who lecture others for vices that they indulge in themselves, particularly clerics. When, flush from finishing his *Enquiries* in 1751, Hume composed another satire, few of his friends could have been surprised that the Scottish clergy were the target.

In the *Petition of the Grave and Venerable Bellmen, or Sextons, of the Church of Scotland to the Honourable House of Commons* Hume pilloried a recent request by Scottish clergy and schoolteachers for a modest increase in their stipend.[84] Stylistically it was a new departure for Hume. Whereas the *Account of Stewart* had blended factual narration with satire, *The Bellmen's Petition* is Swiftian satire the whole way through. It opens with the bellmen pleading that the clerics' request had sanctified the practice of

---

83. Rasmussen, *The Infidel and the Professor*, 145.

84. The mock petition was already a favourite style of Hume's. In February 1751 he circulated among his friends a mock petition 'To the Right Honble [*sic*] the Lord Chief-Justice Reason and the Honble Judges, Discretion, Prudence, Reserve, and Deliberation' by 'The Patients of Westminster, against James Fraser, Apothecary'. Fraser was medical friend who, Hume joked, had endangered the health of his patients by forcing them to swallow his Jacobite political opinions (a 'poison' delivered on a 'wafer, marked patriotism'). Whether Hume wanted this skit published or for it to remain a private prank is unclear. By contrast, Hume most certainly wanted to see *The Bellman's Petition* make into print but could find no publisher in Edinburgh who would take it on. This skit accompanied a letter that Hume wrote to James Abercromby in February 1751. Hume, *The Letters of David Hume*, vol. 2, 340.

demanding money and that they had no desire to be 'backward in this
Holy cause', especially given that 'scripture and reason' have proved that
the 'cause of religion' was 'intimately and inseparably connected with the
temporal interests' of all churchmen.[85] The humour of the subsequent
passages hinges on the fact that the landowners considering the issue of
clerical stipends had good reason to be sympathetic to demands from the
bellmen. For in the Scottish Kirk bellmen also performed the crucial (if
unglamorous) work of grave-digging and so 'are the persons in the world
to whom the present proprietors of land are the most beholden'.[86]

Note that Hume's humour here reverses that of Diogenes as reported
in 'Of Moral Prejudices'. The bellmen rely on the fact that, unlike the
Cynics, most people care deeply about how their bodies fare after death.
Skewering a Christian trope that he would make light of again on his own
deathbed (see below), Hume joked that bellmen could terrorize religious
sceptics into piety more effectively than anyone because they (and not the
priests) had exclusive sway over how physical remains were handled. Consequently, the bellmen insist, even the most determined sceptic 'trembles
when he thinks of us', and 'reflection on us has reformed more lives than all
the sermons in the world'.[87] Pay us fairly, the bellmen implicitly threaten,
or we will not be responsible for what happens to your corpse.

Scholars have generally regarded Hume's *Bellman's Petition* as not only
dark but also uncharacteristically cruel.[88] Certainly it is difficult to reconcile the pamphlet with Smith's claim that Hume's wit was always free of
malice. Rather than expose an outrageous instance of clerical hypocrisy and
greed, Hume had cast doubt on the validity of any monetary demands the
churchmen might make, no matter how modest. Moreover, while we might
expect Hume to be caustic towards clerics, it is striking that he seems no
more sympathetic to the impoverished schoolteachers who were also seeking better conditions. Roger Emerson goes so far as to call *The Bellmen's
Petition* 'distasteful' and claims that it reveals an 'intense social conservatism' on Hume's part.[89] The 'grievances of both ministers and teachers
were real', he argues 'and Hume does not look good ridiculing them'.[90]

85. David Hume, 'Hume's "Bellmen's Petition": The Original Text', ed. M. A. Stewart,
Hume Studies 23, 1 (1997), 5.

86. Ibid., 6.

87. Ibid.

88. Mossner found *The Bellman's Petition* to be 'good fun'. Mossner, *The Life of David
Hume*, 235. Harris is less enthusiastic, calling it 'rather cruel'. Harris, *Hume: An Intellectual
Biography*, 248.

89. Roger L. Emerson, 'Hume and the Bellman, Zerobabel MacGilchrist', *Hume Studies*
23, 1 (1997), 23.

90. Ibid., 10–11.

However, there is another (if not necessarily more flattering) way of reading this pamphlet, one that speaks more to Hume's general attitude towards the clergy than his cruelty. In a letter to Gilbert Elliot explaining his intentions in writing it, Hume announced that he had composed a 'little endeavour at drollery against some people who care not much to be joked upon'.[91] That he chose to do so, he further explained, reflected a long-held ambition to write a 'ridicule of priests' that would serve as a 'supplement' to Swift's *Gulliver's Travels*.[92] Hume goes on to regret that Swift himself was a cleric and so had directed his wit mainly against lawyers and doctors, professions that generally never lacked for satirists to mock them. But priests differ from these other professions, Hume concludes, because they 'are conscious they are really ridiculous'.[93] In other words, ridiculing priests was no cruel abuse, however much they might be put out by it. Instead, it merely exposed them as what they already knew themselves to be. Materially deprived or not, Hume suggests, the Scottish priests had it coming to them. The schoolteachers were merely caught in the crossfire.

Hume's letter to Elliot was audacious, not least because he placed himself in the same league as Swift (as mentioned, the Edinburgh printers were less convinced by Hume's 'good pleasantry and satire' and refused to publish it, probably as a snub to its irreligious content).[94] But the letter also recalled Shaftesbury's argument that the test of ridicule could distinguish those who are 'really ridiculous' from those who merely happen to be mocked. Priests, Hume playfully implied to Elliot, were intrinsically ridiculous in the same way Shaftesbury had found the French Prophets to have been. By hypocritically pretending otherwise, they had made themselves fair game.

Hume's stance on the relationship between humour and hypocrisy was more complex than this squib might suggest, however. Unlike Shaftesbury (and with Hobbes) he appreciated how good humour could not only expose hypocrisy but *enable* it as well.[95] Hume's *History of England* is

---

91. Hume to Gilbert Elliot of Minto. 18 February 1751. Hume, *The Letters of David Hume*, vol. 1, 153.

92. Ibid.

93. Ibid.

94. Hume to John Clephane, 18 February 1751. Ibid., vol. 1, 149.

95. Hume shared this suspicion with Henry Fielding. In his 'Essay on the Knowledge of the Characters of Men', Fielding argued that there was an important difference between good nature and good humour. Whereas good nature was a benevolent disposition towards others, good humour was the 'triumph of the mind' experienced when beholding 'the inferior happiness of others'. And while he stopped short of arguing that laughter was always an expression of pride, Fielding nevertheless conceded that Hobbes had essentially been

replete with characters who strategically make use of their good humour to both conceal their vices and further their political ambitions. Some of the most dangerous hypocrites, Hume observed, had a fondness for witticism, repartee and jokes that made it easier for them to win popularity and, ultimately, power. Oliver Cromwell, he suggested, had a sense of humour that appeared amiable but ultimately served to conceal his malice. In a passage purportedly dedicated to praising Oliver Cromwell's affable nature, Hume describes a number of pranks that the Lord Protector played on his men. These ranged from the relatively innocent, such as the placing of 'burning coals' into his officers' boots and the playful tossing of cushions at his advisers, to the callously casual, as when Cromwell 'bedaubed with ink' the face of the man sitting next to him prior to signing Charles I's death warrant.[96] One incident, however, stands out. While usually sceptical of rumours or hearsay, Hume tells of a 'tradition' whereby

> one day sitting at a table, the protector had a bottle of wine brought to him of a kind which he valued so highly, that he must needs open the bottle himself: But in attempting it, the corkscrew dropped from his hand. Immediately his courtiers and generals flung themselves on the floor to recover it. Cromwell burst out laughing. Should any fool, said he, put his head in at the door, he would fancy from your posture, that you were seeking the Lord; and you are only seeking a corkscrew.[97]

Although presented as evidence of the 'frolic and pleasantry' in Cromwell's character, Hume's account of this incident also functions as an indictment of the state of English liberty in Cromwell's Commonwealth.[98] The sycophancy of Cromwell's inner council as they prostrated themselves on the floor in search of the Lord Protector's fallen corkscrew rivals the behaviour of even the most grovelling of Royal courtiers. Moreover, the laugh that Hume's Cromwell directs at his men on the floor suggests that even he had grown contemptuous of the degree of personal sycophancy the maintenance of his regime seemed to require.

Cromwell was not the only character in Hume's *History* to combine good humour with streaks of intolerance and authoritarianism. After the

---

right and that good humour frequently concealed 'malice and fraud'. Henry Fielding, 'Essay on the Knowledge of the Characters of Men', in *Miscellanies*, vol. 1, 189–90.

96. David Hume, *The History of England from the Invasion of Julius Caesar to the Revolution in 1688* (Indianapolis, IN: Liberty Fund, 1983), vol. 6, 90.

97. Ibid.

98. Ibid.

Restoration many of the courtiers surrounding Charles II seemed similarly determined to give good humour a bad name. A prime example was George Villiers, the Duke of Buckingham and author of *The Rehearsal*, a popular satire on Restoration culture. Shaftesbury had praised Buckingham as an 'author of the highest quality' whose writings had offered the 'most effectual and entertaining method of exposing folly, pedantry, false reason and ill writing' without which the English would have been 'imposed upon'.[99] Hume, by contrast, was both more measured in his praise for the *Rehearsal* and more reluctant to admire Buckingham's wit. Far from undeceiving the English people with his 'ingenious talent for ridicule', Hume found, Buckingham had used it to impose upon anyone who could do him favours, starting with Charles himself.[100] For Hume, Buckingham's wit not only brought him to the king's side but also allowed him to abuse that position once there, particularly in his attempts to undermine Edward Hyde, First Earl of Clarendon. By making Clarendon the 'object of his raillery', Buckingham succeeded in toppling him, with disastrous consequences for the country.[101]

For Hume, Restoration culture was dominated by wits of the most corrupt sort. The tone was set by the king himself. Charles II's habit of doling out wit and treating even important matters of state 'in raillery' gave an impression of good-natured nonchalance.[102] But Charles's inability to endure a witty repartee from someone else revealed just how misleading that impression was. When Parliament tried to pass a levy on playhouses, Hume relates, Charles's courtiers objected on the grounds that the 'players were the king's servants'.[103] An audacious MP, Sir John Coventry, inquired 'whether the king's pleasure lay among the male or the female players?'[104] For Hume it 'might have been expected' that a king as fond of wit as Charles would receive this 'raillery' on his liaisons with actresses in 'good humour'.[105] Instead, Charles's officers had Coventry mutilated, his nose 'cut to the bone' to teach him not to disrespect royal authority by publicly joking at the king's expense.[106] When placed in the context of his overall assessment of Charles's reign, Hume's verdict here is damning. The licentious mirth that Charles encouraged in his court reflected less an

---

99. Shaftesbury, 'Soliloquy, or Advice to an Author', 116.
100. Hume, *History of England*, vol. 6, 32.
101. Ibid., 212.
102. Ibid., 318.
103. Ibid., 248.
104. Ibid.
105. Ibid.
106. Ibid.

atmosphere of tolerance and freedom from Puritan austerity than a corrupted culture in which not all jests were equal.

Ridicule and Religious Controversy

Hume not only shared the Hobbesian suspicion that jokers are often malicious, he also held that those who ridicule others often betray excessive
confidence in themselves and in the superiority of their views. Religious
dogmatists in particular, Hume found, were prone to mocking members of
rival denominations, notwithstanding any reservations they might enter-
tain about the sinfulness of laughter. In his *Natural History of Religion*
(1757) Hume identified the self-certainty displayed by monotheists as
one reason for their intolerance; polytheists were more sociable because
they accepted diversity of creed and worship as a fact of religious life.[107] If
Hume could be a bit facetious in dealing with religious topics, I argue in
this final section, it was not only because he wanted to inject humour into
a subject dominated by the gloomy and grave; he also wished to replace
a ridicule of self-confidence with one that was more sceptical and less
presumptuous.[108] Like Shaftesbury and his followers, Hume hated excessive earnestness in religious debate. But he was also repulsed by the self-
delusions that religious disputants fell into when they thought they could
use ridicule to conclusively dismiss opponents as mistaken.

Hume was not shy about complaining that religion was too often
spoken of with excessive seriousness. In a particularly controversial passage from the fifth volume of the *History*, he declared that when dealing
with religious debate 'history is sometimes constrained to depart a little
from her native and accustomed gravity'.[109] He also castigated those who

---

107. David Hume, 'The Natural History of Religion', in *Principal Writings on Religion
Including Dialogues Concerning Natural Religion and the Natural History of Religion*, ed.
J.C.A. Gaskin (Oxford: Oxford University Press, 2008), 160.

108. As Annette Baier noted, although Hume mocked religion, this did not mean that
he took all religions to be equally objectionable. Annette C. Baier, *Death and Character:
Further Reflections on Hume* (Cambridge, MA: Harvard University Press, 2008), 93.

109. Hume, *History of England*, vol. 5, 69. To the dissenter critic Roger Flexman, this
plea on behalf of what 'history' was 'constrained' to do was little more than a cover for
Hume's own practice of treating religious quarrels with bemusement. Roger Flexman,
'Review of The History of Great Britain, Vol. 1. Containing the Reigns of James I and
Charles I', *Monthly Review*, March 1754. Reprinted in James Fieser, ed., *Early Responses
to Hume's 'History of England'* (Bristol: Thoemmes Press, 2005), 21. Hume removed this
line from subsequent editions. For the thesis that Hume's revisions to the *History* show
that he sought to minimize offence see Graeme Slater, 'Hume's Revisions of the History of
England', *Studies in Bibliography: Papers of the Bibliographical Society of the University
of Virginia* 45 (1992), 130–57. For a characterization of Hume's ridiculing of religion as a

earnestly engaged in theological and liturgical controversies that should never have been imbued with significance. Hume was particularly unforgiving in this regard towards monarchs who, by entering into religious disputes, granted them undeserved importance. One early culprit in this regard was Henry VIII who was vain enough to think himself capable of entering into theological debate but lacked the foresight to see how doing so worked at cross-purposes to his primary aim of ensuring religious uniformity. By publishing his *Defence of the Seven Sacraments*, Hume argued, Henry inadvertently made the controversy with Luther more 'illustrious' and won more converts to the Lutheran side.[110] He repeated the same mistake in the 1540s when, having broken with Rome, he sought to restore religious consensus by promulgating doctrine. Because he entered 'with the greatest earnestness, into all those scholastic disputes', Hume writes, Henry achieved nothing other than encouraging 'the people, by his example, to apply themselves to the study of theology'.[111]

Hume rendered a similarly poor judgment of James I for carelessly missing an opportunity to starve theological controversies of air by refusing to recognize them as significant. Hume initially commends James for rejecting the 'useless austerities' the Puritans tried to push on him and for choosing instead to regard God as a benevolent being 'who created us solely for happiness'.[112] James's cardinal political error, however, was that he came ultimately to treat the Puritans' theological speculations as worthy of serious consideration. 'By entering zealously into frivolous disputes', Hume complains, 'James gave them an air of dignity, which they could not otherwise have acquired'.[113] Still worse, by participating in the theological 'quarrel', James 'could no longer have recourse to contempt and ridicule, the only proper method of appeasing it'.[114] Ultimately, Hume suggests, James's great error lay in failing to recognize that as king his role was not so much to engage with serious matters as to decide what was serious in the first place.

If Hume was wary of the danger of earnestness, however, he refused to join the Shaftesburians in believing that ridicule could test the integrity of religious doctrines. In particular, he challenged the notion that the success that early English reformers enjoyed in using ridicule to discredit their

kind of 'low burlesque' see Donald T. Siebert, *The Moral Animus of David Hume* (Newark: University of Delaware Press, 1990), 121.

110. Hume, *History of England*, vol. 3, 140.

111. Ibid., vol. 3, 290.

112. Ibid., vol. 5, 11.

113. Ibid., vol. 5, 12.

114. Ibid.

rivals proved the truth of Protestantism and the absurdity of Catholicism. In his survey of the strategies used by Henry VIII's regime to discredit monks and friars in advance of dissolving the monasteries, Hume admitted their success in ridiculing the worship of relics. When describing the government's success in this campaign, however, Hume threw some doubt on the self-congratulatory interpretation of these events spun by Protestant historians:

> It is needless to be prolix in an enumeration of particulars: Protestant historians mention on this occasion with great triumph the sacred repositories of convents; the parings of St Edmond's toes; some of the coals that roasted St. Laurence; the girdle of the Virgin shown in eleven several places; two or three heads of St Ursula; the felt of St Thomas of Lancaster, an infallible cure for the head-ach [sic]; part of St Thomas of Canterbury's shirt, much reverenced by big-bellied women; some reliques, an excellent preventative against rain; others a remedy to weeds in corn. But such fooleries, as they are to be found in all ages and nations, and even took place during the most refined periods of antiquity, form no particular or violent reproach to the catholic religion.[115]

An indignant critic, Joseph Towers, in reviewing this passage, regarded it as emblematic of Hume's contempt for religion as such. For while Hume 'seems to have thought that the Protestants have treated the fopperies of the Roman Church with too much ridicule', he wrote, Hume's 'own enumeration of them is sufficiently ludicrous'.[116] It is easy to see how Towers could have arrived at this conclusion. Hume accuses Protestant historians of using detailed lists of relics to make cheap gains at the expense of Catholics and then promptly proceeds to do precisely the same himself. However, rather than align himself with the unnamed historians, Hume ends the passage by clarifying that such 'fooleries' are nothing specific to Catholicism. If ridicule is a test of imposture, Hume implies, then Catholicism will not be the only religion vulnerable to it.

Elsewhere, Hume elaborated on why Catholicism might *appear* more ridiculous than other faiths even if it were not actually so. He did this by revisiting the incident from Burnet's *History of the Reformation* that had proven so bothersome to Brown in his criticism of Shaftesbury. As we have

---

115. Ibid., vol. 3, 252–53.

116. Joseph Towers, *Observations on Mr Hume's History* (London: H. Goldney, for G. Robinson, 1778), 75.

seen, Brown condemned anti-clerical comedies as an irresponsible and self-defeating method for advancing reformation. The best that could be hoped for from them, he had alleged, was that the audiences to such comedies would be temporarily persuaded to despise Catholics. But the English people could never, Brown had insisted, be led this way to embrace Protestantism. In his own assessment of this same episode, Hume was less concerned with admonishing those who encouraged the comedies than in explaining why they were so powerful in the first place. Commenting on the rationale behind the king's decision to outlaw them, Hume argued that the sensuous nature of Catholic liturgical practices was the real reason why Catholics were more easily open to comedic attack than Protestants:

> The king took care about this time to clear the churches from another abuse, which had creeped into them. Plays, interludes, and farces were there often acted in derision of the former superstitions; and the reverence of the multitude for ancient principles and modes of worship was thereby gradually effaced. We do not hear, that the Catholics attempted to retaliate by employing this powerful engine against their adversaries, or endeavoured by like arts to expose that fanatical spirit, by which, it appears, the reformers were frequently actuated. Perhaps the people were not disposed to relish a jest on that side: Perhaps the greater simplicity and the more spiritual abstract worship of the protestants, gave less hold to ridicule, which is commonly founded on sensible representations. It was, therefore, a very agreeable concession, which the king made to the catholic party, to suppress entirely these religious comedies.[117]

Hume here raises questions familiar to any reader versed in the ongoing controversy surrounding the role of ridicule in religious debate. Having acknowledged the potency of ridicule to loosen popular attachment to Catholicism, Hume ponders why Catholics did not return like with like. The first explanation he posits is that the success of ridicule is contingent upon historical circumstances: the English at that particular moment were already predisposed against the old religion, meaning that counter-ridicules from the Catholic side were destined to fall flat (even though Hume hints that some sort of attack on the 'fanatical spirit' of the reformers might have been justified). Hume's second explanation, however, is more psychological. Catholics will always suffer disadvantage in this sort of contest because their images, statuary, relics, vestments and other items

117. Hume, *History of England*, vol. 3, 290.

appealing to the senses makes them especially vulnerable. By banning religious comedies, therefore, Henry spared Catholics further assaults from a weapon that they could never hope to wield as effectively against Protestants.[118]

Crucially, however, there was nothing in Catholic doctrine that made it inherently ridiculous in a way that the Protestant alternative was not. Indeed, for much of the *History*, Hume went out of his way to show how easily Protestant religiosity could be mocked as well. In his summary of English literary achievements at the close of volume 6 of the *History* he highlighted the considerable impact of Butler's *Hudibras* in turning public opinion against the Parliamentarians. By exposing the 'fanaticism and false pretences' of the Parliamentarians, the 'advantage' to the royalists had been 'prodigious'.[119] Moreover, as his critics had indignantly pointed out, Hume's treatment of seventeenth-century Puritans was calculated to show that Catholicism was not the only religion prone to absurdity. In his account of Barebone's Parliament, for example, Hume describes the 'fifth monarchy men, anabaptists, antinomians' and 'independents' chosen to be its members as the 'dregs of the human species' whose 'hearts' became 'dilated' when 'they considered the high dignity to which they supposed themselves to be exalted'.[120] Hume's term 'high dignity' has a mischievous double meaning here, referring at once to the religious radicals' new positions as Parliamentarians and to their personal infusion with the holy spirit. That Hume calls the dignity of the Parliamentarian's 'supposed' suggests that in both cases their selection is dubious: the members of Barebone's Parliament were not elected but instead selected personally by Cromwell, and Hume sarcastically denies that God or Providence could have been 'so kind as to bestow on these men ... supreme authority'.[121] This is precisely the sort of passage that incurred the wrath of Hume's critics, yet in revising it he made just one adjustment, upgrading the Parliamentarians from 'the dregs of the human species' to the 'very dregs of the fanatics', hardly a major concessionary gesture (especially given that 'fanatic' is never a neutral term for Hume).[122] If anything, Hume's substi-

118. This was not the first time that Hume declared Catholicism to be particularly fair game for mockery. In his *Natural History of Religion* he found that the doctrine of the 'real presence' gives greater rise to ridicule than any pagan doctrine. Hume, 'The Natural History of Religion', 167 and 169.
119. Hume, *History of England*, vol. 6, 544–45.
120. Ibid., 60.
121. Ibid.
122. Ibid.

tution only heighted the ridicule by making it unambiguously clear that his later suggestion that 'all fanatics' are 'consecrated by their own fond imaginations' covered the members of Barebone's Parliament.[123]

Although Hume enjoyed ridiculing enthusiasts, he was under no illusions that people who had already fallen into an enthusiasm could ever be laughed out of it. This was the dilemma faced by Charles II, who faced a contagion of anti-Catholic sentiment spurred by rumours of a Jesuit plot to assassinate him. Hume bitterly noted how this panic perverted the public's sense of reality. Visions of a Catholic minority plotting to burn down London, assassinate the king and lay the ground for a recovery of papal supremacy over the English should have been laughed away as 'absurdities'.[124] Instead, anyone who paused to weigh the evidence on its merits risked ostracism or worse: 'To deny the reality of the plot', Hume writes, 'was to be an accomplice: To hesitate was criminal.'[125] By contrast with James, who was presented with a golden opportunity to use ridicule to shape religious politics in his realm and squandered it, Charles here found himself willing to use it but denied even the remotest possibility of a receptive audience. On the few occasions when he could 'speak freely' among friends, Hume notes, Charles threw the 'highest ridicule on the plot and all who believed in it'.[126] But finding the 'torrent' of public opinion 'too strong to be controlled', he could do little more than direct its 'fury'.[127]

Overall then, Hume had a more complex attitude to the relationship between ridicule and religion than his critics assumed. He understood, perhaps better than most of his contemporaries, the powerful temptation to deride views we feel do not merit more serious engagement. More than that, he recognized that to treat seriously was to dignify and that earnest

123. Ibid., 61.
124. Ibid., 341.
125. Ibid., 342.
126. Ibid., 348.
127. Ibid. The case of Charles showed that ridicule was often born of frustration rather than a sense of superiority. In a 1769 letter, written after 'a deluded Multitude' rioted in support of the Whig radical John Wilkes (recently expelled from Parliament), Hume draws an analogy between this present bout of 'Madness' and the enthusiastic hysteria surrounding the 'popish plot' of 1678. His historian's assessment is that the recent 'folly' surrounding Wilkes was the more 'risible' of the two, so much so that all other 'sentiments' he felt towards it were now 'bury'd in Ridicule'. Hume, *The Letters of David Hume*, vol. 2, 197. That the letter opens with a remark that 'History' was now the nation's 'Favourite Reading' suggests a degree of frustration on Hume's part that a public well versed in an 'Absurdity' such as the Popish Plot should fail to repel similar (though not identical) absurdities in the present. Ibid., 196.

forms of engagement could prove just as dangerous to religious peace in the long run as their supposedly uncivil counterparts. But Hume was also more aware of the limits of ridicule than many of his contemporaries. Not only did he give grounds for doubting any easy association of ridicule with truth, he also saw that those who celebrated derision as a way of humbling the pride of their adversaries often hid an unacknowledged pride of their own. Shaftesbury and his followers were so at ease with ridicule in religious debate because they believed that once it had performed its corrosive work their own rationally grounded religion would emerge triumphant. Similarly, the English reformers who mocked Catholics not only tempered the pride of clerics but also displayed their own pride by glorying in the supposed superiority of their own faith. For Hume, that a disputant succeeded in persuading the public to laugh at their adversary might reveal something about their wit or rhetorical skill. But it said nothing about the truth of the claims they used their ridicule to advance. Hume's readers, even if their own convictions were not loosened by his treatment of religion, could at least have learned to look upon religious disputes more as contingent struggles for power than contests from which true religion would emerge victorious.

Conclusion

Perhaps the most famous of Hume's jokes appears in the same obituary letter by Smith with which we began this chapter. According to Smith, Hume on his deathbed began reading Lucian's *Dialogues of the Dead* and tried out several 'jocular excuses' that he might use if prompted by Charon to get into his boat and cross the Styx to Hades.[128] Smith's letter implies that Hume tested a whole series of these excuses but only leaves us with the final two, namely Hume's plea for more time to complete the revisions to his corpus, and his desire to witness the 'downfall of some of the prevailing systems of superstition' (Smith's original letter to Strahan records Hume as wanting the 'churches shut up' and the 'Clergy sent about their business').[129] Several readers of Smith's published letter found this line doubly offensive. In the first place, it seemed to reveal that Hume's last wish was to see organized religion itself tumble, confirming what his critics had suspected all along. Second, and perhaps worse, that Hume was

---

128. Hume, *The Letters of David Hume*, vol. 2, 450.
129. Ibid.

in a joking mood at all challenged the notion that religious sceptics, when faced with death, would fearfully turn towards God and seek absolution. In this sense Hume's jocular mood was more troubling than the actual content of his jokes.

It is far from clear, however, that Hume used his final moments to make one last swipe at religion. He did not speak these words with an eye to publication and there is no evidence that Hume knew that Smith would report his words (or a softened version of them) to a wider audience. Hume, as we have seen, was no Shaftesbury; he was under no illusions that a joke could bring about the downfall of anything, never mind religion. It is more likely that Hume's modest aim was to lighten the mood and make his companions smile at a distressing moment (the contrast with Diogenes, scoffing at his friends for fretting about what would happen to his corpse, could hardly be more marked). As James Harris has remarked in relation to this incident, Hume's joke was 'just a joke'.[130] Recall, moreover, that Smith only provides us with a sample of the 'jocular excuses' that Hume contrived over the course of the conversation. Hume was trying out several different fake excuses to Charon for comic effect, making it difficult to conclude that one was more significant than the others. In other words, if we pause to imagine the specific social setting in which the conversation took place, we can see the comical Hume trying out different lines with his audience, rather than building up to an irreligious punchline.

Finally, even the excuse that he needed more time to revise his works suggests that Hume's tone at this gathering was, above all, self-deprecating. Hume was notoriously precious about his prose and was making fun of himself for believing that he might one day rest content with what he had written and finally cease his tinkering. His remark about superstition should be read in a similar light. Playing again on his reputation (this time for impiety) Hume conjured just the sort of excuse that an irreligious rogue might come up with. In short, if ever there was a text that we should resist the urge to over-interpret, it is a letter reporting the final exchanges of a dying man attempting to cheer up his friends with a bit of banter. Sometimes a joke really is just a joke.

The case of Hume, I have argued, shows how it was possible to be a highly skilled wit and at the same time clear-eyed about the limitations and dangers of humour. Hume appreciated better than many of his contemporaries that scoffers often breed cynicism, that satirists are not always

130. Harris, *Hume: An Intellectual Biography*, 22.

truth-tellers, that ridicule can sour conversation, and that the good-humoured can be duplicitous. In the next chapter we turn to some critics of Hume who saw nothing of that nuance in him. For the Scottish philosophers of Common Sense, Hume was a Diogenes, bent on laughing his readers into scepticism about the external world, morality and religion. To respond effectively to this assault, they reckoned, required returning fire with the same tactics they imagined Hume to have used. To their minds, ridicule was not doomed to be the solvent of common sense. A new, post-Hobbesian, form of ridicule could instead be its shield.

CHAPTER FOUR

Scoffing at Scepticism

RIDICULE AND COMMON SENSE

IN THE MID-1750S Adam Smith made two contributions to the short-lived *Edinburgh Review*. One of these—a survey of current trends in European letters—has received growing scholarly attention, mainly because it reveals the depth of Smith's engagement with Rousseau and Mandeville.[1] Smith's other contribution—a review of Johnson's *Dictionary*—has sparked far less interest. This neglect is understandable. The review is short, dry, and contains fewer clues to Smith's intellectual trajectory for scholars to pour over. Moreover, Smith focuses on Johnson's definitions of just two words. The first of these was 'BUT' (which Smith had a surprisingly lot to say about!). The second was 'HUMOUR'.[2]

A precise account of humour was important, Smith maintained, because too often it was conflated with wit. Humour, he claimed, was something 'wild, loose, extravagant, and fantastical' which 'comes upon a man by fits' and which 'he can neither command nor restrain'.[3] As

---

1. For a sample of this literature see Dennis C. Rasmussen, *The Problems and Promise of Commercial Society: Adam Smith's Response to Rousseau* (College Station: Pennsylvania State University Press, 2008); Sagar, *The Opinion of Mankind*, 139–41; Hont, *Politics in Commercial Society*, 18–22; Charles Griswold, *Jean-Jacques Rousseau and Adam Smith: A Philosophical Encounter* (New York: Routledge, 2018), chapter 3. For a critical (even deflationary) reaction to this scholarship see Mark Hulliung, 'Rousseau and the Scottish Enlightenment: Connections and Disconnections', in *Adam Smith and Rousseau: Ethics, Politics, Economics*, ed. Maria Pia Paganelli, Dennis C. Rasmussen, and Craig Smith (Edinburgh: Edinburgh University Press, 2018), 43–45.

2. Adam Smith, 'Review of Johnson's Dictionary', in *The Glasgow Edition of the Works and Correspondence of Adam Smith*, vol. 3, *Essays on Philosophical Subjects*, 233 and 238.

3. Ibid., 241.

such, it was 'not perfectly consistant [*sic*] with true politeness'.[4] 'Wit', by contrast, was a 'designed, concerted, regular, and artificial' contrivance that required intellect, self-control, and skill.[5] Wit is for gentlemen, Smith concluded, humour is generally more suited to 'buffoons'.[6]

There is a clear Shaftesburian ring to Smith's association of wit with gentlemanly finesse. But Smith also harboured the Hobbesian worry that wit could often be not only clever but contemptuous as well. The satisfaction we gain from ridicule, he argued in *The Theory of Moral Sentiments* (1759), derives ultimately from a mild pleasure in watching the victim squirm. Because there is a 'malice in mankind' which causes us to find the minor discomfort of others 'diverting', we take 'delight' in 'raillery, and in the small vexation which we observe in our companion, when he is pushed, and urged, and teased upon all sides'.[7] Those who are well 'formed to society', Smith continues, realize that the best response to any mishap is to pre-emptively make a joke about it at one's own expense, knowing that others will be only too willing to step in and do it for us.[8]

Contra Hobbes, however, Smith did not believe *all* raillery fitted this mould, a position he made clear when he tackled Hobbes's argument more directly in his *Lectures on Rhetoric and Belles Lettres* (1762–63). In the eighth of these lectures Smith invited his listeners to imagine a well-dressed coxcomb striding through town. The man constantly looks around to check if he is being admired, but only succeeds in drawing a derisive laugh from the crowd he hoped to impress. Eventually this 'fine fellow', presumably distracted by his search for approving faces, slips and falls into a gutter.[9] The accident causes the same onlookers to laugh again, but this time, Smith says, from a 'different motive', namely the incongruity of such a 'fine fellow' ending up in the mud, the 'very condition they in their hearts would have wished him'.[10] A Hobbesian analysis of laughter can

4. Ibid.
5. Ibid.
6. Ibid. Although Smith's review of Johnson was generally well received (the editors of the third edition of the *Encyclopedia Britanica* copied from it for their entry on humour), Dugald Stewart was less than convinced. 'The various significations of the word BUT are very nicely and happily discriminated. The other does not seem to have been executed with equal care.' Stewart, *Biographical Memoirs of Smith, Robertson, and Reid*, 17.
7. Smith, *The Theory of Moral Sentiments*, 52.
8. Ibid.
9. Smith, 'Lectures on Rhetoric and Belles Lettres', 45.
10. Ibid. That the coxcomb displays signs of wealth is not enough to shield him from ridicule. Smith thus exposes how our inclination to admire the rich (later a crucial component of his moral psychology) has its limits. This should qualify Gloria Vivenza's claim that, for Smith, the 'inborn tendency which leads us to respect our superiors also leads us

just about account for the first laugh, Smith implied, but not the second. That first communicates contempt, disapproval, and even 'somewhat of anger', in response to the coxcomb's vanity.[11] The second, by contrast, is sparked purely by the incongruous image of a man in fine clothes suddenly rolling around in filth.[12]

Smith might have chosen a better example with which to refute Hobbes. That the onlookers so clearly take pleasure in seeing the coxcomb get his comeuppance suggests that the separation between laughter from contempt and laughter from incongruity was not nearly neat enough to make his point stick. Perhaps aware of this, Smith followed up with better illustrative examples. A 'tall man amongst a number of small men' makes for laughter and yet 'we don't contemn either'.[13] A mouse ruining the 'effect of an excellent discourse' by running across a chapel floor at an inopportune moment has the same effect, as would a similar occurrence at a funeral.[14] In all these cases, Smith maintains, it is the unexpected incongruity that does the work of generating laughter, leaving our personal sense of worth relative to others untouched.

Smith's alternative to Hobbesian laughter, then, was similar that of his teacher at the University of Glasgow, Francis Hutcheson. While 'great and noble' objects excite admiration and 'little or mean' ones generate contempt, Smith argued, it is the 'blending and joining' of greatness and meanness that makes us laugh.[15] And as with Hutcheson, exposing the shortcomings of Hobbes's argument allowed for the rehabilitation of ridicule as a social corrective. Using ridicule to expose the 'real foibles and blemishes in the characters or behaviour of men', Smith affirmed, contributed in no small way to 'the reformation of manners and the benefit of mankind'.[16]

---

to ridicule only those who are below our station'. Gloria Vivenza, *Adam Smith and the Classics: The Classical Heritage in Adam Smith's Thought* (Oxford: Oxford University Press, 2001), 166.

11. Smith, 'Lectures on Rhetoric and Belles Lettres', 41.

12. Ibid.

13. Ibid.

14. Ibid.

15. Ibid., 43.

16. Ibid., 47. Smith was joined in this view by his fellow teacher of rhetoric, Hugh Blair. 'To render vice ridiculous', Blair proclaimed in his *Lectures on Rhetoric and Belles Lettres*, is 'doing real service to the world'. Blair, *Lectures on Rhetoric and Belles Lettres*, vol. 3, 344–45. For an excellent discussion of how Smith put ridicule to use himself see Jennifer Pitts, 'Irony in Adam Smith's Critical and Global History', *Political Theory* 45, 2 (2015), 141–63.

The focus of this chapter is a group of philosophers in Aberdeen— George Campbell, Thomas Reid, James Oswald and James Beattie— who joined Smith in both disavowing Hobbes and tapping ridicule's corrective potential. The particular service they thought ridicule could perform, however, extended far beyond the correction of manners or the humbling of the vain. Instead, I argue, the Aberdonian philosophers fashioned ridicule into a weapon against modern scepticism, a scepticism that began with Hobbes but was now epitomized by Smith's friend David Hume. Drawing on Shaftesbury's inspiration, they saw in our sense of the ridiculous a distinct faculty, complimentary to reason, that was essential to human sociability. So potent was this faculty that it could even deflect attempts by philosophers to alienate people from the everyday beliefs that oriented their lives. For Beattie especially, all that was required to protect the common beliefs that held society together was for ordinary people to laugh long and disdainfully at sceptics like Hume who, as Beattie saw it, were prepared to deny such beliefs to achieve notoriety. By insisting that anyone with common sense could and should scoff at Hume's scepticism, the Aberdonians invested the laughter of ordinary people with greater philosophical dignity than it had ever enjoyed. Moreover, they turned a weapon long associated with scepticism against the sceptics themselves.

This was not, however, the only novel contribution to the ridicule debate to come out of Aberdeen. Beginning with Beattie's 1776 essay 'On Laughter and Ludicrous Composition', I argue, a new strand of thinking about laughter emerged in Scotland that retained the Hobbesian emphasis on contempt but shifted the focus from individual ridiculers to social groups and classes. For many Scottish philosophers the growth of politeness in modern commercial societies tempered aggressive interpersonal mockery. For Beattie and John Millar, however, the increased social differentiation characteristic of commercial societies generated clashes of manners between professions, classes and guilds that provided fertile ground for mutual derision. The Hobbesian laughter between prideful individuals would, on this new line of argument, eventually be supplanted by mockery between classes.

Shaftesbury in Aberdeen

On 8 March 1758 George Campbell, soon to be principal at Aberdeen's Marischal College, delivered the first Discourse of the Aberdeen Philosophical Society (known colloquially as the Wise Club), an organization of which he was a founding member.[17] Campbell chose as his theme 'The Nature of Eloquence' and would eventually convert what he had to say into the opening three chapters of a major treatise, *The Philosophy of Rhetoric* (1776). Although Campbell's theme was eloquence in general, he expressed a particular interest in what he called the 'eloquence of conversation', of which the essential components were wit, humour and ridicule.[18] Like Smith, Campbell despaired at how these terms were often conflated and made it his task to parse out the differences between them. He wanted to clarify how each of these techniques related to the operations of the mind, while also figuring out how his listeners could make the most effective use of them.

Wit, Campbell explained, works by gratifying the imagination with surprises, or pointing to 'unexpected similarities' between objects that at first glance share little in common.[19] There was nothing particularly novel in this definition, and linking wit to the imagination had been common-place at least since Locke.[20] Campbell's analysis of humour, by contrast, was quite distinct. Just as wit strikes the imagination, he asserts, humour appeals to the passions, making it the comic equivalent of the pathetic eloquence we find in tragedy. A speaker describing 'ardent and durable' passions (such as grief or indignation), he notes, will trigger a sympathetic response and spread the passion to the listener.[21] By contrast, a less potent passion, or one presented 'preposterously', kills 'fellow-feeling' and 'universally awakens contempt'.[22] Having identified contempt as the 'only passion' that humour appeals to, Campbell limited its scope to those 'foibles' of character such as 'jealousies, childish fondness, pertness, vanity,

17. Kathleen Holcomb, 'Wit, Humour and Ridicule: George Campbell's First Discourse for the Aberdeen Philosophical Society', in *Aberdeen and the Enlightenment*, ed. Jennifer J. Carter and Joan H. Pittock (Aberdeen: Aberdeen University Press, 1987), 283.

18. George Campbell, *The Philosophy of Rhetoric*, vol. 1 (London: W. Strahan and T. Cadell, 1776), 42. Campbell's address became chapters 2 and 3 of his 1776 work *The Philosophy of Rhetoric*. Arthur Walzer finds these chapters 'oddly placed' within *The Philosophy of Rhetoric*, which may reflect their origin as a stand-alone essay. Arthur E. Walzer, *George Campbell: Rhetoric in the Age of Enlightenment* (Carbondale: Southern Illinois University Press, 2002), 43.

19. Campbell, *The Philosophy of Rhetoric*, vol. 1, 45.

20. Locke had located wit 'in the assemblage of ideas, and putting those together with quickness and variety, wherein can be found any resemblance or congruity, thereby to make up pleasant pictures and agreeable visions in the fancy'. John Locke, *The Clarendon Edition of the Works of John Locke: An Essay Concerning Human Understanding*, ed. Peter H. Nidditch (Oxford: Oxford University Press, 1975), 156.

21. Campbell, *The Philosophy of Rhetoric*, vol. 1, 57.

22. Ibid., 58.

and self-conceit'.[23] We can experience contempt for more severe vices, Campbell suggests, but we are unlikely to laugh at them.

The central place occupied by contempt in Campbell's analysis makes it look Hobbesian at first glance. As Hutcheson before him had done in his 'Hibernicus' letters, however, Campbell found Hobbes's theory to be, at best, incomplete. For while contempt was integral to the operation of humour, it was not essential to laughter *tout court*. Campbell granted that 'contempt always implies a sense of superiority' which explains our aversion to being laughed at.[24] But Hobbes had failed to see that the 'perception of oddity' was just as likely to make us laugh as the feeling of superiority over another; we can laugh and yet not be 'glorying over anybody'.[25] (To drive the point home, Campbell used the same example a well-dressed man tumbling into a gutter that Smith had used in his *Lectures on Rhetoric and Belles Lettres* and, like Smith, attributed the ensuing laugh to incongruity rather than contempt.[26]) Finally, for Campbell, Hobbes had misunderstood how the proud actually behave. Because pride is an 'unpleasant' passion, Campbell argues, those agitated by it tend to be stiff and 'fastidious' rather than jocular.[27] Far from mocking those they perceive to be beneath them, they 'disdain to laugh' at all for fear of compromising their dignity and joining the 'common herd'.[28]

Campbell's repudiation of Hobbes is further evident in his discussion of the third kind of facetious eloquence: ridicule. For Campbell, ridicule appeals primarily to the judgment and the will and as such is never merely rhetorical but always contains 'an air of reasoning'.[29] Presented like this, the goal of ridicule is not to humiliate or insult but to *convince* an audience by smuggling argumentation under the cover of facetiousness. According to Campbell, this power to convince is partly what separates ridicule from

23. Ibid., 60.
24. Ibid., 88.
25. Ibid., 88 and 90.
26. Campbell, 93. A well-dressed person falling into mud was clearly a favourite example for many eighteenth-century theorists of laughter. In 1776 the poet Elizabeth Gilding included in a volume of her poems an essay by Daniel Turner arguing that the urge to laugh at muddied fine clothes was difficult to overcome, even if the unfortunate was one of our 'greatest intimates, nay our brother'. Turner's example again illustrates how laughter at incongruity could be hurtful to its object and even undermine sociability. Elizabeth Gilding, *The Breathings of Genius. Being a Collection of Poems; to Which are Added, Essays, Moral and Philosophical* (London: W. Faden, 1776), 70.
27. Campbell, *The Philosophy of Rhetoric*, vol. 1, 94.
28. Ibid.
29. Ibid., 69.

wit and humour, which mainly divert their hearers rather than changing their minds.

If Campbell's analysis was anti-Hobbesian, was it also Shaftesburian? As he informed readers in the Preface to *The Philosophy of Rhetoric*, Campbell had begun working out his taxonomy of wit, humour and ridicule in 1750, just before John Brown's *Essays on the Characteristics* reignited the controversy over Shaftesbury's defence of ridicule.[30] Campbell made no mention of Shaftesbury in his Wise Club address or at least in the version of his remarks published in *The Philosophy of Rhetoric*. Kathleen Holcomb has argued that he deliberately avoided engaging in the dispute that Brown provoked, mainly because it revolved around the use of ridicule in religious controversy, rather than in conversation more widely construed.[31] As we saw in the last chapter, however, Brown drew attention not only to the irreligious aspects of Shaftesbury's project, but also to the issue of how ridicule relates to rhetoric, which was precisely Campbell's theme. This makes it unlikely that Campbell was simply uninterested in what Brown had to say. More likely is that by the time Campbell finally published *The Philosophy of Rhetoric* in 1776 the storm Brown caused in Scotland was well and truly over, making engagement with him less necessary.

What is certainly the case, however, is that Campbell was both aware of, and participated in, a long-running discussion in Aberdeen over how Shaftesbury's teachings might be used to refine Scottish manners and taste. George Turnbull, an influential lecturer at Marischal in the 1720s, began the debate. He was drawn to Shaftesbury and the English Deists, and even corresponded with Shaftesbury's friend Robert Molesworth, Hutcheson's sponsor in Dublin.[32] Turnbull made it his business at Marischal to sweep away scholastic pedantry in favour of modern Whig politeness.[33] His *Principles of Moral Philosophy* (1740) defended Shaftesbury's doctrine of natural sociability and held up the Earl's style up as an example of how Mandeville and other modern Epicureans might best be countered.[34]

30. Ibid., iii. On the Brown controversy see chapter 3.

31. Holcomb, 'Wit, Humour and Ridicule', 288.

32. Broadie finds it doubtful that Turnbull would have praised Toland to his students but is certain that he 'would have spoken very respectfully about Shaftesbury'. Alexander Broadie, *A History of Scottish Philosophy* (Edinburgh: Edinburgh University Press, 2010), 239.

33. Paul B. Wood, *The Aberdeen Enlightenment: The Arts Curriculum in the Eighteenth Century* (Aberdeen: Aberdeen University Press, 1993), 40.

34. George Turnbull, *The Principles of Moral Philosophy. An Enquiry into the Wise and Good Government of the Moral World*, vol. 1 (London: A. Millar, 1740), 358.

David Fordyce, Professor of Moral Philosophy at Marischal until his untimely death at sea in 1752, took up where Turnbull left off. According to Paul Wood, it was Fordyce who 'consolidated the Shaftesburian tradition of moralising' in Marischal, using his lectures on ethics to drive home to his students the importance of living in accordance with nature.[35] Fordyce also offered a qualified defence of the Shaftesburian argument that levity can outperform harshness when it comes to reforming unsociable habits. In his *Dialogues Concerning Education* Fordyce held that encouraging wit and humour 'seasons conversation' and that ridicule could usefully correct those minor vices that 'cannot fall under the correction of Law and human Tribunals'.[36] Alexander Gerard, Professor of Moral Philosophy and Logic at Marischal from 1753 and active Wise Club member, similarly limited ridicule to the correction of minor vices in his monumental *Essay on Taste*. For although 'enormous vice' was 'incongruous to the natural system of our minds', he stated, under no circumstances could it be 'ridiculous'.[37]

Campbell entered this discussion by detailing how ridicule could best play the corrective role that Shaftesbury and his followers at Marischal assigned to it. Ridicule, Campbell insisted, must be understood as fundamentally reactive, a check on what should not be done rather than a guide to what should. It is 'fitter for refuting error than for supporting truth' (a certain reference to the controversy over whether ridicule was a test of truth) and was better for keeping people from 'wrong conduct' rather than 'inciting the practice of what is right'.[38] The *faux pas* that ridicule could police were, on Campbell's account, more foolish than malignant and included 'awkwardness, rusticity, ignorance, cowardice, levity, foppery, and pedantry'.[39] When used in debate ridicule has a deflective power,

---

35. Wood, *The Aberdeen Enlightenment*, 55. For a more general account of how eighteenth-century Scottish *literati* absorbed the language of Shaftesburian politeness from their southern neighbour and used it to address a specifically Scottish agenda of commercial modernization see Nicholas Phillipson, 'Politics, Politeness and the Anglicisation of Early Eighteenth-Century Scottish Culture', in *Scotland and England 1286–1815*, ed. Roger A. Mason (Edinburgh: J. Donald Publishers, 1987), 226–46.

36. David Fordyce, *Dialogues Concerning Education*, vol. 2 (London, 1748), 252.

37. Alexander Gerard, *Essay on Taste*, vol. 1 (London: A. Millar, 1759), 68. Gerard was present for the reading of Campbell's discourse to the Wise Club and seems to make an oblique reference to Campbell's taxonomy of wit, humour and ridicule in a footnote. There he clarifies that he is 'well aware' that these three are different, but nevertheless maintains that they share a common foundation in oddness or incongruity. Ibid., 69.

38. Campbell, *The Philosophy of Rhetoric*, vol. 1, 69.

39. Ibid., 70.

blocking more serious arguments by dispelling the gravity they depend on for their persuasiveness. Citing the same passage from Aristotle's *Rhetoric* that Shaftesbury appropriated in *Sensus Communis*, Campbell recommends that speakers use the 'aid of laughter and contempt to diminish, or even quite undo, the unfriendly emotions that have been raised in the minds of the hearers'.[40]

By emphasizing the place of ridicule in persuasion, Campbell seemed to divorce it entirely from philosophical inquiry. Towards the end of his discourse, however, Campbell identifies a species of falsehood that ridicule could negate but that more serious argumentation would miss. 'Dogmas worthy of ridicule', he claimed, are 'beyond the reach of cool reasoning'.[41] Such dogmas were not false per se, but rather 'absurd' and so called for facetious rather than serious refutation. Campbell did not provide many examples of such absurdities or explain what exactly it was that made something absurd rather than false. It was left to two of his colleagues at the Wise Club, Thomas Reid and James Beattie, to furnish an example of a dangerously absurd dogma, and explain why it was important to laugh at it.

Reid, Oswald and the Shaftesburian Defence of Common Sense

Among the attendees at Campbell's discourse to the Wise Club was Thomas Reid, Regent of Arts at King's College, and later Professor of Moral Philosophy at the University of Glasgow. As a student Reid attended Marischal and studied Shaftesbury and Locke under Turnbull.[42] Later, as a minister in the Scottish Kirk, he befriended Campbell and Gerard, and joined them as Wise Club founding members. Although he was a polymath whose interests ranged from mathematics to the natural sciences, Reid's reputation today largely rests on his contributions to a common sense school of philosophy and for offering the most rigorous philosophical response to Hume to come out of Aberdeen.[43]

---

40. Ibid., 236. The passage is *Rhetoric* 3.18. For Shaftesbury's treatment of the same passage see chapter 2 above.

41. Ibid., 69–70.

42. Broadie, *History of Scottish Philosophy*, 239.

43. Whether or not there was a school of common sense philosophy is a matter of controversy. Broadie is happy to refer to a 'school' but defines its membership broadly to include Beattie. Broadie, *A History of Scottish Philosophy*, 236. Others have been less sure. The notion of a coherent common sense school of philosophy is, Paul Wood argues, of 'limited value for the purposes of historical analysis'. Wood allows that Reid, Campbell and Gerard could be said to form a school. Beattie, however, lies on the margins as he

Reid's philosophy was premised on the notion that there were certain first principles that we intuitively know to be true and 'about which it is vain to dispute'.[44] That we exist, that there is an external world, that we learn about that world through smell, hearing, taste, touch and sight, that we have knowledge of space, motion and extension: common sense principles such as these, Reid argued, constitute a kind of epistemological bedrock that no amount of arguing or disputing will be able to shift. Because they reflect the basic constitution of our nature these principles, in Heiner Klemme's helpful phrase, 'cannot be proven to be true, nor do they need such a proof'.[45]

So strong is the natural compulsion to recognize these first principles that denials of them will give rise to a kind of mental revolt frequently expressed in laughter. To support this contention Reid turned to Shaftesbury's *Sensus Communis*, a text he would have encountered during his student days under Turnbull. Shaftesbury's aim in that treatise, Reid argued in his *Essays on the Intellectual Powers of Man* (1785), was twofold: to defend the free use of ridicule in conversation, and to defend common sense against sceptical attack. On Reid's interpretation, however, these tasks went 'hand in hand' in that our sense of the ridiculous functions as a natural defence against the deniers of common sense.[46] As Reid explains: 'To discountenance absurdity nature hath given us a particular emotion . . . that of ridicule, which seems intended for this very purpose of putting out of countenance what is absurd, either in opinion or in practice.'[47]

As Giovanni Grandi has noted, Reid was careful here to stress that the absurdities targeted by ridicule could be practical as much as theoretical.[48] In the case of scepticism, however, the two forms of absurdity were

---

'did not ground his appeal to common sense in a rigorous analysis of human nature'. Paul Wood, 'Thomas Reid and the Common Sense School', in *Scottish Philosophy in the Eighteenth Century*, vol. 1, *Morals, Politics, Art, Religion*, ed. Aaron Garrett and James A. Harris (Oxford: Oxford University Press, 2015), 445.

44. Thomas Reid, *Thomas Reid on Logic, Rhetoric and the Fine Arts: Papers on the Culture of the Mind*, ed. Alexander Broadie (Edinburgh: Edinburgh University Press, 2005), 165.

45. Heiner F. Klemme, 'Scepticism and Common Sense', in *The Cambridge Companion to the Scottish Enlightenment*, ed. Alexander Broadie (Cambridge: Cambridge University Press, 2006), 128.

46. Thomas Reid, *Essays on the Intellectual Powers of Man*, ed. Derek R. Brookes and Knud Haakonssen (Edinburgh: Edinburgh University Press, 2002), 429.

47. Ibid., 462.

48. Giovanni B. Grandi, 'Reid on Ridicule and Common Sense', *Journal of Scottish Philosophy* 6, 1 (2008), 71–90.

intertwined; philosophical absurdities led inexorably to absurd behaviour. As a consequence, Reid affirmed, sceptics who stray too far from the path of common sense to win attention justifiably became laughing stocks. Berkeley's idealism, for instance, was laughed at because people were generally unwilling to 'offer up their common sense as a sacrifice to metaphysics'.[49] In a Latin oration delivered at a graduation ceremony in King's College in Aberdeen, Reid even made it a rule that philosophers should avoid 'overthrowing common notions' lest they make themselves into an 'object of public derision'.[50] Philosophers like Hume who give reasons to doubt first principles, Reid told his audience, should not be seen not as practising philosophy at all but either to be 'playing a game or to be mad'.[51] Elsewhere Reid went so far as to insist that such figures should never be 'reasoned against' but only 'despised or laughed at'.[52]

Unfortunately, Reid warned, even gamesters and madmen could occasionally be persuasive. For while the emotion of ridicule was generally reliable as a test of absurdity, it could be 'stifled'.[53] If an absurd belief or doctrine happened to stir religious dread, for example, then it will be 'no longer a laughable matter'.[54] Similarly, absurdities that conform to popular prejudices or serve powerful interests could also escape detection. Philosophers committed to scepticism, moreover, were adept at disabling common sense or leading it astray.[55] By presenting their arguments with 'gravity and solemnity', Reid held, sceptics like Hume frequently disguised absurdities as propositions worthy of debate and so spared themselves the popular derision that would otherwise moderate their behaviour.[56] Only when that absurdity was 'stripped of the adventitious circumstances from which it borrowed its importance and authority', Reid suggested, could the 'natural emotion of ridicule' have room to once again 'exert its

49. Thomas Reid, *An Inquiry into the Human Mind, On the Principles of Common Sense*, ed. Derek R. Brookes (Edinburgh: Edinburgh University Press, 1997), 75.

50. Thomas Reid, *The Philosophical Orations of Thomas Reid: Delivered at Graduation Ceremonies King's College, Aberdeen, 1753, 1756, 1759, 1762*, ed. D. D Todd, trans. Shirley Darcus Sullivan (Carbondale: Southern Illinois University Press, 1989), 49. In another graduation oration Reid declared it 'difficult to refute' Hume in a 'serious manner'. Ibid., 56.

51. Ibid., 50. An example of such a philosophical absurdity might be de Selby's theory in his *Golden Hours* that night is caused by an accretion of black air from volcanic eruptions.

52. Reid, *Thomas Reid on Logic, Rhetoric and the Fine Arts*, 165.

53. Reid, *Essays on the Intellectual Powers of Man*, 462.

54. Ibid.

55. Our sense of ridicule was thus not unlike Rousseau's general will in that it was incapable of error but prone to being misled or corrupted.

56. Reid, *Essays on the Intellectual Powers of Man*, 462.

force'.[57] All that was required was for 'someone who has the skill or the boldness to pull off the mask'.[58]

It is not clear whether Reid considered himself among those witty and skilful enough to unmask absurdities in this manner.[59] More often than not he summoned others to the task:

> Mere Laughing is surely no Argument & whatever force it has may be employed for Error as well as Truth. [T]hose who deny first Principles may be often Ridiculed in a fair way by displaying the Consequences of their Opinion & the conduct in Life which they naturally lead to. The Sceptical System opens a large field for Wit Humour & Ridicule of this kind which a Lucian or a Swift would know how to improve[.] Should any such Genius ever attempt this manner of confuting Scepticks I think it would be fair dealing. For surely that opinion must be truly ridiculous which has ridiculous consequences & [implies] A Ridiculous Conduct in Life.[60]

Reid begins this passage by scotching the notion, long associated with Shaftesbury, that ridicule is a straightforward test of truth. Whatever else it might be capable of, he says, ridicule cannot substitute for argument and has no intrinsic truth-revealing properties (reason and ridicule have separate 'offices', he elsewhere writes, and just as reason cannot be called on to refute absurdity so ridicule is useless against error[61]). What Reid argues next is of greater interest, however. Not only does he defend ridiculing sceptics, he suggests that the scope for doing so has been so far underexplored. The sceptics, in other words, still await their satirist. Moreover, the style of satire Reid thinks is suitable for such a task is that of two writers, Lucian and Swift, known for ridiculing absurdities in *religion*, suggesting a curious symmetry between religious superstition, on the one hand, and scepticism, on the other. Both sceptics and the superstitious, Reid implies, are equally distanced from common sense and so both are equally in need of a satirist to return them to it.

57. Ibid., 463.

58. Ibid. This should qualify Peter Diamond's claim that Reid 'does not appear to have been very worried about the practical effects of scepticism'. Peter J. Diamond, 'Rhetoric and Philosophy in the Social Thought of Thomas Reid', in *Sociability and Society in Eighteenth-Century Scotland*, ed. John Dwyer and Richard B. Sher (Edinburgh: Mercat Press, 1993), 63.

59. Reid does occasionally take on the role of satirist. See, for instance, his allegory of the Idomenians, a people seduced away from common sense by cunning sceptical philosophers, in chapter 6 of his *Inquiry into the Human Mind*.

60. Reid, *Thomas Reid on Logic, Rhetoric and the Fine Arts*, 171.

61. Reid, *Essays on the Intellectual Powers of Man*, 462.

If sceptics were ridiculous, however, then were they not also harmless? Hume, Reid's likely target in the above passage, had insisted that sceptics could be safely left to their own devices because the demands of common life would eventually compel them to moderate their scepticism. To some extent Reid concurred. For Reid, the fate of Hume's counterparts in the ancient world offered comforting confirmation that scepticism's hold on society was always tenuous and would weaken further if its proponents were simply ignored. Because it was such an obvious 'insult upon the common sense of mankind', Reid assured his readers, Pyrrhonian scepticism had 'died away of itself'.[62] That modern scepticism had already been 'allowed a hearing' demonstrated that it was a more formidable opponent.[63] Even so, Reid expressed confidence that once this new breed of scepticism had 'lost the grace of novelty' it too would 'die away', and for this reason 'should never be refuted'.[64] For Reid, then, ridiculing scepticism in the vein of a Lucian or Swift is permissible, but should also be unnecessary. At best it could accelerate popular dismissal of a philosophy whose noxiousness to common sense condemned it to irrelevance anyway.

Reid was not alone in doubting the wisdom of refuting sceptics. A fellow minister and philosopher, James Oswald (who also studied at King's) issued an even starker warning to this effect in his 1766 *Appeal to Common Sense in Behalf of Religion*.[65] As with Reid, Oswald began by arguing that our taste for the ridiculous reveals something about common sense. The very fact that we laugh at satirical depictions of vice, he argued, was proof of the existence of common sense in matters of morality. Oswald conceded that the 'men of wit and humour' tended to exaggerate human vice.[66] But if they could not depend on a minimal shared understanding of vice and

62. Ibid., 461.

63. Ibid.

64. Ibid. Reid, of course, *did* refute Hume at length in several of his writings, suggesting that Hume was the sort of sceptic that had to be engaged at least somewhat seriously. In his *Essays on the Active Powers of Man* Reid acknowledged that it would be 'disrespectful' of Hume not to engage with its arguments even if the process of proving first principles 'appears ridiculous'. Thomas Reid, *Essays on the Active Powers of Man*, ed. Knud Haakonssen and James A. Harris (Edinburgh: Edinburgh University Press, 2010), 19. For an excellent account of Reid's philosophical arguments against scepticism, one that acknowledges Reid's occasional sympathy with various sceptical positions, see Nicholas Wolterstorff, *Thomas Reid and the Story of Epistemology* (Cambridge: Cambridge University Press, 2000), chapter 8.

65. Richard B. Sher and M. A Stewart, 'James Oswald', *Oxford Dictionary of National Biography* (Oxford: Oxford University Press, 2004).

66. James Oswald, *An Appeal to Common Sense in Behalf of Religion*, vol. 1 (Edinburgh: A. Kincaid and J. Bell, 1766), 302.

virtue then their readers could not be 'entertained and improven [*sic*] as they are by such writings'.[67] The reception of Mandeville's *Fable of the Bees* was a case in point. Mandeville's attempt to expose moral distinctions as 'false and fantastical' caused 'no small alarm' because his portrait of commercial society seemed so worryingly true to life.[68] But this panic, Oswald held, derived from a confusion of common opinion with common sense. Had Mandeville's readers consulted the latter, they could have realized that Mandeville's satire was so disquieting precisely because it triggered our *natural* repugnance to vice, a reaction that demonstrated what Mandeville had denied.

As with Reid, to affirm common sense was also to affirm the futility of arguing with sceptics. For Oswald, 'reasoning with sceptics and infidels about primary truths doth more harm than good' because it increased popular fascination with what the sceptics had to say and encouraged people to treat as debatable propositions truths they had previously taken for granted, particularly in matters of religion.[69] Instead, therefore, of 'heaping up arguments on arguments, and volumes on volumes, in confutation of manifest absurdities', Oswald pleaded, another solution had to be found.[70]

Ridicule was one possibility but by no means the most promising one. Like Reid, Oswald saw nothing wrong with mocking sceptics, but doubted the efficacy of such a tactic in a Scotland dominated, as he saw it, by hypocritically enforced rules of decorum. For although sceptics had already 'seduced the thoughtless' by making the 'capital truths of religion a subject of mirth and drollery' defenders of religion were debarred from hitting back in the same way out of fear being labelled offensive.[71] A 'politeness carried to an excess', Oswald grumbled, would always be hospitable to sceptics and forbidding to their opponents.[72] The only alternative was to try to persuade sceptics that the reasoning they professed to rely on was nothing of the sort, because reasoning itself required belief in certain foundational truths.[73] Because they refused to assent to these primary truths, Oswald claimed, what sceptics

---

67. Ibid., 303.
68. Ibid.
69. Ibid., 312.
70. Ibid., 315.
71. Ibid., 328.
72. Ibid., 329.
73. Reasoning, as Oswald defined it, was the 'skill of tracing the connection between first and secondary truths'. Ibid., 332.

called reasoning was really just 'unmeaning talk'.[74] If they could not be brought to recognize this then there was nothing to be gained from engaging them at all.

Beattie's Essay on Truth *and the Attack on Hume*

For another Aberdeen philosopher, James Beattie, relying on the hope that modern scepticism would fade away on its own was irresponsible, a dereliction of philosophical duty. Beattie, who replaced Gerard as Professor of Moral Philosophy and Logic at Marischal in 1760, placed little faith in Oswald's strategy of urging the sceptics to reconsider their rejection of first principles. Instead, in his own response to Hume, the 1770 *Essay on the Nature and Immutability of Truth; in Opposition to Sophistry and Scepticism*, Beattie opted for all-out *ad hominem* assault. Nothing else, he reckoned, could successfully diminish both sceptical philosophy itself and the man who dared propagate it. The range of mockery he assailed Hume with over the course of the essay was impressive. He accused Hume of only having read the chapter titles of Aristotle, imagined an alien learning about Hume's arguments and dismissing them as absurd, and implied that sceptics like Hume were so suspicious of their own sense experience that only 'insensibility' could permit them to 'endure existence'.[75]

Notwithstanding its huge success at the time (it won plaudits from Johnson's circle in London and earned Beattie both an honorary Oxford degree and a Royal pension) Beattie's *Essay* has often been viewed by philosophers as a bit of an embarrassment, a histrionic screed written by poet clearly out of his depth with philosophical argument.[76] Even Beattie's

---

74. Ibid., 333.

75. James Beattie, *An Essay on the Nature and Immutability of Truth; in Opposition to Sophistry and Scepticism* (London: A. Kincaid & J. Bell, 1770), 460. The virulence of Beattie's assault on Hume casts doubt on Rhona Brown's assertion that 'avoidance of personal attack . . . is a feature of Beattie's philosophical writings'. Rhona Brown, 'The Long-Lost James Beattie: The Rediscovery of "The Grotesquiad"', *The Review of English Studies* 65, 270 (2014), 461.

76. Remarking on Beattie's relationship to metaphysics, Phillipson writes: 'he was neither able to understand nor master the subject on which his career and his fame rested'. Nicholas Phillipson, 'James Beattie and the Defence of Common Sense', in *Festschrift für Rainer Gruenter*, ed. Bernhard Fabian (Heidelberg: Carl Winter, 1978), 151. This brutal verdict is not uncommon. Gavin Ardley thought that Beattie was 'out of his depth' when it came to philosophy, which is why he was 'no match' for Hume. Gavin Ardley, 'Hume's Common Sense Critics', *Revue Internationale de Philosophie* 30, 115–16 (1976), 116. Sophia Rosenfeld similarly regards Beattie as the 'considerably less original and more overheated' popularizer of the philosophy of common sense. Rosenfeld, *Common Sense: A Political*

companions in the Aberdeen Philosophical Society, determined though they might have been to rebut Hume, worried that Beattie had stretched the limits of politeness. But Beattie both anticipated these objections to his approach and (to his mind at least) met them. Those brave enough to aggressively counter a philosophy like scepticism that was popular with polite urbanites of Edinburgh would be 'hooted at' for their 'want of breeding', he predicted.[77] But they should persevere regardless. All methods, short of physical coercion or persecution, were fair game against scepticism. In one ominous passage, Beattie declared that he would be 'extremely sorry to see any other weapon employed' against them than 'reason and ridicule' (a phrase that bears an unfortunate resemblance to a threat) but made clear that both of the latter should be used freely and often.[78]

The rationale behind Beattie's belligerent stance was that a philosophy like Hume's could be absurd and dangerous all at once.[79] That Campbell and Reid, Hume's more formidable philosophical opponents, were prepared to show politeness to Hume even as they expressed disagreement with him was proof to Beattie that they had failed to fully grasp this danger. Campbell's 1762 *Dissertation on Miracles* had balanced its refutation of Hume's argument against miracles with lavish praise for Hume himself.[80] For Campbell, it was precisely Hume's 'justly procur'd' reputation as thinker, historian, and essayist that protected his irreligious arguments from immediate dismissal.[81] Campbell even acknowledged (earnestly) that his own skills in abstract reasoning had been greatly improved by engaging the work of his 'astute and ingenious adversary'.[82] And although

History, 73. Beattie's contemporaries, by contrast, took him seriously as a philosopher and his reputation as a thinker only started to decline in the 1830s. See R.J.W. Mills, 'The Reception of "That Bigoted Silly Fellow" James Beattie's Essay on Truth in Britain 1770–1830', *History of European Ideas* 48, 8 (2015), 1049–79.

77. Beattie, *Essay on Truth*, 360.

78. Ibid., 361.

79. Why 'so much zeal in refuting [scepticism]?' he asked rhetorically. 'Because it is immoral and pernicious, as well as implausible and absurd.' Ibid., 170. Beattie complained to William Forbes that 'Hobbes, Hume, Mandeville, and even Locke' (all sceptics in Beattie's view), were 'votaries of a frivolous yet dangerous philosophy'. Beattie to Sir William Forbes, 17 January 1768. James Beattie, *The Letters of James Beattie, Chronologically Arranged from Sir W. Forbes's Collection*, vol. 1 (London: John Sharpe, 1820), 46.

80. George Campbell, *Dissertation on Miracles* (Edinburgh: A. Kincaid & J. Bell, 1762), v–vi. As Suderman puts it, 'Campbell answered Hume not as an outraged Calvinist minister but as an empirical philosopher'. Jeffrey M. Suderman, 'Religion and Philosophy', in *Scottish Philosophy in the Eighteenth Century*, vol. 1, *Morals, Politics, Art, Religion*, 229.

81. Campbell, *Dissertation on Miracles*, vi.

82. Ibid., vii.

he admitted to occasional and 'unavoidable' lapses into an 'air of ridicule', he nevertheless insisted that he opposed Hume with nothing but argument.[83] Reid too had been careful to juxtapose criticism of the philosophy with praise of the philosopher.

What irked Beattie most was the cosy rapport he perceived Campbell and Reid to have developed with Hume (he was aghast, for example, that they had allowed Hume to review their criticisms of his arguments in manuscript before going to print).[84] In his correspondence Beattie lamented the 'extraordinary adulation' that Reid and Campbell paid to Hume and attacked their decision to pay 'compliments to a man's heart' while at the same time 'proving that his aim [was] to subvert the very principles of truth, virtue, and religion'.[85] But Beattie's complaint here was born of confusion at what Campbell and Reid had done. Their aim had been to spell out what they saw as inconsistencies and fallacies internal to Hume's *arguments*. Neither, however, had speculated about the motives Hume might have had in advancing those arguments. To Beattie's mind this reluctance to impute bad motives to Hume was an act of moral negligence that he was determined not to repeat. He would never 'depart from the Christian and philosophical character' and so would treat Hume with greater 'freedom' than his other critics had done, exposing 'his faults' (as opposed to those of his arguments) for the 'sake of truth and mankind'.[86] Displaying impressive prescience, Beattie was fully aware that adopting such tactics would invite the charge that he was a 'sullen and illiberal bigot'.[87] Sure enough, Hume would later complain to William Strahan of that 'bigoted, silly fellow, Beattie'.[88]

The above criticism of Campbell and Reid was contained in a private letter. In 'The Castle of Scepticism', an allegory written as a graduation address to his students at Marischal, Beattie showed that he was also content to upbraid them publicly.[89] In it, Beattie journeys to a castle where

83. Ibid., viii.

84. 'The courtesies shown to Hume by Reid', Phillipson notes, 'are legendary'. Phillipson, 'James Beattie and the Defence of Common Sense,' 149.

85. Beattie to Thomas Blacklock. 9 January 1769. Beattie, *The Letters of James Beattie*, vol. 1, 61.

86. Ibid., 65.

87. Ibid., 61.

88. Hume to William Strahan. 20 October 1775. Hume, *The Letters of David Hume*, vol. 2, 301.

89. The text is produced in full in James Beattie, 'Beattie's "The Castle of Scepticism": An Unpublished Allegory Against Hume, Voltaire and Hobbes', ed. Ernest Campbell Mossner, *Studies in English* 27, 1 (1948), 108–45.

he encounters several philosophical sceptics engaged in outlandish behaviour, including Voltaire, Hume and Hobbes. Mossner has interpreted this allegory as yet another attack on Hume (with sideswipes along the way at other sceptics), and with good reason. Hume certainly bears the brunt of Beattie's abuse: the allegory opens with Beattie falling asleep while reading a copy of Hume's *Essays* before dreaming that he is among a crowd travelling to a gothic fortress where Humean sceptics are engaged in outrageous experiments (one takes his distrust of sense experience so far as to gouge his own eyes out). But Beattie's tale does much more than make fun of sceptics. It also highlights how dangerously persuasive they can be, their absurdity notwithstanding, and thus calls into question the judgment of those like Reid and Campbell, who were naïve enough to believe that argument alone could discredit it.

The part played by Voltaire in 'The Castle of Scepticism' illustrates the point Beattie was trying to make. This 'lean, little old man' enters the action with a 'strange sarcastic' grin and immediately laughs at Beattie for having some sympathy with the Leibnizian argument that providence has organized the world for the best.[90] Voltaire then tells a 'tedious' tale, the entire humorous effect of which hinges on his repeating the phrase 'the best of all possible worlds' every minute accompanied by what Beattie calls 'droll gesticulations' (we can imagine him waving his arms around and pulling faces).[91] Beattie thus reduces Voltaire's satire to a piece of pitiful buffoonery but at the same time implies that Voltaire's antics not only make people laugh but also *convince* them. So delighted is Voltaire with the warm reception he receives that he offers to write several more pieces of the same sort in order to finally 'exterminate that scoundrel religion from the face of the earth'.[92] Beattie's none-too-subtle point is that even poorly executed or crude satire can prompt an audience to laugh at something that they should really revere with awe. That a sceptic's attack on religion is bereft of wit, Beattie warns, takes little away from its power.

Those, like Reid, who were insufficiently alert to this danger, were just as ridiculous as Voltaire, and so Beattie mocks them too. As Beattie joins the crowd walking in haste towards Hume's castle, he meets a man 'of great learning' (unnamed but identifiable as Reid) who is the 'declared adversary' of Hume.[93] Puzzled as to why Reid would be among those flocking to see a sceptic, Beattie hears from him how 'ingenious' Hume is as a

90. Ibid., 138.
91. Ibid., 140.
92. Ibid., 140.
93. Ibid., 120.

philosopher and how 'wonderful' he is as a man, notwithstanding the fact that his views were 'contrived in absurdity and folly'.[94] Beattie walks away still more perplexed and suggests that Reid may have been 'ironical' in his praise of Hume for fear of causing offence to the 'listening multitude'.[95]

There are numerous ways to interpret this scene, but none are flattering to Reid. On the one hand Beattie seems to believe that alluding to Reid's praise for Hume's character will show how Reid entangled himself in a practical contradiction; by denouncing Hume's philosophy as absurd and yet praising his ingenuity, Reid exposes himself as absurd. By the end, however, a different possibility emerges. Reid might not be ridiculous but more like a cowardly conformist, moving along with the crowd and parroting their praise of Hume (which he knows is unmerited) simply for fear of causing offence to a polite Scottish society taken in by this new philosophical trend. To Beattie this was the height of irresponsibility. For even if Reid's praise for Hume was insincere, it could still mislead the public into believing that Hume was harmless. If Reid had been serious about ridding society of scepticism, then he should at the very least have withheld praise for the philosopher when he refuted the philosophy.

In the end, Beattie's own approach to countering scepticism wavered between faith that its repugnance to common sense would kill it in the end, and alarm that normalizing it as a respectable philosophy could allow its advocates to distort the minds of the public. For while Reid hoped common sense would ultimately prove 'invincible' to sceptical attack, Beattie's *Essay on Truth* showed that he was far less sure of its invulnerability.[96] Building on an earlier insight from Reid, Beattie argued that philosophers who adopt an imposing air of philosophical rigour could cause people to doubt not only what they *believe* but what they actually *know*. Shaftesbury had warned that overbearing clerics frequently adopted a serious demeanour to deceive, and he gave gentlemanly wits the task of puncturing such false gravity with humour. Beattie showed that these clerical tactics could be imitated by the gentleman philosophers themselves. Hume, he warns, 'imposes on us' by the 'solemnity' of his mode of expressing himself.[97] By

94. Ibid., 120. Reid, in one of his own graduation orations at King's, declared that Hume was 'outstanding for his metaphysical acuteness and his genius'. Reid, *Philosophical Orations*, 55.

95. Beattie, 'Castle of Scepticism', 121.

96. Reid, *Essays on the Active Powers of Man*. As James Fieser has shown, Beattie would eventually revise this common sense theory of truth, retreating to a position where common sense is merely a guide to truth and not its criterion. James Fieser, 'The Rise and Fall of James Beattie's Common-Sense Theory of Truth', *Monist* 90, 2 (2007), 287–96.

97. Beattie, *Essay on Truth*, 155.

adopting such a highfalutin tone, Hume sapped his readers' confidence and made them question whether they had 'sagacity enough' to understand him, instead of dismissing his writings as 'absurd and unintelligible'.[98] What Shaftesbury had not anticipated but Beattie insisted on, was that people could be awed into doubt as well as into credulity.

It was clear, for Beattie, that the class of people most likely to be duped in this manner were the polite urbanites of Edinburgh. By contrast, much firmer resistance to scepticism could be expected from the lower orders who could see through Hume's bombast and pre-emptively judge his philosophy ridiculous. It is a striking feature of Beattie's *Essay* that he tempered his distrust of democracy (particularly evident in his later writings) to present the lower classes as having a more solid grasp on common sense than their more refined social superiors. 'In the lower walks of life', Beattie predicted, Hume 'will oftener be the object of ridicule than detestation'.[99] Not that Hume would notice. To philosophers like him, Beattie sneered, the 'vulgar are seldom objects of curiosity'.[100] It followed that the more democratic a society was, the safer common sense would be. 'Democratical governments', he urged, 'are more favourable to simplicity of manners, and consequently to the knowledge of the human mind, than our modern monarchies'.[101] As a teacher at Marischal, Beattie worked hard to polish his students' habits of speech in preparation for polite society. But he was keenly wary that with politeness also came the risk of alienation from common sense, as the fashionable practice of philosophy could loosen high society's grip on even the most fundamental of beliefs.

Commentators on Scottish common sense philosophy have stressed the democratic potential lurking latent within the philosophical programme that Reid inaugurated. If common sense was within the reach of all, then the poor and uneducated could access basic truths just as readily as erudite philosophers conversant in the latest trends from the republic of letters. When judging first principles, Reid asserted, the 'Philosopher and the day-labourer' were 'upon a level'.[102] (The day-labourer may even have a firmer grasp on such principles because they were safely removed from philosophical disputes that bring enjoyment but also foster doubt.) Sophia Rosenfeld has even suggested that eighteenth-century Aberdeen was the

98. Ibid.
99. Ibid., 449.
100. Ibid., 467.
101. Ibid., 468.
102. Reid, *Essays on the Intellectual Powers of Man*, 461. When it came to common sense, therefore, the 'few must yield to the many'. Ibid.

birthplace of a 'populist epistemology', one that democrats on both sides of the Atlantic could later exploit, even if this flew in the face of the social conservatism of the Scots who developed it.[103]

The case of Beattie, however, illustrates that the common sense philosophers were already alert to that democratic potential and did not necessarily seek to hide it. If polite society of Edinburgh and London proved welcoming to Humean scepticism then Beattie preferred to cast his lot in with the vulgar, no matter if he was dismissed as boorish or unrefined as a consequence. Even if Beattie's own ridicule of Hume failed to discredit the latter in the eyes of polite North Britons, their impolite counterparts could be relied on to carry the torch of common sense.

Beattie had democratized ridicule to the point where an incredulous scoff from a day-labourer competed for dignity with the arguments of a philosopher like Hume. The vulgarizing implications of this combination of ridicule and common sense did not go unnoticed or unchallenged. Most influentially, Joseph Priestley retorted that Beattie and company had achieved the exact opposite of what they intended. Rather than securing the bonds of common life from the corrosiveness of scepticism, they had made it easier for individuals to dogmatically regard their own gut instincts as incontestable guides to truth. Because Beattie's common sense 'admits of no appeal to reason', Priestley contended, it permitted 'everyman to think himself authorised to pronounce decisively upon every question according to his present feeling' and denounce anyone whose feelings directed otherwise as ridiculous.[104] Even atheists, Priestley goaded, could convince themselves that their instinctive feeling that God did not exist was the voice of common sense. What was meant to shore up community would thus end either in solipsism, with each individual becoming her own judge of what common sense dictated in any given case, or in a crude epistemological majoritarianism where questions of truth would be decided by 'vote'.[105]

Either way, Priestley predicted, the effect on polite debate would be disastrous. Appealing to common sense in order to dismiss an opponent as absurd 'creates arrogance' among participants and encourages each side to regard the other as made up of 'ideots [sic] and madmen'.[106] Priestley drove

103. Rosenfeld, *Common Sense*, 62.
104. Joseph Priestley, *An Examination of Dr. Reid's Inquiry into the Human Mind on the Principles of Common Sense, Dr. Beattie's Essay on the Nature and Immutability of Truth, and Dr Oswald's Appeal to Common Sense in Behalf of Religion* (London: J. Johnson, 1774), 121.
105. Ibid., 134.
106. Ibid., 122.

the point home by drawing on the story of Elijah's mockery of the priests of Baal. For Priestley, Beattie's appeal to common sense was analogous to hapless priests summoning a false god, a desperate plea to an authority who may be asleep or away on a journey but is in any case absent. In doing so, Priestley showed how the most popular scriptural justification for the use of ridicule to correct error could also be deployed to expose the limits of appealing to any common standard of the ridiculous. Priestley closed his argument with a stinging comparison between common sense philosophers and the man who inspired them: 'There is some doubt whether Shaftesbury was really in earnest in proposing ridicule as the test of truth. . . . Whereas there can be no doubt that this triumvirate of authors are perfectly serious.'[107] Shaftesbury may have been joking; Reid, Beattie and Oswald had no such excuse.

Beattie's Essay on Laughter *and the Modern Sources of Humour*

Beattie's disillusionment with his Wise Club companions did not prevent him from borrowing heavily from their ideas and taking them in new directions. When Beattie published a volume of essays in 1776, he included a long work, 'On Laughter and Ludicrous Composition', that owed much to Campbell in particular. Unlike Reid, Beattie was not in attendance when Campbell delivered his 1758 discourse on wit, humour and ridicule to the Wise Club. Nor is there much evidence that he and Campbell communicated much on the subject before 1776 when they finally exchanged manuscripts before going to press (evidently Beattie had now forgiven Campbell for his politeness towards Hume). Both philosophers were struck by how closely their arguments were aligned. In his *Philosophy of Rhetoric*, Campbell acknowledged a 'remarkable coincidence of sentiments' between his own work and Beattie's. When his *Essays* were published the same year, Beattie returned the compliment, claiming a section he had planned on the distinctions between wit, humour and ridicule was no longer needed because Campbell's 'masterly disquisition' had already covered that ground.[108] Beattie was equally pleased to find that his reflections on the causes of laughter had also been 'fully warranted' by those of his 'learned and ingenious friend'.[109]

107. Ibid., 153.
108. James Beattie, *Essays* (Edinburgh: William Creech; and for E. & C. Dilly, 1776), 326.
109. Ibid.

This mutual backslapping should not disguise the fact that Beattie's essay was a very different kind of work to Campbell's. For starters, Beattie investigated laughter as a subject in its own right, rather than as a piece of a general system of rhetoric. Moreover, Beattie's was a comparative study in the spirit of Montesquieu and included a lengthy analysis of how social and political arrangements determine the level and type of humour found in different societies. They did, however, share a common starting point; a determination to displace Hobbes's theory of laughter with something closer to the incongruity theory that Hutcheson had first defended.

Beattie's antipathy to Hobbes's views on laughter was so intense that he engaged in a kind of meta-critique by making a burlesque of it. In the same 1764 graduation address mentioned above, Beattie caricatured Hobbesian laughter as a sadistic joy at the pain of others. Fittingly for a philosopher who placed great stock in fear, Hobbes appears in Beattie's story stationed behind a ditch and rampart, bedecked with armour, and with a cocked blunderbuss rifle in each hand. As Beattie approaches Hobbes's ditch, he trips on uneven ground, causing Hobbes to burst out laughing. His laughter quickly subsides, however, when Hobbes realizes that Beattie is unhurt. Hobbes immediately makes known his disappointment that Beattie had not broken his neck as if he had done so it would have been 'the prettiest jest' he had seen in a while.[110] He then launches into his definition of laughter (which Beattie reproduces directly from *Leviathan*) before spelling out its consequences. If laughter is sudden glory arising from superiority then

> it is impossible not to be greatly diverted when we see a beast, an idiot, a diseased person, a blind and lame beggar, or a dead man, who are so much and so obviously our inferiors in health, riches, understanding, sense, and activity.[111]

Again, on this caricatured version of Hobbes's argument, the elements of surprise and strangeness that were integral to Hobbes's actual view of laughter are omitted. And once more laughter at others becomes a reflexive response to the perception of pain in another, rather than an altogether avoidable habit of those who bolster their self-esteem through illusory triumphs.

It is easy to dismiss Beattie's allegory as a juvenile attempt to win a few laughs at a graduation ceremony. But Beattie's 'Essay on Laughter'

110. Beattie, 'Castle of Scepticism', 141.
111. Ibid.

shows that he took the need to discredit Hobbes extremely seriously. Echoing Hutcheson and Campbell, Beattie objected that pride usually resulted in a stern demeanour rather than levity and that if Hobbes were correct then the 'wise, the beautiful, the strong, the healthy, and the rich' must 'giggle away a great part of their lives' because they would so often find themselves in the company of inferiors.[112] Isaac Newton himself, Beattie quipped, must have been the 'greatest wag of all time' (again ignoring Hobbes's actual claim that, on the contrary, the great were *less* inclined to laugh than others).[113] In response to these shortcomings Beattie defined the object of laughter as 'an opposition of suitableness and unsuitableness' contained in the same 'assemblage', a refinement of Hutcheson's argument that laughter was grounded in the opposition of meanness and dignity.[114]

To challenge the reductive nature of Hobbes's argument, however, was not to deny the place of contempt in laughter entirely. As Campbell had before him, Beattie recognized that contemptuous laughter was not only possible, but useful for shaming the unsociable and spurring the moral development of those made to laugh at them. 'If', Beattie hoped, 'we can be prevailed on to laugh' at 'follies and vices' then 'our moral reformation may be presumed to be in some forwardness'.[115] Crucially, for Beattie, it was not enough to laugh contentedly at vice; a measure of pride, resentment, or even hatred was necessary as well. In other words, for laughter to have a hope of reforming anyone, it was necessary to make vice ridiculous rather than merely ludicrous. Certainly, treating vice purely as a source of amusement would do more harm than good: 'If we laugh at our faults without despising them, that is, if they appear ludicrous only, and not ridiculous, it is to be feared that one will love rather than hate them.'[116] In other words, if our vices make us laugh without causing us any discomfort, then we will indulge them all the more so that the entertainment may continue.

Beattie not only deemed it inappropriate to laugh at truly vicious acts; he claimed that our mental make-up rendered it nearly impossible. In the event of a clash between serious emotions and the risible, the former will always win out and smother the urge to laugh. Fear, Beattie asserted, will almost always 'repress' laughter (though we might fake a laugh to conceal our fear) no matter how 'incongruous' the frightening object might

112. Beattie, *Essays*, 336.
113. Ibid.
114. Ibid., 348.
115. Ibid., 425.
116. Ibid.

be. Anger too was a 'preservative against risible impressions'.[117] For Beattie, a man with a wooden leg certainly exhibits incongruity, but only the inhumane will laugh at him.[118] Such laughers are not so much ticklish as depraved and will be 'blamed by every good man' for whom pity at the man's plight easily overrides any other sensation.[119] Ultimately, then, the category of behaviours that laughter corrects was ambiguous. Such behaviours had to be objectionable enough to spark *some* kind of negative affect to mix with the laughter, but not so serious that laughter becomes overwhelmed by more powerful, serious emotions. Arrogance and vanity could be ridiculous; malice could not.

In the final part of his essay Beattie went far beyond Campbell by attempting to explain variation in the quantity and type of humour across different societies and époques. Beattie took it for granted that Britain boasted a vibrant and increasingly refined comic culture, one in which cruder and abusive forms of ridicule had been displaced by more polished satires on manners.[120] This was in stark contrast to ancient societies which had either produced little by way of humour, as in the case of Rome (Plautus, Juvenal and Horace were apparently the exceptions that proved the rule), or which preferred coarser forms of farce or character assassination.[121] To account for these differences Beattie looked to the contrasting social structures of ancient and modern societies. Modern commercial societies such as Britain, Beattie argued, were teeming with differences of occupation, class, faction and faith. And while such differences could give rise to friction, they also had explosive comic potential as notions of suitableness and unsuitableness, normalcy and oddity, varied dramatically across different social groupings.

What Beattie called 'modern gallantry' was a particularly potent contributor to the gaiety of modern societies.[122] Beattie remarked approvingly

117. Ibid., 430.

118. Ibid., 431.

119. Ibid.

120. Not everyone agreed with this assumption. William Kenrick, writing in the *London Review*, objected that since the decline of the court jester 'the great' laughed less and that elite culture was in a 'sad, dull state'. William Kenrick, *The London Review of English and Foreign Literature* 5 (1777), 88.

121. Addison in *The Spectator* attributed the increased mirth among the moderns to the demise of ancient simplicity. For Addison, simplicity allowed the ancients to excel in 'noble Sciences' such as 'Poetry, Painting, Oratory, History, Architecture'. Frivolous moderns, by contrast, would have to settle for accomplishments in 'Doggerel, Humour, Burlesque, and all the trivial Arts of Ridicule'. *The Spectator* no. 249 (15 December 1711), 1.

122. Beattie, *Essays*, 472.

on how the legal subordination of women to men in modern societies had been 'amply compensated' for by a culture of gallantry that admitted them to the sphere of polite conversation.[123] As Sylvia Sebastiani has shown, for philosophers like Beattie women were key to the civilizing process, softening the 'rough character of the male' and encouraging a gentler sociability than was to be found in many non-European societies or in previous stages of historical development.[124] For Beattie, a further happy upshot of permitting women to politely converse with men was that they injected diversity into what might otherwise have been a culturally uniform all-male (and humourless) environment. Their presence, as he saw it, would encourage better manners but also better laughs. For the 'freaks and foibles of the female world', Beattie insisted, 'supply a rich fund of humorous entertainment'.[125]

To Beattie's mind the mixing of the sexes encouraged by gallantry was just one more example of how incongruity was humorous. But the matter was not so clear-cut. After all, if laughter at incongruity was all that was at issue then we might expect the women to have been laughing at the men's 'foibles' as well. But in Beattie's example women clearly function as objects of laughter rather than joining in shared laughs at commonly perceived differences. For Beattie, it was vital for women to be admitted to polite conversation, but once there he reduced them to polishers of male speech and sources of male entertainment. The male laughter resulting from these conversations may not have been Hobbesian in its egoism (the men may laugh in a group), but it was a laugh of superiority all the same. The behaviours exhibited by women in Beattie's ideal social universe were not just odd or incongruent; they were also ridiculous.

An important subtext of Beattie's argument was that a shift towards greater equality, whether between classes or sexes, would dry up several rich sources of humour. This was nowhere more apparent than in Beattie's views on how the type of political regime in a country affected the laughing habits of its citizens.[126] Republics in particular were hostile to

123. Ibid.
124. Silvia Sebastiani, *The Scottish Enlightenment: Race, Gender, and the Limits of Progress* (New York: Palgrave Macmillan, 2013), 137.
125. Beattie, *Essays*, 473.
126. Beattie's decision to compare the effects of different political regimes on laughter probably owed something to Montesquieu. For Montesquieu, monarchies were more permissive of satirical writings than other regimes because kings saw value in allowing subjects to harmlessly let off steam in a manner unthreatening to the regime as a whole, even if this meant that the monarch himself might be subjected to satire occasionally. Montesquieu, *The Spirit of the Laws* (Cambridge: Cambridge University Press, 1989), 200.

the ludicrous because the ethos of equality fatally undermined the diversity of manners characteristic of more stratified social orders:

> In a republic, the citizens must often meet together upon the footing of equality and mutual independence; and having nearly the same purposes in view, and enjoying the same privileges, will contract similar habits of thinking, and be animated with similar passions, and marked with a sameness of character, or at least of external deportment.[127]

Equality encourages homogeneity and homogeneity starves humour of fuel. This is why, Beattie continued, despotic societies will experience an even worse dearth of laughter than that encountered in republics. Where 'all subjects are equally insignificant' and where it is safer to 'remain undistinguished', diversity of behaviours and manners will be absent, such that even if the despot were to permit his subjects to compose ludicrous or ridiculous writings, the essential materials needed for such productions would be lacking.[128]

Republics suffered from other crucial deficiencies in respect of laughter. Beattie allowed that one reason we have difficulty assessing comic writing from antiquity was that the 'sphere most favourable to wit and humour is that which is occupied by the middle and lower ranks of mankind', the very social strata whose habits and speech are most often lost to history.[129] His assumption here was that elites in all ages must, given their extensive responsibilities, retain a kind of 'reserve' that militates against humour, a restraint from which their social inferiors were free.[130] Beattie used similar reasoning to account for why republics tended to be dour. For what was true only of elites in other societies held for *all* citizens in a republic where 'important affairs, and consequently important emotions, must ever be present to the sober-minded citizen'.[131] Citizenship, Beattie implied, was a serious business, and the powerful emotions it bred (anxious concern for the public good, fear of corruption, desire for collective glory) would stifle laughter entirely.

If the sober ethos bred by republics was not conducive to humour, the tumult associated with republican politics similarly militated against it. A core element of Beattie's argument was that 'political institutions have an effect on ludicrous writing' by creating the conditions for peace and

127. Beattie, *Essays*, 465.
128. Ibid.
129. Ibid., 459.
130. Ibid.
131. Ibid., 482.

leisure.[132] For Beattie the 'needy and perilous condition' of savage life, combined with the 'violent temper' of the savages themselves, meant that they were 'little addicted to jocularity'.[133] This could only change with the material improvements brought about by civilized government. Because humour concerns 'pleasure rather than necessity', Beattie argued, it could only appear once 'public peace be tolerably secure'.[134] This placed monarchy at an advantage over republics. Because monarchies were less vulnerable to attack or 'intestine commotion', and made few onerous demands upon their subjects for public service, they would always provide fertile ground for humour.[135]

The Return of Hobbesian Laughter: Millar and Preston

Beattie was not the only Scottish philosopher to explore how social differentiation could generate laughter between groups. The Glasgow Professor of Law John Millar offered a more straightforwardly economic explanation for the same phenomenon in his *Historical View of the English Government*. 'The display of comic humour, in any country', Millar argued, 'will depend very much on the varieties which occur in the characters of the inhabitants'.[136] And the 'chief' cause of such diversity was the 'advancement of commerce and manufactures'.[137] In pre-commercial societies, Miller proposed, all have 'the same pursuits and occupations' and have therefore 'similar habits and ways of thinking'.[138] The inevitable consequence of this was that their 'aspect is gloomy and severe', and their 'complexion' is 'melancholy'.[139] Domestic slavery had a similar dampening effect on humour even in the 'most commercial of the Greek states', such as Athens, that were otherwise economically sophisticated.[140] The

132. Ibid., 481.
133. Ibid.
134. Ibid.
135. Ibid.
136. John Millar, *An Historical View of the English Government from the Settlement of the Saxons in Britain to the Revolution in 1688*, ed. Mark Salber-Phillips and Dale R. Smith (Indianapolis, IN: Liberty Fund, 2006), 360. The first two volumes of Millar's *Historical View* were published in 1787 and covered the period up to the Stuarts. A final section of the work was found among Millar's papers upon his death in 1801 and published posthumously in the 1803 edition of Millar's text, from which I quote here.
137. Ibid., 361.
138. Ibid., 363.
139. Ibid., 364.
140. Ibid., 365.

degradation shared by all slaves, Millar suggested, induced among them a 'uniformity of character' which then 'extended to the whole body of the people'.[141] Moreover, because domestic slaves undertook the majority of work only a select few occupations were reserved for the free population. It was therefore vain to expect a rich comic culture in Rome, for instance, as most freemen were confined in their occupations to law or military command, eliminating the 'variety of original character which is the great spur to ridicule'.[142]

In contrast, for Millar, the division of labour found in modern commercial society produced profound differences in social habits. And once the 'materials of humour and ridicule' were in place, the temptation to exploit them would quickly prove great.[143] The result, for Millar, was a society in which nearly all social groups and professions ridicule everyone else:

> Men of robust professions, the smith, the mason, and the carpenter, are apt to break their jests upon the weakness and effeminacy of the barber, the weaver, or the taylor. The poet, or the philosopher in his garret, condemns the patient industry, and the sordid pursuits of the merchant. The silent, mysterious, practitioner in physic, is apt to smile at the no less formal but clamorous ostentation of the barrister. The genteel military man, who is hired, at the nod of his superior, to drive his fellow-creatures out of this world, is ready to sneer at the zeal, and starch-deportment of the Divine, whose profession leads him to provide for their condition and enjoyments in the next. The peculiarities of each individual are thus beheld through a mirror, which magnifies their ludicrous features, and by continually exciting that 'itching to deride', of which all mankind are possessed, affords constant exercise to their humourous talents.[144]

Millar here more or less restates Beattie's argument that increased social differentiation creates opportunities for laughter. Again, however, it would be difficult to describe this as pure laughter at incongruity. The members of the professions Millar lists do not laugh in delighted surprise at the differences between them. Instead, Millar is clear that they laugh derisively at each other. The laughter of the carpenter at the barber, however good-naturedly intended, is nevertheless tinged with an attitude

141. Ibid., 366.
142. Ibid., 368.
143. Ibid., 361.
144. Ibid., 362.

of belittlement. Millar replaces the interpersonal comparisons between individuals emphasized by Hobbes with intergroup comparisons between different professions in a commercial society. This is, in other words, a Hobbesian account of laughter but with sociological content.

If variety of occupation was a pre-requisite for humour, however, an overly advanced division of labour could push in the opposite direction. For Millar such a division of labour could create a working population whose tasks were so minutely divided that there were no longer any great differences between them to fuel laughter. With a nod to his teacher Adam Smith, Millar found that the worker who rounds the head of the pin and his colleague who sharpens the point 'present nothing different to the eye of the comic observer'.[145] At this stage we reach a tipping point; the 'field of humour and ridicule . . . ceases to encrease' (*sic*) and may eventually be 'worn out and exhausted'.[146] In other words the phenomenon that Smith had identified as conducive to wealth creation was in the long run destructive of humour, leading eventually to its terminal decline.

Millar was indebted to the Hobbesian tradition of basing laughter in contempt rather than to Hobbes himself. Other students of modern laughter, by contrast, were prepared to rehabilitate Hobbes himself and explicitly endorse his theory. The Dubliner William Preston, a founder of the Royal Irish Academy, insisted that Hobbes's theory had been dismissed far too hastily. Vouching for its ancient pedigree, Preston wrote that an adequate understanding of the role of laughter in social life could only be obtained if we 'recur to the theory of Hobbes', a theory that was 'conformable' to Aristotle's.[147] Only following Hobbes in acknowledging the ineradicable element of contempt in laughter, Preston argued, could explain our intense aversion to being laughed at, and the power of ridicule as a disciplinary force:

> Why do men not chuse to be laughed at? Certainly because it indicates that they are objects of contempt. How happens it that a sportive word is more severely felt, and excites more lasting resentment, than the keenest reproaches? Why do we hold it indecorous and profligate to laugh at our parents, benefactors, and seniors? Why is it held impious

145. Ibid., 374.
146. Ibid.
147. William Preston, 'Essay on Ridicule, Wit, and Humour', in *Transactions of the Royal Irish Academy* (Dublin: George Bonham, 1788), 71. In an iconic article Aldridge declared Preston's essay the 'most authoritatively worded pronouncement on the subject of ridicule'. Alfred Owen Aldridge, 'Shaftesbury and the Test of Truth', *PMLA* 60, 1 (1945), 154.

and profane to laugh at things divine and holy? Why do public speakers and controversial writers endeavor to turn the laugh against their
opponents? Why is ridicule so powerful an engine of debate, even while
it disclaims an appeal to sober argument? Surely because the very
essence of mirth is a latent contempt, and there is a sort of general
intuitive perception that ridicule degrades and vilifies its object.[148]

That the contempt was 'latent' was crucial to Preston's argument. Unlike
Beattie, Preston recognized that on Hobbes's account it was not sufficient
to feel superior to another in order to experience mirth in their presence.
Glory alone is not productive of mirth; only *sudden* glory is. Once the centrality of surprise to Hobbes's theory was appreciated, Preston averred, the
objections raised by his Scottish critics melted away, including Beattie's
complaint that Hobbes's position committed him to predicting that the
wise would laugh often. Correctly understood, Preston argued, Hobbes's
account of laughter allowed for variation in what counts as ridiculous
across specific contexts, while at the same time locating laughter's fundamental source in the 'conscious triumph of self-superiority, either real
or imaginary.'[149] A century and a half after Hobbes first speculated on the
moral psychology of laughter, his theory still had its vocal defenders.

Conclusion

Writing in the *Elements of Criticism* (1762), the Edinburgh writer and jurist
Henry Home (Lord Kames) predicted that ridicule would eventually prove
'too rough an entertainment for those who are polished and refined' and so
would gradually decline in polite commercial societies.[150] So advanced was
this process in the principal commercial societies of Europe, Kames suggested, that ridicule had already 'banished France' and was 'losing ground
daily in England'.[151] The philosophers examined in this chapter offered two
reasons for why this verdict was premature. For champions of common
sense such as Reid, Beattie and Oswald, ridicule was a permanent and indispensable check against the scourge of scepticism, a form of philosophy that
modern commercial society (as they saw it) was increasingly susceptible to.
Particularly for Beattie, it was not enough to stand aside and wait for the

148. Preston, 'Essay on Ridicule, Wit, and Humour', 72.
149. Ibid., 89.
150. Henry Home (Lord Kames), *Elements of Criticism* (Dublin: Sarah Cotter, 1762),
vol. 2, 83.
151. Ibid.

absurdity of scepticism to become manifest to the public. Instead, the public must be made to laugh at it, lest they be tempted to embrace its conclusions.

By linking ridicule to social and economic organization Beattie and Millar offered an additional reason for why ridicule would never become redundant, even in polite societies. As the members of commercial society organized themselves into social classes and group identities solidified, the potential for finding their fellow citizens ridiculous could only increase. In addition to the wealth it generated, the division of labour in commercial society could throw up abundant clashes between groups who, no matter how well versed in politeness, would never be able to resist deriding each other. So long as commercial society existed, the Hobbesian laughter of contempt would have its place.

CHAPTER FIVE

'Too Solemn for Laughter'?

SCOTTISH ABOLITIONISTS AND THE MOCK APOLOGY FOR SLAVERY

Laughter against real evil is bitter.[1]

—REINHOLD NIEBUHR

STARTING WITH SHAFTESBURY, the philosophers we have examined in this book realized that considerations of civility placed restraints on how ridicule should be used. But they also acknowledged a natural limitation to ridicule imposed by the human mind itself. Because strong passions such as anger, fear and pity overwhelmed the weaker feeling of mirth, ridicule was powerless as a response to major crimes or moral abominations. Folly, unsociability and impropriety could be checked by ridicule; inhumanity required more earnest condemnation and an altogether more severe form of punishment.

This chapter examines a group of Scottish polemicists who pushed against this limitation by deploying ridicule against what they took to be the gravest of social evils: the European enslavement of Africans. Like abolitionists as a whole they were varied in their origins, aims and professional pursuits. Not all were straightforwardly radical in their politics (humanitarianism could sit comfortably alongside a commitment to social hierarchy). One, James Ramsay, studied at Aberdeen's King's College under Reid and served as a minister and a naval surgeon. Two others, William Dickson and James Tytler, were products of the University of Edinburgh and

---

1. Reinhold Niebuhr, 'Humour and Faith', in *Holy Laughter: Essays on Religion in the Comic Perspective*, ed. M. Conrad Hyers (New York: Seabury Press, 1969), 138.

became writers and editors. A fourth, Alexander Geddes, emerged from the Catholic community of Rathven on the north Aberdeenshire coast and devoted much of his life to producing a new scholarly edition of the Bible in English for the use of British Catholics. They were united not only by their detestation of slavery but also by a shared a polemical approach. Each saw potential in ridicule as a weapon of enlightened criticism. Equally, each was determined to expose defenders of African slavery as not merely mistaken but contemptible, and their arguments as absurd. Taking their cue from Montesquieu's *Spirit of the Laws*, their preferred form of ridicule was often a mock endorsement of the very pro-slavery arguments they sought to discredit. In adopting this strategy these abolitionists conceded that some prejudiced or self-interested claims on behalf of slavery could not be countered by argument alone but should instead be derided as *beneath* refutation. This was Hobbesian laughter infused with moral disgust.

There is no doubt that this was a brazen strategy and one that set these writers apart from many of their contemporaries in Enlightenment Scotland. As Iain Whyte notes, many Scottish intellectuals kept 'as quiet as possible about the slave trade' lest 'too many questions were asked, and Scottish self-image suffer'.[2] Certainly there was no shortage of critics of slavery within Scottish intellectual circles, but most refrained from actively participating in the campaign for abolition. Hume called domestic slavery 'more cruel and oppressive than any civil subjection whatsoever', and declared it incompatible with modern commercial society.[3] But he had relatively little to say about the modern plantation system of slavery and the imperial trade that supplied it with bodies. Smith similarly judged slavery to be unsuited to commercial society, but never forcefully exerted himself for the trade's abolition.[4] An elderly Reid expressed satisfaction that the University of

2. Iain Whyte, '"The Upas Tree, Beneath Whose Pestiferous Shade All Intellect Languishes and All Virtue Dies": Scottish Public Perceptions of the Slave Trade and Slavery, 1756–1833', in *Recovering Scotland's Slavery Past: The Caribbean Connection*, ed. T. M. Devine (Edinburgh: Edinburgh University Press, 2015), 190.

3. Hume, 'Of the Populousness of Ancient Nations', in *Essays Moral, Political and Literary*, 383. For an excellent account of how Hume elided modern commercial slavery in order to focus on its 'feudal, Ancient, and Asiatic variants' see Onur Ulas Ince, 'Between Commerce and Empire: David Hume, Colonial Slavery, and Commercial Incivility', *History of Political Thought* 39, 1 (2012), 109.

4. Adam Smith, *The Glasgow Edition of the Works and Correspondence of Adam Smith*, vol. 2, *An Inquiry into the Nature and Causes of the Wealth of Nations, Vol. 1*, ed. William B. Todd (Oxford: Oxford University Press, 1975), 99. As Lisa Hill notes, Smith lambasted slavery as economically inefficient but was 'complacent' when it came to the slave trade itself and 'probably thought it was pointless to press for reform'. Lisa Hill, *Adam Smith's Pragmatic Liberalism: The Science of Welfare* (Cham: Palgrave Macmillan, 2020), 205 and

Glasgow had sent a contribution to the petition campaign 'in favour of the African slaves' but did so in a private letter.[5] Millar made a humanitarian case for suppressing the slave trade and attended meetings of the Glasgow abolitionists, but kept clear of the pamphlet wars between abolitionists and defenders of the trade.[6] By comparison, Ramsay, Dickson, Tytler and Geddes were more willing to go out on a limb by composing screeds against the slave trade and mocking those who had the gall to defend it.

Recovering this turn to ridicule among Scottish abolitionists will, I hope, accomplish two things. First, it will expand our understanding of the range of rhetorical resources adopted by those involved in one of the most consequential political campaigns of late eighteenth-century Britain. In particular, it will help dispel the notion that the campaign for abolition was monopolized by the earnest evangelical piety of William Wilberforce and his Quaker allies.[7] Solemn denunciations of slavery and providential warnings of the divine punishments that would befall the British if they continued to uphold it were common in the abolitionist movement.[8] But they were not the only rhetorical tactic available to those who sought to impress upon the British public the moral imperative to end the slave trade. As Kwame Anthony Appiah has noted, 'what galvanizes the movement against slavery [in the 1780s] is not moral argument', but a complex set of rhetorical appeals designed to convert public disgust at the slave trade into popular demands for its elimination.[9] Ridicule, I suggest, represented a particularly potent example of such a rhetorical appeal.

---

207. Daniel Luban finds a plausible explanation for such pessimism in Smith's fear that the slave masters' love of domination would encourage them to perpetuate the institution long after its ceased to deliver economic benefits. Daniel Luban, 'Adam Smith on Vanity, Domination, and History', *Modern Intellectual History* 9, 2 (2012), 177.

5. Thomas Reid to James Gregory, 25 February 1788, in *Electronic Enlightenment*.

6. John Millar, *The Origin of the Distinction of Ranks*, ed. Aaron Garrett (Indianapolis, IN: Liberty Fund, 2006), 275–79. For an account of how Millar's humanitarian case against slavery went beyond the more lukewarm condemnations of his teacher, Smith, see Fred Ablondi, 'Millar on Slavery', *Journal of Scottish Philosophy* 7, 2 (2009), 163–75. According to his biographer, Millar took a 'most active part' in the Glasgow campaign, attended abolitionist meetings, and drew up a petition. John Craig, 'Account of the Life and Writings of the Author', in *The Origin of the Distinction of Ranks*, 68.

7. On this see Markus Rediker, 'Slave Trade Satire Shows Dark Abolitionist "Humour"', *NPR*, 7 October 2004. https://www.npr.org/transcripts/14993517.

8. John Coffey, '"Tremble, Britannia!": Fear, Providence and the Abolition of the Slave Trade, 1758–1807', *The English Historical Review* 127, 527 (2012), 844–81.

9. Appiah, *The Honor Code*, 110. As Christopher Brown aptly puts it, the challenge abolitionists faced was to bridge the 'chasm that distinguished moral opinion from moral action'. Christopher Leslie Brown, *Moral Capital: Foundations of British Abolitionism* (Chapel Hill: University of North Carolina Press, 2006), 2. Less sympathetically, Rice finds

Second, this episode spotlights a difficulty faced by political reformers of all stripes in the eighteenth century and beyond; namely how to counter claims that seemed unworthy of refutation but that had sufficient traction with the public such that *some* kind of response to them was necessary. As the Scottish abolitionists discovered, squibs written in mock support of slavery could easily backfire, not least because careless or malicious readers could misinterpret ironic advocacy as genuine. They also ran the risk of trivializing the moral wrong of slavery or presenting it as just one more topic on which wits could try out their skills. Finally, appealing to the public's sense of the ridiculous risked revealing the potential hollowness of all such appeals by demonstrating that what to some was plainly absurd was to others not only true, but self-evidently so.

The chapter will proceed as follows. I begin with the text that inspired much of the Scottish parodying of pro-slavery argument: Montesquieu's *Spirit of the Laws* and in particular book 15, chapter 5 where Montesquieu attacks the slave trade indirectly by ironically endorsing it. I then return to the writings of James Beattie, one of the first of the Scottish philosophers to systematically dismantle the case for African slavery but who, like other Scottish philosophers, proved reticent about publicly calling for abolition. Beattie mined Montesquieu's *Spirit of the Laws* for arguments against slavery but conspicuously distanced himself from Montesquieu's embrace of ridicule, insisting instead on the need to refute the pro-slavery case in a manner more respectful to those who advanced it (in this respect he extended to slave traders the polite treatment he had conspicuously denied to Hume). By contrast, the polemicists Ramsay, Dickson, Geddes and Tytler all saw promise in reviving Montesquieu's approach and, if anything, darkened his humour still further. I conclude by examining the persistence of ridicule as a rhetorical practice in later abolitionist polemics of the nineteenth century.

Montesquieu and the Mock Defence of Slavery

Scottish abolitionists interested in using ridicule to unsettle pro-slavery argument found inspiration in one of the most important texts to influence the Scottish Enlightenment: Montesquieu's *Spirit of the Laws*. Montesquieu followed the English debate on ridicule, but had little confidence

---

that Scottish intellectuals 'conspicuously failed to make it seem either immoral or abnormal to maintain the individual or national commitment to slavery' and in most cases simply 'shrugged off any responsibility to put theory into practice'. C. Duncan Rice, *The Scottish Abolitionists 1833–1861* (Baton Rouge: Louisiana State University Press, 1981), 20–21.

in the Shaftesburyian doctrine that ridicule qualified as a form of reasoning or test of truth (this 'method of proving or combating decides nothing',
he insisted, 'because a joke is not a reason').[10] Nonetheless, few Enlightenment figures wielded ridicule more effectively than Montesquieu did
against the cruelties of the Atlantic slave trade. In a chapter of *The Spirit
of the Laws* entitled 'Of the Slavery of the Negroes', Montesquieu adopted
a savagely ironical tone, inviting his readers to imagine that he has been
tasked with defending the European treatment of Africans: 'If'—the use
of the conditional is key—'I had to defend the right we had of making
Negroes slaves, here is what I would say.'[11] What follows is a catalogue
of slave trade apologetics that Montesquieu ironically presents as bluntly
self-evident and in need of no elaboration.

Beginning with the economic case for slavery, Montesquieu declares it
obvious that enslaved Africans will be needed to clear American forests as
Europeans had already 'exterminated the Americans'.[12] The price of sugar
too would soar to exorbitant levels if free rather than slave labour was
employed on the sugar plantations. Montesquieu even tried on a version
of the religious justification for slavery. God, after all, could hardly have
placed an immortal soul in a 'body that was entirely black'.[13] Commenting
next on the European fixation on skin colour, Montesquieu commends
Asians for reinforcing physical markers of inferiority by castrating Black
men. The ancient Egyptians too win his ironic praise for having the good
sense to kill all redheads they happened to get their hands on, having

10. Montesquieu, *My Thoughts*, trans. Henry C. Clark (Indianapolis, IN: Liberty Fund,
2012), #1262, 337. (Citations of the *Pensée* include the number of each 'thought' and the
page number in the Liberty Fund edition.) Montesquieu agreed with Shaftesbury that ridicule was the best antidote to religious extremism, and alleged that fanaticism in England
had been 'destroyed' by it. Unlike Shaftesbury, Montesquieu did not view the growing taste
for ridicule in public debate as heralding greater freedom of thought, regarding it instead
as the by-product of a culture addicted to frivolity. Mankind, Montesquieu thought, could
be divided into 'those who think and those who amuse' and that the latter were beginning
to prevail in France was of no comfort to him. Ibid., #972, 273. Nor did Montesquieu share
Shaftesbury's faith that anything undeserving of ridicule was safe from its effects. French
society was buzzing with wits 'turning good and even virtuous things to ridicule', a habit
associated with intellectual slackness and presumption. Ibid., #1006, 280.

11. Montesquieu, *The Spirit of the Laws*, 250. Nancy Morrow calls this chapter a 'misleading satirical attack on black slavery' that 'could be taken literally, by some, as a defence
of slavery'. Nancy V. Morrow, 'The Problem of Slavery in the Polemic Literature of the
American Enlightenment', *Early American Literature* 20, 3 (1985), 238.

12. Montesquieu, *The Spirit of the Laws*, 250.

13. Ibid.

recognized hair colour as equal in moral significance to skin colour. In a move reminiscent of his approach in the *Persian Letters* (1721), Montesquieu even presents the failure of Africans to be besotted with gold in the manner of Europeans as a sure sign that they lack common sense.

Finally, Montesquieu (still in ironic mood) anticipates the humanitarian case against slavery and refutes it. The Black skin and 'flat noses' of the slaves, he alleges, represent insurmountable barriers to sympathy with their plight.[14] In any case, to recognize 'these people' as human would be unacceptably risky because it would raise the troubling possibility that Europeans had failed to be 'Christians' towards them.[15] Fortunately such a moment of self-reckoning was unnecessary, Montesquieu concludes, because accounts of slave suffering were surely exaggerated anyway, the proof being that the 'princes of Europe' had not yet convened to address the matter.[16] If those princes, who had not hesitated to enter into 'so many useless agreements with one another', had not addressed the matter of the inhumane treatment of slaves then, *ipso facto*, there was no matter to address.[17]

Montesquieu's tactics in this chapter were nothing if not audacious. As Diana Schaub notes, rather than 'sermonize on the injustice of race slavery', he 'simply mouths the self-incriminating arguments of its proponents', making those arguments in the process 'appear as what they are: brutal, prideful, and absurd'.[18] By choosing parody rather than refutation, Montesquieu encouraged his readers to regard the case for African slavery as *beneath* reasoning and those who advanced it as worthy of contempt.[19] For some early readers, Montesquieu's willingness to apply ridicule to the particular case of slavery was both unprecedented and daring. Dupont de

14. Ibid.

15. Ibid.

16. Ibid.

17. Ibid.

18. Diana J. Schaub, 'Montesquieu on Slavery', *Perspectives on Political Science* 34, 2 (2005), 73.

19. Such, at least, is how Montesquieu's French contemporaries interpreted this chapter. For some of those familiar with his writings, Montesquieu's turn to ridicule when discussing African slavery was very much within character. D'Alembert insisted that the *Persian Letters* should not be considered the Baron's only satirical work, arguing that Montesquieu frequently chose to make opponents look 'ridiculous' when he had the option of presenting them as 'odious' instead. D'Alembert, 'An Eulogium on President Montesquieu', in *The Complete Works of M. de Montesquieu*, vol. 1 (London: T. Evans, 1777), xxiv.

Namours, in a 1771 article for the *Ephémérides*, was adamant that this tactic had not been tried before. 'Montesquieu', de Namours wrote, 'was the first to attack with ridicule the pretended reasoning, not less absurd than atrocious, that the oppressors of the blacks used to excuse their slavery'.[20] The Abbé Raynal, principal author of the influential *Philosophical and Political History of the Settlements and Trade of the Europeans in the East and West Indies*, was likewise struck by the novelty of Montesquieu's approach. Raynal, however, attributed it less to rhetorical cunning than to Montesquieu's solicitous concern for reason itself, which would suffer if called upon to rebuff pro-slavery arguments. 'Montesquieu', Raynal proclaimed, 'could not prevail upon himself to treat the question concerning slavery in a serious light' because he saw that it would be 'degrading reason to employ it . . . in refuting an abuse repugnant to it'.[21] As for those who dared to justify slavery regardless, for Raynal they deserved a dual punishment: 'the utmost contempt from a philosopher' (like Montesquieu) and 'from the negro a stab from his dagger!'[22]

Before the Scottish abolitionists imitated Montesquieu's example, anglophone critics of the British trade realized the significance of what he had done and credited him with offering a fresh approach to anti-slavery polemics. Benjamin Rush quoted the entirety of book 15, chapter 5 in a

20. Cited in Vickie Sullivan, *Montesquieu and the Despotic Ideas of Europe: An Interpretation of 'The Spirit of the Laws'* (Chicago: University of Chicago Press, 2017), 259–60. This is a view echoed in Montesquieu scholarship today. Vickie Sullivan finds that Montesquieu's attack 'stands out as courageous denunciation and satire . . . which was to have a decisive effect on the anti-slavery movement in France'. Ibid., 260. According to Sue Peabody, these are Montesquieu's 'most ironic passages' and advanced 'propositions that are intended to be self-evidently narrow minded or preposterous'. Sue Peabody, *'There Are No Slaves in France': The Political Culture of Race and Slavery* (Oxford: Oxford University Press, 1996), 66–67. For Judith Shklar, Montesquieu's 'deepest scorn and blackest humour . . . were reserved for racist defences of slavery'. Judith Shklar, *Montesquieu* (Oxford: Oxford University Press, 1987), 96. According to Roger Anstey, Montesquieu offered a 'splendidly ironical condemnation of slavery'. Roger Anstey, 'A Reinterpretation of the Abolition of the British Slave Trade', *The English Historical Review* 87, 343 (1972), 307. Claudine Hunting noted how Montesquieu 'unabashedly carried' the traditional defences of slavery to 'untenable excess' and argued that, together with Voltaire, Montesquieu's satire dealt 'one of the most effective blows to the yet undecided or to the last of those resisting the abolition of slavery'. Claudine Hunting, 'The Philosophes and Black Slavery', *Journal of the History of Ideas* 39, 3 (1978), 416 and 418. For James Walvin, Montesquieu 'embraced a criticism of slavery, though couching its denunciations in ironic terms'. James Walvin, *England, Slaves and Freedom 1776–1838* (London: Macmillan, 1986), 98.

21. Abbé Raynal, *Philosophical and Political History of the Settlements and Trade of the Europeans in the East and West Indies*, vol. 3 (London: T. Cadell, 1776), 166.

22. Ibid.

footnote of his *Address to the Inhabitants of the British Settlements in America upon Slave-keeping*, applauding how Montesquieu had treated the argument that Black skin was a mark of inferiority 'with the ridicule it deserves'.[23] Another critic of the British trade, James Otis, found that the potency of Montesquieu's chapter lay in how the arguments he presented, weak as they might be, were nevertheless the best that could be made on slavery's behalf: 'No better reasons can be given, for enslaving those of any colour, than such as baron Montesquieu has humorously given, as the foundation of that cruel slavery exercised over the poor Ethiopians.'[24] An argument that rested on a contrast between 'short hair curl'd like wool' and 'Christian hair', Otis continued, could hardly 'help' the pro-slavery cause.[25] But, as Montesquieu had shown, such weak arguments were all that those 'whose hearts are as hard as the nether millstone' had available to them.[26]

None of these commentators interpreted Montesquieu's irony as a form of esoteric writing necessitated by censorship. Instead, they agreed that Montesquieu was either too repulsed by those who defended African slavery to engage them in serious debate or (more likely) thought they could be more effectively countered by subjecting them to ridicule. It was an approach that some (but by no means all) of Montesquieu's Scottish readers would enthusiastically embrace.

Beattie and the Sober Refutation of Pro-Slavery Arguments

Among the first of the Scots to pick up on Montesquieu's ironic endorsement of treatment of African slavery was the Presbyterian minister and philosopher George Campbell. Like other Scottish intellectuals, Campbell situated Montesquieu in the same tradition of Stoic moralism as Shaftesbury and pointed to *The Spirit of the Laws* as an example of how ridicule could serve as an effective method of moral criticism.[27] Producing an

23. Benjamin Rush, *An Address to the Inhabitants of the British Settlements in America, upon Slave-Keeping* (Boston: John Boyles, 1773), 3–4.

24. James Otis, *The Rights of the British Colonists Asserted and Proved* (Boston: Edes and Gill, 1764), 29.

25. Ibid.

26. Ibid.

27. Most notably, Adam Ferguson placed Montesquieu alongside Shaftesbury in a list of thinkers who embodied the 'real spirit' of Stoic philosophy. Adam Ferguson, *Principles of Moral and Political Science* (Edinburgh: A. Strahan and T. Cadell, London; and W. Creech, Edinburgh, 1792), 8. This reading of Montesquieu as a 'Stoic moralist' is more neglected than other aspects of his Scottish reception. See Iain McDaniel, *Adam Ferguson in the Scottish Enlightenment* (Cambridge, MA: Harvard University Press,

'absurd argument for an opinion', Campbell argued, could usefully convey to an audience that 'no good motive or argument' could be given in its favour.[28] An 'excellent specimen' of this tactic, he continued, was Montesquieu's book 15, chapter 5, 'where the practice of Europeans in enslaving the negroes, is ironically justified in a manner which does honour to the author's humanity and love of justice, at the same time that it displays a happy talent in ridicule'.[29] By classifying Montesquieu's intervention in this way, Campbell suggested that the Frenchman had wisely refused to reason with slavery's defenders, choosing instead a different method to counter arguments that lay 'beyond the reach of cool reasoning'.[30] As with Raynal, then, Campbell found in Montesquieu's chapter a signal that to offer a serious reply to defenders of slavery would debase not only its victims but also reason itself.

Not all Scottish readers of Montesquieu were so convinced by the merits of his approach, however. James Beattie was overtly critical of it, despite both his abhorrence of slavery and his reputation as a pugnacious polemicist who, in attacking David Hume (as we saw in the last chapter) considered no rhetorical tactic out of bounds. Beattie's case is of special interest because in his writings on laughter he had reflected on when ridicule was appropriate as a mode of criticism. We can be confident, therefore, that Beattie's oscillations between facetious and serious modes of critique were deliberately chosen with considerations of appropriateness in mind.

In his first interventions in the slavery debate Beattie's main preoccupation was not the African trade per se but rather European claims to racial superiority that were used to justify it. Beattie attributed the prevalence of such claims to modern philosophers who were sceptical in their metaphysics but overly self-assured in proclaiming the superiority of their own civilization over others. Again, for Beattie, it was Hume who embodied this combination of epistemological modesty and cultural or racial chauvinism.[31] In a notorious footnote added to his essay 'On National Characters', Hume had

2013), 12. For a general overview of Montesquieu's influence on Scottish Enlightenment thinking see James Moore, 'Montesquieu and the Scottish Enlightenment', in *Montesquieu and His Legacy*, ed. Rebecca E. Kingston (Albany: State University of New York Press, 2009).

28. Campbell, *Philosophy of Rhetoric*, vol. 1, 78.

29. Ibid., 78–79.

30. Ibid., 69–70.

31. For Rice, Beattie used slavery as a 'lever in clerical controversies' and attacked Hume's stance of the racial inferiority only to 'discredit him and his moderate admirers'. This is unconvincing. Beattie's antipathy to slavery was long standing and outlasted his battle with Hume. Rice, *The Scottish Abolitionists*, 120.

asserted the superiority of white Europeans to 'negroes' on the basis that no great civilizational accomplishments had ever come out of Africa:

> I am apt to suspect the negroes to be naturally inferior to the whites. There scarcely was a civilized nation of that complexion, nor even any individual eminent either in action or speculation. No ingenious manufactures amongst them, no arts, no sciences. . . . Not to mention our colonies, there are negroe slaves dispersed all over Europe, of whom none ever discovered any symptoms of ingenuity; though low people, without education, will start up amongst us, and distinguish themselves in every profession. In Jamaica, indeed, they talk of one negroe as a man of parts and learning; but it is likely he is admired for slender accomplishments, like a parrot, who speaks a few words plainly.[32]

Beattie was incensed by this passage and twice responded to it. The differences between his two responses reveal how divergent Beattie's approach to countering racist prejudice was to that of Montesquieu, who had usually served as his authority on all matters related to slavery.

Beattie first took aim at Hume's footnote in 1768 at a meeting of Aberdeen's Wise Club. There he made known his disdain for Hume's argument with the most withering of put-downs, ridiculing Hume for failing to see that it was the institution of slavery itself that was responsible for the deficiencies in civilization he observed among Africans. Hume himself would never have amounted to much if forced to endure anything like the hardship of slavery:

> Tell me, Mr Hume, in what department of genius you would expect a Negroe slave to distinguish himself? Would you have him be a Philosopher, Historian, or Poet? Surely you must know that all such professions are as far beyond his sphere as the condition of royalty is beyond your owne [sic]? . . . Learn, Mr Hume, to prize the blessings of Liberty and Education, for I will venture to assure you that had you been born and bred a slave, your Genius, whatever you may think of it, would never have been heard of.[33]

32. Hume, *Essays Moral, Political and Literary*, 208. That Hume revised the footnote in reply to Beattie's objections while at the same time retaining its core claim of Black inferiority shows that this was his settled view on the matter rather than an unfortunate lapse. For a convincing treatment that foregrounds the tensions between Hume's position on race and his determination to account for variation in human societies by moral as opposed to physical causes see Aaron Garrett and Silvia Sebastiani, 'David Hume on Race', in *The Oxford Handbook of Philosophy and Race*, ed. Naomi Zack (Oxford: Oxford University Press, 2017), 31–43.

33. Beattie cited in Sebastiani, *The Scottish Enlightenment: Race, Gender, and the Limits of Progress*, 114.

The irony here was that Hume's aim in 'Of National Characters' had been to challenge climate-based explanations for differences in national cultures by affirming the primacy of social–environmental or moral causes in the development of human cultures.[34] When Hume failed to apply his own reasoning to the case of African slaves, Beattie pounced.

However, when Beattie took this argument public in his 1770 *Essay on Truth*, he converted his *ad hominem* sneer into a more generalized objection to European claims to racial superiority. Misleadingly presenting Hume's argument as a justification for slavery (Beattie would have known that Hume was a critic of slavery in spite of his views on race), Beattie opted, on this occasion at least, not to belittle Hume personally. The sarcasm was quietly dropped, as was the direct upbraiding of 'Mr Hume'. Instead, Beattie turned the logic of Hume's argument back on Europe in order to highlight Hume's unrealistic expectations of what humans could achieve in servitude: 'To suppose [the negro] of an inferior species because he does not distinguish himself, is just as rational, as to suppose any private European of an inferior species, because he has not raised himself to the condition of royalty.'[35] More significantly, when Beattie turned to a direct critique of slavery itself, he preferred exhortation to denunciation. Instead of attacking the defenders of slavery, he played on British patriotism and fondness for liberty to inspire his readers to reject slavery as an institution unworthy of a people who were the most 'generous on earth'.[36]

In his later interventions on the subject of slavery, Beattie more explicitly singled out ridicule as inappropriate when sparring with pro-slavery advocates. One such advocate who came to prominence in the 1780s was the Liverpool-based pamphleteer Raymond Harris, an ex-Jesuit whose religious defence of slavery eventually earned him a financial award from Liverpool Council for services to the city's commerce. The particular occasion for this prize was Harris's *Scriptural Researches on the Licitness of the Slave Trade, Shewing its Conformity with the Principles of Natural and Revealed Religion, Delineated in the Sacred Writings of the Word of God* (1788).[37]

34. This hatred, however, 'did not impinge upon' his views on the 'natural hierarchy of peoples'. Garrett and Sebastiani, 'David Hume on Race', 38.

35. Beattie, *Essay on Truth*, 482.

36. Ibid., 484.

37. Harris's real name was Don Raymondo Hormaza. Liverpool Council paid him one hundred pounds for his services to the town and its trade. See David Brion Davis, *The Problem of Slavery in the Age of Revolution, 1770–1823* (Oxford: Oxford University Press, 1999), 542–43.

Pressed to answer this pamphlet, Beattie pondered the approach he would take in a letter to Beilby Porteus, Bishop of London and eventual abolitionist. Beattie was utterly dismissive of Harris's scriptural arguments for slavery but, crucially, he promised to give his opponent a 'fair hearing'.[38] Confident that Harris's arguments could have 'no influence upon a candid and rational mind', Beattie predicted that they would instead only 'provoke indignation: for the matter is too solemn for laughter'.[39] Precisely because it was a defence of so grave a moral crime as slavery, Beattie suggested, Harris's pamphlet could be repugnant and outrageous but *not* ridiculous. In the end, he chose not to answer Harris at all, pleading to William Forbes (Beattie's friend and later biographer) that his 'health' was a 'great hindrance' to all his 'projects'.[40]

In his later *Elements of Moral Science*, Beattie again disavowed the use of ridicule in the abolitionist cause, this time alluding directly to the example of Montesquieu and his admirers. In the lengthy discussion of slavery that dominates Part 3 of the text, Beattie drew frequently on *The Spirit of the Laws* (though not, notably, on the chapter relating specifically to the enslavement of Africans) to the extent that one scholar judged his views to be 'little more than a recapitulation of Montesquieu's'.[41] Beattie is also held to have shared the French philosopher's sense that it was 'irksome to be coldly rational' when discussing this particular social evil.[42] While this might be true in part, Beattie distanced himself from those who approved of Montesquieu's tactics. 'In protesting against such a practice' as slavery, Beattie admitted,

> it is not easy to preserve that lenity of language, and coolness of argument, which philosophy recommends: and one eminent author has not sought to preserve it, but explicitly declares, that he who can seriously

38. James Beattie to Beilby Porteus 3 July 1788, in Beattie, *The Letters of James Beattie*, vol. 2, 165.

39. Ibid., 166.

40. James Beattie to William Forbes, 3 May 1788. Ibid., 165. Beattie was not entirely inactive against the slave trade at this time. In 1788 he drafted a petition from Marischal College to Parliament calling for abolition of the slave trade and in 1792 encouraged Aberdeen City Council to do the same. Iain Whyte, *Scotland and the Abolition of Black Slavery, 1756–1838* (Edinburgh: Edinburgh University Press, 2006), 60. In his biography of Beattie, Forbes remarked that the abolition of the slave trade was Beattie's 'favourite topic' and that he felt the 'strongest and warmest interest in favour of the poor Africans'. Beattie made his repugnance towards slavery known to his students, many of whom then carried his 'principles' with them to the West Indies. William Forbes, *An Account of the Life and Writings of James Beattie* (Edinburgh: H.S. Baynes and Co., 1824), 401–2.

41. F.T.H Fletcher, 'Montesquieu's Influence on Anti-Slavery Opinion in England', *Journal of Negro History* 18, 4 (1933), 423.

42. Ibid.

argue in vindication of slavery deserves no other answer than the stab of a poniard. I am not, however, so bloody-minded; and shall endeavour to justify what I have said [against slavery], by an appeal to the reason, rather than to the passions, of mankind.[43]

The 'eminent author' in the above passage must be Raynal who, as we have seen, believed that slavery's advocates should be met with Montesquieu's philosophical contempt and a dagger-thrust from the enslaved themselves. Beattie embraced a more polite approach, presenting pro-slavery arguments not as monstrous absurdities to be met with scorn but as serious claims to truth that must be rationally examined. He took seriously, for example, the economic case for slavery but ultimately fell back on the argument, popularized by Adam Smith, that free labourers were more productive than slaves. To the argument that Africans had enslaved each other prior to the arrival of Europeans, Beattie responded that European demand fuelled domestic African slavery and that, in any case, African slave-mongers were only imitating European example. As for the claim that slaves were happier in bondage than they would be otherwise, Beattie both presented evidence to the contrary and urged that an unlawful practice that produced happiness was no less unlawful as a result. He even gave a hearing to arguments for the natural inferiority of Black people based upon, *inter alia*, polygenesis, the scriptural story of the curse of Ham, differentials in skull size, and the degree of civilization achieved by Europeans. In each case Beattie regarded the pro-slavery argument as easily refuted but as requiring refutation all the same.[44] If he sometimes considered such arguments absurd, Beattie nevertheless accepted that their absurdity would not be self-evident to his readers.

Moreover, Beattie went out of his way to avoid impugning his opponents or causing offence to anyone invested in the institution of slavery itself. His 'censure' was not to be 'leveled at any individuals', including slave-masters who refused to liberate their slaves for fear of the tumult that would follow an overly sudden emancipation.[45] Slavery was an institution so central to British political economy that effectively the whole society bore responsibility for it, a radical argument with wide implications, but one that could be construed as letting individual slave-holders

43. James Beattie, *Elements of Moral Science*, vol. 2 (Edinburgh: William Creech, 1793), 156.

44. Only when confronting the claim that the ubiquity of slavery across history must mean that it is lawful and natural does Beattie relax his commitment to earnest engagement; this argument 'deserves no answer'. Ibid., 160.

45. Ibid., 166.

off the hook. Rather than exhort slave-masters to treat their slaves more humanely, Beattie proposed that outlawing the importation of new slaves into the West Indies (the only immediate legal change he called for) would inevitably result in the better treatment of those already enslaved.[46]

As we saw in the previous chapter, when writing against the dangers of scepticism Beattie was of the view that the philosopher's mission was to boldly galvanize public opinion rather than tread softly for fear of a backlash. Why then did he adopt a different approach when publicly engaging defenders of slavery? One explanation concerns the nature of the work that contained his most extensive criticism of the slave trade. The *Elements of Moral Science* was a compilation of the lectures that Beattie developed over the course of his teaching career at Marischal College. As such, it lacked the polemical swagger of the *Essay on Truth*. However, a fear of shocking or offending may also have played a considerable part in his decision. Whereas Beattie had lost little time in publishing his *Essay on Truth*, he was unhurried about sending his denunciation of slavery to the press. In a footnote in the *Elements of Moral Science* Beattie admitted that most of the anti-slavery material had been written in 1778, twenty-five years earlier. He went on to plead that this delay was due to his not having access at the time to 'all the books I wished to consult' and to a related anxiety that the information on which he based his arguments might be 'partial'.[47] However, as he later informed his Bluestocking correspondent and fellow abolitionist, Elizabeth Montagu, Beattie had initially intended his critique of slavery to form part of his *Dissertations Moral and Critical* (1783) but decided instead to suppress it. His reasons for doing so, he now confided, had more to do with anxiety at causing offence than with inadequate access to sources. For although the piece was written with a 'good intention towards White men as well as Negroes' the outcome, he feared, would ultimately have been to 'create enemies to the author' rather than achieve anything worthwhile in terms of 'justice and benevolence'.[48]

---

46. Beattie's determination to avoid individual offence did, however, admit of one exception. Clergy who refused to educate the enslaved in Christianity (or who would only do so for a fee) Beattie not only chastised but mocked as well. The clergy had pleaded that the plantation owners had denied them permission to teach their slaves, thereby absolving them of the charge that they had neglected their Christian duty. Beattie's advice to these clerics dripped with sarcasm: 'I hope I shall give no offence by saying, that when a planter's prohibition and the express command of Jesus Christ happen to contradict each other, it may be worth clergyman's while to consider, which of these two deserves the precedence.' But towards the slave-holders themselves Beattie never strayed from politeness. Ibid., 221–22.

47. Ibid., 218.

48. James Beattie to Elizabeth Montagu, 21 December 1779. Aberdeen UL MS 30/1/177, as cited in Glen Doris, 'An Abolitionist Too Late? James Beattie and the Scottish

Ramsay's Restraint

Beattie's reluctance to become embroiled in disputes over the issue of slavery was in stark contrast to the other Aberdeenshire abolitionists. Another student and friend of Reid's at Kings, James Ramsay, proved himself far more willing to go out on a limb in attacking the slave trade, even if doing so dragged him into personal spats. Unlike his friend Beattie, Ramsay had first-hand experience of the West Indian sugar plantations, having spent nearly two decades serving as a minister and surgeon on the island of St Kitts. He distilled that experience into the *Essay on the Treatment and Conversion of African Slaves* (1784), a hugely influential work that proved foundational for Wilberforce's parliamentary campaign to end the trade and earned Ramsay a place among Olaudah Equiano's 'Saints' of the abolitionist movement.[49]

Ramsay's status as an eyewitness to the abuses of the West Indian plantocracy allowed him to adopt a two-pronged strategy against the slave trade, one that combined philosophical refutation of pro-slavery arguments with vivid descriptions of planter cruelty that he could personally attest to. Following Beattie's lead, Ramsay picked out Hume's racist arguments as representative of the kind of pseudo-philosophy that had been a boon to the pro-slavery cause. Unlike Beattie, however, Ramsay had few qualms about mocking (the now deceased) Hume for his prejudice. If Hume truly believed that physical attributes could reveal anything about intellectual capability, Ramsay asserted in the *Essay*, then he might as well have declared that only men of similar heft to himself could be philosophers:

> Mr Hume, because a tall bulky man, and also a subtile [*sic*] philosopher, might have denied a capacity for metaphysical subtilty to all who wanted his great bodily attributes, as well as suppose capacity and vigor of mind incompatible with a flat nose, curling hair, and a black skin.[50]

Enlightenment's Lost Chance to Influence the Slave Trade Debate', *Journal of Scottish Thought* 2, 1 (2009), 87.

49. Olaudah Equiano, *The Interesting Narrative of the Life of Olaudah Equiano, or Gustavus Vassa, the African. Written by Himself*, vol. 2 (New York: W. Durrell, 1791), 187. For more on Equiano's appreciation for Ramsay see Folarin Shyllon, *James Ramsay: The Unknown Abolitionist* (Edinburgh: Canongate, 1977), 98–100.

50. James Ramsay, *An Essay on the Treatment and Conversion of African Slaves in the British Sugar Colonies* (London: James Phillips, 1784), 214. No other treatise 'approached the importance and influence' of Ramsay's *Essay*. Brown, *Moral Capital*, 364.

If Hume's 'great bodily attributes' were associated with his intellectual abilities, then the thin were condemned to stupidity. By presenting this *reductio ad absurdum* Ramsay not only turned the tables on Hume but also exposed the European tendency to only ever relate physical attributes to ability when discussing non-European peoples. To be consistent, Ramsay joked, would require puzzling over the significance of high Scottish cheekbones as a potential sign of Scottish intellect.[51]

It was Ramsay's eyewitness accounts of planter cruelty, however, that seemed to confirm Beattie's prediction that to criticize the slave trade was necessarily to make enemies.[52] Despite the fact that Ramsay's proposals were modest (*The Monthly Review* was puzzled that Ramsay sought mainly to improve the condition of slaves rather than castigate the whole system with the 'ardour and enthusiasm of Rousseau or Reynall') he found himself subjected to violent abuse and even death threats.[53] Planters and pro-slavery advocates went to great lengths to cast doubt on Ramsay's character and, by extension, his reliability as a witness of slave suffering. The tone he adopted towards the planters themselves came in for particularly close scrutiny, particularly when he had the temerity to reply to his accusers with sarcasm.[54] In a reply to an attack from James Tobin, a particularly determined representative of the planter class, Ramsay insinuated that there must be several James Tobins (including 'J. Tobin, Duellist', a nod to the method Tobin had proposed to settle their dispute), as this was the only explanation for how works under the same name could contradict themselves so frequently.[55] Tobin complained of Ramsay's

51. The reference to cheekbones seems to have been a trope and was used by pro-slavery writers as well. Bryan Edwards, a defender of the planter position, argued that skin colour was 'no more to be considered as a proof of degradation, than the red hair and high cheek bones of the Natives of the North of Europe'. Bryan Edwards, *The History, Civil and Commercial, of the British Colonies in the West Indies*, vol. 2 (Dublin: Luke White, 1793), 69. Edwards's rejection of any idea of racial inferiority did not stop him defending slavery and the slave trade as 'necessary evils' for the empire's economy. See Peter Kitson, '"Candid Reflections": The Idea of Race in the Debate over the Slave Trade and Slavery in the Late Eighteenth and Early Nineteenth Century', in *Discourses of Slavery and Abolition: Britain and Its Colonies, 1760–1838*, ed. Brycchan Carey, Markman Ellis, and Sara Salih (New York: Palgrave Macmillan, 2004), 18.

52. Ramsay had no shortage of enemies already. His humane treatment of slaves when working as a doctor on St Kitts angered their masters and quickly made him a 'marked man'. Whyte, *Scotland the Abolition of Black Slavery*, 108.

53. Anon., 'Ramsay's *Essay on the Treatment of Slaves*', in *Monthly Review or Literary Journal* 70 (1784), 418. On the threats of assassination see Shyllon, *James Ramsay*, 5.

54. His biographer, Shyllon, calls Ramsay's wit 'caustic' but also occasionally 'tactless'. Shyllon, *James Ramsay*, 82 and 84.

55. James Ramsay, *A Letter to James Tobin, Esq. Late Member of His Majesty's Council in the Island of Nevis* (London: James Phillips, 1787), 5.

lack of 'decorum' and that his description of the conditions under which slaves lived more closely resembled the 'impotent railing of a deranged old woman' than the 'manly resentment of a liberal mind'.[56] It was precisely the kind of bruising, personalized clash that Beattie strove to avoid.

The situation worsened when Ramsay took his case to Parliament in 1788 and provided testimony to a Privy Council inquiry into slavery and the slave trade. From that point on, pro-slavery interests escalated the campaign to impugn his character and motives. Undaunted, Ramsay continued to wade in where Beattie had feared to tread by rubbishing the religious justification for the slave trade. Like Beattie, he was incensed by Harris's scriptural distortions and published the kind of forceful rebuttal that Beattie had contemplated but never delivered. His *Examination of the Rev. Mr. Harris's Scriptural Researches on the Licitness of the Slave-Trade* (1788) questioned Harris's motivation, implying that only a hired propagandist could extract a justification for the Liverpool slave trade from the fact that 'Abraham possessed servants'.[57] For Ramsay, the notion that God would sanction such an inhumane practice was risible and he sarcastically implored Harris to specify the 'high purposes answered by slavery' such that it could become an 'act of piety to violate our benevolent feelings'.[58]

Despite his reputation for personal invective, however, Ramsay remained closer to Beattie's approach to criticism of the slave trade than at first appears. By staking so much on his credibility as a witness of planter barbarity, Ramsay ran the risk of converting his anti-slavery work into a test of his own character. But he also sought to depersonalize the debate by stressing that the case against the slave trade did not hinge on whether the behaviour of individual planters was as bad as he presented. Like Beattie, Ramsay's preference was to argue against the defenders of slavery on their own terms and focus on how planter behaviour would be altered by the abolition of the trade rather than dwell on their prior inhumane conduct. In one of his last pamphlets on the subject, he even painstakingly

---

56. James Tobin, *A Farewel Address to the Rev. Mr. James Ramsay: From James Tobin, Esq.* (London: G. and T. Wilkie, 1788), 1–2. Brown argues that the 'venom' of Ramsay's replies to Tobin 'often undermined an otherwise powerful case'. Brown, *Moral Capital*, 373. The character assaults on Ramsay eventually took their toll. According to Eric Williams, when Ramsay died in 1789, one of his planter opponents boasted that he had 'killed him'. Eric Williams, *Capitalism and Slavery* (Richmond, VA: William Byrd Press, 2007), 181.

57. James Ramsay, *Examination of the Rev. Mr. Harris's Scriptural Researches on the Licitness of the Slave-Trade* (London: James Phillips, 1788), 12

58. Ibid., 15.

considered seventy-seven 'objections' to abolition and refuted them one by one.[59] In only a single case, when he considered the charge that African slaves in the West Indies were happier than peasants in England, did Ramsay dismiss the claim as one that 'insults common sense'.[60] As we shall see in the next section, some of his fellow travellers in the early abolitionist movement displayed far less patience with pro-slavery argument than either Beattie or Ramsay could muster.

Dickson, Shaftesbury and the Orang Outang Philosophers

Beattie and Ramsay's approach to attacking the slave trade differed markedly from that of three other participants in the Scottish Enlightenment who shared his abolitionist sympathies, at least two of whom he knew personally (though he likely crossed paths with the third as well): William Dickson, Alexander Geddes and James Tytler. Educated at the University of Edinburgh, Dickson was one of only a handful of Scottish abolitionists to have first-hand experience of the slave trade in the colonies, having emigrated to Barbados in 1772 (Beattie would comment glowingly on Dickson's 'acute and authentic observations' of the plantations).[61] Upon his return in 1785, Dickson threw himself into the abolitionist campaign which would soon gather steam in London and eventually published a formidable tract, the *Letters on Slavery* (1789), which called for an immediate halt to the slave trade and picked apart the notion that Europeans enjoyed natural superiority to Africans (the work would ultimately earn him, on Beattie's initiative, an honorary LLD degree from Marischal College).

In a post-script to his ninth *Letter* Dickson insisted that when countering denials of the Africans' humanity it was necessary to 'apply the test of truth', a direct allusion to the Shaftesburian argument that ridicule could expose falsehood.[62] Dickson considered himself on solid ground in applying this maxim to the subject of slavery partly because Montesquieu had done so before him. Before he could follow Montesquieu's example, however, Dickson had to clear up a misunderstanding concerning the Frenchman's true intention. Dickson's worry was that inattentive readers had mistaken Montesquieu's endorsement of slavery as genuine.

59. James Ramsay, *Objections to the Abolition of the Slave Trade, with Answers* (London: James Phillips, 1788).

60. Ibid., 33.

61. Beattie, *Elements of Moral Science*, vol. 2, 201.

62. William Dickson, *Letters on Slavery* (London: J. Philips, 1789), 81.

The particular inattentive reader that he had his sights on was Gordon Turnbull whose 1786 *Apology for Negro Slavery* cited the 'justly admired' Montesquieu as having argued that slavery in hot climates was 'founded on natural causes'.[63] For Dickson, Turnbull had gullibly taken as literal what was patently intended as sarcastic. 'This author', he scoffed, 'has *seriously* quoted *The Spirit of the Laws* in support of slavery' and so failed to see that 'Montesquieu has treated that subject in an admirable strain of severe, but deserved, irony'.[64] Turnbull had not been quite as dull-witted as Dickson alleged in that he had selectively quoted from book 15, chapter 7 (in which Montesquieu purports to explain why slavery in hot climates 'runs less counter to reason') and so bypassed the mock defence of slavery altogether.[65] Nevertheless, for Dickson, it was precisely that mock defence that rendered Montesquieu ineligible for enlistment to the pro-slavery cause, whatever else he might have written on the subject. It was the 'ridiculous arguments' that Montesquieu advanced in its favour that would serve as a 'lasting monument' to his 'detestation of slavery'.[66]

Putting the method he had just praised into practice, Dickson offered his own sarcastic demolition of racist arguments. The idea that Africans have a 'fetid smell' was plainly wrong, Dickson argued, but even if correct, there was no connection between odour and intellect.[67] (If British philosophers discovered such a connection, he added, then they should be congratulated, as such 'intellectual ferrets' would be useful to have around.[68]) Dickson admitted that 'negroes' did 'have flat noses' but he could no more easily account for that fact than he could for the 'high cheek bones of the Scotch' (a possible allusion to an earlier joke by Ramsay).[69] Parodying Turnbull's citation of Montesquieu, Dickson then looked to a 'certain French *apologist* for slavery', this time citing Montesquieu's facetious claim that because Africans had flat noses they ought not to be pitied.[70] For Dickson, this was no different than suggesting that elderly women with wrinkles were obviously witches and should be burned as such.

Hume too was not to be spared Dickson's contempt. Alluding to Beattie's mockery of Hume's argument in the *Treatise of Human Nature* that

63. Gordon Turnbull, *Apology for Negro Slavery* (London: J. Stephenson, 1786), 7.
64. Dickson, *Letters on Slavery*, 81.
65. Turnbull, *Apology for Negro Slavery*, 7.
66. Dickson, *Letters on Slavery*, 81.
67. Ibid., 82.
68. Ibid.
69. Ibid.
70. Ibid.

the self was a bundle of perceptions, Dickson declared that: 'If a certain philosopher formed his "perceptions", alias *doubtful doubts* into bundles, why may not we pack up the *refuse* of our objections, in the same way, and thus dispatch them in the lump.'[71] For Dickson, some arguments did not merit careful treatment but should instead be gathered up *en masse* and swept aside as rubbish. Hume's claims about the inferiority of non-Whites clearly fell into that category. Finally, Dickson turned to Montesquieu one last time. To Montesquieu's worry that if Africans were acknowledged to be human then the Europeans who enslaved them would have to doubt their own Christianity, Dickson had this to say: 'If this be not irony it is something very like it.'[72]

Part of Dickson's justification in using ridicule was the need to counter pre-emptively the contempt that would meet his own proposals. This was particularly the case in Letter 17, where Dickson proposes that evidence provided by Black witnesses should be admissible in colonial courts and that Black people should be eligible to sit on juries and serve in the police. Dickson imagines that these arguments, far from being granted a fair hearing, will be subjected to laughter, and he promises to return like with like.

> Black jurors and black constables! This proposition I know will be considered in the West Indies treason to the sacred majesty of a white skin. I see the sarcastic grin of ridicule and the malignant scowl of asperity already formed. Asperity to individual men (not individual cruelties and absurdities) I will not willingly deal in; but ridicule I will not scruple to retort.[73]

Dickson makes clear that ridicule is something of a last resort; it is the refuge of those who are themselves contemned and so are justified in firing back rather than enduring the scorn patiently. He promises general restraint in his dealings with individuals but will have no qualms about showing contempt for those he cannot hope to convince otherwise or (more likely) at all.

Crucially, however, Dickson recognized that not everyone, least of all the enslaved, was in a position to retaliate in this way. That ridicule was a weapon unavailable to the enslaved was made clear in the final section of the *Letters*, where Dickson turned to address to them directly. Adopting the tone of the author of a conduct manual, Dickson implores the 'free negroes' and 'more enlightened and regular slaves' to avoid any behaviour

71. Ibid., 84. Emphasis in original.
72. Ibid., 85.
73. Ibid., 148.

that might jeopardize the passage of an abolition bill through Parliament.[74] In particular, he insisted that they should settle for the abolition of the slave trade and not agitate for an immediate end to slavery itself, if only because a people 'totally ignorant of Christianity' would not be ready to enjoy the 'blessings of liberty'.[75]

In the meantime both slaves and freed Black people must consider themselves duty-bound to show 'respectful deference to the whites' and demonstrate their humanity by improving themselves to a level at which 'monkeys and *orang outangs* never will arrive'.[76] Evidence of such improvement could, Dickson argued, come in many forms, including through a 'vindication of African capacity by the pen of an African'.[77] Ridiculing the very notion of their natural inferiority in the manner Dickson himself had pursued, by contrast, was sure to fail. Dickson's Black readers, he suggests, may well scoff at those who claimed orangutans to be 'as good and as clever as most black men' but doing so would not improve their condition.[78] On the contrary, it would only serve to confirm European suspicions that Africans were insolent and that contemplating even a gradual emancipation would encourage them to revolt. 'You laugh', Dickson warns them, 'but you must now prove yourself to orang outang philosophers and "shew yourselves men", otherwise than by *merely laughing*.'[79]

Dickson's precise intent in this last sentence is difficult to fathom but it is likely that he had several ends in view. One was clearly to take a swipe at the offensive stupidity of interspecies comparisons and at the pretensions of the philosophers who endorsed them. His particular target was the English planter Edward Long who in his *History of Jamaica* (1774) suggested that an orangutan husband would be no 'disgrace' to a 'Hottentot female', an argument that Dickson sarcastically applauded.[80] Such

74. Ibid., 172.
75. Ibid.
76. Ibid., 174.
77. Ibid., 176.
78. Ibid., 175.
79. Ibid. Emphasis in original.
80. Ibid., 83. Dickson slightly misquotes here. Long's exact words were: 'Ludicrous as the opinion may seem, I do not think that an oran-outang husband would be any dishonour to an Hottentot female.' Edward Long, *The History of Jamaica, or, General Survey of the Ancient and Modern State of That Island. With Reflections on Its Situation, Settlements, Inhabitants, Climate, Products, Commerce, Laws, and Government*, vol. 2 (London: T. Lowndes, 1774), 364. Dickson's decision to focus his attack on Long was understandable given that the latter was the leading influence on polygenist views of racial difference, views that could be used to defend the enslavement of Black people. Most defenders of the slave trade, however, preferred economic arguments to those based on racial difference. Brown agrees that

cross-breeding, after all, could result in useful '*anthropomorphite* mules-
animals' which could be herded more easily and worked harder than other
beasts of burden.[81] By referring to 'orang outang philosophers' Dickson
implied that writers like Long were the sub-humans, not the people whose
humanity they set out to deny.

At the same time, however, Dickson also stresses that at least one common means of proving one's humanity would not be open to Africans, that of
laughter itself. For several abolitionists, the fact that Africans laugh served
as crucial evidence of their humanity. In the first volume of his *Elements
of Moral Science*, for example, Beattie followed Aristotle in proclaiming
'risibility' to be 'one of distinguishing characteristics of man' and cited the
African slaves' laughter as proof that they were part of the human family.[82]
Dickson's suggestion was that British prejudice against Black people was
so extreme that this particular proof of their humanity would never pass
muster with a White British audience. Finally, having earlier affirmed the
Shaftesburian proposition that ridicule was a 'test of truth', Dickson now
heavily qualified it. Black ridicule of the White refusal to recognize their
humanity, Dickson dismally accepted, would do nothing to expose the
absurdity or injustice of that refusal. Only Black-authored works of high
literature, Dickson suggests, could even stand a chance of doing so.

Dickson's sarcasms are a useful illustration of how appeals to the ridiculous are also appeals to a consensus, in this case concerning the boundaries
of humanity. As Sebastiani observes, planters such as Long had humanized
the orangutan only to open up a gulf *within* humanity between orangutans
and barbarous Africans, on the one hand, and civilized Europeans, on the
other.[83] Dickson's ridicule appealed to an alternative vision of humanity,
one that cast the orangutans back into animality, while elevating humans
as a whole into a species whose members should enjoy equal status.[84] To
those who shared Dickson's view, Long's attempt to align Africans with
humanized primates should have been 'indecent' and 'shocking'.[85] Dickson's task was to prod them into acknowledging what they already knew.

'pro-slavery writers made almost no attempt to defend slavery in the abstract'. Instead they
mainly relied on the economic case for its continuation. Brown, *Moral Capital*, 372.

81. Dickson, *Letters on Slavery*, 83.

82. Beattie, *Elements of Moral Science*, vol. 1, 158.

83. Silvia Sebastiani, 'A "Monster with Human Visage": The Orangutan, Slavery, and
the Borders of Humanity in the Global Enlightenment', *History of the Human Sciences* 32,
4 (2019), 92.

84. Ibid., 93.

85. Dickson, *Letters on Slavery*, 83.

Geddes and the Danger of Irony

Although Dickson endorsed Montesquieu's ridicule as an abolitionist tactic, he never attempted a full-on parody of pro-slavery argument in the vein of the French baron. It was another Scot, Alexander Geddes, who revived Montesquieu's tactic and took it to new heights. A radical Catholic priest who opposed 'the mummeries of popery as heartily as any Presbyterian', Geddes showed an affinity for satire from his first publication, a version of Horace's *Satires* 'adapted to the present times and manners' that ultimately won him a doctorate from Aberdeen University and the acquaintance of Beattie and Reid.[86] In it, Geddes made plain that the right to use ridicule against vice was sacrosanct and that he saw no reason why

> when fools or knaves provoke,
> I should refuse myself a joke—
> Or you this freedom should deny—
> I really see no reason why.[87]

Most of Geddes' satirical powers were deployed in an ongoing dispute with Catholic bishops who repeatedly censored him for attempting a translation of the Bible into English for the use of English Catholics. In the preface to an open letter to these bishops, Geddes launched into a full-throated defence of ridicule as a weapon of dispute, this time with added assurances that he would use it with restraint:

> Good natured, seasonable ridicule has always been considered as the Satellite of reason, and has often done her great and important services. Here I could have made his blade much more tranchant [*sic*], if I had chosen it: but I have more than once compelled him to sheath his sword, when he was most eager to brandish it, because I wished him to tickle only, not to slash.[88]

Geddes's description of himself as a polite humourist who intended only to 'tickle' was one that even his admirers struggled to recognize. According

86. David Irving, *The Lives of the Scottish Poets; with Preliminary Dissertations on the Literary History of Scotland and the Early Scottish Drama* (London: Longman et al., 1810), 363. For details of Geddes's heterodox Catholicism see Mark Goldie, 'Alexander Geddes at the Limits of the Catholic Enlightenment', *The Historical Journal* 53, 1 (2010), 61–86.

87. Alexander Geddes, *Select Satires of Horace, Translated into English Verse and, for the Most Part, Adapted to the Present Time and Manners* (London: T. Cadell, 1779), 48.

88. Alexander Geddes, *Letter from the Reverend Alexander Geddes to the Rev. John Douglass* (London: J. Johnston, 1794), iii.

to an otherwise sympathetic contemporary, Geddes's lapses into irony usually propelled him into a 'violence of controversy not perfectly consistent with the polished manners of the day'.[89] This was certainly the case when, in 1792, Geddes placed his talent for ridicule at the service of the anti-slavery cause. While moving in radical circles in London, Geddes concluded that every attempt to argue against slavery had been 'in vain'.[90] A new approach was therefore needed, one that that mixed 'humour and severity'.[91] The result was the anonymous *An Apology for Slavery; or, Six Cogent Arguments against the Immediate Abolition of the Slave-Trade*, forty-seven pages of mock advocacy for the 'trade in human blood' published by the radical printer Joseph Johnson.[92]

The opening lines of Geddes's tract situated it as part of the response to another of Johnson's publications from that year, Thomas Paine's *Rights of Man*. The *Apology*'s anonymous narrator bemoans how some of Paine's over-eager readers had pushed his argument 'so far as to maintain that the vile and barbarous *Blacks* of Africa have an equal claim to freedom as the rest of the human race' before pleading that the abolitionists had been granted too easy a time of it and that the embattled defenders of slavery must be allowed a right of reply.[93] Geddes thus began by reversing Montesquieu's formula; rather than voicing pro-slavery arguments, the *Apology* first demolished the abolitionist case, taking aim specifically at claims that slavery was unnatural, inhumane and prohibited by religion. To say that slavery was contrary to nature, the *Apology*'s narrator insists, was to forget that nature was also responsible for destructive storms, volcanoes and floods. Appealing to humanity was hardly more promising, as the history of humanity itself was a story of crime, violence, war and oppression. Religion was even less available as an authority against slavery, for while individual clerics had denounced the slave trade as a matter of conscience, the established Church had not, and it was that Church alone that spoke for religion. (Here Geddes blended his concern for the

---

89. John Mason Good, *Memoirs of the Life and Writings of the Reverend Alexander Geddes, L.L.D* (London: G. Kearsley, 1803), 530. Some of the more heated of these confrontations took place between Geddes and Henry Fuseli at the printer Joseph Johnson's house. So infuriated was he by Fuseli's 'ready wit' that Geddes took to walking twice around St Paul's Churchyard to cool off before returning to the fray. John Knowles, *The Life and Writings of Henry Fuseli*, vol. 1 (London: Henry Colburn & Richard Bentley, 1831), 73.

90. Good, *Memoirs of the Life and Writings of the Reverend Alexander Geddes*, 270.

91. Ibid.

92. Ibid., 271.

93. Alexander Geddes, *An Apology for Slavery; or, Six Cogent Arguments Against the Immediate Abolition of the Slave-Trade* (London: Joseph Johnson, 1792), 7.

plight of slaves with the frustration of a heterodox Catholic critical of the British Church and state.)

Having dismissed the abolitionist case Geddes reproduced a version of Montesquieu's sarcastic imitation of pro-slavery arguments.[94] Continuing its facetious subversion of Paine, the *Apology* presents as commonsensical a series of claims antithetical to radicals like Geddes himself and others in the Johnson circle: 'That man is born in Slavery, lives in Slavery, and dies in Slavery, is a truth too obvious to be seriously called into question.'[95] For each person born passes from the 'lightless dungeon' of the womb to the control of a 'female slave driver' (midwives and nannies) to the tyranny of schoolteachers, of work (if poor), or of luxury (if rich).[96] But even if slavery is humanity's general condition, the *Apology* asserts, the African is condemned by Ham's curse to be especially suited to it: 'A Black and a Slave have become synonymous terms', such that 'African Freedom would be a solecism in language.'[97] The laws of nations likewise sanction the practice, and the exception of some American states (such as Rhode Island) that had recently abolished the slave trade could be summarily dismissed. 'What influence', after all, 'should one dirty republic have on the world?'[98]

The *Apology's* closing argument revealed how Geddes wished to provoke readers far beyond defenders of slavery. It made perfect sense that slavery was lawful under the British constitution, Geddes claimed, because that constitution *already* distributed liberty in 'unequal parcels' to Catholics and dissenters.[99] To abolish slavery, therefore, would only encourage other subjects with less than full freedom to press their grievances, an outcome that even the arch-abolitionist Wilberforce could not have intended. This was an argument that risked diluting the pamphlet's antislavery message by establishing an equivalence between chattel slaves and Catholics who were denied full civil liberties. By expanding the *Apology* into a wider attack on the British reluctance to tolerate Catholics, Geddes also risked presenting himself as a disaffected subversive warring with the church–state establishment as a whole rather than attacking the particular evil of the slave trade. Such linkage between slavery and other issues on the reform agenda was precisely what most members of the London

94. It has been claimed, with good reason, that the tone of Geddes's pamphlet is 'reminiscent' of Montesquieu's satirical chapter. Fletcher, 'Montesquieu's Influence on Anti-Slavery Opinion in England', 423.

95. Geddes, *Apology for Slavery*, 20.

96. Ibid., 21.

97. Ibid., 24.

98. Ibid.

99. Ibid., 35.

Committee of the Society for the Abolition of the Slave Trade had been trying to avoid and may explain why Geddes's pamphlet never entered the canon of abolitionist literature.[100]

Throughout his *Apology* Geddes echoed not only not Montesquieu's style but also his specific mock arguments. Both authors satirically assert that the indispensable role played by slave labour in keeping the cost of sugar down was reason enough to defend it in accordance with what Geddes called the 'law of self-interest' and the 'law of luxury'.[101] Both, moreover, present abolition as inconsistent with the interests of the state, as revenue flows indirectly linked to the trade would be disrupted, resulting in a violation of the 'maxims' of 'state expediency'.[102] Unlike Montesquieu, however, Geddes's mock apology for slavery made for unsettling reading for abolitionists as well as for the defenders of slavery, and not only because he linked abolition to toleration for Catholics. By grounding his apology for slavery in an appeal to common sense, Geddes (deliberately or not) exposed the hollowness of all such appeals. This was troubling not only to Mr *Common Sense* himself, Thomas Paine, but also to common sense philosophers like Beattie who relied heavily on the notion that slavery was repugnant to common sense and so self-evidently objectionable. The impression Geddes left on his readers was that common sense was never quite common enough. He might even have been mimicking actual slave-traders who invoked common sense at the very moment the tide of public opinion in Britain began to move against them. In 1788, the Colonial Agent for Jamaica, Stephen Fuller, recognized that the 'stream of popularity' was running against the slave trade but had faith nonetheless that 'common sense is with us'.[103]

Tytler, Sharks and Rhetorical Distancing

In Edinburgh, during the same year as Geddes published his *Apology for Slavery*, the polymath and 'hack writer' James Tytler adopted a different set of satirical tactics.[104] Tytler, if anything, surpassed Geddes

100. On the aversion of the London Committee to the conflating of abolition with other radical causes see Seymour Drescher, *Abolition: A History of Slavery and Anti-Slavery* (Cambridge: Cambridge University Press, 2009), 220. Radicalism was the 'Achilles heel' of the early abolitionist movement. J. R. Oldfield, *Popular Politics and British Anti-Slavery: The Mobilisation of Public Opinion Against the Slave Trade 1787–1807* (New York: Routledge, 1998), 4.

101. Geddes, *Apology for Slavery*, 20.

102. Ibid., 31.

103. Drescher, *Abolition: A History of Slavery and Anti-Slavery*, 216.

104. Richard Yeo, *Encyclopaedic Visions: Scientific Discourses and Enlightenment Culture* (Cambridge: Cambridge University Press, 2001), 11.

for eccentricity. The poet Robert Burns memorably described him as an 'obscure, tippling' printer who 'drudge[d] about Edinburgh in leaky shoes'.[105] Tytler's earliest and most lasting contribution to Enlightenment intellectual culture came when he was entrusted with producing the second edition of the *Encyclopaedia Britannica* from 1777 to 1784. It was a remarkable feat that he undertook on meagre pay and in conditions of near-penury. At the time of the invitation to edit *Britannica* Tytler was languishing in a debtors' sanctuary—Burns thought it astonishing that this 'unknown drunken mortal' could have been the 'author and compiler of three-fourths of Elliot's pompous Encyclopaedia Britannica' while fetching a measly 'half a guinea a week!'[106]

During this brief editorial career, Tytler revealed himself an avid proponent of Scottish common sense philosophy. In the entry for 'Sense, Common' in his edition of the *Encyclopaedia* he departed from its advertised neutrality on philosophical matters to heartily endorse Reid, Beattie and Campbell's efforts to undermine the scepticism of Hume, the 'British Bayle'.[107] Tytler was similarly taken with Scottish Enlightenment theories of ridicule. His entry on 'Ridicule' (new to his edition) consisted in little more than an abridgement of chapter 12 of Kames's *Elements of Criticism*.[108] Kames's chapter contained a robust defence of ridicule as the only means of testing what is 'really grave' and held that it should be deployed freely and widely without fear of adverse consequences.[109] Employing the familiar Shaftesburian motif, Tytler (via Kames) insisted that if 'something is neither risible nor improper it will not be vulnerable to an attack from ridicule'.[110] Provided it could be brought 'under proper culture', therefore, ridicule was an indispensable method for ensuring that truth will prevail even among the 'vulgar'.[111]

This was a lesson that Tytler would retain during his turn to radicalism in the 1790s, a turn that would ultimately result in his having to flee Britain for fear of prosecution during Pitt's anti-sedition drive. Following

105. Robert Burns, *The Oxford Edition of The Works of Robert Burns*, vol. 1, *Commonplace Books, Tour Journals, and Miscellaneous Prose*, ed. Nigel Leask (Oxford: Oxford University Press, 2014), 316–17.

106. Ibid., 318.

107. Kathleen Hardesty Doig et al., 'James Tytler's Edition (1777–1784): A Vast Expansion and Improvement', in *The Early Britannica: The Growth of an Outstanding Encyclopedia*, ed. Frank A. Kafker and Jeff Loveland (Oxford: Voltaire Foundation, 2009), 134–35.

108. Ibid., 93.

109. Home (Lord Kames), *Elements of Criticism*, vol. 1, 55.

110. Ibid., 56.

111. Ibid., 57.

defeat in Parliament of a motion to abolish the slave trade in 1791, the London Committee orchestrated a massive popular mobilization, resulting in a deluge of petitions before Parliament. Rather than add one more earnest voice to this chorus, Tytler instead published a mock petition to Parliament that drew attention to the fate of a maritime constituency who would be adversely affected by abolition. The result was the '*PETITION of the SHARKS of Africa* to the House of Commons', an astonishingly daring satire even by the standards of the day, which Tytler published in a short-lived periodical he edited called *The Historical Register*.[112] The petition begins by informing the members of Parliament that African sharks are currently in a 'flourishing condition' thanks to the nourishment provided by slave ships.[113] The shark petitioners then proceed to explain in grim detail how they come to be fed. Not only do the ships' captains dump the bodies of dead slaves overboard, but the sharks also feast on the 'bodies of living negroes' who 'voluntarily plunge' into the sea, preferring 'instant destruction' by the sharks' jaws to continued enslavement.[114] The destruction of slavers by shipwreck was likewise a source of 'many a delicious meal'.[115] The petition ends by imploring members of Parliament to turn a deaf ear to the 'wild ravings' of the abolitionists and expressing confidence that Britain's political elite will 'not suffer sharks to starve in order that negroes may be happy'.[116]

Tytler's pamphlet was a departure from Montesquieu's model and brought him closer to the macabre tone of Swift's *Modest Proposal*. Rather than parody pro-slavery opinion, Tytler uses the sharks as a distancing device, allowing his readers to imagine, in gruesome terms, the non-human beneficiaries of the slave trade and how they might make the case for perpetuating it. Importantly, however, aside from evoking sympathy for the enslaved, Tytler's petition collapses the distance between races by contrasting *all* humans with the sharks. Tytler's sharks do not discriminate on the basis of race; to the extent that all human flesh is delicious, all humans are equal. At the same time, the shark petitioners are also aware of White racial prejudice and seek to exploit it for their own benefit,

---

112. James Fergusson, *Balloon Tytler* (London: Faber and Faber, 1972), 114.

113. Anon. [Tytler], 'The Petition of the Sharks of Africa' (May 1792), University of Bristol DM211. On the provenance of this satire see Marcus Rediker, 'History from below the Water Line: Sharks and the Atlantic Slave Trade', *Atlantic Studies* 5, 2 (2008), 285–97. Fergusson notes that Tytler's periodical 'castigated the slave trade' although he makes no specific mention of the shark satire.

114. [Tytler], 'The Petition of the Sharks of Africa', 1.

115. Ibid.

116. Ibid.

playing on White disdain for Black people and so encouraging them to prolong a trade that benefits both Whites and sharks.

By the time he published this satire, Tytler's association with the *Encylopaedia Britannica* had come to an end, possibly owing to his need to flee England back to Scotland to escape a divorce suit. He contributed several articles to the third edition but by now had passed on the principal editorial graft to George Gleig. Assuming that Tytler kept up with a project he had devoted so much time and labour to, he must have been galled to read a new article on 'Slavery', authored by Gleig himself, that attacked the tone used by uncompromising abolitionists like himself. Gleig's article acknowledged the inhumanity and injustice of the slave trade, predicted its eventual demise, welcomed the fact that Parliament had finally taken up the issue, and insisted that the enslaved be Christianized before manumission could be seriously tabled. Not only did the article fall short of calling for immediate abolition, however, it also castigated those abolitionists whose detestation of slavery had led them to treat defenders of the slave trade with incivility. Gleig opened his objection by burnishing his own anti-slavery credentials: 'To a cause truly Christian', Gleig asked rhetorically, 'who could not pray for success?'[117] But that success, he continued, would be delayed by the immoderation of the abolitionists' attacks: 'Language calculated to exasperate the planters cannot serve the negroes.'[118] When Parliament voted narrowly to defeat Wilberforce's abolitionist petition, Gleig attributed this setback in part to the 'insulting epithets indiscriminately heaped upon the slave-holders'.[119] Given that Tytler published his satire anonymously, it is highly unlikely that Gleig was targeting him specifically. But that the two *Encyclopaedia* editors had opposed visions of abolitionist strategy there can be no doubt.

Conclusion

Judging the success of these experiments in using ridicule to combat racial prejudice and advance the abolitionist cause is difficult. Even the London Society for the Abolition of the Slave Trade deemed Dickson's *Letters on Slavery* 'too strong' and initially declined to print it.[120] Geddes's *Apology*

---

117. George Gleig, *Encyclopaedia Britannica; or, a Dictionary of Arts, Sciences, and Miscellaneous Literature on a Plan Entirely New*, 3rd edn, vol. 17 (Dublin: James Moore, 1790), 532.
118. Ibid.
119. Ibid.
120. Whyte, *Scotland and the Abolition of Black Slavery*, 115.

for Slavery met the fate of many satires in that it was interpreted by some as sincere and applauded by the very anti-abolitionists it was supposed to undermine (Johnson was obliged to add the word 'Ironical' to the title of subsequent editions to prevent readers from interpreting it as anything other than an anti-slavery tract).[121] Tytler's shark satire appeared at the culmination of an abolitionist campaign that was already five years old and that had been gradually winning over public opinion to the cause. His intention may thus have been to cement a consensus already formed rather than make new converts.

Yet, whatever the limitations of the tactic, the notion that ridicule should frequently replace argument in countering the prejudices that have upheld slavery never waned. Perhaps the most celebrated abolitionist orator of the nineteenth century, Frederick Douglass, placed it at the heart of his 4 July address to the Ladies Anti-Slavery Society of Rochester in 1852. There has been no shortage of analysis of what Douglass *did* in that speech: his invocation of scripture, his rehabilitation of the United States constitution as an anti-slavery document, and his denunciation of the hypocrisy behind White American boasts of freedom, have all been rightly regarded as central planks of his rhetorical strategy. Just as important as what Douglass did, however, was what he *refused* to do and what he demanded be done. At the culmination of the speech Douglass made plain that White claims to superiority over Black people should be regarded as beneath engagement and that he would not be refuting them 'by the rules of logic and argumentation'.[122] Instead Douglass declared that 'scorching irony' was called for and that if he had the requisite talent he would release a 'fiery stream of biting ridicule, blasting reproach' and 'withering sarcasm' upon those who clung to such claims.[123] For Black people to have to argue that they merited equal dignity to White people would itself, Douglass implied, be a demeaning experience. Not only would it treat as contestable (and hence uncertain) a claim to human equality that should be regarded as axiomatic, but it would also elevate a bigoted prejudice to the status of a seriously debatable proposition. That the case for the equal humanity of Black people would easily win out in such a debate, Douglass suggested, was beside the point. To stage the contest at all would be to commit the

121. David Whitford, *The Curse of Ham in the Early Modern Era: The Bible and the Justifications for Slavery* (London: Routledge, 2009), 161.

122. Frederick Douglass, 'What to the Slave Is the Fourth of July?', in *The Essential Douglass: Selected Writings and Speeches*, ed. Nicholas Buccola (Indianapolis, IN: Hackett, 2016), 59.

123. Ibid.

fallacy of treating as commensurable (and so capable of critical comparison) what was in reality incommensurable.

By contrast, to counter such claims with ridicule, Douglass insinuated, would accomplish two things. In the first place, it would belittle the claim that Black people are naturally inferior and so put it back in its proper place (or rather keep it there). Second, it would signal to those who treat such a claim as a serious proposition that the debate they wish to have will not happen on terms of their choosing or may not even happen at all. In reality, of course, this was rarely the case. As Montesquieu saw, the power of ridicule to settle debate or fix the boundaries of permissible argument was severely limited. No matter how convinced a speaker might have been that his or her mockery has decisively defeated the opponent, this was rarely (if ever) the case. But it is precisely this limitation that made ridicule appropriate on just such occasions. If ridicule really could decide an issue as suddenly and completely as some of its Enlightenment advocates claimed, then this very potency would render it unsuitable for debate, much as the devastation wrought by nuclear weapons renders them—one hopes, still—unusable in conventional warfare. A rhetorical move that could quash further debate would not be a rhetorical move at all but something external to the realm of persuasion. It is precisely because it lacked such power that ridicule was appropriate for debate— exposing moments when one side disguises raw assertions of prejudice or self-interest as arguments—but never bringing debate to a halt entirely.

CHAPTER SIX

An Education in Contempt

RIDICULE IN WOLLSTONECRAFT'S POLITICS

We must each of us wear a fool's cap; but mine, alas! has lost its bells,
and is grown so heavy, I find it intolerably troublesome . . . I have been
persuing [sic] a number of strange thoughts since I began to write, and
have actually both wept and laughed immoderately—Surely I am
a fool.[1]

—MARY WOLLSTONECRAFT TO JOSEPH JOHNSON, 1792

Laughter can be [a] kind of wilful and rebellious noise.[2]

—SARA AHMED

IN THE DRAMATIC OPENING PAGES of her *Vindication of the Rights of Men* (1790), Mary Wollstonecraft accused Edmund Burke of passing off ridicule as a 'test of truth'.[3] In doing so she obliquely referenced the Shaftesburian defence of ridicule as a mechanism for discerning truth and correcting vice.[4] For Wollstonecraft, few works better exposed the hollowness

---

1. Mary Wollstonecraft, 'Letters to Joseph Johnson', in *The Works of Mary Wollstonecraft*, ed. Marilyn Butler and Janet Todd, 7 vols (London: Pickering and Chatto, 1989), vol. 6, 359.

2. Sara Ahmed, *Living a Feminist Life* (Durham, NC: Duke University Press, 2017), 204.

3. Mary Wollstonecraft, *A Vindication of the Rights of Men*, in *The Works of Mary Wollstonecraft*, vol. 5, 9.

4. Wollstonecraft's work for Joseph Johnson's *Analytical Review* reveals her familiarity with Shaftesbury's writings. Although she admired his argument that 'virtue is desirable for its own sake' she took issue, like so many others, with the Earl's 'affected' writing style. Mary Wollstonecraft, 'Contributions to the *Analytical Review*', in *The Works of Mary Wollstonecraft*, vol. 7, 347.

of this claim than Burke's *Reflections on the Revolution in France* (1790). Far from leading his readers towards truth, Burke's ridicule was in her view motivated by, and designed to elicit, nothing but contempt. The objects of that contempt, in Wollstonecraft's eyes, ranged from the poor, to the dissenting minister Richard Price (whose sermon welcoming the revolution had served as the catalyst for Burke's polemic), to the members of the *Assemblée Nationale* itself.[5] Burke's repeated attempts to raise a 'horse laugh', Wollstonecraft suggested, had far more to do with despising his opponents as unworthy than with proving the truth of any claim.[6]

Yet, as several readers of the *Vindication* have pointed out, Wollstonecraft's attack on Burke is itself laced with ridicule. Time and again she heaps mock pity on Burke's 'infantile sensibility', pleading that she must handle him delicately for fear that an overly rigorous debate on a 'metaphysical' topic like the rights of man would 'derange' his 'nervous system'.[7] Moreover, she made clear to her readers that her ridicule of Burke was calculated and deliberate. The *Vindication* mimics the epistle form of Burke's *Reflections*, with Burke himself as the letter's addressee. But in sharp contrast to the warm opening salutation with which Burke greeted Charles-Jean-Francois Depont (his correspondent in *Reflections*), the *Vindication*'s greeting places Burke firmly on guard. In what follows, Wollstonecraft warns, she will not only 'express contempt' for Burke but will do so overtly, rather than concealing her feelings as the 'equivocal idiom of politeness recommends'.[8]

How are we to make sense of Wollstonecraft's upbraiding of Burke for ridiculing his opponents, on the one hand, and her unapologetic determination to do precisely the same towards him, on the other? And what might answering this question reveal about the place of ridicule within her political project as a whole? From the moment of its publication a matter of weeks after Burke's *Reflections*, both sympathetic and hostile readers of the *Vindication* have agreed that Wollstonecraft erred by choosing to match Burke's expression of contempt with one of her own. One generous early

---

5. Wollstonecraft twice reprimands Burke for treating Price with contempt. Wollstonecraft, *A Vindication of the Rights of Men*, 18 and 44. She also accosts him twice for the contempt he shows towards the poor. Ibid., 55. For her criticism of Burke's disrespectful treatment of the *Assemblée Nationale* see ibid., 40.

6. Ibid., 7.

7. Ibid., 16. On the 'wry sense of humor' that pervades Wollstonecraft's writings see Eileen Hunt Botting, 'The Personal Is the Political: Wollstonecraft's Witty, First Person Feminist Voice', in *The Vindication of the Rights of Woman*, ed. Eileen Hunt Botting (New Haven, CT: Yale University Press, 2014), 262.

8. Ibid., 7.

critic in the *English Review* worried that Wollstonecraft would be accused of having 'repaid' Burke too much 'in his own coin'.[9] William Godwin, who in his own much earlier engagement with Burke had been careful to combine criticism of Burke's 'principles' with respect for his character, called the work 'too contemptuous and intemperate'.[10] More recent critics have concurred.[11] Janet Todd goes so far as to find something of a double standard at work in Wollstonecraft's criticism of Burke's 'sarcasms', suggesting that 'Burke's attack on Price never stoops to the kind of personal abuse that Wollstonecraft levels at Burke'.[12] At best, it would seem, Wollstonecraft's ridicule of Burke distracted from her arguments for the rights of man and her defence of the French Revolution. At worst, it revealed her to have been an injudicious or even wantonly abusive critic.

These criticisms, I aim to show in this chapter, posit a misleading equivalence between Wollstonecraft's and Burke's modes of address and in so doing occlude the positive role played by ridicule in Wollstonecraft's political project. Over the course of her writing career, I argue, Wollstonecraft

9. Anon., *The English Review, or an Abstract of English and Foreign Literature* 17 (1791), 95.

10. William Godwin, *Memoirs of the Author of the Vindication of the Rights of Woman* (London: J. Johnson, 1798), 76. In his *Defence of the Rockingham Party*, Godwin expressed disagreement with Burke's 'aristocratic principles' but went out of his way not to 'question the integrity of any man, upon account of his tenets, whether in religion or politics'. He even expressed concern that Burke had been the victim of 'superficial raillery and abuse'. William Godwin, *A Defence of the Rockingham Party* (London: J. Stockdale, 1783), 30, 35. Other early readers of the *Vindication* were more sympathetic. For Francis Stone, it was Burke alone who was guilty of treating ridicule as a test of truth. Wollstonecraft, by contrast, had 'defeated' him in the 'fair fought field of argument'. Francis Stone, *An Examination of the Right Hon. Edmund Burke's Reflections on the Revolution in France* (London: sold by G.G.J. and J. Robinson and others, 1792), 7.

11. Ralph Wardle maintained that Wollstonecraft subjected Burke to 'sheer abuse' rather than arguing with him. Ralph Wardle, *Mary Wollstonecraft: A Critical Biography* (Lawrence: University of Kansas Press, 1951), 118. Virginia Sapiro similarly saw 'haste' and 'anger' in Wollstonecraft's rhetorical choices. Virginia Sapiro, *A Vindication of Political Virtue: The Political Theory of Mary Wollstonecraft* (Chicago: University of Chicago Press, 1992), 201. Not everyone has taken issue with Wollstonecraft's tone. Recently, Amartya Sen has praised Wollstonecraft for her 'quite remarkable' way of 'combining wrath and reasoning in the same work'. Amartya Sen, *The Idea of Justice* (Cambridge, MA: Harvard University Press, 2009), 392. I share Sen's admiration but disagree that 'wrath' is the only or even predominant passion on display in Wollstonecraft's *Vindication*.

12. Janet Todd in Mary Wollstonecraft, *A Vindication of the Rights of Woman and A Vindication of the Rights of Men*, ed. Janet Todd (Oxford: Oxford University Press, 1993), 380, editor's note 45. Mary Beth Tegan suggests that the 'contemptuous tenor' of Wollstonecraft's commentary 'arguably weakens her position as a champion for women's rights'. Mary Beth Tegan, 'Mocking the Mothers of the Novel: Mary Wollstonecraft, Maternal Metaphor, and the Reproduction of Sympathy', *Studies in the Novel* 42, 4 (2010), 367.

endowed ridicule with two definite and defensible purposes. First, she used ridicule to express a dignified contempt for those who sought to demean others from a position of social privilege. Though never shedding her reservations about ridicule entirely, Wollstonecraft thus recognized its value as a form of 'active non-identification', that is, a way of signalling to oneself and one's audience that an opponent is unworthy of the dignity to which they lay claim.[13] Second, Wollstonecraft recommended that young women be trained to ridicule writings (and their authors) that reinforce the prejudices that contribute to women's subordination. A female student educated under Wollstonecraft's principles, in other words, would not shun ridicule entirely but would instead direct it at the authors whose writings compounded the notion that women were incapable of the independence that Wollstonecraft summoned them to exercise.

The chapter begins by examining the place of ridicule within eighteenth-century education and conduct manuals, a literature that was fundamental to Wollstonecraft's formation as a thinker and writer. I show how many of the educational theorists who influenced Wollstonecraft considered ridicule a bad social habit that needed to be corrected through civility and self-restraint. I turn next to Wollstonecraft's own condemnation of ridicule as needlessly cruel, a poor substitute for reasoned argument, and a vice peculiar to vain aristocrats struggling with status anxiety. Turning, in the third section, to her contest with Burke, I show how Wollstonecraft's understanding of ridicule as both abusive and anxiety-laden informed her rhetorical choices in the *Vindication of the Rights of Men*, and in particular her controversial decision to attack Burke *ad hominem* rather than engage his arguments on their own terms. Finally, in the fourth section, I offer an analysis of ridicule within Wollstonecraft's most celebrated text, the *Vindication of the Rights of Woman* (1792). There I examine the significance of Wollstonecraft's recommendation that young women be taught to ridicule cultural narratives that, if taken too seriously by female readers, would reinforce male domination of women.

Ridicule in the Education and Conduct Literature

Getting to grips with the eighteenth-century education and advice literature is essential to understanding Wollstonecraft's views on ridicule. Much of this literature was driven by a fear that Britain was spiralling into

13. I take the term 'active non-identification' from Macalester Bell. Macalester Bell, *Hard Feelings: The Moral Psychology of Contempt* (Oxford: Oxford University Press, 2013), 53.

a state of cultural decay and political corruption. One symptom of this decline was an increased fondness for jesting among social elites, a vice attributed to French influence. 'The infection of French levity', the schoolmaster Vicesimus Knox complained in *Liberal Education* (1781), 'has pervaded the whole mass of the English body politic'.[14] For Knox and others like him, the combination of witty conversation with moral seriousness that had been a hallmark of the Shaftesburian programme was a chimera. Instead, 'levity in conversation' was inexorably associated with moral laxity or 'levity of principle'.[15] Educational reform was needed to arrest the first and thereby prevent the second.

A key assumption shared by educational reformers who took up this challenge was that the habit of ridiculing others was a sign of an abusive temperament. The Whig historian Catherine Macaulay, whose *Letters on Education* Wollstonecraft admired intensely, was unequivocal that children should be reproached for mocking others and that tutors should 'discourage every attempt to ill-natured raillery'.[16] Macaulay's worry was not only that mocking others was hurtful but also that children who were too fond of it would mistake the infliction of pain as the purpose of all ridicule. An addiction to 'sarcastic censoriousness' would prevent the child from recognizing that 'honest satire never wounds but to amend'.[17] If someone is to be mocked, there had better be good reason for it. Macaulay's fear was that children permitted to mock others unchecked would fail to heed this limitation.

Particularly of concern in this respect were young women who might be tempted to fire off repartees to demonstrate their wit in front of male company, causing undue offence in the process. The poet and social reformer Hannah More, whose writings on female education are often compared with Wollstonecraft's, considered this 'fatal fondness for indulging the spirit of ridicule' a devastating character flaw among young women that could 'never be condemned more severely than it deserves'.[18] Even if the put-down was timely and merited, she argued, women should learn to smother it and content themselves with the 'inner triumph' that comes

14. Vicesimus Knox, *Liberal Education: Or, a Practical Treatise on the Methods of Acquiring Useful and Polite Learning* (London: C. Dilly, 1783), 404.

15. Ibid., 412–13.

16. Catherine Macaulay Graham, *Letters on Education: With Observations on Religious and Metaphysical Subjects* (London: C. Dilly, 1790), 170.

17. Ibid., 169.

18. Hannah More, *Essays on Various Subjects Principally Designed for Young Ladies* (London: J. Wilkie, 1778), 48.

from successfully suppressing a 'lively but severe remark'.[19] This was not least because female ridicule was automatically more wounding to men than a comparable jibe from a fellow man. When mocked by a woman, More urged, the male target might well 'join in the laugh' but would do so to cover up 'how much he is hurt' rather than share in the mirth.[20]

Male vulnerability to female ridicule extended far beyond sensitivity to offence, however. Women with a penchant for ridicule, More argued, could also turn impressionable young men away from an earnest commitment to religion. 'Ridicule', More affirmed in her *Strictures on the Modern System of Female Education*, was the 'most dangerous weapon in the whole arsenal of impiety', and she echoed the early High Church response to Shaftesbury ('a noble sceptic of the last age') by declaring that ridicule was 'no test of truth'.[21] What More added, however, was that ridicule became even more sinister in its effects when 'directed by a fair and fashionable hand'.[22] Because women of high social standing were often arbiters of what was fashionable they could corrupt an unsuspecting young man by treating with 'levity or derision [religious] subjects which he has been used to hear named with respect'.[23] Men witnessing this impious derision would quickly adopt a similar attitude in order to escape mockery themselves and so weaken their attachment to religion. More's suggestion is that ridicule produces effects that more overt attacks on religion could never accomplish. For while a young man might be able to 'confute an argument or unravel a sophistry' he 'cannot stand a laugh' and the potential embarrassment that comes from being exposed as unfashionably pious.[24]

The improper use of ridicule could also sour relations between classes. It was common for education writers to complain about the habitual contempt shown towards the socially disadvantaged and the jokes that were made at their expense. Dampening the taste for such humour, the education writers reasoned, required the early inculcation of a respectful attitude towards others. John Locke's *Some Thoughts Concerning Education* and James Burgh's *Thoughts on Education* (forerunners to Wollstonecraft's own *Thoughts on Female Education*) particularly stressed the need to counteract the socially learned contempt that the children of

19. Ibid., 49.
20. Ibid., 51.
21. Hannah More, *Strictures on the Modern System of Female Education* (London: T. Cadell, 1799), 12.
22. Ibid.
23. Ibid., 14.
24. Ibid., 14.

the wealthy directed toward those representatives of the poor they most came into contact with, namely domestic servants. Locke regretted that so many children were in the habit of inflicting upon servants 'domineering Words, Names of Contempt, and an imperious Carriage; as if they were of another Race, and Species beneath them' and recommended that such behaviour be 'weeded out' by accustoming children to act with 'civility' towards 'meaner sorts of people'. Failure to do so, Locke warned, would eventually result in adults prone to 'Oppression and Cruelty'.[25] Burgh similarly deplored how 'the most laborious, industrious and useful part of mankind' were 'generally treated with neglect and contempt' while 'the idle, the inactive and most useless part of the species, I mean, the rich' were 'adored as Gods upon earth'.[26]

Even if contemptuous attitudes persisted beyond childhood, these critics reasoned, adults could still be trained to exercise self-restraint and conceal their disdain for those they deemed beneath them. This was the view strenuously defended by William Godwin in his own contribution to the advice and conduct literature. Against those pretending to 'do homage at the shrine of sincerity' by arguing that hiding disregard for others amounted to hypocrisy, Godwin held that refraining from contemptuous talk was in fact a *precondition* for frank and open debate among equals.[27] A true 'freedom of opinion', he insisted, required not only the absence of legal restraint on thought, but also that a certain 'forebearance' be 'moulded into the manners of the community'. As for the argument that ridicule or other frank expressions of contempt could be used to educate or reform the morally deviant, Godwin was especially scathing towards it: 'Who ever thought', he asked with ample sarcasm of his own, 'of enlightening his pupil in the truths of geometry . . . by the cool and biting sarcasms of contempt?'[28]

If most educational theorists saw ridicule as simply abusive, others saw in it traces of an anxious dependence or even servility. Hester Chapone, a writer whose influence upon Wollstonecraft looms particularly large, advanced this argument with special force.[29] In the eighth of her *Letters*

25. Locke, *Some Thoughts Concerning Education*, 92.

26. James Burgh, *Thoughts on Education* (Boston: Rogers and Fowle, 1749), 17.

27. William Godwin, *Reflections on Education, Manners, and Literature* (Philadelphia: Robert Campbell and John Bioren, 1793), 272.

28. Ibid., 275.

29. Wollstonecraft selected numerous passages from Chapone's *Letters on the Improvement of the Mind* when compiling her *Female Reader*, a compendium of 'Miscellaneous Pieces, in Prose and Verse' chosen 'from the Best Writers for the Improvement of Young Women'. Mary Wollstonecraft, *The Female Reader*, in *The Works of Mary Wollstonecraft*,

on the Improvement of the Mind (from which Wollstonecraft cited copiously in her *Female Reader*) Chapone shared the apprehension of other educational writers that the 'desire of laughing' could induce impressionable young women to callously make fun of the 'most respectable of characters'.[30] However, in another of her letters Chapone made clear that that those who belittle others only do so to anxiously cover up their deficiencies. 'Pride', she begins,

> is, I think, an high opinion of one's self, and an affected contempt of others. I say *affected*, for that it is not a *real* contempt is evident from this, that the lowest object of it is of importance enough to torture the proud man's heart only by refusing him the homage and admiration he requires. . . . The proud man's contempt of others is only assumed with a view to awe them into a reverence by his pretended superiority, so it does not preclude an extreme inward anxiety about their opinions and a slavish dependence on them for all his gratifications.[31]

In this passage contempt is not (or at least not only) an expression of power; it also exposes the uneasy dependence of the person expressing it on the very people he is trying to degrade. A vain man's 'airs of insolence and contempt', Chapone went on to write, really only succeed in displaying just how desperately he 'depend[s] on the breath of the person he would be thought to despise'.[32] On Chapone's analysis, real contempt, a contempt thoroughly detached from any desire for recognition, is rare. It is the preserve, the achievement even, of a truly independent agent.

---

vol. 4, 53. More telling still, Wollstonecraft exempted Chapone from some of the more scathing criticisms she made of female educational theorists in chapter 5 of the *Vindication of the Rights of Woman*, a chapter devoted to censuring 'writers who have rendered women objects of pity, bordering on contempt'. While Wollstonecraft saw most educational manuals as complicit in the degrading of women, Chapone's *Letters*, she there remarks, 'contain so many useful observations that I only mention them to pay the worthy writer this tribute of respect', a remarkable endorsement given the generally critical tone of this portion of the *Vindication*. Wollstonecraft, *A Vindication of the Rights of Woman*, in *The Works of Mary Wollstonecraft*, vol. 5, 147 and 174. For Betty Schellenberg, this praise is evidence of Wollstonecraft's affinities with the Bluestocking movement, of which Chapone was a prominent member. Betty A. Schellenberg, 'The Bluestockings', in *Mary Wollstonecraft in Context*, ed. Nancy E. Johnson and Paul Keen (Cambridge: Cambridge University Press, 2020), 236.

30. Hester Chapone, *Letters on the Improvement of the Mind, Addressed to a Young Lady* (London: J. Walter and E. and C. Dilly, 1778), vol. 2, 106–7. Cited by Wollstonecraft in *The Female Reader*, 76.

31. Ibid., vol. 1, 106–7. Emphasis in original.

32. Ibid., vol. 1, 110.

Notice, however, that Chapone's analysis also suggested an effective method for throwing a puffed-up gentleman anxious about his status off balance. Simple refusal of the signs of reverence such a man 'requires' suffices to lay his dependence bare. A tactical form of withholding attention, in other words, could itself be a useful manner of turning the tables on vain elites and exposing their anxieties. When Wollstonecraft pointedly refused to engage Burke's arguments in the *Vindication of the Rights of Men* and chose to ridicule him instead, I will argue below, she used a version of this strategy to puncture the assumed superiority of her adversary. Before turning to the *Vindication*, however, I look in the beginning of the next section at how Wollstonecraft developed her own analysis of ridicule as brutally harmful, on the one hand, and a symptom of anxious dependence, on the other.

Wollstonecraft's Critique of Ridicule

Concerns about the potential of ridicule for cruelty and abuse can be found all over Wollstonecraft's corpus. She particularly regretted that young society girls often compensated for their lack of self-respect by a contemptuous treatment of those they considered inferior, a contempt often expressed through ridicule. In the *Female Reader*, Wollstonecraft singled out ridicule as a particularly abusive form of utterance, portraying it as the preferred weapon of dependent characters anxiously craving recognition. Under the heading 'Ridicule' she placed an excerpt from James Usher's 1767 *Clio, or a Discourse on Taste* which presented mockery as the refuge of those lacking in genuine self-esteem (or 'noble pride') and who mistakenly believed that they could 'rise out of contempt only by the depression of others'. By contrast, the excerpt continues, those who are 'conscious of their own superior merit . . . seldom affect ridicule'.[33] Dignified awareness of one's own self-worth, Wollstonecraft (via Usher) implied, needs no reward, least of all the recognition of others.

Laughing at physical blemishes was a particularly odious habit. The governess in Wollstonecraft's *Original Stories* (1788) chastises one of her young charges (who happens to be called Mary) for failing to indulge her fondness for ridicule 'in the right place' and in particular for laughing at an old woman's 'bodily infirmities and accidental defects'.[34] It was a theme Wollstonecraft would return to in the *Young Grandison*, an

33. Wollstonecraft, *The Female Reader*, 145.
34. Wollstonecraft, 'Original Stories', in *The Works of Mary Wollstonecraft*, vol. 4, 394.

educational manual originally composed in Dutch by Madame de Cambon that Wollstonecraft effectively rewrote with significant 'alterations and improvements' in 1790.[35] A lady who ridiculed a 'modest young gentleman who was a little deformed' (calling him a 'spider' and a 'little ape') and who 'continued to laugh' even when her victim showed signs of discomfort will eventually meet her comeuppance, Wollstonecraft grimly warns, when the 'ignorant' in turn 'laugh at her' after the physical charms that ground her self-esteem have faded.[36] This problem was exacerbated by the fact that girls were encouraged to regard conformity to fashion as a gauge of a person's worth, leading them to mock the 'most respectable characters' for not keeping up with arbitrary shifts in form or etiquette. Because women, Wollstonecraft observed elsewhere, were 'more accustomed to observe manners than actions' they were 'too much alive to ridicule'.[37] Learning to base esteem (both of themselves and others) on virtue and reason, Wollstonecraft implied, would eradicate such behaviour.

Ridicule was not only cruel; it was also profane. Nowhere in Wollstonecraft's writings do we find approval for the Shaftesburian doctrine that wit and religion could mix or that a scriptural warrant for ridicule could be found in the behaviour of the prophet Elijah or Christ. Instead, she saw Christ's own experience at the hands of the Romans as emblematic of how mockery was incompatible with Christian love. In the *Young Grandison* a sensible mother warns her son that even the innocent pranks played on April Fool's day bore the taint of Christ's humiliation. The 'custom of making fools of each other' could be traced, she maintained, to the 'abuse and scoffing' Christ suffered from those who 'put on him a scarlet robe by way of derision'.[38] To 'mock the wretched' or make a joke that 'gives a fellow creature pain', therefore, was only another way to 'insult' Christ himself.[39] As we shall see shortly, Wollstonecraft would lean heavily on this Gospel

35. Wollstonecraft's translations can safely be read as expressing her own views. As Sylvana Tomaselli writes: 'the texts she produced were as if her own, not just because she agreed with the ideas put forward, but because she more or less re-wrote their contents'. Sylvana Tomaselli, 'Mary Wollstonecraft: The Reunification of the Domestic and Political Spheres', in *Geschlechterordnung und Staat: Legitimationsfiguren der politischen Philosophie (1600–1850)*, ed. Marion Heinz and Sabine Doyé (Berlin: Oldenbourg, 2012), 237.

36. Mary Wollstonecraft, *Young Grandison*, in *The Works of Mary Wollstonecraft*, vol. 2, 286.

37. Mary Wollstonecraft, *The Wrongs of Woman*, in *The Works of Mary Wollstonecraft*, vol. 1, 163.

38. Wollstonecraft, *Young Grandison*, 299.

39. Ibid.

anecdote with its message about the cruelty inherent in ridicule when con-demning Burke's own proclivity to embarrass opponents with his wit.

Wollstonecraft was similarly sceptical that young people could be trained to use ridicule responsibly in conversation or debate. In her 1787 *Thoughts on the Education of Daughters* she remarked that if ridicule lived up to its reputation as the 'boasted test of truth' then women should excel at increas-ing human knowledge.[40] It quickly becomes apparent that even at this early stage in her career Wollstonecraft had little faith in ridicule's truth-revealing capacities. On the contrary, proneness to ridicule among young women results, she observed, in 'trifling conversations'.[41] Worse still was when young women reached for ridicule as a kind of cheap substitute for argument. Like Hannah More, Wollstonecraft bemoaned the fact that young women denied opportunities to exercise their reason would make use of other weapons at their disposal rather than shy away from debate entirely. Scoring points with ridicule or a 'smart turn of expression' would grant them the illusion of hav-ing won an argument when in reality they had failed to convince anybody of anything.[42] In the *Vindication of the Rights of Woman* she would renew this critique, this time associating it more with elite men. While the ability to fire off repartees and timely put-downs might win ephemeral praise, she there argued, it could never secure lasting respect. Wittiness resembled beauty as an unstable basis for esteem and in this respect gentlemen wits and society women trying to lure prospective husbands had more in common than at first appeared. The 'vain fooleries of wits and beauties to obtain attention, and make conquests are', she says, 'much upon a par.'[43]

If indulging in ridicule was a bad habit for girls, viewing comedy performed on stage was comparatively safer. Unlike other cultural crit-ics of her day Wollstonecraft was relatively sanguine about the state of comedy on the English stage and would eventually compose an autobio-graphical comedy herself (the manuscript of which Godwin unfortunately destroyed, having deemed it too 'crude' to be worth preserving).[44] It could, she argued, be 'very improving' for young viewers to see 'follies pointed out' and 'vanity ridiculed' on stage, provided those in attendance were paying

40. Wollstonecraft, *Thoughts on the Education of Daughters*, in *The Works of Mary Wollstonecraft*, vol. 4, 13.
41. Ibid.
42. Ibid, 32.
43. Wollstonecraft, *A Vindication of the Rights of Woman*, 110.
44. She presented the draft to two publishers but found neither willing to take it. Janet M. Todd, *Mary Wollstonecraft: A Revolutionary Life* (New York: Columbia Univer-sity Press, 2000), 359.

attention to the performance and not just trying to attract the attention of male onlookers.[45] But in these approving remarks Wollstonecraft made clear that this was the exception that proved the rule. The theatre, she insisted, was 'the only place where ridicule is useful'.[46] In other contexts, she implied, it was either useless or harmful.

The desire to laugh could also encourage immodest behaviour in both men and women. Throughout her writings Wollstonecraft unequivocally condemns 'bodily wit', suggesting that a 'libertine' who simply 'obeys the call of appetite' demonstrates greater modesty than the 'lewd joker who sets the table in a roar'.[47] One consequence of confining young girls in single-sex institutions such as nurseries, schools, or convents is that they quickly learn to play 'jokes and hoiden tricks' on each other, a behaviour that she unfavourably compares to sexual double entendres that 'shake the convivial table when the glass has circulated freely'.[48] Reflecting on her personal experience, Wollstonecraft even hints that she, 'an awkward rustic', was victim to such pranking in her youth.[49]

There was also an aristocratic tinge to ridicule that Wollstonecraft could not abide. Across her published works and correspondence, Wollstonecraft frequently pointed to the penchant for ridicule among the English and French aristocracies as a sign of their vanity, foppishness, and shallow understanding of the world. She found Eton insufferable because the students sharpening their wits on each other ('puns flying about like crackers') made it little more than an arena for aristocratic male posturing. Writing to her sister Everina, she complained that the 'fondness for ridicule' prevalent there tended to make everyone 'affected', the end result being that 'vanity in one shape or another reigns triumphant'.[50] She observed similar things of the French. Court culture under the *ancien régime*, she noted in her *Historical and Moral View of the French Revolution*, encouraged participants to sacrifice 'depth of thought' for the 'shrewdness of sharpened wit'.[51] In this respect they resembled the young girls who pounce with a witticism when they have no other response to

45. Wollstonecraft, *Thoughts on the Education of Daughters*, 47.

46. Ibid.

47. Wollstonecraft, *The Vindication of the Rights of Woman*, 198 and 195.

48. Ibid., 198.

49. Ibid.

50. Wollstonecraft, *The Collected Letters of Mary Wollstonecraft*, ed. Janet Todd (New York: Columbia University Press, 2003), 80.

51. Wollstonecraft, *Historical and Moral View of the French Revolution*, in *The Works of Mary Wollstonecraft*, vol. 6, 228.

an argument. The French, she complained, 'never miss an opportunity of saying a pertinent thing, or tripping up, by a small retort, the arguments with which they have not strength fairly to wrestle'.[52]

The indirectness of ridicule also made it conducive to the kind of hypocrisy Wollstonecraft identified with aristocratic culture. The French courtiers who enjoy banter, she remarked, often did so at the expense of those they had complimented the day before. In some cases they even attempted to 'appear polite' at the 'very moment they are ridiculing a person'.[53] Far from being a test of truth, then, ridicule was a tool of deception wielded by backstabbers who tried to gain the confidence of others only to make their fall more exquisite. Appalled at such a culture, Wollstonecraft was broadly in agreement with Robespierre (who she would later demonize as the architect of the Terror), who called for a new morality that would substitute 'genius for wit' and 'truth for glamour'.[54] A regenerated political culture in which such a morality predominated would privilege transparency, simplicity, and honesty ahead of what Wollstonecraft called the 'knack' of 'uttering sprightly repartees'.[55]

Although aristocratic wit was symptomatic of intellectual feebleness, for Wollstonecraft, it could nevertheless have a potent effect on affairs of state. When the *Assemblée Nationale* proclaimed freedom of the press with Declaration of the Rights of Man and the Citizen, royalists trained in court wit were poised to put their skills to good use against their political opponents. Wollstonecraft was particularly alarmed at how quickly and effectively satirical publications such as the *Journal en vaudevilles* and the *Actes des Apôtres* mobilized for counter-revolutionary purposes. In this case she conceded that earnestness and simplicity, qualities she otherwise admired, placed the revolutionaries at a distinct disadvantage. When the political neophytes that Burke disparaged in the *Reflections* arrived at Versailles, she lamented, their 'rustic gait' and 'awkward figures' made them immediately vulnerable to court wits.[56] Wollstonecraft even chided the leaders of the constituent assembly for allowing their 'passion for liberty' to blind them to the need to restrain hostile caricaturists by means of libel laws:

> Some of these satires were written with considerable wit, and such a happy turn of caricature, that it is impossible not to laugh with the

52. Ibid.

53. Ibid., 122.

54. Maximilien Robespierre, *Report on the Principles of Public Morality* (Philadelphia, 1794).

55. Wollstonecraft, *Historical and Moral View of the French Revolution*, 230.

56. Ibid., 186.

author, though indirectly ridiculing the principles you hold sacred. The most respectable decrees, the most important, and serious discussions, were twisted into jests; which divided the people without doors into two distinct parties; one, speaking of the assembly with sovereign contempt, as a set of upstarts and babbling knaves; and the other, setting up new thrones for their favourites, and viewing them with blind admiration, as if they were a synod of demigods. The countenancing of this abuse of freedom was ill-judged.[57]

The converting of 'serious discussions' into 'jests' was mostly performed by the *Journal en Vaudevilles*, which translated the debates of the *Assemblée Nationale* into witty songs.[58] As if to pay personal tribute to the persuasive power of these caricatures, Wollstonecraft admits that she was made to laugh at the very same figures she had criticized Burke for demeaning, and whose 'principles' she shared.[59] The satirists succeeded in stoking contempt for the *Assemblée Nationale* and, to make matters worse, encouraged its supporters to become so uncritical in their political affiliations that they exalted the deputies as 'demigods'. Caricature operates, Wollstonecraft here realizes, by exaggeration and simplification. The danger is that such distortions can spill over into politics as such, trivializing what is actually important and amplifying what could otherwise be negotiable differences into causes for enmity. It was for this reason that allowing the freedom of the press continue unabated was 'ill-judged' in Wollstonecraft's estimation, especially when issuing a 'decree respecting libels' could have easily curbed such 'licentious' abuse.[60]

What emerges from the above is that Wollstonecraft, like her predecessors in the education literature, blended a concern with the cruelty of ridicule with recognition that it could also be a badge of dependence, the default mode of address for those whose sense of superiority was buoyed by arbitrary differences of appearance or social status. We might suspect therefore that Wollstonecraft saw no value in ridicule whatsoever. However, a critique of how it had conventionally been abused need not translate into a disavowal of ridicule as such. Even setting aside for a moment her explicit

---

57. Ibid.

58. Laura Mason, *Singing the French Revolution: Popular Culture and Politics, 1787–1799* (Ithaca, NY: Cornell University Press, 1996), 67.

59. Wollstonecraft was far from alone in this. The *Actes des Apôtres* 'infuriated revolutionaries, not least because the newspaper's 100 per-cent oppositionism was often genuinely funny and attracted a broad audience'. Colin Jones, *The Smile Revolution in Eighteenth-Century Paris* (Oxford: Oxford University Press, 2014), 144.

60. Wollstonecraft, *Historical and Moral View of the French Revolution*, 186.

embrace of contempt in responding to Burke (to which I return below) Wollstonecraft's writings yield ample evidence that she saw value in having the subordinated channel a dignified contempt towards the very people or structures of power that oppressed them, a contempt that was often best expressed through ridicule. By implying that those who lorded it over them from a superior social vantage point are in fact beneath them according to some alternative measure of worth, the subordinated could both assert their own dignity and call into question the very basis upon which social status is allocated in the first place. In this manner, ridicule could be refashioned from a kind of abuse into a lever of social and moral reform.

Sneering at the Privileged: The Vindication of the Rights of Men

By the 1790s, several writers in the radical London circles Wollstonecraft inhabited were coming to appreciate the potential for ridicule to express a dignified contempt for the aristocracy and other social elites. Thomas Paine's *Rights of Man* (1791) went to great lengths to expose hereditary monarchy as not only a deficient form of government but also a ridiculous one, claiming that if the British public would only agree to laugh at it and at the aristocratic system that propped it up, then both would soon crumble. Paine even went so far as to argue that ridiculing aristocratic privileges would obviate the need to formally abolish them. There was 'no need to take titles away', he asserted, 'because they take themselves away when society concurs to ridicule them'.[61] Paine's use of 'concur' was telling. It suggested that the people needed to *decide* that titles were ridiculous rather than recognize that they always had been. It was down to writers like Paine to nudge them towards that decision.

Others in Wollstonecraft's milieu approvingly noted how ordinary people were already taking matters into their own hands and using ridicule to defy their social superiors in a manner that, far from being abusive, both expressed and nourished a new sense of civic equality. Godwin happily observed how mockery by the poor increasingly disturbed the 'tranquillity' of the upper classes and inspired the ridiculers themselves with the 'consciousness of citizenship'.[62] For Godwin, reversing the usual flow

---

61. Thomas Paine, *The Complete Works of Thomas Paine*, ed. Philip Foner, vol. 1 (New York: The Citadell Press, 1969), 287.

62. William Godwin, *An Enquiry Concerning Political Justice, and Its Influence on General Virtue and Happiness* (Dublin: Luke White, 1793), 40.

of contempt by directing it against the privileged, in other words, did not have to be an empty consolation for the lower orders. It could also go some small way towards redressing imbalances of social power, placing the privileged in some degree of discomfort and refusing them the homage their own contempt was designed to extort. In counteracting the psychosocial effects of elite scorn, ridicule itself was often the best remedy.

Wollstonecraft similarly came to see greater value in using ridicule to expose the vanity and corruption of Britain's social elites. In a favourable review of Samuel Hoole's 1790 satire *Modern Manners; or The Country Cousins* she welcomed any attempt to 'laugh vice out of countenance'.[63] Hooles's poem was a classic clash of manners tale about the Rusty family from the 'wilds' of the north of England who pay a surprise visit to their relatives in London and, agog at what they find, report home in a series of letters.[64] To Wollstonecraft's mind, Hoole succeeded well enough in caricaturing the vices of London society but she held back from praising him too highly because his task had been so easy. So 'unnatural' were the habits of the upper classes in the capital that only minor exaggerations were needed to render them ridiculous.[65] Tellingly, Wollstonecraft's favourite stanza in the poem, which she quotes to round off her review, features a dog fouling a copy of a book by William Dodd, a spendthrift preacher who won over many with his feigned piety but was ultimately hanged for forgery.[66] Hoole's suggestion, seconded by Wollstonecraft, is that even a dog can spot a character corrupted by high society. Wollstonecraft's hope was that 'shafts of ridicule' such as this would have a salutary shaming effect, and make vanity 'shrink back' as if it were 'wounded'.[67]

Wollstonecraft's growing appreciation for ridicule as a corrective to the vices of the rich should prompt us to reassess her chosen mode of attack on Burke. More specifically, the opening criticism of Burke in the *Vindication of the Rights of Men* for ridiculing others from a place of privilege should brace us for a treatment of him in subsequent pages as simultaneously abusive but also pitifully dependent, anxious, and even vulnerable to ridicule himself. My aim next is to show that this is indeed what Wollstonecraft presents us with.

63. Wollstonecraft, 'Contributions to the *Analytical Review*', 254.
64. Samuel Hoole, *Poems: Consisting of Modern Manners, Aurelia, The Curate, and Other Pieces Never before Published*, vol. 1 (London: J. Dodsley, 1790), 7.
65. Wollstonecraft, 'Contributions to the *Analytical Review*', 254.
66. The dog has 'done what she should not' on a copy of Dodd's *Mediations and Contemplations*. Wollstonecraft, 'Contributions to the *Analytical Review*', 254.
67. Ibid.

Finding evidence in the *Vindication* of Wollstonecraft's concern with the abusiveness of Burke's ridicule is not especially difficult. 'Glow[ing]', as she puts it, 'with indignation', she indicts Burke repeatedly for casting down 'thundering censures' and the 'bushfiring of ridicule' upon his opponents. In identifying this flaw she was hardly alone. Even Burke's friend Philip Francis had warned him to cut down on the 'jest and sneer and sarcasm' before sending his *Reflections on the Revolution in France* to press.[68] Wollstonecraft particularly takes umbrage to Burke's treatment of Richard Price, who had been her close friend and mentor during her time managing a school at Newington Green.[69] Burke had confessed in his reply to Francis that one of his principal aims in writing the *Reflections* had been to expose Price to the 'hatred, ridicule and contempt of the whole world' and it was this (as Wollstonecraft saw it) gratuitous decision to abuse an elderly man that Wollstonecraft sought to expose and condemn.[70]

In Wollstonecraft's eyes, however, Burke's mockery of the weak or infirm extended far beyond his dissenter opponents to the king himself. Commentators on the *Vindication* who focus on Wollstonecraft's indignation over Burke's attacks on Price often miss her surprisingly sympathetic portrayal of George III, whose treatment at the hands of Burke during the mental illness that sparked the Regency crisis similarly draws Wollstonecraft's ire. In the debates over the Regency Bill that took place in February 1789, Burke had insisted that the king had been thoroughly incapacitated and pleaded that God, by inflicting him with such an illness, had effectively 'hurled' him 'from his throne'.[71] Unsurprisingly, Burke's critics seized upon this speech as evidence of his scant respect for the monarch. More interesting to Wollstonecraft, however, was what Burke said next. To pretend that the king had not been stricken by madness might look humane, Burke suggested, but effectively it would amount to 'putting a

68. Philip Francis to Edmund Burke, 19 February 1790. Edmund Burke, *The Correspondence of Edmund Burke*, ed. Alfred Cobban and Robert A. Smith, vol. 6 (Chicago: University of Chicago Press, 1967), 86.

69. Towards Price, Wollstonecraft seethed, Burke was a bully, showing no qualms about subjecting an ageing minister then 'tottering on the verge of the grave', to 'willful' and 'wanton abuse'. Wollstonecraft, *A Vindication of the Rights of Men*, 18–19.

70. Burke to Philip Francis, 19 February 1790. Burke, *The Correspondence of Edmund Burke*, vol. 6, 92. See also Richard Bourke, *Empire and Revolution: The Political Life of Edmund Burke* (Princeton, NJ: Princeton University Press, 2015), 707.

71. Edmund Burke, *The Writings and Speeches of Edmund Burke*, vol. 4, *Party, Parliament, and the Dividing of the Whigs: 1780–1794*, ed. P. J. Marshall, Donald C. Bryant and William B. Todd (Oxford: Oxford University Press, 2015), 271.

crown of thorns on his head, a reed in his hand . . . dressing him in a rai-ment of purple' and crying 'Hail King of the British!'[72]

In drawing this analogy between George III and the Romans' mockery of Christ, Burke sought to show that to expect the king to exercise even limited executive power when his mental state was so impaired would be to humiliate him. Wollstonecraft, however, chose to read Burke's inten-tions very differently. As we saw above, Wollstonecraft considered the mockery of Christ as encapsulating the cruelty of a ridicule that had no other purpose than to hurt its target. Aware that Burke's allusion to this episode in the Regency debate had embarrassed him before, Wollstone-craft now used it to accuse him of inhumanely exploiting the king's illness to press for political advantage against the government of William Pitt.[73] Burke's words, Wollstonecraft alleged, were not a plea to spare the king but instead amounted to a 'cruel mockery' of a suffering monarch, one that that was 'insulting to God and man'.[74] Burke, of course, had intended to cast Pitt's ministers as the Romans dressing Christ in purple robes. Woll-stonecraft's response was to place Burke himself in that role, and present him as the mocker who had blasphemously compared a man who had experienced a 'loss of reason' to Christ.[75] In doing so, she reinforced the image of Burke as abusive in his use of ridicule and (what was worse) will-ing to direct it wherever it was politically advantageous for him to do so.

Indignation at Burke's ridicule of others, however, fuels only a por-tion of Wollstonecraft's response to Burke. Martha Nussbaum has argued that indignation generally spurs the harmed to protest against, or attempt to reform, the afflicter of the harm. More visceral emotional reactions like contempt, by contrast, want simply 'to get the person out of sight'.[76] Wollstonecraft adopts a similar line of reasoning in the *Vindication* by presenting indignation and contempt as 'opposite passions' which clash with each other in the mind.[77] When Wollstonecraft announces to Burke that his abusive ridicules have earned her contempt, or when she detects an anxious eagerness on his part to 'convince the world' of his contempt

72. Ibid.

73. Burke's performance in the regency crisis debates was widely perceived to have been a humiliating experience. His speeches were frequently interrupted by laughter. John W. Derry, *The Regency Crisis and the Whigs 1788–9* (Cambridge: Cambridge University Press, 1963), 157.

74. Wollstonecraft, *A Vindication of the Rights of Men*, 26.

75. Ibid., 27.

76. Martha Nussbaum, *Hiding From Humanity: Disgust, Shame, and the Law* (Prince-ton, NJ: Princeton University Press, 2004), 106.

77. Wollstonecraft, *A Vindication of the Rights of Men*, 28.

for the revolutionaries, we should expect nothing else than that she will regard Burke thereafter as unworthy of engagement and pass over much of what he wrote as not worth her attention.[78] True to that initial promise, Wollstonecraft time and again sidesteps substantial engagement with the details of Burke's arguments and does so unapologetically.

Readers of the *Vindication* are treated to an example of such a deliberate withholding of attention in the very first sentence. Wollstonecraft, again making her intention explicit, dispenses with the marks of respect usually prefaced to replies of this sort, especially from authors of a social standing inferior to that of the addressee. She will not apologize for 'intruding' on his 'precious time'.[79] Nor will she declare that it is 'an honour' to discuss the rights of man with someone of Burke's literary abilities. Her opening sally then, is not an indignant complaint, but a calm withholding of pleasantries conventionally due on such occasions. The refusal of honorifics, however, has only just begun. Even after such an opening, Wollstonecraft's readers might still have expected her to actually refute the 'specious' arguments from Burke that roused her 'indignation' in the first place.[80] But they would be largely disappointed. In spite of the damage his arguments have wrought in her eyes, she ultimately concludes that it would be too 'tedious' to try her own patience and that of her readers by pointing out their flaws.[81]

In Wollstonecraft's eyes, Burke's habit of ridiculing his opponents, while cruel, also revealed him to be pitifully weak and insecure.[82] In selecting the Regency debate to criticize him, she would have known that Burke's vehemence in opposing Pitt had given rise to the accusation that it was he, rather than the king, who was teetering on the brink of madness. For Wollstonecraft, Burke's heavy reliance on wit, far from revealing his prowess as a speaker, actually revealed his dependence on a faculty that was separated from madness by a 'thin partition' and that thrived only where judgment was missing.[83] Drawing on the Lockean distinction between wit and judgment, Wollstonecraft denigrates the former, reducing it to little more than a 'lucky hit' that follows when those with florid

78. Ibid., 44.

79. Ibid., 7.

80. Ibid., 5. There is little evidence to suggest that Burke himself ever read the *Vindication*.

81. Ibid., 59.

82. For an account of how 'Burke became contemptible by holding others in contempt' see Don Herzog, *Poisoning the Minds of the Lower Orders* (Princeton, NJ: Princeton University Press, 1998), xv.

83. Wollstonecraft, *A Vindication of the Rights of Men*, 28.

imaginations experience a 'momentary inspiration'.[84] Burke's wit, she thus implied, was exactly of the sort she associated with aristocratic males too puffed-up and vain to engage in reasoned debate. As such, it offered one more reason not to debate him. Normally, Wollstonecraft insists, she would 'respect an opponent' with fundamentally different views to her own.[85] But Burke's contempt for his opponents meant that anything that passed for argument in his work could be left unanswered.

This strategy of evasion frustrated early critics of the *Vindication* and continues to bother readers today.[86] It is a strategy, however, that Wollstonecraft amply justified over the course of the text. The *Vindication* contains a coherent argument as to why most members of the upper classes should be denied the esteem they so anxiously crave from their social inferiors. So long as the prevailing system of unnatural social distinctions persists, Wollstonecraft argued, the middle class in particular will have *prima facie* grounds for regarding themselves as superior in dignity to, rather than the mere equals of, the rich and privileged. The *Vindication* thus served not only as an example of how propertied elites *can* be treated with contempt by a social inferior, but also presented a case for why they usually *should* be. In other words, Wollstonecraft attempted more than merely cutting Burke down to size; she argued for a wholesale rethinking of the manner in which contempt and esteem should be distributed in a class-based society.[87]

Upon what grounds did she so argue? As with so many of Wollstonecraft's arguments, this one concerned education (broadly conceived as the set of environmental factors that contribute to a person's moral and intellectual development). At the core of the argument was the following claim: the pampered upbringing enjoyed by the rich actually deprived them of sufficient opportunities to develop the capacities necessary for a rational exchange between citizens on matters of public importance. In this respect, the very rich and very poor have something in common. The social conditions of both groups (a complete lack of material want for the one and debasing physical labour for the other) have conspired to

84. Ibid., 54.
85. Ibid., 30.
86. An anonymous reviewer complained that from Wollstonecraft's title page 'we expected this work would have been confined to an examination of Mr Burke's political principles. This, however, occupies but a small part of the whole.' Anon., 'Art. 41. A Vindication of the Rights of Men', *Monthly Review or Literary Journal*, no. 4 (January 1791), 95.
87. Miller has coined the phrase 'upward contempt' to describe the contempt shown by those lower on the social spectrum towards their social superiors. William Ian Miller, 'Upward Contempt', *Political Theory* 23, 3 (1995), 476.

deny them an education adequate to the demands of a free society and left them in a state of dependence. Yet in spite of the fact that both groups were dependent, only the poor were routinely contemned. The deference granted as a matter of course to the rich allowed them to overlook their own debility and artificially propped up their self-esteem. By continuing to revere the rich in this manner, Wollstonecraft claimed, her contemporaries reinforced wealth as an artificial basis of social esteem, contributed to the further debasement of the most vulnerable in society, and lent overall legitimacy to a corrupt social order.

It is this argument that propelled Wollstonecraft's insistence, early in the *Vindication*, that the category of the 'vulgar' (a term Burke regularly deployed in the *Reflections* to describe the poor or uneducated) be expanded to include the rich. 'By this epithet', she declared, 'I mean not only to describe a class of people, who, working to support the body, have not had time to cultivate their minds' but 'likewise those who, born in the lap of affluence, have never had their invention sharpened by necessity' and so have become 'creatures of habit and impulse'.[88] Poverty and affluence, Wollstonecraft here claimed, each work to mould individuals into dependence, albeit by different means. By recasting an upbringing in a wealthy home as both a privilege *and* a disadvantage from which it is extremely difficult to recover, Wollstonecraft thus made a case in the *Vindication* for treating the rich not with the signs of homage to which they accustomed, but rather with the same kind of contempt that she had poured down on Burke.[89]

It might immediately be objected that if Wollstonecraft had wanted to justify contempt towards an idle upper class incapacitated by their pampered upbringings, then she could have chosen a better target than Edmund Burke. As she herself concedes, Burke was born without title and his rise to prominence was achieved largely on merit.[90] Moreover, he was

---

88. Wollstonecraft, *A Vindication of the Rights of Men*, 16.

89. It was a case she would make again two years later when composing the *Vindication of the Rights of Woman*. The 'middle classes', she there argued, 'appear to be in the most natural state'. They have been spared both the debilitating effect of poverty and the enfeebling effects of wealth. The 'great', by contrast, 'have the strongest claim to pity'. Denied the chance to 'practice the duties which dignify the human character' they are left 'vain and helpless'. Consequently, Wollstonecraft proposed adopting 'a separate view of the different ranks of society' rather than pretending that characters produced by each will possess equal dignity. Wollstonecraft, *A Vindication of the Rights of Woman*, 75.

90. Whereas most gain prominence through 'fortune and hereditary office', Wollstonecraft writes, 'you [Burke] have raised yourself by exertion and abilities'. Wollstonecraft, *A Vindication of the Rights of Men*, 43.

repeatedly and savagely ridiculed on account of his Irishness, with satirists such as James Gillray and Thomas Rowlandson frequently depicting him as a closet Jesuit owing to his efforts to relieve Irish Catholics from civic exclusion.[91] However, in Wollstonecraft's eyes, this only made his defection to the side of property and privilege all the more troubling. Burke had made that defection explicit in the *Reflections*, urging that possession of landed property be retained as the primary basis for the distribution of esteem within English society over and against claims of ability. Against the Marquis de Barentin's proclamation at the opening of the Estates General that 'all occupations were honourable', Burke bluntly retorted that the 'occupation of an hair-dresser' or a 'working tallow-chandler' simply 'cannot be a matter of honour to any person'.[92] To suggest otherwise was not to challenge a 'prejudice' but to 'war with nature' itself.[93] Burke's immediate rhetorical purpose in these lines was to subject arguments for equal rights to a *reductio ad absurdum*: to press for political equality is to press eventually for even those in the lowliest of occupations to take up the reins of government. But though he would later clarify that he did not wish to exclusively 'confine power, authority and distinction to blood, and names, and titles', Burke continued in the *Reflections* to weigh in heavily on the side of property against what he called the 'invasion of ability'.[94] Thus even if Burke had not been born into the idle upper class, Wollstonecraft had reason to believe he had opted to make himself a tool of it. When she accused Burke of lacking 'enlightened self-love' she meant precisely that he had lost the self-esteem that came from living a dignified, independent existence.[95] Having embraced the dependence that came from being at or near the apex of a corrupt social order, Wollstonecraft maintained, Burke could no longer be expected to reason as an equal. Indeed, it would be 'cowardice' on her part to ask him to do so.[96]

Wollstonecraft thus built a case for treating the rich as fundamentally deprived by their upbringing of a dignity that lay within reach of the majority. As such, far from being entitled to the esteem they claimed, the rich were deserving of the very same level of disregard they normally exhibited towards the poor and vulnerable. Once this is borne in mind,

91. For a selection of such satires see Nicholas K. Robinson, *Edmund Burke: A Life in Caricature* (New Haven, CT: Yale University Press, 1996).

92. Burke, *Reflections on the Revolution in France*, 49.

93. Ibid.

94. Ibid., 50–51.

95. Wollstonecraft, *A Vindication of the Rights of Men*, 34.

96. Ibid., 10.

then Wollstonecraft's ridicule of Burke appears less like an intemperate outburst than an exemplary mode of address that she wished others to imitate.

Educating Women through Ridicule: The Vindication of the Rights of Woman

In *A Vindication of the Rights of Woman* (1792) Wollstonecraft renewed her critique of the ridicule practised by elite men and associated it once more with the insidious manners a social world centred on gallantry. More so than in earlier writings, however, Wollstonecraft now more steadily emphasized the deforming effects that such ridicule could have on those already suffering domination. She stressed that if women in particular were subjected to ridicule, even from well-intentioned reformers hoping to shame them into altering their conduct, then the result would be humiliation and further erosion of their self-esteem rather than moral improvement. It is for this reason that Wollstonecraft herself, although often unsparing in her criticism of the foppishness and superficiality of high-society women, carefully refrained from ridiculing them. What is more, she explicitly warned against the dangers of doing so. Throughout the *Vindication of the Rights of Woman* Wollstonecraft held firm to the conviction that even women who surrender their independence through an unhealthy 'attachment to rakes' should not be 'satirized' on the basis of faults that were the result of their education.[97] For, she wrote, to 'laugh at . . . or satirize the follies of a being who is never allowed to act freely from the light of her own reason is as absurd as cruel'.[98] It is absurd because it implies that the women in question could have achieved the impossible; that is, exercising their reason in a way that has been systematically denied them. It is cruel for a similar reason. Shaming women for behaving in precisely the way that they have been socialized to behave would only aggravate the injury of denying them an adequate education in the first place.

Readers of the *Vindication of the Rights of Woman* who are tempted to accuse Wollstonecraft of feminist misogyny may well consider her plea for women to be spared ridicule as disingenuous. After all, even if she did not mock women directly, Wollstonecraft nevertheless painted portraits of female vices that often matched the stereotyped view adopted by their male detractors. If anything, *A Vindication of the Rights of Woman*

---

97. Wollstonecraft, *A Vindication of the Rights of Woman*, 118.
98. Ibid., 260.

exaggerated tales of female superficiality, coquettishness and vanity in a manner that borders on parody. Nor did Wollstonecraft limit her criticisms to the women of her own time. To study history, she maintained, was to discover just how few women had managed to free themselves from the 'galling yoke of sovereign man' to excel (there was little suggestion that exceptional women had been passed over or misrepresented by male historians).[99] So few were the exceptions that Wollstonecraft jokingly relaxed her insistence that souls had no sex to speculate that the 'few extraordinary women' who had successfully escaped the 'orbit prescribed to their sex' must have been '*male* spirits' mistakenly trapped in 'female frames'.[100] Notwithstanding her warnings about the cruelty of much satire, moreover, she conceded that even the 'severest satirists' of women often had a point.[101] The problem, as Wollstonecraft saw it, was not that female inferiority was a lie but rather that an actual inferiority (albeit artificially produced) had been compounded by a society that treated women as amounting to even less than they had historically been permitted to attain.

Given her sympathy with satirical portrayals of women it is tempting to concur with her critics that Wollstonecraft replicated many of the abuses of ridicule for which she castigated others. Such a reading, however, overlooks the extent to which Wollstonecraft not only called for writers to hold back from satirizing women but also defended the women of her day from those who had already done so. The 'severest satirist' whose views on female inferiority she felt compelled to endorse remained a hypothetical one. Whenever Wollstonecraft engaged with *actual* satirists known to her readers, by contrast, she was unequivocally critical of what they had written. In other words, Wollstonecraft did not just take issue with how women had been ridiculed; she also confronted the satirists whose representations of female incompetence and vice had reinforced sexist prejudices.

This is nowhere better illustrated than in Wollstonecraft's treatment of Jonathan Swift. In a contribution to Johnson's *Analytical Review* Wollstonecraft had dismissed Swift as a 'misanthrope' who took out his frustrations on the world through satire.[102] Now she took him to task for not only misrepresenting female vices but also for misidentifying the sources of the defects he *did* accurately describe. For Wollstonecraft, Swift's *The*

99. Ibid., 103.
100. Ibid.
101. Ibid.
102. Ibid., 104.

Furniture of a Woman's Mind was emblematic of the contradiction that satirists fell into when trying to expose the failings of women.[103] The poem begins by presenting women as mindlessly parroting clichés and fixating on the latest fashions: 'A SET of Phrases learn't by Rote / A Passion for a Scarlet-Coat.'[104] To Wollstonecraft these lines were objectionable on two levels. In the first place, that women were forced to have recourse to 'rote' learning was damning evidence of the poverty of the education they typically received, not, as Swift implied, a poor reflection on their mental capabilities. As for the fixation with dressing up, Swift here mistakenly ascribed to women a vice that is by no means limited to one sex. 'Why', Wollstonecraft wryly asked, 'should women be censured with petulant acrimony, because they seem to have a passion for a scarlet coat?'[105] After all, military officers, those paragons of masculinity, were 'also particularly attentive to their persons' and preened over their scarlet uniforms as much as women did over their coats.[106] As with Burke, then, Wollstonecraft's judgment was that Swift's satire revealed more about his own petulance than about the supposed vanity of its target.

The charge that Wollstonecraft was complicit in demeaning women also passes over the extent to which she encouraged women to *retaliate* against authors who scorned them. 'The being who patiently endures injustice or silently bears insults' would soon, she warned, either become 'unjust' or 'unable to discern right from wrong'.[107] Insults, Wollstonecraft thus implied, were themselves a form of injustice, and to put up with them either out of Stoicism or Christian meekness was not only insufficient as a response but also facilitative of further injustice. The very epitome of a dependent woman was one that will 'silently endure injuries' (whether verbal, emotional, or physical) for fear of what would happen if she responded otherwise.[108] The problem here was not only that those who received little pushback when they insult women would be undeterred from repeating the offence. It was also that the 'undeserved contempt' to which women were continually subjected could render them

---

103. Ibid. In her *Thoughts on the Education of Daughters* she similarly described Swift as a man who 'hated the world' whose 'foolish wish of rising superior to the common wants and desires of the human species made him singular, but not respectable'. Wollstonecraft, *Thoughts on the Education of Daughters*, 30.

104. Jonathan Swift, *The Poetical Works of Dr. Jonathan Swift*, vol. 2 (London: J. Bell, 1787), 152.

105. Wollstonecraft, *A Vindication of the Rights of Woman*, 108.

106. Ibid., 93.

107. Ibid, 153.

108. Ibid, 102.

truly 'contemptible' over time, making it urgently necessary for women to set aside the desire to appear meek and instead counter undeserved aspersions from the very start.[109] In any case, the kind of endurance that was usually praised as a mark of a well-moderated temper was nothing of the sort. Meekness and 'docility', Wollstonecraft complained, were more often than not the 'stamp of fear' rather than self-mastery.[110]

Rather than ignoring insulting claims that women were inherently vicious or frail, therefore, Wollstonecraft was adamant that women should respond with a dignified contempt of their own. Such a response, however, would not take the form of the empty retorts or witticisms that Wollstonecraft so despised as the product of gallantry. Instead, women needed to learn how to inoculate themselves from the literary productions that demeaned them by ridiculing the texts *as they read* them. To a degree often unacknowledged, the *Vindication of the Rights of Woman* was first and foremost a book about books and the pernicious effects they could have if their readers treated their contents as too authoritative and their authors too seriously.[111] But simply identifying the flaws in such works was not enough to counteract their influence. Arousing contempt towards them was equally important.

Wollstonecraft's proposal for how such a dignified contempt could be cultivated constitutes one of the most ambitious elements of her educational programme for young women. In chapter 13 of the *Vindication of the Rights of Woman* she offered a preliminary sketch of how educating women capable of challenging their subordination to men should involve instruction in ridicule. Confronting the specific problem of how girls could be discouraged from reading 'flimsy' novels that reinforced the Swiftian vision of women as unthinking, coquettish and dependent on arbitrary male power, Wollstonecraft offered the following by way of advice:

> The best method, I believe, that can be adopted to correct a fondness for novels is to ridicule them: not indiscriminately, for then it would have little effect; but, if a judicious person, with some turn for humour, would read several to a young girl, and point out both by tones, and apt

109. Ibid., 219.
110. Ibid., 153.
111. Even though Wollstonecraft went to great pains to emphasize the sheer variety of social, economic and cultural factors that contributed to the warping of women's characters, the focus of her critical attention was nearly always textual, and she circled back repeatedly to criticism of the novels, poems and education manuals responsible for propagating the 'mistaken notions that enslave my sex'. Ibid., 105.

comparisons with pathetic incidents and heroic characters in history, how foolishly and ridiculously they caricatured human nature, just opinions may be substituted instead of romantic sentiments.[112]

This is a remarkable proposal on a number of fronts. In the first place, having expressed concern in her educational writings that women too often indulge an appetite for ridicule when young, she now created a role for what is, in essence, a tutor in ridicule. Whether the tutors or governesses responsible for other aspects of the student's education can play this role depends on whether they can combine their judiciousness with a suitable 'turn for humour'. Admittedly, the ridicule in which the students were to be coached is not of the personalized or abusive sort Wollstonecraft so often criticized, but this endorsement of instruction in ridiculing is no less extraordinary for that. It essentially amounts, as one recent commentator has put it, to Wollstonecraft choosing to 'put a bad social habit to good use'.[113] Second, given the centrality of a Lockean association of ideas to her educational thought as a whole, we know that Wollstonecraft intended by this scheme to build ridiculing habits for life, or to begin an 'habitual association of ideas', that 'grows with our growth'.[114] If it remained the case that young women should refrain from ridiculing undeserving others, it is also evident that confrontations with the deservedly contemptible should have triggered in Wollstonecraft's students a response of disdain.

It is difficult to imagine how exactly these tutoring sessions in ridicule would proceed, particularly as Wollstonecraft provided no details beyond this brief sketch. It would have been insufficient for the tutor in question to simply tell the students that they should experience contempt for what is being read to them, otherwise it would not be necessary to recruit a tutor with a 'turn for humour'. Clearly some humorous representation of the material was required, or at least something to make the students laugh. The reference to history suggests that the mockery could be followed up by reference to a more suitable set of exemplars from the past. Even in endorsing ridicule as a method of instruction, therefore, Wollstonecraft stresses the need to balance it with what she calls the 'sober dignity' of history.[115]

112. Ibid., 258.

113. Tegan, 'Mocking the Mothers of the Novel', 366.

114. Wollstonecraft, *A Vindication of the Rights of Woman*, 186. Commenting on this passage Saba Bahar notes that the students would in time 'internalize this authoritative counsel and ridicule'. Saba Bahar, *Mary Wollstonecraft's Social and Aesthetic Philosophy* (New York: Palgrave, 2002), 115.

115. Wollstonecraft, *A Vindication of the Rights of Woman*, 258.

Although Wollstonecraft did not elaborate on how exactly ridicule might be deployed in developing a student's critical faculties, we can nevertheless look to her own practice of reviewing books to see how she thought it might be done. Throughout most of her writing career Wollstonecraft supported herself by reviewing a vast range of books for Johnson's *Analytical Review*. As Fiore Sireci has shown, this work allowed her to cultivate a distinctive reviewing style that carried over into the *Vindication of the Rights of Woman*.[116] It was a style that hinted at what her tutorials in ridiculing books might look like. In her review of *Edward and Harriet, or the Happy Recovery*, for example, Wollstonecraft dismissed the novel as a 'heterogeneous mass of folly, affectation, and improbability' before explaining to her readers why it was necessary to not only point out these flaws but to laugh at them.[117] The '*cant* of sensibility', she wrote, cannot be 'tried by any criterion or reason'. Instead, it is 'ridicule' that 'should direct its shafts against this fair game'.[118] Her reasoning here perfectly anticipated her proposal in the *Vindication*. Ridicule was called for, she argued, because it alone could 'deter the thoughtless from imbibing the wildest notions' and 'most pernicious prejudices'.[119]

Part of the explanation behind Wollstonecraft's more upbeat assessments of ridicule's pedagogical potential was her conviction that to *seriously* denounce sentimentalist depictions of social life would be to grant them too much weight. As with Burke, Wollstonecraft went out of her way in the *Vindication of the Rights of Woman* to present those she argued with most as being unworthy of the time she dedicated to refuting them. In some extreme cases this active dismissal took the form of performing forgetfulness of the names of her opponents. Dr John Gregory, whose influential *Father's Legacy to his Daughters* Wollstonecraft repeatedly attacked for educating women to be the dependent playthings of men, was reduced in chapter 4 to 'some author' despite being named elsewhere in the text.[120] Another author who claimed that women had nothing to do in the world after the age of forty became a 'lively writer' whose 'name' she cannot 'recollect'.[121] Given the haste with which Wollstonecraft wrote it is entirely possible that these memory lapses were genuine. But she made no attempt to correct for

---

116. Fiore Sireci, "'Writers Who Have Rendered Women Objects of Pity": Mary Wollstonecraft's Literary Criticism in the Analytical Review and A Vindication of the Rights of Woman', *Journal of the History of Ideas* 79, 2 (2018), 243–65.

117. Wollstonecraft, 'Contributions to the *Analytical Review*', 19.

118. Ibid.

119. Ibid.

120. Wollstonecraft, *A Vindication of the Rights of Woman*, 133.

121. Ibid., 108.

them in later editions. More likely she wanted to convey that authors like Gregory were insignificant enough to be easily forgotten.

Wollstonecraft's ability to deflate texts purporting to be serious was nowhere better illustrated than in chapter 5, which Wollstonecraft devoted to a critical survey of the 'writers who have rendered women objects of pity, bordering on contempt'.[122] Such writers, Wollstonecraft argued, had conjured up images of women that are, paradoxically, extremely powerful and yet so vulnerable to criticism that they wither under the slightest examination. Much of Rousseau's description of female education in *Emile* fell into that category. Wollstonecraft repeatedly enjoins her readers to dismiss Rousseau's proposals for how young women should be groomed as dependable (and dependent) helpmeets to men as 'nonsense!' These are proposals that should only have to be glanced at to be despised, meaning that any earnest attempt to refute them would bestow on them an undeserved dignity. A good example of this is Rousseau's argument that girls have a natural fondness for dolls and dresses. Such an argument, Wollstonecraft scoffs, is so 'puerile as not to merit a serious refutation'.[123]

An *unserious* refutation, on the other hand, was perfectly appropriate. Throughout chapter 5 Wollstonecraft's strategy is to quote liberally from the texts in question, imply that the contents of what she has cited should be self-evidently absurd to the reader, and then take the extra step (as she had with Burke) of making the author in question seem insecure, vain and intellectually impaired. Quoting at length a sermon by James Fordyce (a popular Scottish moralist and brother of the Marischal College philosopher David Fordyce) that depicts girls as 'frail' and in constant need of male protection, Wollstonecraft interjects to mock not only Fordyce's views but also the sanctimonious manner in which he delivers them.[124] At the climax of his sermon, Fordyce condemns the behaviour of rakes and cads by rhetorically asking his readers whether they 'can be such barbarians, so supremely wicked, as to abuse [a girl's trust]?' This rhetorical question is quickly followed by another: 'Can you', he continues, 'find it in your hearts to despoil the gentle, trusting creatures of their treasure, or do any thing to strip them of their native robe of virtue?'[125] As with Rousseau, Wollstonecraft professes not to know 'any comment that can be made seriously on this curious passage'.[126] Another form of comment, therefore, is needed. And so to the phrase 'Can you find it in your hearts . . . ?' Wollstonecraft replies: 'Can

122. Ibid., 147.
123. Ibid., 111.
124. Ibid., 163.
125. Ibid.
126. Ibid.

you?—Can you? Would be the most emphatical comment, were it drawled out in a whining voice.'[127] We can here glimpse an example of the kind of mimicry that Wollstonecraft's tutor in ridicule could attempt when trying to build resistance in their students to the narratives that contribute to their subordination. Pointing out the flaws in Fordyce's portrayal of women is one way to sap his sermon of its potency. Another is to parody aloud the sanctimonious 'whining' of its author.

Wollstonecraft selected Fordyce's *Sermons* because they have 'long made part of a young woman's library' and she anticipates the objection that the popularity of the work must reflect some merit in its author.[128] Wollstonecraft's retort is that James Hervey's *Meditations* were also read widely, even though Hervey had 'sinned against sense and taste'.[129] But herein lies the tension in Wollstonecraft's strategy. She must acknowledge that the narratives spun by Rousseau and Fordyce have not only been popular but also *powerful*—how else could they have contributed so much to women's degradation? And yet, in ridiculing them, she treats them as if they were of no consequence at all. In recommending that young women be educated in ridicule, Wollstonecraft sought to empower them not only to recognize sentimentalized portraits of female frailty as ridiculous but also to *make* them ridiculous; to take something powerful, make it appear small, and thus gradually chip away at whatever made it powerful in the first place. Paradoxically, then, in order to be prepared for what she called the 'serious business of life', whether that was shouldering the responsibilities of citizenship or providing for themselves materially, Wollstonecraft's women had first to learn how to laugh.[130] For only by contemptuously dismissing what had been written about them in the past could women finally become independent agents, refuse the roles scripted for them, and instead become authors of their own lives.

Conclusion

The audacity and even ferocity with which Wollstonecraft mocks her opponents can appear to be in tension with her general commitment to the equal dignity of all and her abhorrence for cruelty. To her mind, however, there was a danger in treating all ridicule, mockery and sarcastic

127. Ibid., 110.
128. Ibid., 162. As Vivien Jones notes, most of Wollstonecraft's targets in the education and conduct literature were authors that she had elsewhere praised or acknowledged as influences. For Fordyce, by noted contrast, she reserved nothing but 'vitriol'. Vivien Jones, 'Conduct Literature', in *Mary Wollstonecraft in Context*, 244.
129. Wollstonecraft, *A Vindication of the Rights of Woman*, 164.
130. Ibid., 98.

dismissal as equally objectionable. Ridicule of women or the poor compounded their subjection and undermined their capacity for independence. As such, it was a different kind of injury than anything a seasoned Parliamentarian like Burke ever had to endure.

A final word on how Wollstonecraft's analysis of ridicule might be situated within her politics as a whole. Recent scholarship has folded Wollstonecraft's two *Vindications* into a republican tradition that conceptualizes freedom as non-domination and associates citizenship with independence from arbitrary power.[131] Less examined in that literature, however, have been the specific resources Wollstonecraft offered for resisting domination and establishing the social conditions under which freedom may be enjoyed. Wollstonecraft's educational programme for young girls suggests how a training in ridicule may enable the oppressed to recognize (and defy) the cultural narratives that render them more vulnerable to domination. That this has been largely overlooked may be partly due to Wollstonecraft's own success in exposing the ways in which ridicule often facilitated domination by (especially) the socially privileged. Once we come to better appreciate the multiple uses to which ridicule could be put, however, then it becomes apparent that those who were debased by ridicule were often the same people who stood to gain most from learning to exercise it themselves.

131. On Wollstonecraft's republican understanding of freedom see especially Alan M.S.J. Coffee, 'Mary Wollstonecraft, Freedom and the Enduring Power of Social Domination', *European Journal of Political Theory* 12, 2 (2013), 116–35 and Lena Halldenius, 'The Primacy of Right: On the Triad of Liberty, Equality, and Virtue in Wollstonecraft's Political Thought', *British Journal for the History of Philosophy* 15, 1 (2013), 75–99.

Conclusion

IN 1796 THE PREACHER Thomas Scott penned a response to the second part of Thomas Paine's *Rights of Man*. Among Scott's many complaints was that Paine's book was so 'replete with wit' that it was effectively an 'attempt to reduce Lord Shaftsbury's [*sic*] maxim to practice, and to make *ridicule the test of truth*'.[1] Scott followed up this criticism with a general warning to the God-fearing among his readers not to pay the 'least regard' to wit or ridicule because they 'obscure truth' and 'confuse and mislead the mind'.[2] The notion of using ridicule to test authority was still causing shudders nearly ninety years after Shaftesbury composed the *Letter Concerning Enthusiasm*.

By the end of the eighteenth century, however, it was increasingly common to express alarm about ridicule without invoking Shaftesbury at all. In his *Ridicule the Most Successful Adversary of Truth* (1798) the rector of Creeting in Suffolk, John Roberts, warned that the 'philosophy of France' was rapidly replacing homegrown Deism as the principal source of dangerous levity.[3] The most fiendish wits were now Jacobins rather than Earls (Roberts preferred to be a 'prodigy of dullness than the brightest Jacobin, that ever ingeniously scoffed').[4] By the nineteenth century the stir Shaftesbury had caused was well and truly over and his reputation as both philosopher and

---

1. Thomas Scott, *A Vindication of the Divine Inspiration of the Holy Scriptures, and of the Doctrines Contained in Them: Being an Answer to Two Parts of Mr T. Paine's Age of Reason* (London: D. Jaques, 1796), ii. Emphasis in original.

2. Ibid., 157.

3. John Roberts, *Ridicule the Most Successful Adversary of the Truth* (Ipswich: George Jermyn, 1798), 23.

4. Ibid., 9.

wit was on the wane. The poet Thomas Gray's verdict, recorded by Samuel Johnson, summed up the growing indifference towards him:

> You say you cannot conceive how lord Shaftesbury came to be a philosopher in vogue; I will tell you: first, he was a lord; secondly, he was as vain as any of his readers; thirdly, men are very prone to believe what they do not understand; fourthly, they will believe anything at all, provided they are under no obligation to believe it; fifthly, they love to take a new road, even when that road leads nowhere; sixthly, he was reckoned a fine writer, and seems always to mean more than he said. Would you have any more reasons? An interval of above forty years has pretty well destroyed the charm. A dead lord ranks with commoners: vanity is no longer interested in the matter; for a new road is become an old one.[5]

There is more than a bit of anti-aristocratic pique in these remarks, but Gray set a tone for later critics to follow. In 1873 Stephen Leslie included the *Characteristics* among those books that are 'allowed to slumber peacefully on the shelves of dusty libraries' having been 'dragged into oblivion' by the weight of their own faults.[6] Part of the explanation for the work's fall from grace, Leslie noted, was that although Shaftesbury had made the 'best defence that can be made' for ridicule, he was 'very unskilful in its application' and irksome to read as a result.[7] Laughter and humour would continue to be investigated, discussed, and fretted about, but not in the terms Shaftesbury had set.

Although the specific debate that Shaftesbury set in motion has long petered out, the problems that inspired it are very much still with us. We still inhabit societies in which ridicule appears to vex and oppress some while bouncing off others. We still debate the limits of permissible speech in political communities ostensibly committed to the equal dignity of their members. We still worry about humiliation and public shaming, while simultaneously insisting that something more than argument is needed in response to contemptible ideas and behaviours. Given these continuities, I conclude by arguing that the ridicule debate in Enlightenment Britain can spur political theorists to rethink their approach to these problems or,

---

5. Samuel Johnson, 'Life of Gray', in *The Lives of the Most Eminent English Poets; with Critical Observations on Their Works*, vol. 4 (London: C. Bathurst and others, 1781), 474–75.

6. Stephen Leslie, *Essays on Freethinking and Plain Speaking* (Cambridge: Cambridge University Press, 2012), 198.

7. Ibid., 215–16.

at the very least, confront complexities that their eighteenth-century fore-bears brought into focus. Taking the complexities of the politics of ridicule seriously, I argue, requires avoiding the extremes of Hobbesian pessimism and Shaftesburian optimism while preserving the insights of both.

To begin, the history we have examined in this book should place us on guard against the temptation to essentialize ridicule as either civil or unsociable, inclusive or exclusionary. To celebrate or denigrate ridicule *as such* not only neglects nuanced differences of style and content, it also fails to heed the importance of social context.[8] Whether a given taunt is civil or not depends as much on who the ridiculer and ridiculed are as on the content of what was written or said. As a thoroughly social (if not always sociable) practice, ridicule cannot be evaluated in a vacuum. Its appro-priateness hinges a great deal on its environment, or more specifically on differences of power between those who laugh and those laughed at. In short, ridicule needs to be evaluated less moralistically as a virtue or vice and more *politically* as a form of speech capable of producing an array of context-dependent benefits or harms.

Participants in the ridicule debate who leaned more to the Shaftes-burian side of the argument stressed that ridicule had an in-built ten-dency to civilize itself because speakers would learn to refine their use of it through practice, education and a bit of trial and error. These mecha-nisms would in time produce responsible speakers who could be trusted to keep their mirth civil and target only the arrogant, conceited, or deluded. Those who strayed from civility by mocking the innocent or undeserving would be sanctioned by society, perhaps by being jeered at themselves. On the Shaftesburian view, then, jesting need not be insulting or abusive but could instead widen the space for civil disagreement while pushing the boundaries of acceptable debate.

The powerful Hobbesian retort to this optimistic vision is that the operation of pride can distort the identification of both responsible ridi-culer and worthy target. Those inflamed by pride will satisfy themselves that *they* and their allies are responsible ridiculers striking out at oppo-nents whose contemptible or disgusting behaviour cries out for censure. Those same opponents will make the opposite assessment, bemoan the

8. A good example is the set of Danish cartoons of the prophet Mohammed that pro-voked violence in 2005. As Lars Toender astutely shows, the cartoons cannot be treated as a uniform set. While some of the cartoons were anti-Islamic, others were directed against the editor who commissioned the cartoons in the first place. Lars Toender, 'Humility, Arro-gance and the Limitations of Kantian Autonomy: A Response to Rostbøll', *Political Theory* 39, 3 (2011), 378–85.

incivility of those who mock them, and return like with like, resulting in mutual resentment and the steady coarsening of political life. Urging self-restraint, the Hobbesian continues, will go some way towards arresting this spiral but heavier-handed methods may be needed as well, including libel laws or other statutory correctives to hateful or abusive speech. Such interventions may alleviate conflict temporarily but because humans are incurably irascible, the cycle of mockery and counter-mockery must be interminable.

But this Hobbesian perspective, taken to its extreme, generates its own difficulties. There is merit to the Shaftesburian view that it is unsustainable to always suppress our mockery for fear of escalating conflict, not least because this would gift unmerited security to the powerful. Moreover, one way of checking whether the powerful are worthy of the respect they demand is to probe them with ridicule and see how well they hold up. If they respond by getting flustered then this may not tell us much, but it will at least convey that the authority in question lacks confidence in their claims to deference and should be scrutinized further. To declare such a practice off limits out of concern for civility would be to embrace submissiveness for the sake of peace. And even if we accept that ridicule is often born of pride and expresses contempt, not all assertions of pride are illegitimate and not all contempt is unjustified. When a victim expresses contempt for their abuser, they are not trying to gain an arbitrary positional advantage in the economy of esteem; they are declaring the abuser truly contemptible and themselves uncowed by the treatment they have endured. Any perspective that rejects such speech on the grounds that contempt endangers civility should itself be rejected.

The ridicule debate in Enlightenment Britain can be informative beyond what it suggests about the civility or incivility of ridicule. It can also secure us against any easy association of ridicule with freedom. This is another case where Shaftesburian optimism and Hobbesian pessimism must temper each other. Shaftesbury sometimes treated ridicule as a kind of index of freedom and implied that despotic societies were relatively humourless. Only the coarsest buffoonery, for him, could be expected in contexts of intellectual and spiritual repression (it was the only way the 'poor cramped wretches' in Italy could 'discharge a free thought') because it afforded an outlet to spirits that would otherwise be muffled.[9] On the Shaftesburian view, ridicule can even *bring about* freedom by fomenting an atmosphere that is inhospitable to the domineering and imperious.

9. Shaftesbury, 'Sensus Communis', 35.

But such optimism cannot long survive contact with the reality of a world in which elites barely register the mockery levelled against them or even encourage it to allow those they rule to harmlessly let off steam. The Italian novelist Elena Ferrante, delivering a dose of anti-Shaftesburian pessimism, argues persuasively that laughter is 'overrated' as a critical force because people mistakenly believe that to make fun of power is to hurt it.[10] 'Ridicule, yes, annoys the powerful', she writes, but it cannot 'bury them'.[11] At best it can give us a fleeting sensation of freedom or a 'short, very short, sigh of relief'.[12]

The problem is not just that laughter offers only a transient, compensatory freedom. In some cases it signals degradation rather than a free spirit fleeing restraint. For many of the thinkers we have looked at, citizens who used ridicule to forensically dissect claims to authority may have been free spirited, but those who mocked indiscriminately were servile, insecure and pitifully dependent. Worse still, humourists could prove the most despotic characters of all. Hume's Cromwell was the perfect religious hypocrite who feigned an austere piety to gain the trust of sectarians. But he was also a prankster whose gaiety complemented the very worst of his authoritarian instincts. The court of Charles II was more welcoming to humour than the Puritans had been, but to Hume it was more a space of licence than liberty. For Wollstonecraft, bantering cultures such as Eton or Versailles were oppressively male and haughty. A genuinely free society would not be without laughter, she held, but it would concern itself more with cultivating genius than wit.

Finally, attending to the ridicule debate should make political theorists think twice about the relationship between ridicule and democracy. Ever since the publication of Bakhtin's iconic study of Rabelais, we have been accustomed to thinking of humour as carnivalesque and demotic, a joyous upsurge that permits the people to momentarily invert a stratified social order and loosen the grip of hierarchy on their imaginations.[13] More recently, democratic theorists have considered democracies more hospitable to humour than any other kind of regime. The 'liberal democratic polity',

10. Elena Ferrante, *Incidental Inventions*, trans. Ann Goldstein (New York: Europa, 2019), 26.

11. Ibid.

12. Ibid. For the philosopher Justin Smith, ridicule is rarely more than a 'palliative', a shot of giddiness that quickly passes and disturbs nothing. Justin E. H. Smith, *Irrationality: A History of the Dark Side of Reason* (Princeton, NJ: Princeton University Press, 2019), 236.

13. Mikhail Bakhtin, *Rabelais and His World*, trans. Helene Iswolsky (Bloomington: Indiana University Press, 1984), chapter 1.

Sammy Basu has written in a Shaftesburian vein, is 'uniquely friendly to humorous citizens'.[14] For William Connolly, laughter and humour are integral to the ethos of agonistic respect on which democratic politics thrives.[15]

The democratic pedigree of humour looks, admittedly, impeccable. Comedy had its origins in the raucous festivals of Dionysus where the Athenian *demos* was given the chance to laugh at political elites, pretentious *parvenus* and effete philosophers. The bodily humour characteristic of these comedies had a levelling quality to it and brought their targets down to the level of the ordinary citizen (even the rich and powerful piss and fart). The critics of Shaftesbury who were appalled at his blasé treatment of Socrates's fate at the hands of Aristophanes were adamant that laughter was demotic and could have fatal consequences for the wise. For these critics, ridicule was unsafe regardless of the user's refinement or skill because a laughing *demos* was nearly always a dangerous one.

To say that ridicule is *demotic*, however, is not to say that it is *democratic*. For Hume, aspirants to political power in democratic states must persuade the common citizen of their usefulness if they are to be elected to office or win support for their policies.[16] In a stratified monarchical order, by contrast, ambitious subjects have to make themselves entertaining to those above them, making wit and banter the currencies of preferment. Beattie, for all his other spats with Hume, agreed. The egalitarian ethos of democracies, Beattie argued, blended citizens into a homogenous mass, removing the incongruous clashes between social groups that made feudal states or aristocracies so mirthful. But democracies were also more sombre on Beattie's account because they concentrated the citizens' minds on the kind of public business that would otherwise have been left to aristocrats or monarchs. In a society where citizens are shouldered with the obligations of ruling, they have little energy for diversion.

The argument that democracy dampens humour enjoyed greater longevity than much of what Shaftesbury wrote about ridicule. Perhaps the most astute observer of democratic societies, Alexis de Tocqueville, offered a version of it in his *Democracy in America* (1835–40). 'In aristocratic

14. Sammy Basu, 'Dialogic Ethics and the Virtue of Humor', *Journal of Political Philosophy* 7, 4 (1999), 385.

15. William E. Connolly, *Identity/Difference: Democratic Negotiations of Political Paradox* (Minneapolis: University of Minnesota Press, 2002), 180. For a critical comparison of Connolly's agonistic laughter and Aristotelian wittiness see John Lombardini, 'Civic Laughter: Aristotle and the Political Virtue of Humor', *Political Theory* 41, 2 (2013), 203–30.

16. Hume, 'Of the Rise and Progress of the Arts and Sciences', 126.

societies', Tocqueville observed, 'people freely let themselves go in bursts of tumultuous, boisterous gaiety'.[17] The reason was that subjects in aristocratic societies enjoy some freedom and security while at the same time remaining 'untroubled by the major cares of life'.[18] Even under despotisms, Tocqueville alleged, people will occasionally experience 'mad fits of gaiety' despite the fear bred by such regimes.[19] Democratic citizens, by contrast, were far more seriously minded because they were so busy providing for themselves and attending to public business. Constantly occupying themselves with 'serious questions of government' or some scheme to further their private interests, they had neither leisure nor inclination for humour.[20] So strong was the sobering effect of democracy that it could even force people to be serious who might otherwise be jocular. For in a democracy, 'gravity' becomes a 'national trait'.[21]

What all this suggests is that an explosion of ridicule is probably not a sign that democracy is robust. An upsurge in ridicule can reflect an atmosphere of intolerant moral absolutism rather than scepticism. And in a raucous public sphere where everything can be turned into a joke, ridicule quickly loses whatever limited critical purchase it may have had. Moreover, greater frivolity, gaiety and wit are all perfectly compatible with a loss of freedom and an erosion of democracy. Disempowered citizens who are unable or unprepared to cooperate with each other in defence of their interests may be more inclined to ridicule than those endowed with more collective purpose and the freedom to govern themselves. Finally, when the jokers start scaling the ladders of power this may augur, not a playful opening up of the political realm or a burst of critical *esprit*, but rather a steady waning of political freedom.

17. Alexis de Tocqueville, *Democracy in America*, ed. J. P. Mayer, trans. George Lawrence (New York: Harper Perennial Modern Classics, 2000), 609.
18. Ibid., 610.
19. Ibid.
20. Ibid.
21. Ibid.

Manuscripts

Shaftesbury's Notes on Hieronymus Wolf's translation of Epictetus. Shaftesbury Papers, National Archives at Kew, PRO 30/24/27/16.

Shaftesbury to Jacques Basnage, 21 January 1707. Shaftesbury papers, National Archives, Kew, PRO 30/24/22/4.

Pierre Coste to Shaftesbury, 26 September 1709. Hampshire Record Office. Malmesbury Papers 9M73/G255/29.

John Toland to Shaftesbury, December 1709. Hampshire Record Office. Malmesbury Papers 9M73/G258/7

John Cropley to James Stanhope, 17 June 1710. Kent History and Library Centre U1590/C9/31

University of Bristol DM211. Anon. (Tytler). 'The Petition of the Sharks of Africa', May 1792.

Primary Sources

Aelianus, Claudius. *Historical Miscellany*. Edited by N. G. Wilson. Cambridge, MA: Harvard University Press, 1997.

Akenside, Mark. *The Pleasures of Imagination*. London: R. Dodsley, 1744.

Anderson, George. *An Estimate of the Profit and Loss of Religion, Personally and Publicly Stated*. Edinburgh, 1753.

Anon. *An Account of the Tryal, Examination and Conviction of the Pretended French Prophets*. London: J.B, 1707.

———. 'Art. 41. A Vindication of the Rights of Men', *Monthly Review or Literary Journal*, no. 4 (January 1791), 95–97.

———. *The English Review, or an Abstract of English and Foreign Literature* 17 (1791).

———. *An Epitaph on the French Prophet*. London, 1707.

———. *An Essay on Laughter, Wherein Are Displayed, Its Natural and Moral Causes, with the Arts of Exciting It*. London: T. Davies, and L. Davis, 1769.

———. *A Full and True Account of the Apprehending and Taking Six French Prophets*. London, 1707.

———. *The Grouler, or Diogenes Robbed of His Tub*. London: S. Popping, 1711.

———. *Pillory Disappointed, or the False Prophets Advancement*. London: Robert du Chemin, 1707.

———. *The Priest Turn'd Poet or, The Best Way of Answering Dr. Sacheverell's Sermon . . . Being His Discourse Paraphras'd in Burlesque Rhime*. London: The booksellers of London and Westminster, 1709.

———. *The Printers Petition to the Poetical Senate Assembled in Grub-Street*. Dublin, 1726.

———. 'Ramsay's *Essay on the Treatment of Slaves*'. In *Monthly Review or Literary Journal* 70 (1784).

———. *Reviews of Literature and Spirit of Foreign Magazines*, vol. 8. Philadelphia: John P. Watson, 1812.

———. *Some Late Opinions Concerning the Foundation of Morality, Examined*. London: R. Dodsley; and M. Cooper, 1753.

Arbuckle, James. *A Collection of Letters and Essays on Several Subjects, Lately Publish'd in the Dublin Journal*. London: J. Darby and T. Browne, 1729.

———. *Hibernicus's Letters: Or, a Philosophical Miscellany*, vol. 1. London: printed for J. Clark, T. Hatchet, E. Symon; J. Gray; C. Rivington; and 6 others, 1734.

Astell, Mary. *Bart'lemy Fair, or An Inquiry After Wit; in Which Due Respect Is Had to a Letter Concerning Enthusiasm, to My Lord: Answer a Fool According to His Folly, Lest He Be Wise in His Own Conceits*. London: R. Wilkin, 1709.

Balfour, James. *A Delineation of the Nature and Obligation of Morality*. Edinburgh: Hamilton, Balfour, and Neill, 1753.

Barclay, Robert. *An Apology for the True Christian Divinity: Being an Explanation and Vindication of the Principles and Doctrines of the People Called Quakers*. London, 1678.

Barrow, Isaac. *The Theological Works of Isaac Barrow*, vol. 1. Oxford: Clarendon, 1818.

Bayle, Pierre. 'Bion'. In *A General Dictionary, Historical and Critical: In Which a New and Accurate Translation of That of the Celebrated Mr. Bayle . . . Is Included*. Edited and translated by John Peter Bernard, Thomas Birch and John Lockman, vol. 3. London: James Bettenham, 1735.

———. 'Diogenes'. In *A General Dictionary Historical and Critical*. Edited and translated by John Peter Bernard, Thomas Birch and John Lockman, vol. 4. London: James Bettenham, 1736.

———. 'Shaftesbury', In *A General Dictionary, Historical and Critical*. Edited and translated by John Peter Bernard, Thomas Birch and John Lockman, vol. 9 (London: James Bettenham, 1739.

Beattie, James. 'Beattie's "The Castle of Scepticism": An Unpublished Allegory against Hume, Voltaire and Hobbes'. Edited by Ernest Campbell Mossner. *Studies in English* 27, 1 (1948), 108–45.

———. *Elements of Moral Science*, vol. 1. Edinburgh: William Creech, 1790.

———. *Elements of Moral Science*, vol. 2. Edinburgh: William Creech, 1793.

———. *An Essay on the Nature and Immutability of Truth; in Opposition to Sophistry and Scepticism*. London: A. Kincaid & J. Bell, 1770.

———. *Essays*. Edinburgh: William Creech; and for E. & C. Dilly, 1776.

———. *The Letters of James Beattie, Chronologically Arranged from Sir W. Forbes's Collection*, 2 vols. London: John Sharpe, 1820.

Bellegarde, Jean. *Reflexions Upon Ridicule and the Means to Avoid It*. London: Tho. Newborough, D. Midwinter, and Benj. Tooke, 1706.

Berkeley, George. *Alciphron: Or, the Minute Philosopher*. Dublin: William Williamson, 1757.

Bisset, William. *The Modern Fanatick. With a Large and True Account of the Life, Actions, Endowments, Etc of the Famous Dr. Sacheverell*. London: printed and sold by A. Baldwin and T. Harrison, 1710.

Blackall, Ofspring. *The Way of Trying Prophets*. London: W. Rogers, 1707.

Blair, Hugh. *Lectures on Rhetoric and Belles Lettres*, vol. 3. Basel: J. J. Tourneisen, 1788.

Brown, John. *An Estimate of the Manners and Principles of the Times*. London: L. Davis, and C. Reymers, 1757.

──. *Essays on the Characteristics*. London: C. Davis, 1751.

Bulkley, Charles. *A Vindication of My Lord Shaftesbury, on the Subject of Ridicule. Being Remarks upon a Book, Intitled, Essays on the Characteristics*. London: John Noon, 1751.

Burgess, Daniel. *Foolish Talking and Jesting Described and Condemned*. London: Andrew Bell and Jonas Lumley, 1694.

Burgh, James. *Thoughts on Education*. Boston: Rogers and Fowle, 1749.

Burke, Edmund. *The Correspondence of Edmund Burke*. Edited by Alfred Cobban and Robert A. Smith, 10 vols. Vol. 6. Chicago: University of Chicago Press, 1967.

──. *Reflections on the Revolution in France*. Edited by L. G. Mitchell. Oxford: Oxford University Press, 1993.

──. *The Writings and Speeches of Edmund Burke, Vol. 4: Party, Parliament, and the Dividing of the Whigs: 1780–1794*. Edited by P. J. Marshall, Donald C. Bryant, and William B. Todd. Oxford: Oxford University Press, 2015.

Burns, Robert. *The Oxford Edition of The Works of Robert Burns, Vol. 1: Commonplace Books, Tour Journals, and Miscellaneous Prose*. Edited by Nigel Leask. Oxford: Oxford University Press, 2014.

Campbell, George. *Dissertation on Miracles*. Edinburgh: A. Kincaid & J. Bell, 1762.

──. *The Philosophy of Rhetoric*, 2 vols. Vol. 1. London: W. Strahan and T. Cadell, 1776.

Carlyle, Alexander. *Autobiography of the Rev. Dr. Alexander Carlyle, Minister of Inveresk: Containing Memorials of the Men and Events of His Time*. W. Blackwood and sons, 1860.

Chapone, Hester. *Letters on the Improvement of the Mind, Addressed to a Young Lady*. 2 vols. London: J. Walter and E. and C. Dilly, 1778.

Charpentier, François. *Vie de Socrate*. Amsterdam: Chez F. L'Honore, 1650.

Collections of Passages Referr'd to by Dr. Henry Sacheverell in His Answer to the Articles of His Impeachment. London, 1710.

Collins, Anthony. *A Discourse Concerning Ridicule and Irony in Writing, in a Letter to the Reverend Dr. Nathaniel Marshall*. London: J. Brotherton, 1729.

Colman, Benjamin. *The Government and Improvement of Mirth According to the Laws of Christianity*. Boston: B Green, 1707.

Coste, Pierre. 'The Life and Character of Mr. Locke in a Letter to the Author of the Nouvelles de La Republique Des Lettres by Mr. P. Coste'. In *A Collection of Several Pieces of Mr. John Locke. Publish'd by Mr. Desmaizeaux, under the Direction of Anthony Collins, Esq*. London: R. Francklin, 1739.

Cunningham, Alexander. *The History of Great Britain: From the Revolution in 1688, to the Accession of George the First*, 2 vols. Vol. 2. London: Thomas Hollingbery, 1787.

D'Alembert. 'An Eulogium on President Montesquieu'. In *The Complete Works of M. de Montesquieu*, by Montesquieu, vol. 1. London: T. Evans, 1777.

Defoe, Daniel. *An Essay on the Regulation of the Press*. London, 1704.

──. *The Shortest-Way with the Dissenters*. London, 1702.

Descartes, René. *The Passions of the Soul*. Oxford: Oxford University Press, 2015.

Dickson, William. *Letters on Slavery*. London: J. Philips, 1789.

Distaff, John. *A Character of Don Sacheverellio, Knight of the Firebrand; in a Letter to Isaac Bickerstaff, Esq; Censor of Great Britain*. Dublin: printed and sold by Francis Higgins, 1710.

Douglass, Frederick. 'What to the Slave Is the Fourth of July?' In *The Essential Douglass: Selected Writings and Speeches*. Edited by Nicholas Buccola. Indianapolis, IN: Hackett, 2016.

Dunton, John. *The Bull-Baiting: Or, Sacheverell Dress'd up in Fire-Works*. London: John Morphew, 1709.

Edwards, Bryan. *The History, Civil and Commercial, of the British Colonies in the West Indies*, vol. 2. Dublin: Luke White, 1793.

Edwards, John. *Theologica Reformata, or the Body and Substance of the Christian Religion*. London: John Lawrence, 1713.

Epictetus. *Discourses, Fragments, Handbook*. Translated by Robin Hard. Oxford: Oxford University Press, 2014.

Essays and Observations, Physical and Literary. Read before a Society in Edinburgh, and Published by Them. Edinburgh: G. Hamilton and J. Balfour, 1754.

Equiano, Olaudah. *The Interesting Narrative of the Life of Olaudah Equiano, or Gustavus Vassa, the African. Written by Himself*, vol. 2. New York: W. Durrell, 1791.

Ferguson, Adam. *Principles of Moral and Political Science*. Edinburgh: A. Strahan and T. Cadell, London; and W. Creech, Edinburgh, 1792.

Fielding, Henry. 'A Dialogue Between Alexander the Great and Diogenes the Cynic'. In *Miscellanies*, vol. 1. London: A. Millar, 1743.

———. 'An Essay on Conversation'. In *Miscellanies*, vol. 1. London: A. Millar, 1743.

———. 'Essay on the Knowledge of the Characters of Men'. In *Miscellanies*, vol. 1. London: A. Millar, 1743.

Flexman, Roger. 'Review of The History of Great Britain, Vol. 1. Containing the Reigns of James I and Charles I'. *Monthly Review*, March 1754.

Fordyce, David. *Dialogues Concerning Education*, vol. 2. London, 1748.

Fowler, Edward. *Reflections upon a Letter Concerning Enthusiasm*. London: H. Clemens, 1709.

Geddes, Alexander. *An Apology for Slavery; or, Six Cogent Arguments Against the Immediate Abolition of the Slave Trade*. London: Joseph Johnson, 1792.

———. *Letter from the Reverend Alexander Geddes to the Rev. John Douglass*. London: J. Johnston, 1794.

———. *Select Satires of Horace, Translated into English Verse and, for the Most Part, Adapted to the Present Time and Manners*. London: T. Cadell, 1779.

Gerard, Alexander. *Essay on Taste*. London: A. Millar, 1759.

Gilding, Elizabeth. *The Breathings of Genius. Being a Collection of Poems; to Which are Added, Essays, Moral and Philosophical*. London: W. Faden, 1776.

Gleig, George. *Encyclopaedia Britannica; or, a Dictionary of Arts, Sciences, and Miscellaneous Literature on a Plan Entirely New*, vol. 17. Dublin: James Moore, 1790.

Godwin, William. *A Defence of the Rockingham Party*. London: J. Stockdale, 1783.

———. *An Enquiry Concerning Political Justice, and Its Influence on General Virtue and Happiness*. Dublin: Luke White, 1793.

———. *Memoirs of the Author of the Vindication of the Rights of Woman*. London: J. Johnson, 1798.

———. *Reflections on Education, Manners, and Literature*. Philadelphia: Robert Campbell and John Bioren, 1793.

Good, John Mason. *Memoirs of the Life and Writings of the Reverend Alexander Geddes, L.L.D.* London: G. Kearsley, 1803.

Gordon, Thomas. *Cato's Letters*, no. 53. London, 1721.

Gregory, John. *A Comparative View of the State and Faculties of Man. With Those of the Animal World.* London: J. Dodsley, 1765.

Hobbes, Thomas. *The Elements of Law: Human Nature and De Corpore Politico.* Edited by J.C.A Gaskin. Oxford: Oxford University Press, 1994.

———. Letter to Charles Cavendish, 1 September 1638. In *Electronic Enlightenment Scholarly Edition of Correspondence.* Edited by Robert McNamee et al. University of Oxford. https://www.e-enlightenment.com.

———. *Leviathan.* Edited by Richard Tuck. Cambridge: Cambridge University Press, 1991.

———. *Man and Citizen (De Homine and De Cive).* Edited by Bernard Gert. Indianapolis, IN: Hackett, 1991.

Hoole, Samuel. *Poems: Consisting of Modern Manners, Aurelia, The Curate, and Other Pieces Never before Published*, vol. 1. London: J. Dodsley, 1790.

Home (Lord Kames), Henry. *Elements of Criticism*, 2 vols. Vol. 1. Dublin: Sarah Cotter, 1762.

Horace. *Satires and Epistles.* Translated by John David. Oxford: Oxford University Press, 2011.

How, John. *Some Thoughts on the Present State of Printing and Bookselling.* London: How, 1709.

Hume, David. *Enquiries Concerning Human Understanding and Concerning the Principles of Morals.* Edited by L. A. Selby-Bigge. Oxford: Clarendon Press, 1975.

———. *Essays Moral, Political and Literary.* Edited by Eugene F. Miller. Indianapolis, IN: Liberty Fund, 1987.

———. *The History of England from the Invasion of Julius Caesar to the Revolution in 1688*, 6 vols. Indianapolis: Liberty Fund, 1983.

———. 'Hume's "Bellmen's Petition": The Original Text'. Edited by M. A. Stewart. *Hume Studies* 23, 1 (1997), 3–4.

———. 'A Letter from a Gentleman to His Friend in Edinburgh'. In *A Treatise of Human Nature.* Edited by David Fate Norton and Mary J. Norton. Oxford: Clarendon Press, 2011.

———. *The Letters of David Hume*, ed. J.Y.T Greig, 2 vols. Oxford: Clarendon Press, 1932.

———. 'My Own Life'. In *Essays Moral, Political and Literary.* Edited by Eugene F. Miller. Indianapolis, IN: Liberty Fund, 1987.

———. 'The Natural History of Religion'. In *Principal Writings on Religion Including Dialogues Concerning Natural Religion and the Natural History of Religion.* Edited by J.C.A. Gaskin. Oxford: Oxford University Press, 2008.

———. 'Of Moral Prejudices'. In *Essays Moral, Political, and Literary.* Edited by Eugene F. Miller. Indianapolis, IN: Liberty Fund, 1987.

———. 'Of Simplicity and Refinement in Writing'. In *Essays Moral, Political, and Literary.* Edited by Eugene F. Miller. Indianapolis, IN: Liberty Fund, 1987.

———. 'Of the Populousness of Ancient Nations'. In *Essays Moral, Political, and Literary.* Edited by Eugene F. Miller. Indianapolis, IN: Liberty Fund, 1987.

———. 'Of the Rise and Progress of the Arts and Sciences'. In *Essays Moral, Political and Literary*. Edited by Eugene F. Miller. Indianapolis, IN: Liberty Fund, 1987.

———. 'Of Superstition and Enthusiasm'. In *Essays Moral, Political, and Literary*. Edited by Eugene F. Miller. Indianapolis, IN: Liberty Fund, 1987.

———. *Principal Writings on Religion Including Dialogues Concerning Natural Religion and the Natural History of Religion*. Edited by J.C.A. Gaskin. Oxford: Oxford University Press, 2008.

———. 'The Sceptic'. In *Essays Moral, Political, and Literary*. Edited by Eugene F. Miller. Indianapolis, IN: Liberty Fund, 1987.

———. *A Treatise of Human Nature*. Edited by David Fate Norton and Mary J. Norton. Oxford: Clarendon Press, 2011.

———. 'A True Account of the Behaviour and Conduct of Archibald Stewart Esq; Late Lord Provost of Edinburgh'. In *The Ironic Hume*. By John Vladimir Price. Austin: University of Texas Press, 1965.

Hutcheson, Francis. *An Inquiry into the Original of Our Ideas of Beauty and Virtue*. London: John Darby, 1725.

———. *Logic, Metaphysics, and the Natural Sociability of Mankind*. Edited by James Moore and Michael Silverthorne. Translated by Michael Silverthorne. Indianapolis, IN: Liberty Fund, 2006.

———. 'Nos 10–12'. In *Hibernicus's Letters: Or, a Philosophical Miscellany*, vol. 1. London: J. Clark, T. Hatchet, E. Symon; J. Gray; C. Rivington; and 6 others, 1734.

Irving, David. *The Lives of the Scottish Poets; with Preliminary Dissertations on the Literary History of Scotland and the Early Scottish Drama*. London: Longman et al., 1810.

Johnson, Samuel. 'Life of Gray'. In *The Lives of the Most Eminent English Poets; with Critical Observations on Their Works*, vol. 4. London: C. Bathurst and others, 1781.

Joubert, Laurent. *Treatise on Laughter*. Translated by Gregory David de Rocher. Tuscaloosa: University of Alabama Press, 1980.

Kenrick, William. *The London Review of English and Foreign Literature* 5 (1777).

Kingston, Richard. *Enthusiastick Impostors No Inspired Prophets*. London: J. Morphew, 1707.

Knowles, John. *The Life and Writings of Henry Fuseli*, vol. 1. London: Henry Colburn & Richard Bentley, 1831.

Knox, Vicesimus. *Liberal Education: Or, a Practical Treatise on the Methods of Acquiring Useful and Polite Learning*. London: C. Dilly, 1783.

Lee, William. *Daniel Defoe: His Life and Recently Discovered Writings: Extending from 1716 to 1729*, 3 vols. Vol. 1. London: John Camden Hotten, Piccadilly, 1869.

Leibniz, Gottfried Wilhelm Freiherr von. 'Remarques Sur Le Livre Anglois Intitulé, Lettre Sur l'Enthousiasme'. In *Recueil de Diverses Pieces, Sur La Philosophie, La Religion Naturelle, l'histoire, Les Matematiques, Etc. Par Mrs. Leibniz, Clarke, Newton, et Autres Auteurs Célèbres*, vol. 2. Amsterdam: François Changuion, 1740.

Leland, John. *A View of the Principal Deistical Writers That Have Appeared in England in the Last and Present Century*, vol. 1. London: W. Richardson and S. Clark, for R. and J. Dodsley, and T. Longman, 1766.

Leng, John. *Natural Obligations to Believe the Principles of Religion, and Divine Revelation: In XVI Sermons, Preached in the Church of St. Mary Le Bow*. London: W.B. for Robert Knaplock, 1719.

Leslie, Charles. *Reflections upon a Late Scandalous and Malicious Pamphlet Entitul'd, The Shortest Way with the Dissenters; or Proposals for the Establishment of the Church. To Which the Said Pamphlet Is Prefix'd Entire by It Self*. London, 1703.

Leslie, Stephen. *Essays on Freethinking and Plain Speaking*. Cambridge: Cambridge University Press, 2012.

Locke, John. *The Clarendon Edition of the Works of John Locke: An Essay Concerning Human Understanding*. Edited by Peter H. Nidditch. Oxford: Oxford University Press, 1975.

———. *Some Thoughts Concerning Education*. Edited by Nathan Tarcov. Indianapolis, IN: Hackett, 1996.

———. *Writings on Religion*. Edited by Victor Nuovo. Oxford: Clarendon Press, 2004.

Long, Edward. *The History of Jamaica, or, General Survey of the Ancient and Modern State of That Island. With Reflections on Its Situation, Settlements, Inhabitants, Climate, Products, Commerce, Laws, and Government*, vol. 2. London: T. Lowndes, 1774.

Lucian. *Chattering Courtesans and Other Sardonic Sketches*. Translated by Keith Sidwell. London: Penguin, 2004.

Lynde, Humphrey. *The Ancient Doctrine of the Church of England Maintained in Its Primitive Purity*. London: Austin Rice, 1660.

Macaulay Graham, Catherine. *Letters on Education: With Observations on Religious and Metaphysical Subjects*. London: C. Dilly, 1790.

MacQueen, Daniel. *Letters on Mr Hume's History of Great Britain*. Edinburgh, 1756.

Mandeville, Bernard. *The Fable of the Bees: or, Private Vices, Publick Benefits*, 2 vols. Edited by F. B. Kaye. Oxford: Clarendon Press, 1924.

———. *Free Thoughts on Religion, the Church, and National Happiness*. London: T. Jauncy, 1720.

Mendelssohn, Moses. *Philosophical Writings*. Edited by Daniel Dahlstrom. Cambridge: Cambridge University Press, 1997.

Millar, John. *An Historical View of the English Government from the Settlement of the Saxons in Britain to the Revolution in 1688*. Edited by Mark Salber-Philips and Dale R. Smith. Indianapolis, IN: Liberty Fund, 2006.

———. *The Origin of the Distinction of Ranks*. Edited by Aaron Garrett. Indianapolis, IN: Liberty Fund, 2006.

Montesquieu. *My Thoughts*. Translated by Henry C. Clark. Indianapolis, IN: Liberty Fund, 2012.

———. *The Spirit of the Laws*. Cambridge: Cambridge University Press, 1989.

More, Hannah. *Essays on Various Subjects Principally Designed for Young Ladies*. London: J. Wilkie, 1778.

———. *Strictures on the Modern System of Female Education*. London: T. Cadell, 1799.

More, Henry. *Enthusiasmus Triumphatus; or, A Brief Discourse of The Nature, Causes, Kinds, and Cure of Enthusiasm*. Los Angeles: William Andrews Clark Memorial Library, University of California, 1966, repr. of 2nd edn., 1662.

Oswald, James. *An Appeal to Common Sense in Behalf of Religion*, vol. 1. Edinburgh: A. Kincaid and J. Bell, 1766.

Otis, James. *The Rights of the British Colonists Asserted and Proved*. Boston: Edes and Gill, 1764.

Paine, Thomas. *The Complete Works of Thomas Paine*, 2 vols. Edited by Philip Foner. Vol. 1. New York: The Citadell Press, 1969.

Parker, Samuel. *Censura Temporum*. London: John Morphew, 1708.

Preston, William. 'Essay on Ridicule, Wit, and Humour'. In *Transactions of the Royal Irish Academy*. Dublin: George Bonham, 1788.

Priestley, Joseph. *A Course of Lectures on Oratory and Criticism*. London: Joseph Johnson, 1777.

——. *An Examination of Dr. Reid's Inquiry into the Human Mind on the Principles of Common Sense, Dr. Beattie's Essay on the Nature and Immutability of Truth, and Dr Oswald's Appeal to Common Sense in Behalf of Religion*. London: J. Johnson, 1774.

Quintilian. *The Orator's Education*. Translated by Donald A. Russell. Cambridge, MA: Harvard University Press, 2001.

Ramsay, Allan. *Essay on Ridicule*. London, 1753.

Ramsay, James. *An Essay on the Treatment and Conversion of African Slaves in the British Sugar Colonies*. London: James Phillips, 1784.

——. *Examination of the Rev. Mr. Harris's Scriptural Researches on the Licitness of the Slave-Trade*. London: James Phillips, 1788.

——. *A Letter to James Tobin, Esq. Late Member of His Majesty's Council in the Island of Nevis*. London: James Phillips, 1787.

——. *Objections to the Abolition of the Slave Trade, with Answers*. London: James Phillips, 1788.

Rand, Benjamin, ed. *The Life, Unpublished Letters, and Philosophical Regimen of Anthony, Earl of Shaftesbury*. New York: Macmillan, 1900.

Raynal, Abbé. *Philosophical and Political History of the Settlements and Trade of the Europeans in the East and West Indies*, vol. 3. London: T. Cadell, 1776.

Reid, Thomas. *Essays on the Active Powers of Man*. Edited by Knud Haakonssen and James A. Harris. Edinburgh: Edinburgh University Press, 2010.

——. *Essays on the Intellectual Powers of Man*. Edited by Derek R. Brookes and Knud Haakonssen. Edinburgh: Edinburgh University Press, 2002.

——. *An Inquiry into the Human Mind, On the Principles of Common Sense*. Edited by Derek R. Brookes. Edinburgh: Edinburgh University Press, 1997.

——. *The Philosophical Orations of Thomas Reid: Delivered at Graduation Ceremonies King's College, Aberdeen, 1753, 1756, 1759, 1762*. Edited by D. D. Todd. Translated by Shirley Darcus Sullivan. Carbondale: Southern Illinois University Press, 1989.

——. *Thomas Reid on Logic, Rhetoric and the Fine Arts: Papers on the Culture of the Mind*. Edited by Alexander Broadie. Edinburgh: Edinburgh University Press, 2005.

Roberts, John. *Ridicule the Most Successful Adversary of the Truth*. Ipswich: George Jermyn, 1798.

Robespierre, Maximilien. *Report on the Principles of Public Morality*. Philadelphia, 1794.

Ruffhead, Owen. 'Review of The History of England under the House of Tudor'. *The Monthly Review* 20 (May 1759).

Rush, Benjamin. *An Address to the Inhabitants of the British Settlements in America, upon Slave-Keeping*. Boston: John Boyles, 1773.

Sacheverell, Henry. *The Perils of False Brethren Both in Church and State: Set Forth in a Sermon Preach'd before The Right Honourable, The Lord Mayor, Alderman, and Citizens of London, at the Cathedral Church of St Paul, on the 5th of November, 1709.* London: Henry Clements, 1709.

Scott, Thomas. *A Vindication of the Divine Inspiration of the Holy Scriptures, and of the Doctrines Contained in Them: Being an Answer to Two Parts of Mr T. Paine's Age of Reason.* London: D. Jaques, 1796.

Shaftesbury. 'The Ainsworth Correspondence'. In *Standard Edition: Complete Works, Correspondence and Posthumous Writings*, vol. 2,4, *Moral and Political Philosophy. Select Sermons of Dr. Whichcote u.a.* Edited by Wolfram Benda, Christine Jackson-Holzberg, Friedrich A. Uehlein and Erwin Wolff. Stuttgart/Bad Cannstatt: Frommann-Holzboog, 2004.

———. 'Askêmata'. In *Standard Edition: Complete Works, Correspondence and Posthumous Writings*, vol. 2,6. *Moral and Political Philosophy. Askemata I (Englisch).* Edited by Wolfram Benda, Christine Jackson-Holzberg, Patrick Müller and Friedrich A. Uehlein, Stuttgart/Bad Cannstatt: Frommann-Holzboog, 2011.

———. 'Chartae Socraticae'. In *Standard Edition: Complete Works, Correspondence and Posthumous Writings*, vol. 2,5. Edited by Wolfram Benda, Christine Jackson-Holzberg, Friedrich A. Uehlein and Erwin Wolff. Stuttgart/Bad Cannstatt: Frommann-Holzboog, 2008.

———. *Correspondence. Letters 1–100 (December 1683–February 1700). Standard Edition: Complete Works, Correspondence and Posthumous Writings*, vol. 3,1. Edited by Christine Jackson-Holzberg, Patrick Müller, and Friedrich A. Uehlein. Stuttgart/ Bad Cannstatt: Frommann-Holzboog, 2017.

———. 'An Inquiry Concerning Virtue or Merit'. In *Characteristics of Men, Manners, Opinions, Times*. Edited by Lawrence E. Klein. Cambridge: Cambridge University Press, 1999.

———. 'A Letter Concerning Enthusiasm'. In *Characteristics of Men, Manners, Opinions, Times*. Edited by Lawrence E. Klein. Cambridge: Cambridge University Press, 1999.

———. 'Miscellaneous Reflections'. In *Characteristics of Men, Manners, Opinions, Times*. Edited by Lawrence E. Klein. Cambridge: Cambridge University Press, 1999.

———. 'The Moralists'. In *Characteristics of Men, Manners, Opinions, Times*. Edited by Lawrence E. Klein. Cambridge: Cambridge University Press, 1999.

———. 'Sensus Communis, An Essay on the Freedom of Wit and Humour'. In *Characteristics of Men, Manners, Opinions, Times*. Edited by Lawrence E. Klein. Cambridge: Cambridge University Press, 1999.

———.'Shaftesbury's Index'. In *Characteristics of Men, Manners, Opinions, Times*. Edited Douglas J. Den Uyl, vol. 3. Indianapolis, IN: Liberty Fund, 2001.

———. 'Soliloquy, or Advice to an Author'. In *Characteristics of Men, Manners, Opinions, Times*. Edited by Lawrence E. Klein. Cambridge: Cambridge University Press, 1999.

Shaftesbury, The Fourth Earl of. 'A Sketch of the Life of the Life of the Third Earl of Shaftesbury by His Son, the Fourth Earl'. In *The Life, Unpublished Letters, and Philosophical Regimen of Anthony, Earl of Shaftesbury*. Edited by Benjamin Rand. New York: Macmillan, 1900.

Shorey, William. *Reason, and Not Raillery, the Proper Test of Religion*. London: W. and J. Innys, 1720.

Smith, Adam. *The Glasgow Edition of the Works and Correspondence of Adam Smith*, vol. 2, *An Inquiry into the Nature and Causes of the Wealth of Nations, Vol. 1*. Edited by William B. Todd. Oxford: Oxford University Press, 1975.

———. *The Glasgow Edition of the Works and Correspondence of Adam Smith*, vol. 6, *Correspondence*. 2nd edition. Edited by Ernest Mossner and Ian Simpson Ross. Oxford: Oxford University Press, 1987.

———. 'Lectures on Rhetoric and Belles Lettres'. In *The Glasgow Edition of the Works and Correspondence of Adam Smith*, vol. 4. Edited by J. C. Bryce. Oxford: Oxford University Press, 1983.

———. 'A Letter to the Authors of the Edinburgh Review'. In *The Glasgow Edition of the Works and Correspondence of Adam Smith*, vol. 3, *Essays on Philosophical Subjects*. Edited by W.P.D. Wightman, J. C. Bryce and I. S. Ross. Oxford: Oxford University Press, 1980.

———. 'Review of Johnson's Dictionary'. In *The Glasgow Edition of the Works and Correspondence of Adam Smith*, vol. 3, *Essays on Philosophical Subjects*. Edited by W.P.D. Wightman, J. C. Bryce and I. S. Ross. Oxford: Oxford University Press, 1980.

———. *The Theory of Moral Sentiments*. Edited by Knud Haakonssen. Cambridge: Cambridge University Press, 2002.

The Spectator No. 249. London: Sam Buckley, 1711.

Stanhope, Philip Dormer. *Miscellaneous Works of the Late Philip Dormer Stanhope, Earl of Chesterfield*, vol. 4. London: Edward and Charles Dilly, 1779.

———. *Letters written by the late Right Honourable Philip Dormer Stanhope, Earl of Chesterfield, to his son Philip Stanhope*, vol. 1. Dublin: John Chambers, 1776.

Stone, Francis. *An Examination of the Right Hon. Edmund Burke's Reflections on the Revolution in France*. London: sold by G.G.J. and J. Robinson and others, 1792.

Swift, Jonathan. *The Poetical Works of Dr. Jonathan Swift*, vol. 2. London: printed under the direction of J. Bell, 1787.

Tobin, James. *A Farewel Address to the Rev. Mr. James Ramsay: From James Tobin, Esq*. London: G. and T. Wilkie, 1788.

Tocqueville, Alexis de. *Democracy in America*. Edited by J. P. Mayer. Translated by George Lawrence. New York: Harper Perennial Modern Classics, 2000.

Toland, John. 'Introduction'. In *Letters from the Right Honourable the Late Earl of Shaftesbury, to Robert Molesworth*. London: W. Wilkins, 1721.

———. *The Jacobitism, Perjury, and Popery of High Church Priests*. London: J. Baker, 1710.

Tottie, John. *Ridicule, so Far as It Affects Religion, Consider'd and Censur'd*. Oxford, 1735.

Towers, Joseph. *Observations on Mr Hume's History*. London: H. Goldney, for G. Robinson, 1778.

Turnbull, Gordon. *Apology for Negro Slavery*. London: J. Stephenson, 1786.

———. *The Principles of Moral Philosophy. An Enquiry into the Wise and Good Government of the Moral World*, vol. 1. London: A. Millar, 1740.

Warburton, William. *The Divine Legation of Moses Demonstrated*. London: Mr. Fletcher Gyles, 1742.

——. *Remarks on Several Occasional Reflections*. London: John and Paul Knapton, 1744.

Watts, Isaac. *Sermons on Various Subjects*. London: John and Barham Clark, Eman. Mathews, and Richard Ford, 1723.

White, James. *The Clouds: A Comedy. Written by Aristophanes, the Wittiest Man of His Age, against Socrates*. London: T. Payne, 1759.

Witherspoon, John. *The Ecclesiastical Characteristics, or the Arcana of Church Policy, Being an Humble Attempt to Open Up the Mystery of Moderation*. Glasgow, 1753.

——. *The Moderator*, no. 2 (1757).

——. *A Serious Apology for the Ecclesiastical Characteristics*. Edinburgh: William Gray, 1753.

Wollstonecraft, Mary. *The Collected Letters of Mary Wollstonecraft*. Edited by Janet Todd. New York: Columbia University Press, 2003.

——. 'Contributions to the *Analytical Review*'. In *The Works of Mary Wollstonecraft*. Edited by Marilyn Butler and Janet Todd, 7 vols. Vol. 7. London: Pickering and Chatto, 1989.

——. *The Female Reader*. In *The Works of Mary Wollstonecraft*. Edited by Marilyn Butler and Janet Todd, 7 vols. Vol. 4. London: Pickering and Chatto, 1989.

——. *An Historical and Moral View of the French Revolution*. In *The Works of Mary Wollstonecraft*. Edited by Marilyn Butler and Janet Todd, 7 vols. Vol. 6. London: Pickering and Chatto, 1989.

——. 'Letters to Joseph Johnson'. In *The Works of Mary Wollstonecraft*. Edited by Marilyn Butler and Janet Todd, 7 vols. Vol. 6. London: Pickering and Chatto, 1989.

——. *Original Stories*. In *The Works of Mary Wollstonecraft*. Edited by Marilyn Butler and Janet Todd, 7 vols. Vol. 4. London: Pickering and Chatto, 1989.

——. *Thoughts on the Education of Daughters*. In *The Works of Mary Wollstonecraft*. Edited by Marilyn Butler and Janet Todd, 7 vols. Vol. 4. London: Pickering and Chatto, 1989.

——. *A Vindication of the Rights of Men*. In *The Works of Mary Wollstonecraft*. In *The Works of Mary Wollstonecraft*. Edited by Marilyn Butler and Janet Todd, 7 vols. Vol. 5. London: Pickering and Chatto, 1989.

——. *A Vindication of the Rights of Woman*. In *The Works of Mary Wollstonecraft*. In *The Works of Mary Wollstonecraft*. Edited by Marilyn Butler and Janet Todd, 7 vols. Vol. 5. London: Pickering and Chatto, 1989.

——. *A Vindication of the Rights of Woman and A Vindication of the Rights of Men*. Edited by Janet Todd. Oxford: Oxford University Press, 1993.

——. *The Wrongs of Woman: or, Maria*. In *The Works of Mary Wollstonecraft*. Edited by Marilyn Butler and Janet Todd, 7 vols. Vol. 1. London: Pickering and Chatto, 1989.

——. *The Young Grandison*. In *The Works of Mary Wollstonecraft*. Edited by Marilyn Butler and Janet Todd, 7 vols. Vol. 2. London: Pickering and Chatto, 1989.

Xenophon. *Conversations of Socrates*. Edited by Hugh Tredennick and Robin Waterfield. London: Penguin, 1990.

Secondary Sources

Ahmed, Sara. *Living a Feminist Life*. Durham, NC: Duke University Press, 2017.

Ahnert, Thomas. *The Moral Culture of the Scottish Enlightenment: 1690–1805*. New Haven, CT: Yale University Press, 2014.

Aldridge, Alfred Owen. 'Shaftesbury and the Test of Truth'. *PMLA* 60, 1 (1945).

———. 'Shaftesbury Rosicrucian Ladies'. *Anglia*, no. 103 (1985), 297–319.

Amir, Lydia B. *Humor and the Good Life in Modern Philosophy: Shaftesbury, Hamann, Kierkegaard*. New York: State University of New York Press, 2015.

Anselment, Raymond A. 'Socrates and the Clouds: Shaftesbury and a Socratic Tradition'. *Journal of the History of Ideas* 39, 2 (1978), 171–82.

Anstey, Roger. 'A Reinterpretation of the Abolition of the British Slave Trade'. *The English Historical Review* 87, 343 (1972), 304–32.

Appiah, Kwame Antony. *The Honor Code: How Moral Revolutions Happen*. London: Norton, 2010.

Ardley, Gavin. 'Hume's Common Sense Critics'. *Revue Internationale de Philosophie* 30, 115–16 (1976), 104–25.

Bahar, Saba. *Mary Wollstonecraft's Social and Aesthetic Philosophy*. New York: Palgrave, 2002.

Baier, Annette C. *Death and Character: Further Reflections on Hume*. Cambridge, MA: Harvard University Press, 2008.

Bakhtin, Mikhail. *Rabelais and His World*. Translated by Helene Iswolsky. Bloomington: Indiana University Press, 1984.

Basu, Sammy. 'Dialogic Ethics and the Virtue of Humor'. *Journal of Political Philosophy* 7, 4 (1999), 378–403.

Baumstark, Moritz. 'The End of Empire and the Death of Religion: A Reconsideration of Hume's Later Political Thought'. In *Philosophy and Religion in Enlightenment Britain: New Case Studies*. Edited by Ruth Savage, 231–57. Oxford: Oxford University Press, 2012.

Bejan, Teresa. *Mere Civility: Disagreement and the Limits of Toleration*. Cambridge, MA: Harvard University Press, 2017.

Bejan, Teresa, and Bryan Garsten. 'The Difficult Work of Liberal Civility'. In *Civility, Legality and Justice in America*. Edited by Austin Sarat, 15–45. Cambridge: Cambridge University Press, 2014.

Bell, Macalester. *Hard Feelings: The Moral Psychology of Contempt*. Oxford: Oxford University Press, 2013.

Berger, Peter L. *Redeeming Laughter: The Comic Dimension of Human Experience*. Berlin: Walter de Gruyter, 1997.

Bergson, Henri. 'Laughter'. In *Comedy*. Edited by Wylie Sypher. Garden City, NY: Doubleday Anchor Books, 1956.

Berry, Helen. 'Rethinking Politeness in Eighteenth-Century England: Moll King's Coffee House and the Significance of "Flash Talk": The Alexander Prize Lecture'. *Transactions of the Royal Historical Society* 1 (2001), 65–81.

Bevis, Matthew. *Comedy: A Very Short Introduction*. Oxford: Oxford University Press, 2012.

Billig, Michael. *Laughter and Ridicule: Towards a Social Critique of Humour*. London: Sage Publications, 2005.

Bourke, Richard. *Empire and Revolution: The Political Life of Edmund Burke*. Princeton, NJ: Princeton University Press, 2015.

Box, M. A. *The Suasive Art of David Hume*. Princeton, NJ: Princeton University Press, 2014.

Brion Davis, David. *The Problem of Slavery in the Age of Revolution, 1770–1823*. Oxford: Oxford University Press, 1999.

Broadie, Alexander. *A History of Scottish Philosophy*. Edinburgh: Edinburgh University Press, 2010.

Brooke, Christopher. *Philosophic Pride: Stoicism and Political Thought from Lipsius to Rousseau*. Princeton, NJ: Princeton University Press, 2012.

Brown, Christopher Leslie. *Moral Capital: Foundations of British Abolitionism*. Chapel Hill: University of North Carolina Press, 2006.

Brown, Michael. 'The Biter Bitten: Ireland and the Rude Enlightenment'. *Eighteenth-Century Studies* 45, 3 (2012), 393–407.

———. *Francis Hutcheson in Dublin, 1719–1730*. Dublin: Four Courts Press, 2002.

———. 'Swift, Satire, and the Problem of Whig Regeneration'. *Restoration: Studies in English Literary Culture, 1660–1700* 39, 1–2 (2015), 83–99.

Brown, Rhona. 'The Long-Lost James Beattie: The Rediscovery of "The Grotesquiad"'. *The Review of English Studies* 65, 270 (2014), 456–73.

Brown, Wendy. *Regulating Aversion: Tolerance in the Age of Identity and Empire*. Princeton, NJ: Princeton University Press, 2008.

Carey, Daniel. *Locke, Shaftesbury and Hutcheson: Contesting Diversity in the Enlightenment and Beyond*. Cambridge: Cambridge University Press, 2006.

Cerny, Gerald. *Theology, Politics, and Letters at the Crossroads of European Civilization: Jacques Basnage and the Baylean Hugenot Refugees in the Dutch Republic*. Dordrecht: Martinus Nijhoof, 1987.

Champion, Justin. *Republican Learning: John Toland and the Crisis of Christian Culture, 1696–1722*. Manchester: Manchester University Press, 2003.

Coe, Jonathan. 'Sinking Giggling into the Sea'. *London Review of Books* 35, 14 (2013).

Coffee, Alan M.S.J. 'Mary Wollstonecraft, Freedom and the Enduring Power of Social Domination'. *European Journal of Political Theory* 12, 2 (2013), 116–35.

Coffey, John. '"Tremble, Britannia!": Fear, Providence and the Abolition of the Slave Trade, 1758–1807'. *The English Historical Review* 127, 527 (2012), 844–81.

Collis, Karen. 'Shaftesbury and Literary Criticism: Philosophers and Critics in Early Eighteenth-Century England'. *The Review of English Studies* 67, 279 (2015), 294–315.

Condren, Conal. *Hobbes, the Scriblerians and the History of Philosophy*. London: Pickering and Chatto, 2012.

Connell, Philip. *Secular Chains: Poetry and the Politics of Religion from Milton to Pope*. Oxford: Oxford University Press, 2016.

Connolly, William E. *Identity/Difference: Democratic Negotiations of Political Paradox*. Minneapolis: University of Minnesota Press, 2002.

Conti, Greg. 'Hume's Low Road to Toleration'. *History of Political Thought* 36, 1 (2015), 165–91.

Cosmos, Georgia. *Huguenot Prophecy and Clandestine Worship in the Eighteenth Century: 'The Sacred Theatre of the Cévennes'*. Burlington, VT: Ashgate, 2005.

Craig, John. 'Account of the Life and Writings of the Author', in *The Origin of the Distinction of Ranks*, ed. Aaron Garrett. Indianapolis, IN: Liberty Fund, 2006.

Crisp, Roger. *Sacrifice Regained: Morality and Self-Interest in British Moral Philosophy from Hobbes to Bentham*. Oxford: Oxford University Press, 2019.

Curtis, Catherine 'From Sir Thomas More to Robert Burton: The Laughing Philosopher in the Early Modern Period'. In *The Philosopher in Early Modern Europe: The Nature of a Contested Identity*. Edited by Conal Condren, Stephen Gaukroger and Ian Hunter, 90–112. Cambridge: Cambridge University Press, 2006.

Darnton, Robert. 'To Deal with Trump, Look to Voltaire'. *New York Times*, 27 December 2018.

Darwall, Stephen. *The British Moralists and the Internal 'Ought': 1640–1740*. Cambridge: Cambridge University Press, 1995.

Davison, Kate. 'Occasional Politeness and Gentlemen's Laughter in 18th-Century England'. *The Historical Journal* 57, 4 (2014), 921–45.

Derry, John W. *The Regency Crisis and the Whigs 1788–9*. Cambridge: Cambridge University Press, 1963.

Diamond, Peter J. 'Rhetoric and Philosophy in the Social Thought of Thomas Reid'. In *Sociability and Society in Eighteenth-Century Scotland*. Edited by John Dwyer and Richard B. Sher, 57–80. Edinburgh: Mercat Press, 1993.

Dickie, Simon. *Cruelty and Laughter: Forgotten Comic Literature and the Unsentimental Eighteenth Century*. Chicago: University of Chicago Press, 2011.

Doris, Glen. 'An Abolitionist Too Late? James Beattie and the Scottish Enlightenment's Lost Chance to Influence the Slave Trade Debate'. *Journal of Scottish Thought* 2, 1 (2009), 83–98.

Douglass, Robin. 'Mandeville on the Origins of Virtue'. *British Journal for the History of Philosophy* 28, 2 (2020), 276–95.

Drescher, Seymour. *Abolition: A History of Slavery and Anti-Slavery*. Cambridge: Cambridge University Press, 2009.

Dworkin, Ronald. 'The Right to Ridicule'. *New York Review of Books*, 23 March 2006.

Eagleton, Terry. *On Humour*. New Haven, CT: Yale University Press, 2019.

Elias, Norbert. 'Essay on Laughter'. Edited by Anca Parvulescu. *Critical Inquiry* 43, (Winter 2017), 281–304.

Emerson, Roger L. 'Hume and the Bellman, Zerobabel MacGilchrist'. *Hume Studies* 23, 1 (1997), 9–28.

Ewin, R. E. 'Hobbes on Laughter'. *The Philosophical Quarterly* 51, 202 (2001), 29–40.

Fergusson, James. *Balloon Tytler*. London: Faber and Faber, 1972.

Ferrante, Elena. *Incidental Inventions*. New York: Europa, 2019.

Fieser, James. 'Hume's Wide View of the Virtues: An Analysis of His Early Critics'. *Hume Studies* 24, 2 (1998), 295–311.

———. 'The Rise and Fall of James Beattie's Common-Sense Theory of Truth'. *Monist* 90, 2 (2007), 287–96.

———. ed. *Early Responses to Hume's 'History of England'*. Bristol: Thoemmes Press, 2005.

Fletcher, F.T.H. 'Montesquieu's Influence on Anti-Slavery Opinion in England'. *Journal of Negro History* 18, 4 (1933), 414–25.

Forbes, William. *An Account of the Life and Writings of James Beattie*. Edinburgh: H.S. Baynes and Co., 1824.

Fricker, Miranda. *Epistemic Injustice: Power and the Ethics of Knowing*. Oxford: Oxford University Press, 2007.

Gadamer, Hans-Georg. *Truth and Method*. London: Continuum, 2004.

Gantar, Jure. *Pleasure of Fools: Essays in the Ethics of Laughter*. Montreal: McGill-Queen's University Press, 2005.

Garrett, Aaron and Sebastiani, Silvia. 'David Hume on Race'. In *The Oxford Handbook of Philosophy and Race*. Edited by Naomi Zack, 31–43. Oxford: Oxford University Press, 2017.

Gatrell, Vic. *City of Laughter: Sex and Satire in Eighteenth-Century London*. London: Atlantic Books, 2006.

Gay, Peter. *The Enlightenment: The Rise of Modern Paganism*. New York: Norton, 1966.

Gill, Michael. 'Shaftesbury on Politeness, Honesty, and Virtue'. In *New Ages, New Opinions: Shaftesbury in His World and Today*. Edited by Patrick Müeller, 167–84. Frankfurt am Main: Peter Lang, 2014.

Gilmore, Jr., Thomas B. 'The Eighteenth-Century Controversy over Ridicule: A Reconsideration'. *Georgia State University School of Arts and Sciences Research Papers*, no. 25 (1970).

Goldie, Mark. 'Alexander Geddes at the Limits of the Catholic Enlightenment'. *The Historical Journal* 53, 1 (2010), 61–86.

Graham, Gordon. 'Francis Hutcheson and Adam Ferguson on Sociability'. *History of Philosophy Quarterly* 31, 4 (2014), 317–29.

Grandi, Giovanni B. 'Reid on Ridicule and Common Sense'. *Journal of Scottish Philosophy* 6, 1 (2008), 71–90.

Grean, Stanley. *Shaftesbury's Philosophy of Religion and Ethics*. Athens: Ohio University Press, 1967.

Griswold, Charles. *Jean-Jacques Rousseau and Adam Smith: A Philosophical Encounter*. New York: Routledge, 2018.

Hadot, Pierre. *Philosophy as a Way of Life: Spiritual Exercises from Socrates to Foucault*. Oxford: Blackwell, 1995.

Haley, K.H.D. *The First Earl of Shaftesbury*. Oxford: Clarendon University Press, 1968.

Halldenius, Lena. 'The Primacy of Right. On the Triad of Liberty, Equality, and Virtue in Wollstonecraft's Political Thought'. *British Journal for the History of Philosophy* 15, 1 (2013), 75–99.

Halliwell, Stephen. 'Comic Satire and Freedom of Speech in Classical Athens'. *The Journal of Hellenic Studies* 111 (1991), 48–70.

——. *Greek Laughter: A Study of Cultural Psychology from Homer to Early Christianity*. Cambridge: Cambridge University Press, 2008.

Hanvelt, Marc. *The Politics of Eloquence: David Hume's Polite Rhetoric*. Toronto: University of Toronto Press, 2012.

Hardesty Doig, Kathleen, Frank Kafker, and Jeff Loveland. 'James Tytler's Edition (1777–1784): A Vast Expansion and Improvement'. In *The Early Britannica: The Growth of an Outstanding Encyclopedia* Edited by Frank Kafker and Jeff Loveland, 69–155. Oxford: Voltaire Foundation, 2009.

Harris, James A. *Hume: An Intellectual Biography*. Cambridge: Cambridge University Press, 2015.

Herzog, Don. *Poisoning the Minds of the Lower Orders*. Princeton, NJ: Princeton University Press, 1998.

Heyd, David. 'The Place of Laughter in Hobbes's Theory of Emotions'. *Journal of the History of Ideas* 43, 2 (1982), 285–95.

Heydt, Colin. 'Hume's Innovative Taxonomy of the Virtues'. In *Reading Hume on the Principles of Morals*. Edited Jacqueline Taylor, 118–36. Oxford: Oxford University Press, 2020.

Hill, Lisa. *Adam Smith's Pragmatic Liberalism: The Science of Welfare*. Cham: Palgrave Macmillan, 2020.

Hoekstra, Kinch. 'Hobbesian Equality'. In *Hobbes Today: Insights for the 21st Century*. Edited by S. A. Lloyd, 76–112. Cambridge: Cambridge University Press, 2013.

Holmes, Geoffrey. *The Trial of Doctor Sacheverell*. London: Eyre Methuen, 1973.

Holmes, Richard. 'James Arbuckle and Dean Swift: Cultural Politics in the Irish Confessional State'. *Irish Studies Review* 16, 4 (2008), 431–44.

Hont, Istvan. 'The Early Enlightenment Debate on Commerce and Luxury'. In *The Cambridge History of Eighteenth-Century Political Thought*. Edited by Mark Goldie and Robert Wokler, 377–418. Cambridge: Cambridge University Press, 2008.

———. *Politics in Commercial Society*. Cambridge, MA: Harvard University Press, 2015.

Hulliung, Mark. 'Rousseau and the Scottish Enlightenment: Connections and Disconnections'. In *Adam Smith and Rousseau: Ethics, Politics, Economics*. Edited by Maria Pia Paganelli, Dennis C. Rasmussen and Craig Smith, 32–52. Edinburgh: Edinburgh University Press, 2018.

Hunt Botting, Eileen. 'The Personal Is the Political: Wollstonecraft's Witty, First Person Feminist Voice'. In *The Vindication of the Rights of Woman*. Edited by Eileen Hunt Botting, 261–79. New Haven, CT: Yale University Press, 2014.

Hunting, Claudine. 'The Philosophes and Black Slavery'. *Journal of the History of Ideas* 39, 3 (1978), 405–18.

Ince, Onur Ulas. 'Between Commerce and Empire: David Hume, Colonial Slavery, and Commercial Incivility'. *History of Political Thought* 39, 1 (2012), 107–34.

Israel, Jonathan. *A Revolution of the Mind: Radical Enlightenment and the Intellectual Origins of Modern Democracy*. Princeton, NJ: Princeton University Press, 2011.

Jaffro, Laurent. 'The Passions and Actions of Laughter in Shaftesbury and Hutcheson'. In *Thinking about the Emotions: A Philosophical History*. Edited by Alix Cohen and Robert Stern, 13–149. Oxford: Oxford University Press, 2017.

———. 'Shaftesbury on the Natural Secretion and the Philosophical Personae'. *Intellectual History Review* 18, 3 (2008), 349–59.

———. 'Le Socrate de Shaftesbury: Comment raconter aux modernes l'histoire de Socrate'. In *Socrate in Occidente* Edited by Ettore Lojacono, 66–90. Florence: Le Monnier Università, 2004.

Jaffro, Laurent, Christian Maurer, and Alain Petit. 'Pathologia, A Theory of the Passions'. *History of European Ideas* 39, 2 (2013), 221–40.

Jones, Clyve. 'Debates in the House of Lords on "The Church in Danger", 1705 and on Dr Sacheverell's Impeachment, 1710'. *The Historical Journal* 19, 3 (1976), 759–71.

Jones, Colin. *The Smile Revolution in Eighteenth-Century Paris*. Oxford: Oxford University Press, 2014.

Jones, Vivien. 'Conduct Literature'. In *Mary Wollstonecraft in Context*. Edited by Nancy E. Johnson and Paul Keen, 238–45. Cambridge: Cambridge University Press, 2020.

Kapust, Daniel J. *Flattery and the History of Political Thought: That Glib and Oily Art*. Cambridge: Cambridge University Press, 2018.

Keymer, Thomas. *Poetics of the Pillory: English Literature and Seditious Libel, 1660–1820*. Oxford: Oxford University Press, 2019.

Kitson, Peter. '"Candid Reflections": The Idea of Race in the Debate over the Slave Trade and Slavery in the Late Eighteenth and Early Nineteenth Century'. In *Discourses of Slavery and Abolition: Britain and Its Colonies, 1760–1838*. Edited by Brycchan Carey, Markman Ellis, and Sara Salih, 11–25. New York: Palgrave Macmillan, 2004.

Klein, Lawrence E. 'Ridicule as a Tool for Discovering Truth'. In *The Oxford Handbook of Eighteenth-Century Satire*. Edited by Paddy Bullard, 575–94. Oxford: Oxford University Press, 2019.

———. *Shaftesbury and the Culture of Politeness: Moral Discourse and Cultural Politics in Early Eighteenth-Century England*. Cambridge: Cambridge University Press, 1994.

Klemme, Heiner F. 'Scepticism and Common Sense'. In *The Cambridge Companion to the Scottish Enlightenment*. Edited by Alexander Broadie, 117–25. Cambridge: Cambridge University Press, 2006.

Knights, Mark. *The Devil in Disguise: Deception, Delusion and Fanaticism in the Early English Enlightenment*. Oxford: Oxford University Press, 2011.

Kuin, Inger N. I. 'Diogenes vs. Demonax: Laughter as Philosophy in Lucian'. In *Laughter, Humor, and Comedy in Ancient Philosophy*. Edited by Pierre Destrée and Franco V. Trivigno, 263–84. Oxford: Oxford University Press, 2019.

Laborie, Lionel. *Enlightening Enthusiasm: Prophecy and Religious Experience in Early Eighteenth Century England*. Manchester: Manchester University Press, 2015.

———. 'The Huguenot Offensive against the Camisard Prophets in the English Refuge'. In *The Huguenots: France, Exile and Diaspora*. Edited by Jane McKee and Randolph Vigne, 125–34. Brighton: Sussex Academic Press, 2013.

Laerke, Mogens. 'G. W. Leibniz: Moderation and Censorship'. In *The Use of Censorship in the Enlightenment*. Edited by Mogens Laerke, 155–78. Leiden: Koninkliike Brill NV, 2009.

Locke, Jill. *Democracy and the Death of Shame: Political Equality and Social Disturbance*. Cambridge: Cambridge University Press, 2016.

Lombardini, John. 'Civic Laughter. Aristotle and the Political Virtue of Humor'. *Political Theory* 41, 2 (2013), 203–30.

———. *The Politics of Socratic Humor*. Oakland, CA: University of California Press, 2018.

Livingston, Donald W. *Philosophical Melancholy and Delirium: Hume's Pathology of Philosophy*. Chicago: University of Chicago Press, 1998.

Luban, Daniel. 'Adam Smith on Vanity, Domination, and History'. *Modern Intellectual History* 9, 2 (2012), 275–302.

Lund, Roger D. *Ridicule, Religion and the Politics of Wit in Augustan England*. Burlington, VT: Ashgate, 2012.

Mandelbrote, Scott. 'The Heterodox Career of Nicolas Fatio de Duillier'. In *Heterodoxy in Early Modern Science and Religion*. Edited by John Hedley Brooke and Ian Maclean, 263–97. Oxford: Oxford University Press, 2005.

Marcuse, Herbert. 'Repressive Tolerance'. In *A Critique of Pure Tolerance*. Edited by Robert Paul Wolff, Barrington Moore and Herbert Marcuse, 95–137. Boston: Beacon Press, 1969.

Margalit, Avishai. *The Decent Society*. Cambridge, MA: Harvard University Press, 1996.

Markovits, Elizabeth. *The Politics of Sincerity*. University Park: Pennsylvania State University Press, 2008.

Marshall, Ashley. 'The Generic Context of Defoe's The Shortest Way with the Dissenters and the Problem of Irony'. *The Review of English Studies* 61, 249 (2009), 234–58.

Mason, Laura. *Singing the French Revolution: Popular Culture and Politics, 1787–1799*. Ithaca, NY: Cornell University Press, 1996.

Maurer, Christian, and Laurent Jaffro. 'Reading Shaftesbury's *Pathologia*: An Illustration and Defense of the Stoic Account of the Emotions'. *History of European Ideas* 39, 2 (2013), 207–20.

Mazella, David. *The Making of Modern Cynicism*. Charlottesville: University of Virginia Press, 2007.

McDaniel, Iain. *Adam Ferguson in the Scottish Enlightenment*. Cambridge, MA: Harvard University Press, 2013.

Merrill, Thomas W. *Hume and the Politics of Enlightenment*. Cambridge: Cambridge University Press, 2015.

Miller, William Ian. 'Upward Contempt'. *Political Theory* 23, 3 (1995), 476–99.

Mills, R.J.W. 'The Reception of "That Bigoted Silly Fellow" James Beattie's Essay on Truth in Britain 1770–1830'. *History of European Ideas* 48, 8 (2015), 1049–79.

Minois, Georges. *Histoire du Rire et de la Dérision*. Paris: Librairie Arthème Fayard, 2000.

Moore, James. 'Montesquieu and the Scottish Enlightenment'. In *Montesquieu and His Legacy* Edited by Rebecca E. Kingston, 179–95. Albany: State University of New York Press, 2009.

———. 'The Two Systems of Francis Hutcheson: On the Origins of the Scottish Enlightenment'. in *Studies in the Philosophy of the Scottish Enlightenment*. Edited by M. A. Stewart, 37–59. Oxford: Oxford University Press, 1990.

Moore, Sean. 'Swift's Financial Satires and the Bank of Ireland Controversy of 1720–1'. *Eighteenth-Century Ireland / Iris an Dá Chultúr* 17 (2002), 26–56.

Morreall, John. *Taking Laughter Seriously*. Albany: State University of New York Press, 1983.

Morrow, Nancy V. 'The Problem of Slavery in the Polemic Literature of the American Enlightenment'. *Early American Literature* 20, 3 (1985), 236–55.

Morton, Adam. 'Laughter as a Polemical Act in Late Seventeenth-Century England'. In *The Power of Laughter and Satire in Early Modern Britain*. Edited by Mark Knights and Adam Morton, 107–32. Woodbridge: The Boydell Press, 2018.

Mossner, Ernest. *The Life of David Hume*. Oxford: Oxford University Press, 2001.

Niebuhr, Reinhold. 'Humour and Faith'. In *Holy Laughter: Essays on Religion in the Comic Perspective*. Edited by M. Conrad Hyers, 134–49. New York: Seabury Press, 1969.

Nussbaum, Martha. *Hiding From Humanity: Disgust, Shame, and the Law*. Princeton, NJ: Princeton University Press, 2004.

———. 'Stoic Laughter: A Reading of Seneca's Apocolocyntosis'. In *Seneca and the Self*, edited by Shadi Bartsch and David Wray, 84–112. Cambridge: Cambridge University Press, 2009.

Oldfield, J.R. *Popular Politics and British Anti-Slavery: The Mobilisation of Public Opinion Against the Slave Trade 1787–1807*. New York: Routledge, 1998.

Parkin, Jon. 'Straw Men and Political Philosophy: The Case of Hobbes'. *Political Studies* 59, 3 (2011), 564–79.

Paulson, Ronald. *Don Quixote in England: The Aesthetics of Laughter*. Baltimore, MD: Johns Hopkins University Press, 1998.

Peabody, Sue. *'There Are No Slaves in France': The Political Culture of Race and Slavery*. Oxford: Oxford University Press, 1996.

Peltonen, Markku. *The Duel in Early Modern England: Civility, Politeness and Honour*. Cambridge: Cambridge University Press, 2003.

Phillipson, Nicholas. 'Hume as a Moralist: A Social Historian's Perspective'. *Royal Institute of Philosophy Supplements* 12 (1978), 140–61.

———. 'James Beattie and the Defence of Common Sense'. In *Festschrift für Rainer Gruenter*. Edited by Bernhard Fabian. Heidelberg: Carl Winter, 1978, 145–54.

———. 'Politics, Politeness and the Anglicisation of Early Eighteenth-Century Scottish Culture'. In *Scotland and England 1286–1815*. Edited Roger A. Mason. Edinburgh: J. Donald Publishers, 1987, 226–46.

Pitts, Jennifer. 'Irony in Adam Smith's Critical and Global History'. *Political Theory* 45, 2 (2015), 141–63.

Price, John Vladimir. *The Ironic Hume*. Austin: University of Texas Press, 1965.

Prince, Michael B. *The Shortest Way with Defoe: Robinson Crusoe, Deism, and the Novel*. Charlottesville: University of Virginia Press, 2020.

Rasmussen, Dennis C. *The Infidel and the Professor: David Hume, Adam Smith, and the Friendship That Shaped Modern Thought*. Princeton, NJ: Princeton University Press, 2017.

———. *The Problems and Promise of Commercial Society: Adam Smith's Response to Rousseau*. College Station: Pennsylvania State University Press, 2008.

Rediker, Marcus. 'History from below the Water Line: Sharks and the Atlantic Slave Trade'. *Atlantic Studies* 5, 2 (2008), 285–97.

———. 'Slave Trade Satire Shows Dark Abolitionist 'Humour', *NPR*, 7 October 2004. https://www.npr.org/transcripts/14993517.

Redwood, John. *Reason, Ridicule and Religion: The Age of Enlightenment in England 1660–1750*. London: Thames and Hudson, 1976.

Rice, C. Duncan. *The Scottish Abolitionists 1833–1861*. Baton Rouge: Louisiana State University Press, 1981.

Rivers, Isabel. *Reason, Grace and Sentiment: A Study of the Language of Religion and Ethics in England, 1660–1780*, vol. 2, *Shaftesbury to Hume*. Cambridge: Cambridge University Press, 2000.

Robinson, Nicholas K. *Edmund Burke: A Life in Caricature*. New Haven, CT: Yale University Press, 1996.

Rosenfeld, Sophia. *Common Sense: A Political History*. Cambridge, MA: Harvard University Press, 2011.

Sabl, Andrew. *Hume's Politics: Coordination and Crisis in the History of England*. Princeton, NJ: Princeton University Press, 2012.

Sagar, Paul. *The Opinion of Mankind: Sociability and the Theory of the State from Hobbes*. Princeton, NJ: Princeton University Press, 2018.

Sapiro, Virginia. *A Vindication of Political Virtue: The Political Theory of Mary Wollstonecraft*. Chicago: University of Chicago Press, 1992.

Schaub, Diana J. 'Montesquieu on Slavery'. *Perspectives on Political Science* 34, 2 (2005), 70–78.

Schellenberg, Betty A. 'The Bluestockings'. In *Mary Wollstonecraft in Context*. Edited by Nancy E. Johnson and Paul Keen, 230–37. Cambridge: Cambridge University Press, 2020.

Schneewind, Jerome. *The Invention of Autonomy: A History of Modern Moral Philosophy*. Cambridge: Cambridge University Press, 1998.

Schwartz, Hillel. *The French Prophets: The History of a Millenarian Group in Eighteenth-Century England*. Berkeley: University of California Press, 1980.

———. *Knaves, Fools, Madmen, and That Subtile Effluvium: A Study of the Opposition to the French Prophets in England, 1706–1710*. Gainesville: University of Florida Press, 1978.

Sebastiani, Silvia. 'A "Monster with Human Visage": The Orangutan, Slavery, and the Borders of Humanity in the Global Enlightenment'. *History of the Human Sciences* 32, 4 (2019), 80–99.

———. *The Scottish Enlightenment: Race, Gender, and the Limits of Progress*. New York: Palgrave Macmillan, 2013.

Sen, Amartya. *The Idea of Justice*. Cambridge, MA: Harvard University Press, 2009.

Sharpe, Kevin. *Rebranding Rule: The Restoration and Revolution Monarchy, 1660–1714*. New Haven, CT: Yale University Press, 2013.

Shea, Louisa. *The Cynic Enlightenment: Diogenes in the Salon*. Baltimore, MD: Johns Hopkins University Press, 2010.

Sher, Richard B. and Stewart, M. A. 'James Oswald'. *Oxford Dictionary of National Biography*. Oxford: Oxford University Press, 2004.

Shklar, Judith. *Montesquieu*. Oxford: Oxford University Press, 1987.

Shyllon, Folarin. *James Ramsay: The Unknown Abolitionist*. Edinburgh: Canongate, 1977.

Siebert, Donald T. *The Moral Animus of David Hume*. Newark: University of Delaware Press, 1990.

Sireci, Fiore. '"Writers Who Have Rendered Women Objects of Pity": Mary Wollstonecraft's Literary Criticism in the Analytical Review and A Vindication of the Rights of Woman'. *Journal of the History of Ideas* 79, 2 (2018), 243–65.

Skinner, Quentin. *From Humanism to Hobbes: Studies in Rhetoric and Politics*. Cambridge: Cambridge University Press, 2018.

———. 'Hobbes and the Classical Theory of Laughter'. In *Visions of Politics*, vol. 3, *Hobbes and Civil Science*, 142–76. Cambridge: Cambridge University Press, 2001.

Slater, Graeme. 'Hume's Revisions of the History of England'. *Studies in Bibliography: Papers of the Bibliographical Society of the University of Virginia* 45 (1992), 130–57.

Sleat, Matt. ed., *Politics Recovered: Realist Thought in Theory and Practice*. New York: Columbia University Press, 2018.

Smith, Justin E. H. *Irrationality: A History of the Dark Side of Reason*. Princeton, NJ: Princeton University Press, 2019.

Sonenscher, Michael. *Sans-Culottes: An Eighteenth-Century Emblem in the French Revolution*. Princeton, NJ: Princeton University Press, 2008.

Speck, W. A. 'The Current State of Sacheverell Scholarship'. In *Faction Displayed: Reconsidering the Impeachment of Dr Henry Sacheverell*. Edited by Mark Knights, 16–27. Singapore: Wiley-Blackwell, 2012.

Stewart, Dugald. *Biographical Memoirs of Smith, Robertson, and Reid*. Edinburgh: George Ramsay and Company, 1811.

Stewart, M. A. 'Hume's Intellectual Development, 1711–1752'. In *Impressions of Hume*. Edited by Marina Frasca-Spada and P.J.E. Kail, 11–58. Oxford: Oxford University Press, 2005.

Stohr, Karen. 'Our New Age of Contempt'. *New York Times*, 23 January 2017.

Stuart-Buttle, Tim. *From Moral Theology to Moral Philosophy: Cicero and Visions of Humanity from Locke to Hume*. Oxford: Oxford University Press, 2019.

——. 'Shaftesbury Reconsidered: Stoic Ethics and the Unreasonableness of Christianity'. *Locke Studies* 15 (2015), 163–213.

Suderman, Jeffrey M. 'Religion and Philosophy'. In *Scottish Philosophy in the Eighteenth Century*, vol. 1, *Morals, Politics, Art, Religion*. Edited by Aaron Garrett and James A. Harris, 196–238. Oxford: Oxford University Press, 2015.

Sullivan, Vickie. *Montesquieu and the Despotic Ideas of Europe: An Interpretation of 'The Spirit of the Laws'*. Chicago: University of Chicago Press, 2017.

Tave, Stuart. *The Amiable Humorist: A Study in the Comic Theory and Criticism of the Eighteenth and Early Nineteenth Centuries*. Chicago: University of Chicago Press, 1960.

Taylor, Charles. *Sources of the Self: The Making of the Modern Identity*. Cambridge, MA: Harvard University Press, 1989.

Taylor, Jacqueline. *Reflecting Subjects: Passion, Sympathy, and Society in Hume's Philosophy*. Oxford: Oxford University Press, 2015.

Tegan, Mary Beth. 'Mocking the Mothers of the Novel: Mary Wollstonecraft, Maternal Metaphor, and the Reproduction of Sympathy'. *Studies in the Novel* 42, 4 (2010), 357–76.

Todd, Janet M. *Mary Wollstonecraft: A Revolutionary Life*. New York: Columbia University Press, 2000.

Toender, Lars. 'Humility, Arrogance and the Limitations of Kantian Autonomy: A Response to Rostbøll'. *Political Theory* 39, 3 (2011), 378–85.

Tomaselli, Sylvana. 'Mary Wollstonecraft: The Reunification of the Domestic and Political Spheres'. In *Geschlechterordnung und Staat: Legitimationsfiguren der politischen Philosophie (1600–1850)*. Edited by Marion Heinz and Sabine Doyé, 235–49. Berlin: Oldenbourg, 2012.

Vivenza, Gloria. *Adam Smith and the Classics: The Classical Heritage in Adam Smith's Thought*. Oxford: Oxford University Press, 2001.

Voitle, Robert. *The Third Earl of Shaftesbury 1671–1713*. Baton Rouge: Louisiana State University Press, 1984.

Waldron, Jeremy. *The Harm in Hate Speech*. Cambridge, MA: Harvard University Press, 2012.

Wallace, Robert. 'Law, Attic Comedy, and the Regulation of Comic Speech'. In *Cambridge Companion to Ancient Greek Law*. Edited by Michael Gagarin and David Cohen, 357–73. Cambridge, Cambridge University Press, 2005.

Walsh, Ashley. *Civil Religion and the Enlightenment in England, 1707–1800*. Woodbridge: The Boydell Press, 2020.

Walvin, James. *England, Slaves and Freedom 1776–1838*. London: Macmillan, 1986.

Walzer, Arthur E. *George Campbell: Rhetoric in the Age of Enlightenment*. Carbondale: Southern Illinois University Press, 2002.

Wardle, Ralph. *Mary Wollstonecraft: A Critical Biography*. Lawrence: University of Kansas Press, 1951.

Whitford, David. *The Curse of Ham in the Early Modern Era: The Bible and the Justifications for Slavery*. London: Routledge, 2009.

Whyte, Iain. *Scotland and the Abolition of Black Slavery, 1756–1838*. Edinburgh: Edinburgh University Press, 2006.

———. '"The Upas Tree, Beneath Whose Pestiferous Shade All Intellect Languishes and All Virtue Dies": Scottish Public Perceptions of the Slave Trade and Slavery, 1756–1833'. In *Recovering Scotland's Slavery Past: The Caribbean Connection*. Edited by T. M. Devine, 187–205. Edinburgh: Edinburgh University Press, 2015.

Wigelsworth, Jeffrey R. *Deism in Enlightenment England*. Manchester: Manchester University Press, 2009.

Williams, Bernard. 'Hume on Religion'. In *The Sense of the Past: Essays in the History of Philosophy*. Edited by Myles Burnyeat, 267–76. Cambridge: Cambridge University Press, 2007.

Williams, Eric. *Capitalism and Slavery*. Richmond, VA: William Byrd Press, 2007.

Wolf, Richard B. 'The Publication of Shaftesbury's "Letter Concerning Enthusiasm"'. *Studies in Bibliography: Papers of the Bibliographical Society of the University of Virginia* 32 (1979), 236–41.

———. 'Shaftesbury's Just Measure of Irony'. *Studies in English Literature, 1500–1900* 33, 3 (1993), 565–85.

Wolterstorff, Nicholas. *Thomas Reid and the Story of Epistemology*. Cambridge: Cambridge University Press, 2000.

Wood, Paul B. *The Aberdeen Enlightenment: The Arts Curriculum in the Eighteenth Century*. Aberdeen: Aberdeen University Press, 1993.

———. 'Thomas Reid and the Common Sense School'. In *Scottish Philosophy in the Eighteenth Century*, vol. 1, *Morals, Politics, Art, Religion* Edited by Aaron Garrett and James A. Harris, 404–52. Oxford: Oxford University Press, 2015.

Woolhouse, Roger. 'Lady Masham's Account of Locke'. *Locke Studies* 3 (2003), 167–93.

Yeo, Richard. *Encyclopaedic Visions: Scientific Discourses and Enlightenment Culture*. Cambridge: Cambridge University Press, 2001.

Young, Iris Marion. 'Communication and the Other: Beyond Deliberative Democracy'. In *Democracy and Difference: Contesting the Boundaries of the Political*. Edited by Seyla Benhabib, 120–36. Princeton, NJ: Princeton University Press, 1996.

Zaretsky, Robert, and John T. Scott. *The Philosopher's Quarrel*. New Haven, CT: Yale University Press, 2009.

Common Sense (Paine), 176

Common Sense philosophers. *See*
Aberdeen Philosophical Society

contagiousness, of laughter, 81

contempt, ridicule as, 83–84, 108;
Aberdeen Philosophical Society
members on, 120–25, 142, 147–50;
abusiveness, of ridicule, 53, 60–61,
186, 190–96, 198–204, 216; dignified
contempt, by women, 185, 207–11; as
excitement of contempt, 28–29, 96;
as expression of contempt, 5–10, 14,
26–28, 183; humiliation, ridicule as
tool of, 12, 15, 17, 19, 103–5; indignation, contempt *versus*, 199–200; latent
contempt, 149; political use of contemptuous speech, 14–15; on slavery,
152, 156, 170; undeserved contempt
of women, 206–7; upward contempt,
201n87. *See also* prideful superiority

control, laughter as relinquishment
of, 76

contumely, 68n69

conversation, art of, 86–87, 89–90, 123

Cooper, Anthony Ashley. *See* Shaftesbury,
Earl of

correcting smaller faults, through ridicule, 10n40, 31, 81–82, 121–22, 126,
140, 142–43, 197–98. *See also* vice

Coste, Pierre, 1, 36n64, 39n77, 46–47

countering ridicule with ridicule, 63–66,
196–204, 216. *See also* Aberdeen Philosophical Society; Wollstonecraft, Mary

courtly humour, 93n26, 193–94, 218; jesters, 28, 143n120

Coventry, John, 109

Cromwell, Oliver, 108, 114–15, 217

cultured insolence, 11n41

Cynic ridicule, 17, 24, 40, 56, 91–92; dangers of, 40–41; Shaftesbury's tactics of,
41–47. *See also* Diogenes

d'Alembert, Jean-Baptiste le Rond, 104,
156n19

Daudé, Jean, 32

De Cive (Hobbes), 8–9

Declaration of the Rights of Man and the
Citizen (1789), 194–95

A Defence of the Rockingham Party
(Godwin), 184n10

Defence of the Seven Sacraments (Henry
VIII), 111

deflective powers, of ridicule, 126–27

Defoe, Daniel, 54, 63–66

De Homine (Hobbes), 7

Deism, 10, 23, 125, 213

democracy, 138–40, 144–45, 217–19

Democracy in America (Tocqueville),
218–19

Demonax, 37, 38nn72–73

de Namours, Dupont, 156–57

dependence, 201–2, 203, 208–10

Depont, Charles-Jean-Francois, 183

Design of a Socratick History (Shaftesbury), 42

Dialogues (Eachard), 96

Dialogues Concerning Education
(Fordyce), 126

Dialogues of the Dead (Lucian), 116

Dickson, William, 18, 151–52, 153, 154,
168–72, 173, 179

A Dictionary of the English Language
(Johnson), 119–21

dignity and meanness, contrast between,
81, 142

Diogenes, 41n84, 45–47, 51, 91–93, 98, 106,
118; "divine facetiousness" of, 35–41

Dionysus, 218

disability, laughter at, 28, 38, 82, 143,
198–99

Discourses (Arrian), 38–39

Discourses Concerning Ridicule and Irony
(Collins), 69n71, 96–99

disinterested affection for others, 77

dissenters, religious, 11, 62–65, 71, 78–79,
86–87, 96, 198

Dissertation on Miracles (Campbell),
134–35

Dissertations Moral and Critical
(Beattie), 164

dissolute mirth, 93

divine messenger (angelos), 39

Dodd, William, 197

Douglass, Frederick, 180–81

Dryden, John, 27

Dublin Weekly Journal (newspaper), 55,
77–83

Eachard, John, 96

earnestness. *See* seriousness

A NOTE ON THE TYPE

THIS BOOK has been composed in Miller, a Scotch Roman typeface designed by Matthew Carter and first released by Font Bureau in 1997. It resembles Monticello, the typeface developed for The Papers of Thomas Jefferson in the 1940s by C. H. Griffith and P. J. Conkwright and reinterpreted in digital form by Carter in 2003.

Pleasant Jefferson ("P. J.") Conkwright (1905–1986) was Typographer at Princeton University Press from 1939 to 1970. He was an acclaimed book designer and AIGA Medalist.

The ornament used throughout this book was designed by Pierre Simon Fournier (1712–1768) and was a favorite of Conkwright's, used in his design of the *Princeton University Library Chronicle.*